MW00824321

COOPERATION

COOPERATION

A Political, Economic, and Social Theory

BERNARD E. HARCOURT

Columbia University Press

New York

Columbia University Press
Publishers Since 1893
New York   Chichester, West Sussex
cup.columbia.edu

Cataloging-in-Publication Data is available from the Library of Congress.
ISBN 9780231209540 (hardback)
ISBN 9780231557993 (ebook)

LCCN 2022046588

Columbia University Press books are printed on permanent
    and durable acid-free paper.
Printed in the United States of America

Cover design: Elliott S. Cairns

Contents

Getting Started

Scientists at NASA's Goddard Institute for Space Studies report that the average global temperature on planet Earth has increased by at least 1.1° Celsius (1.9° Fahrenheit) since 1880. The trend lines on all the graphs and plots rise upward in an oscillating linear fashion. The overwhelming consensus among scientists is that any warming beyond an additional 0.4° Celsius, or beyond a total increase of 1.5° Celsius from 1880, would threaten human existence on Earth.[1]

The overwhelming scientific consensus, also, is that humans have caused the planet to warm through industrialization and the emission of heat-trapping greenhouse gases.[2] Despite the consensus, there are some who deny that global warming is caused primarily by human activity. But even if there are nonhuman factors contributing to global warming, there is no question that it will take coordinated action by everyone on planet Earth to avoid imminent catastrophe.

Humans have become interdependent in a way that could not have been imagined by earlier political thinkers, economists, or social theorists, even forty years ago. As a result, most of our inherited political ideas and economic models are now outdated or not up to the task. Enlightenment ideals of individual autonomy, of man mastering nature, of growth maximization, of the wealth of nations—all those political, economic, and social theories have proven to be illusory and deceptive, if not perilous, in the face of the new reality of complete human interdependence.

The two dominant responses oscillate between rugged individualism and governmental coordination: at one extreme, many argue that we can solve the crises only if the government leaves us to our own devices and ingenuity; at the other extreme, many argue that only governments working together can control the developing crises. But as new crises pile on, such as the rise of pandemics

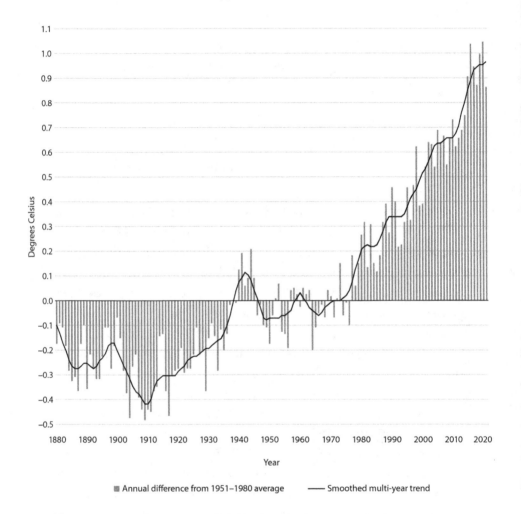

Figure 1 Temperatures are rising: Global land-ocean temperature index (1880–2021)

Data source: NASA's Goddard Institute for Space Studies (GISS). Credit: NASA/GISS.

This graph uses data from the NASA Goddard Institute for Space Studies to compare the annual average surface temperature each year from 1880 to 2021 with the long-term average surface temperature 1951–1980. The data shown in the bar chart are the average surface temperature for each year; the line shows the LOWESS regression (smoothed multiyear trend) for the same period. "Global Temperature," NASA Global Climate Change, accessed September 15, 2022, https://climate.nasa.gov/vital-signs /global-temperature/.

and increasing threats to democracy, the dueling positions have hit an impasse. They have reached a point of polarization that has become paralyzing in many countries. Interdependent, and now gridlocked, we desperately need a different way of thinking and acting: a new political, economic, and social model for the twenty-first century.

That model is hidden in plain sight. It rests on cooperation: on people cooperating and working with one another, throughout all aspects of their lives, for the well-being of all the people and the environment. It has been around for decades, even centuries, but receives scant attention by contrast to the two polar extremes. In a concentrated, combined, and compounded form, it offers a new political, economic, and social theory and practice that might be called "coöperism."

Coöperism allows us to embrace our newfound interdependence and, together, to confront the shared threats to humanity. It is time to embrace it—before it is too late. Please join me in thinking through its theory and practice, and its larger implications for cooperation democracy.

Bernard E. Harcourt
New York City
November 10, 2022

COOPERATION

CHAPTER 1

The Urgency of Cooperation

A round the world, we face an unprecedented constellation of crises: extreme climate events and the menace of global climate change; COVID-19, Mpox, and a new plague of pandemics; threats to fair elections and democracy; the increased polarization and radicalization of politics. We are familiar with the litany. Many of us share a sense of dread; many, a feeling of hopelessness. Today, there is no need nor time to dwell on the crises. We know them all too well. What we need instead is a way forward. What we need is constructive thinking and action—before it is too late.

STUCK IN A RUT

But we are stuck with wheels spinning because people are headed in two radically different directions. There is a tug-of-war pulling us apart, with no possible victor. As a result, conflict and tensions are mounting, further eroding our trust in one another and dramatically increasing the divide in many liberal democracies. Often things are becoming so polarized that they are causing the collapse of stable political structures and party oppositions, and new, more radical factions are emerging in many countries. More democracies are failing, even sliding into autocracy, than at any time in the past century.[1] As the polarization increases, many people are beginning to wonder whether it will lead to civil strife at home—where it hasn't already.

On one side, many people are turning increasingly to an ideal of individualism and self-sufficiency that is accompanied by a deep distrust of government. "Get the government out of our hair," some say, "and we'll be stronger, more resilient, and better able to deal with the problems, whether it is an extreme climate event or a virus." On this view, if everyone just minded their own business, focused on themselves and their families, on their own lives, we would all be better off. Individual strength is what will save us. So we should just hunker down and tend to our own affairs, not those of others. As for the government, it needs to be shrunk: lower taxes, less regulation, fewer mandates, no more redistribution of wealth. The government needs to get out of our way. All we need the state to do is police those who break the rules and, at the international level, fend off those who are attacking our way of life. All we need is local police and an army at the border—that's about it. Other than that, we need to be left alone.

On the other side, many people are turning increasingly to government to implement the kind of regulations they believe are necessary to address the global crises we face and resolve collective action problems. This is accompanied by greater faith in the ability of the state to assess, coordinate, and impose the kinds of public policies that will make us all better off. "We need to act together, through our elected representatives," many say, "to pass legislation and enact public policies that will lessen the spread of pandemics and reduce carbon emissions." According to this view, we need reliable, neutral experts to figure out what is best practice and legislators to enact them. After all, a mask mandate from a competent health agency is no more problematic than wearing seatbelts in an automobile. The path forward is a well-regulated state that relies on experts and science to look out for our best interests—and for the people to both respect those mandates and keep a watchful eye on our representatives so that they do their job properly.

Both sides accuse the other of inconsistencies and hypocrisy, which makes matters only more hostile and polarized and fuels conspiracy theories. The "individualists," let's call them, accuse their opponents of lining their pockets with pork-belly legislation and redistributing their well-earned money to those who don't work. For individualists, all the talk of "general welfare" just translates into the enrichment of liberal urban elites, the empowerment of the political class, and handouts to the poor; nothing good comes of it for the hardworking folks in between. Plus, when it comes to topics like reproduction or sexuality, then all of a sudden the other side is for individual choice and self-determination. And vice versa, of course. Those who favor government regulation, let's call them "statists" for now, accuse the individualists of relying on all kinds of government services to entrench their privileges. For the statists, all the talk of hard work, self-sufficiency, and well-earned merit hides forms of privilege that have been acquired over decades or centuries through conquest, colonization, slavery, and apartheid. The individualists, they say, want to have reliable utilities, high-speed communications, first responders, and good roads to drive on, all of which require a functioning government. It's not really that they want "no government" or "small government"; they just fail to recognize how much organization it takes to have a functioning society. Plus, the talk of individualism masks racial prejudice and in the end only serves the superwealthy. Of course, the accusations of racism go both ways—with the individualists claiming they are being discriminated against whenever the statists take race into account, implicitly or explicitly, in policy making.

As the accusations grow—and as the global crises mount—the tension is getting worse and worse because both sides need a supermajority to realize their vision of the just society. The individualists need a solid majority in government in order to dismantle the state. So long as the state is imposing mandates on them, they cannot just mind their own business. They need a supermajority across all the branches of government in order to tear it down—or an armed revolution and civil war. On the other hand, the statists also need a supermajority to pass their legislation and get their regulations upheld in court. If the individualists get control of any one of the branches of government, they can obstruct the policies and create gridlock. Neither side can achieve their ultimate objective—scaling the state up or down—unless they have control of all the branches of government. So each side needs to convince or coerce their fellow citizens.

As the tensions rise, so does the volume. With everything from supersized flags flying off the back of giant four-by-four pickup trucks and on highway overpasses, to convoys of tractors and eighteen-wheelers blocking borders and cities, to massive die-ins and occupations, the two opposing sides are getting louder and louder. They control the leading media outlets—with giants on one side like Fox News, the *Wall Street Journal*, the *Times of London*, the Murdoch media empire in Australia, England, and the United States; CNews TV, Vivendi, Hachette and the media empire of Vincent Bolloré in France; and the *Estadão* and *O Globo* news outlets in Brazil, for instance. On the other side there are stations and newspapers like MSNBC, the *Washington Post*, the *New York Times*, the *Guardian* in the UK, and *Libération* in France.[2] The two sides dominate the party structure in most liberal democracies, alternating and mostly sharing power. And they both depend on wealthy elites from either side of the political spectrum to gain a supermajority and enact their political vision. One need only mention here

Donald Trump or the Koch brothers in the United States or Silvio Berlusconi in Italy or again Vincent Bolloré in France—these are vast financial empires that fund politics, control media, and influence culture. The discourse of individualism may be widespread in the popular classes now, but it is fueled—financially and politically—by superwealthy elites who have a real stake in lower taxes and less government redistribution. And they are not alone: the statists as well are funded by wealthy elites and corporate contributions, with party elites raking in contributions. This means that the government's regulatory efforts are often captured by those wealthy contributors and their investments in multinational corporations so that the public policies often end up resulting in bonanzas for the liberal elite, investors, managers, and big business.

Today, the polarization and conflict consume all our attention. But they are not likely to address the constellation of crises we face, because both sides ultimately need large-scale collective action to prevail. The individualists, paradoxically, cannot just mind their own business. They must convince a supermajority of their peers and win electoral victories to achieve their objective of dismantling the state, which explains why they are becoming more vocal, loud, and aggressive— and so nationalistic. They have to claim the nation and the people. On the other side, the statists also need to convince a supermajority in order to gain control of all the branches of government and implement their public policies. Otherwise, they cannot get anything done. Both sides face deep collective-action problems: neither side can accomplish its goal unless it dominates the political sphere. Assuming for the sake of argument that either one of them could actually resolve the crises we face—global climate change, pandemics, democratic threats—neither one has the supermajority necessary to get it done. The result is a stalemate in many countries and gridlock in the face of crises, which is pushing many liberal democracies to the brink of civil discord.

The conflict between these two dominant worldviews—and the resulting paralysis—takes on a different character in different democracies around the world. Each country has its own unique history, customs, and traditions that structure the opposition. The clash may take the shape of competition between centrists and socialists in France, conservatives and the Labour Party in the United Kingdom, the BJP and the center-left Congress in India, the nationalist conservative Jubilee Party and the Orange Democratic Movement in Kenya, or the Law and Justice versus the New Left in Poland. The labels and the rhetoric differ somewhat, but the conflict is similar and often plays out in parallel ways.

The United States: A Case Study

In the United States, the growing polarization aggravates a decades-long struggle over the economic organization of American society. Since the turn of the twentieth century at least, two main paradigms have emerged and now prevail, represented today by the two largest political parties: a "deregulatory" model that effectively delegates to nongovernmental entities the power to set the terms of economic exchange; and an "administrative state" model that relies on policy makers in Washington, DC (or Sacramento, Albany, and other state capitals), to regulate our economic and social organization. The first presents itself as championing individualism and freedom; the second presents itself as more reasonable, inclusive, and protective of the disadvantaged members of society. They are now each closely tied to the two major political parties—Republican and Democratic—and easily identified on the American political spectrum.

On the political right, Republicans have fought against governmental regulation of business and commerce for decades, with the stated intention of liberating the entrepreneurial and productive ambition of individuals. Republicans favor small government in economic affairs, and they have used governmental institutions to achieve that goal. In the early twentieth century, many industrialists used the federal courts to oppose social movements intended to improve the conditions of working men and women. They relied primarily on the Supreme Court's *Lochner* line of decisions, which used the device of a federal constitutional right to "freedom of contract" as a way to strike down state and federal regulations. Later, President Ronald Reagan brought about a wave of "deregulation,"[3] this time operating directly through executive departments and agencies. In the twenty-first century, President Donald Trump similarly tried to reduce the size of the federal government, primarily by failing to appoint people to key positions of authority or appointing others who promised to dismantle the federal agencies of which they were in charge.

On the political left, Democrats have predominantly relied on federal governmental regulation to organize economic exchange, with the stated intention of spreading wealth and providing a social safety net for the least advantaged.[4] President Franklin Delano Roosevelt created a range of governmental agencies and projects during the New Deal with the goal of employing and ensuring the safety and well-being of many Americans.[5] President Lyndon B. Johnson launched a number of governmental programs and initiatives under the banner

of the Great Society. President Barack Obama set up a complex federal regulatory system to encourage state health insurance markets to increase the number
of Americans covered by health insurance. President Joe Biden, emulating FDR,
sought to create public works projects and governmental social programs in the
wake of the COVID-19 pandemic and put in place a large federally funded infrastructure renewal program and energy and climate tax program.

For decades, the struggle between these two competing paradigms of economic
organization has structured American politics. It has taken on many forms in
addition to party politics, including popular uprisings such as the Tea Party and
MAGA (Make America Great Again) movements on the right, and the DSA
(Democratic Socialists of America) and Occupy Wall Street movements on the
left. Both political parties at times have exploited social, cultural, and racial cleavages as a way to advance their cause, pitting people of different backgrounds
against one another and courting different subgroups and communities. The conflict was, in a way, baked into the origins of American liberalism—the idea that
people should be allowed to pursue their own vision of the good life as long as they
do not interfere with others and that the government should be there simply to
enforce the hedges between people and resolve some collective-action problems.[6]
Republicans emphasize the individual liberty side of this equation, Democrats the
need for government regulation and enforcement. The two poles are the result,
and the mounting crises are pushing them further and further apart—without
either side being able to garner a strong majority.

With a solid conservative supermajority now in the United States Supreme
Court, the fulcrum of the fight has shifted back to the federal judiciary. On June
30, 2022, a supermajority of the Supreme Court struck down as unconstitutional
regulations proposed by the U.S. Environmental Protection Agency intended to
combat global climate change. The regulations, originally promulgated by the
Obama administration, targeted carbon-dioxide emissions from coal and natural-
gas power plants. Those regulations were projected to reduce America's depen-
dence on coal from 38 percent in 2014 to 27 percent by 2030 and to result in the
forced retirement of dozens of existing coal power plants. Chief Justice John Roberts, writing for the six-justice majority, concluded that the magnitude of the
regulations demanded a more explicit delegation of authority from Congress to
the EPA. Roberts wrote that, in extraordinary cases, common sense dictates the
need for clearer congressional buy-in.[7] Justice Neil Gorsuch penned a more radical
concurring opinion, joined by Justice Samuel Alito, that raised broader questions

about the propriety of Congress's delegating regulatory power to agencies. Gorsuch intimated that congressional delegation of power might encroach on the constitutional design of separation of powers—in his words, might "dash" the whole scheme of enumerated powers. "In a world like that," Gorsuch wrote, "agencies could churn out new laws more or less at whim. Intrusions on liberty would not be difficult and rare, but easy and profuse."[8]

The Supreme Court's decision in *West Virginia v. EPA* is the product of a decades-long campaign by Republicans to enlist the federal courts again in the struggle over the economic organization of American society—a campaign dating back at least to the famous memorandum written by Lewis F. Powell Jr. in 1971 to the U.S. Chamber of Commerce warning of the threat of government regulation to American business.[9] Once again, the effort to "deregulate" is being pursued under principles of constitutional law. My colleague at Columbia Law School, Philip Hamburger, charted a blueprint for the dismantling of the administrative state in books such as *Is Administrative Law Unlawful?* (2014) and *The Administrative Threat* (2017).[10] The justices in the supermajority are, in part, following Philip Hamburger's script and striking down federal regulations under a separation-of-powers theory that places on Congress greater responsibility to legislate the content of regulations. In fact, Justice Gorsuch explicitly refers to Philip Hamburger's book *Is Administrative Law Unlawful?* in his concurring opinion.[11] Naturally, the justices in the supermajority know the political consequences of their actions. They know, just as well as the rest of us, that Congress is in gridlock. They also know, as well as all of us, that constitutional adjudication is malleable, as evidenced by their deft treatment of precedent in overruling *Roe v. Wade*.[12] The justices know the consequences of what they are doing. Because of gridlock, Congress will be unable to respond with legislation to make explicit the delegation of authority. Prior to the 2022 midterms, the Democratic majority in Congress could act only through budget reconciliation measures, which are not subject to the Senate filibuster—as evidenced by the climate tax package passed by a razor-thin Democratic Senate majority a few months later, on August 7, 2022.[13] As this book went to press, the 2022 midterm elections resulted in a slim Republican majority in the House, which will likely vitiate even the possibility of legislating through the budget for the next two years. With a stroke of the pen, the Supreme Court successfully undermined regulatory efforts to address climate change, tying one hand behind the back of the Democratic presidential administration and handing coal and natural-gas companies and the fossil-fuel industry—or, more specifically, their equity shareholders—a financial bonanza. The battle between the two competing economic paradigms has returned to the Supreme Court. This should not be a surprise; both models use governmental institutions to achieve their ends.

With a slim majority in Congress and a Democratic president in office, the Democrats responded in the only way they could, by passing climate measures through a budget reconciliation process. The Inflation Reduction Act of 2022, signed into law on August 16, 2022, includes about $360 billion in tax credits and incentives to address climate change. It operates through fiscal measures such as tax rebates for clean energy, including wind and solar power. It makes billions of dollars available to fossil-fuel companies to cut down their emissions and develop new technologies to achieve net-zero emissions targets. The legislation is essentially an industrial, corporate, and tax bill cloaked as a climate and clean energy bill.[14] It includes more than $60 billion to support "on-shore clean energy manufacturing in the U.S.," as well as "production tax credits to help U.S. manufacturers accelerate production of solar panels, wind turbines, batteries, and process key minerals; $10 billion investment tax credits for new manufacturing facilities that make clean tech like EVs, wind turbines and solar panels; $2 billion in grants to help automaker facilities transition to clean vehicle production; up to $20 billion in loans to construct new manufacturing facilities for clean vehicles," and other tax incentives to help manufacture heat pumps and other devices.[15] It is a bonanza for energy companies. But barring a supermajority in the Senate, and having lost the Supreme Court, that is the only way for the Democrats to move forward on climate. Direct government regulations will not stick.[16]

Although these developments should not surprise us, at the same time they should not distract us from the larger conflict over the two competing paradigms. The constitutional controversy at the Supreme Court is a red herring. Constitutional interpretations will vary over time. The Court has already gone back and forth a few times and will likely continue to swing, like a pendulum, depending on its political composition—that is, on how many justices are appointed by Republican or Democratic presidents. At each pivot, the justices will pen elaborate and finely reasoned judicial opinions. They will claim to have reached the only proper and correct method of constitutional decision making—whether it is fundamental rights, originalism, textualism, judicial restraint, or the living Constitution—and will maintain that they alone are defending our constitutional scheme. But their conclusions will simply align with their political views, with the rare exception of the rogue justice, like David Souter, who goes in a completely unexpected direction. The constitutional interpretations are and will continue to be politically motivated—as evidenced by the *West Virginia v. EPA* decision. In that case, the justices in the supermajority hang their decision on vague and malleable terms like "common sense," a "reason to hesitate," "extraordinary" cases, and "ordinary" circumstances—all the telltale words of legal manipulation.[17] Lawyers know well how to deploy those terms. Roberts writes that the case falls within instances where "agencies [are] asserting highly consequential power beyond what Congress could *reasonably* be understood to have granted";[18] and that "a decision of *such magnitude and consequence* rests with Congress itself."[19] But we all know those words are merely conclusory. Roberts is the one who decides on whether the "magnitude and consequence" are too great, or what Congress could "reasonably" be understood to have done. There are no metrics, no objective, neutral, or scientific measures of any of this. It is all made of whole cloth. There is no need to get bogged down in these constitutional interpretations and fabrications. They will vary depending on the composition of the Court. To focus on the constitutional questions is to miss the crux of the matter.

THE CRUX OF THE PROBLEM

The real problem is that neither paradigm of economic organization in the United States—neither the deregulatory model nor the administrative-state model—is able to achieve a supermajority and, as a result, neither is able to address our impending crises. Instead, both models merely serve the financial interests of the wealthy and are augmenting inequality in American society, fueling another crisis of inequity that is compounding the others.

The fact is, neither model benefits the vast majority of the American people. The first is more open about it. Republicans are not shy about speaking of the "trickle-down" economic effects of their proposed economic policies or of federal deregulation. In large part, their model functions explicitly and primarily through the increased wealth of American business and wealthy Americans. They often advocate explicitly for lifting taxes on the wealthy, lowering corporate taxes, and eliminating the estate tax. The second model favors the wealthy more indirectly, by consistently defaulting to business and corporate interests. Democrats see themselves as more redistributive but almost always fall back on large corporations to make their policies work. So, for instance, Obamacare ends up relying on large private health insurance companies to create health-care options for Americans. It defaults to huge American corporations like Aetna, Cigna, Humana, and UnitedHealthcare, whose values have skyrocketed in the process.[20] The Biden climate legislation, as we just saw, operates through tax credits that end up extending billions of dollars in tax breaks to energy companies. The real beneficiaries are oil and gas multinationals, alternative energy companies, automobile corporations—and all their shareholders. The result is that corporate wealth and interests get center stage in the Democratic model as well. Plus, in today's world of campaign finance, the Democratic Party has no good alternative but to court big business and the extremely wealthy to bankroll their election campaigns and to support their lobbying efforts.

Both paradigms benefit primarily people who already have accumulated wealth and investments, at the expense of the vast majority of people living in the United States, because both models privilege the interests of wealthy investors in big business and multinational corporations, which prioritize shareholder return over the welfare of consumers, workers, suppliers, and other stakeholders. Both models rest on the logic of the corporate investor, namely, that economic activity should maximize the return on investment. This logic of profit maximization to boost investor returns may seem intuitive and obvious, but it has deeply detrimental consequences for consumers, workers, and other stakeholders in the enterprise. It means that workers are often not paid a living wage or afforded proper health care in order to minimize business expenses. It means that consumer welfare takes second seat to profits. It means that treating suppliers more equitably reduces the bottom line.

The logic of the shareholder investor is, simply, to maximize return on investment. The well-being of others is not of primary concern. The shareholder has one main interest: to draw a larger dividend or sell their investment at a higher value. As a result, they have every interest in extracting more from the enterprise, squeezing out more from the other stakeholders, eking out more from the workers and suppliers, and augmenting the value of their holdings through share-price strategies. These logics of profit detach the shareholder from any real investment in the lives of all those who are associated with the enterprise. They operate at a distance. Most individuals who own investments today, whether directly as stock or indirectly through retirement accounts, hold them as a form of speculation to increase the overall return on their savings and to increase their wealth—if possible, to increase their wealth more than others and more than the market, since that is the only effective way to get richer. But this ends up being an effort to extract wealth from an enterprise, from its consumers or workers, from all the people whose livelihoods depend on the business. It ends up, in many cases, being a form of gambling on the livelihoods of others. These logics elevate investor profit over human welfare.

As an economic matter, the shareholder logics thrive on the old maxim that "private vice creates public benefits." This is the idea that when people pursue their own selfish financial interests, they put into place practices, mechanisms, and institutions that end up benefiting others even more. This logic undergirds both paradigms—the deregulatory paradigm very explicitly, the administrative state paradigm because it almost always falls back on corporate incentives and tax breaks. But what the reality of our economic condition demonstrates today is not public benefits but growing inequality within American society—and abroad as well. Today, the three wealthiest American individuals (all men) have more aggregated wealth than the bottom 50 percent of the American population, or about 160 million people.[21] The eight wealthiest individuals in the world (again, all men) own more than the poorest half of humanity.[22] And the gap is getting bigger.

Thomas Piketty, my colleague at the École des hautes études en sciences sociales (EHESS), details the rise in inequality in the United States and other countries. Piketty and his colleagues, Facundo Alvaredo, Lucas Chancel, Emmanuel Saez, Gabriel Zucman, and others, meticulously demonstrate that trickle-down economic theories have only worsened the uneven distribution of wealth. Not just in the United States but in country after country—France, UK, Canada, Australia, Germany, Sweden, India, Japan, and more—Piketty and his colleagues show an increasing curve of inequality since the mid-twentieth century and the height of the welfare state, what is now referred to as the U-curve of inequality.[23] Piketty and his colleagues' descriptive claims have undergone close scrutiny by the social science community and have withstood peer reviews and critiques from the left and the right.[24] Their conclusions are unimpeachable: wealth inequality has been on a steep rise since the mid-twentieth century. The top-down growth models mostly benefit the top.

The problem, in the end, is that both dominant paradigms today—the deregulatory and the administrative-state models—place corporate shareholder interests above those of the other stakeholders, the first explicitly, the second by default. They benefit only the wealthy. The rest of the people are feeling increasingly vulnerable and becoming further polarized in the face of mounting global crises. Pushed further and further apart, without the possibility of compromise—without the possibility of reaching across the aisle or of achieving a supermajority—the two opposite poles are veering into conflict at the same time that they have become two dead ends.

ANOTHER PATH: COOPERATION

There is, however, another path forward, far less loud, far less confrontational, far less aggressive, in fact far less known in large part because it does not need to convince a majority of other people. It can thrive simply in small groups—a few friends who come together to create a consumer cooperative, a few farmers who start sharing equipment and producing together, a few engineers who found a worker cooperative, some community friends who start making ice cream for justice, neighbors who provide mutual aid and support to one another, home health-care aides who get together to form a worker-owned enterprise. These forms of cooperation have a long history and tradition, and they are a growing force around the world. They rest, very simply, on people cooperating with one another across different aspects of their lives—consumption, production, work, housing, finance, insurance, mutual support—in order to improve the well-being of all the stakeholders and the environment. Cooperation works within existing governmental structures, so it does not need to dismantle the state. Cooperation also embraces self-determination and is the product of a lot of individual initiative, so it is not fundamentally at odds with the idea of individual freedom either. And it requires no more than a handful of dedicated people to ignite a project.

Cooperation has taken many forms, from early purchasing societies like the Rochdale Society of Equitable Pioneers started in 1844 outside Manchester, England, to large consortiums of industrial cooperatives like the Mondragón Group in the Basque region, to employee-managed stock ownership companies (ESOPs) like King Arthur Flour in Vermont today. What they all have in common is the ambition to be, in the words of the International Cooperative Alliance (ICA), "an autonomous association of persons united voluntarily to meet their common economic, social and cultural needs and aspirations through a jointly-owned and democratically-controlled enterprise."[25] Much of the thinking around cooperation has taken place in the context of cooperatives—but cooperation applies as well to insurance mutuals, credit unions, mutual aid projects, and more broadly to certain nonprofits and community organizations. The values and principles originally formulated for cooperatives—for instance, by the Rochdale Society in 1844 or more recently by the ICA in 1937—apply generally to all forms of cooperation.

Democratic participation, self-determination, equity in distributions and obligations, inclusiveness, solidarity, and caring for the welfare of all the stakeholders and for the environment: those are the guiding stars of cooperation. Often formulated in the context of cooperatives—for instance, by the ICA in its "Statement on the Cooperative Identity: the Values and Principles"—these are the central values shared by all the varied forms of cooperation. They are articulated in terms of seven core principles: first, that cooperation must be open to all without discrimination and based on voluntary membership; second, that the cooperative organization should be run democratically by the members themselves and that members should have equal say and an equal vote in the decision-making process; third, that the members should contribute and benefit equitably from the running of the enterprise; fourth, that the cooperation should remain autonomous and self-determining, under the control of the members only; fifth, that it must strive to provide training and education for the members; sixth, that there be cooperation among cooperative enterprises; and finally, that the cooperative enterprises strive toward the sustainable development of their environment and communities. As the ICA statement also emphasizes, "members believe in the ethical values of honesty, openness, social responsibility and caring for others."[26] These values and principles have been distilled from the myriad experiments and charters of cooperative enterprises over centuries. They are reflected as well in the legal codification of cooperatives around the world, including in the United States. The Tax Court of the United States, for instance, defines cooperatives, for purposes of the federal tax code, as enterprises that are democratically controlled by the members themselves and equitably allocate among the members the "fruits and increases arising from their cooperative endeavor" in relation to the members' participation in the cooperative endeavor.[27]

Today, there are cooperative efforts across the political spectrum. Some cooperatives aim to maintain a traditional way of life; others are more utopian or seek to achieve a solidarity economy. The Kingston Cheese Cooperative, for instance, is an Amish community dairy cooperative set up to support and sustain the traditional Amish community in Wisconsin. According to the *Wisconsin State Farmer*, the Amish community settled in Green Lake County, Wisconsin, in 1978 when families moved there from northern Indiana. When they arrived, there were four creameries that serviced dairy farmers, but those creameries closed. So the Amish community got together and decided to allow its members to work with electricity so that a few of them could take over one of the creameries and start an Amish dairy cooperative. They did so in 1984. When the COVID-19 pandemic hit, their sales plummeted, but the Amish community exercised its cooperative rights to buy the dairy plant, which employed at the time about thirty-five Amish men and women, to prevent mass layoffs and further disruption of life during the pandemic. They chose to further their collective mission: "protecting their way of life, keeping younger farmers in business and providing employment for all the men and women who work at the plant." This proved successful. "When the co-op began in 1984 there were 20 patrons with an average of 10 cows in their herds; back then 10,000 pounds of milk per day came into their cheese factory in cans to make blue cheese," the *Wisconsin State Farmer* reports. "Today there are about 87 patrons with an average of 15 cows; 40,000 pounds of milk comes into their plant each day."[28] The Kingston Cheese Cooperative emerged from the pandemic with new vibrancy.

At the other end of the country—and of the political spectrum—Cooperation Jackson is an ambitious effort to create a self-sustaining, self-determining, solidarity economy within the African American community of Jackson, Mississippi. Founded by Kali Akuno and others in 2014, Cooperation Jackson was established in a poor African American neighborhood with high rates of unemployment and poverty. The neighborhood had been abandoned by the municipality and private enterprise, leading to many abandoned buildings and lots. Cooperation Jackson raised funds and bought land to set up an agricultural cooperative, a food cooperative, and other cooperative enterprises. It expanded to create a shop with equipment, such as a 3-D printer, to create a makers' space. Today, Cooperation Jackson includes Freedom Farms Cooperative, a worker-owned urban-farming cooperative that grows and sells organic vegetables; Nubia's Place Café and Catering Cooperative, a worker-owned health-oriented catering business and café that coordinates with Freedom Farms; the Green Team, a worker-owned yard-care and composting cooperative that sells composted organic yard waste to farmers, hardware stores, and home-supply outlets; the Center for Community Production, a cooperative print manufacturing shop and fabrication lab with a 3-D printer; land held in common through the Fannie Lou Hamer Community Land Trust to serve the community; and educational and organizing spaces including the Kuwasi Balagoon Center for Economic Democracy and Development. In addition, Cooperation Jackson has set up the Jackson Human Rights Institute, which engages in human-rights training and organizing, with the ambition of turning Jackson into a "Human Rights City."[29]

Cooperation Jackson is part of a growing movement toward "solidarity economies." The U.S. Solidary Economy Network, organized in 2009, an outgrowth of a forum held at the University of Massachusetts, Amherst, defines a solidarity economy as an "alternative development framework" grounded in the values of cooperation, equity, mutualism, and solidarity, and in the following principles: "the primacy of social welfare over profits and the unfettered rule of the market; sustainability; social and economic democracy; [and] pluralism and organic approach, allowing for different forms in different contexts, and open to continual change driven from the bottom up."[30] As Ethan Miller explains, a solidarity economy seeks to get us beyond the simplicity of binary contradictions—for instance, jobs versus the environment—by rethinking the terms of the debate.[31] Networks of solidarity economy initiatives are growing across the globe, as evidenced by the Intercontinental Network for the Promotion of the Social Solidarity Economy, known as RIPESS, for "Réseau Intercontinental de Promotion de l'Économie Social Solidaire," organized in Lima, Peru, in 1997.

Popular support for cooperation is widespread. Polling data show broad support for worker cooperatives across the political spectrum. A survey conducted by Data for Progress in 2021 found that nearly 79 percent of Democrats and 66 percent of Republicans support "transition where small businesses become worker cooperatives." There is as well broad bipartisan support for programs that assist states in establishing or expanding worker cooperatives. Of all likely voters, 66 percent supported such programs, and only 20 percent opposed them. By the same token, voters across the political spectrum support the idea of creating a U.S. Employee Ownership Bank under the Department of the Treasury that would promote either employee stock-ownership plans or worker cooperatives.[32] There are even articles in conservative media, such as the *American Conservative* magazine, that speak favorably about cooperative businesses and how they can save communities—including, for instance, how the Democracy Brewing cooperative in the Dorchester neighborhood of Boston helped revive a depressed neighborhood or how the Democracy Collaborative, an organization dedicated to democratic initiatives, helped expand the Market Driven Community Cooperatives Initiative in Rochester, New York. "The number of worker co-operatives in the United States has been growing for two decades," the *American Conservative* reports; "the higher wages and shared ownership of co-ops have also helped them and their members stabilize and rebuild their communities."[33] This should not be entirely surprising. You may recall that even President Ronald Reagan supported employee ownership and said "I can't help but believe that in the future we will see in the United States . . . an increasing trend toward the next logical step, employee ownership. It is a path that befits a free people."[34]

Not only does the sentiment extend across the political spectrum, but cooperative efforts can be found throughout American commerce. There are forms of cooperation hidden in plain sight. They exist even in mainstream sectors and permeate the American economy: Land O'Lakes, Sunkist, and Ocean Spray are producer cooperatives; State Farm and Liberty Mutual are mutual insurance companies; REI is a consumer cooperative, and Ace Hardware a retailer cooperative. Isthmus Engineering and Manufacturing in Madison, Wisconsin, Cooperative Home Care in the Bronx, King Arthur Flour in Vermont, and AK Press in California are worker cooperatives. The Navy Federal Credit Union, with more than $125 billion in assets and eight million members, is a member credit union. And nonprofit educational, cultural, and social institutions, as well as community organizations, surround us.[35]

The insurance industry has been home to large and resilient mutual societies for a long time. Benjamin Franklin founded the oldest property insurance company in the country, a mutual that is considered the first recognized cooperative business in the United States.[36] Half of the largest ten property and casualty insurance companies today are mutuals; together, those five mutual insurance companies serve 25 percent of the entire market (by contrast, the five largest nonmutual insurance companies serve only 21 percent of the market). Most of the household-name insurance companies—State Farm, Liberty Mutual, New York Life, Nationwide, Northwestern Mutual, Mutual of Omaha, etc.—are mutuals and are extremely resilient. The median age of a U.S. mutual insurance company is about 120 years.[37]

Farmer and producer cooperatives, consumer cooperatives, worker cooperatives, and retailer cooperatives thrive across economic sectors today—despite everything being stacked against them. In fact, and quite surprisingly, cooperatives in the United States "survive through their first six to 10 years at a rate 7 percent higher than traditional small businesses."[38] Cooperatives can even thrive in the financial sector, where credit unions developed starting in 1920 with the Massachusetts

Association of Credit Unions and in 1934 with federal laws enabling their formation. Credit unions gained lasting status by surviving the Great Depression and the financial crises in the 1980s, and today have more than 100 million members in the United States.[39] In a country like France, the Crédit Agricole Group, which was formed by thirty-nine regional banks that are full-fledged cooperative entities, serves more than 21 million customers and has more than 9.3 million member-clients at the local level.[40] As of September 2018, Crédit Agricole had 23.3 percent of French household deposits and total assets of 1.7 trillion euros.[41]

Existing cooperative enterprises can be as large as multinationals. The Mondragón cooperative consortium, headquartered in the Basque region of Spain— a diversified enterprise manufacturing heavy equipment—employs more than 74,000 workers and brings in annual revenues in the billions of euros, 12.5 billion euros in 2016.[42] Mondragón is the seventh largest corporate group in Spain. Cooperative enterprises can dominate the competition and be technological leaders in their field. Swann-Morton, a worker cooperative in Sheffield, England, is a world leader in manufacturing and selling surgical blades and scalpels; it exports to more than one hundred countries around the globe. Founded in 1932 on the principle that "claims of individuals producing in an industry come first," Swann-Morton has estimated annual revenues today in the range of $50 million.[43] Cooperatives can also be small and local. Justice Cream is a community-owned, women-of-color-led, nonprofit, nondairy ice cream cooperative in Chicago that makes flavors like "snactivist," "flower to the people," "berry the colonizer," and "whole latte justice." Incorporated in Illinois in 2017, their mission, they write, is "to develop a solidarity economy through nondairy ice cream, while cultivating a collective consciousness through liberatory education." They donate 100 percent of their profits to grassroots community organizations that work toward collective liberation. (It's pronounced "justice cream," not "just ice cream.")[44]

Mutual-aid projects have also arisen organically throughout the United States, especially in response to the COVID-19 pandemic. Local mutual-aid efforts, some of which have grown to be nationwide, offer free home delivery of groceries by mutual-aid volunteers to the elderly and infirm confined at home and at great risk of contagion. One of the associations, Invisible Hands—note the ironic reference to Adam Smith—was set in motion by a college junior, Liam Elkind, and attracted more than 1,200 volunteers in its first ninety-six hours in early March 2020. It spawned chapters around the country, delivering groceries to those in need. By mid-April 2020, Invisible Hands had more than 12,000 volunteers and had served about 4,000 requests for aid.[45] Many people have been deeply involved in the mutual-aid movement during the pandemic, including Mariame Kaba, who is a devoted advocate of mutual aid, and Dean Spade, who has spearheaded mutual-aid efforts and written about them in a book titled *Mutual Aid: Building Solidarity During This Crisis (and the Next)*. It represents, Spade writes, an ideal of "Solidarity, Not Charity."[46]

The Reach of Cooperation

The reach of cooperation—and awareness—is also growing around the world. The United Nations declared 2012 the International Year of Cooperatives.[47] Today, almost 12 percent of the world's population are cooperative members, and there are at least 3 million cooperatives operating around the globe.[48] In 2012, the three hundred largest cooperatives in the world had revenues reaching $2.2 trillion.[49] In the United Kingdom alone, more than 7,100 cooperatives contribute more than $45 billion to the British economy.[50] In the United States, agricultural cooperatives have about 2.2 million farm memberships, with gross business volume of all farmer cooperatives reaching $170.1 billion in 2010. More broadly, in the United States, as of 2011, 48,000 cooperatives directly served about 120 million people, almost 40 percent of the total population. These include 8,334 credit unions with more than 91 million members and $760 billion in assets; 930 rural electric cooperatives serving 42 million people; 2,723 property casualty mutual insurance companies; and more than 50,000 families using cooperative day-care centers daily.[51] The number of worker cooperatives in the United States has nearly doubled over the past decade.[52]

Cooperation is flourishing around the world, from Manhattan, Brooklyn, and the Bronx, where Cooperative Home Care Associates, a worker-owned cooperative of home-care aides, has become one of the largest worker cooperatives in the United States (around 1,700 workers) and has consistently lower turnover than other home-care businesses, to farm-machinery cooperatives (called CUMAs in French, for *coopératives d'utilisation de matériel agricole*) that mutualize plows, tractors, and combine harvesters for their member farmers and now total more than 11,000 in France, representing almost 50 percent of French farmers.[53] Networks of cooperation are thriving across the globe from the Co-operative and Policy Alternative Center in South Africa, to the U.S. Solidarity Economy Network in Belchertown, Massachusetts, to RIPESS in Africa, Asia, Europe, Latin America and the Caribbean, North America, and Oceania.

A quiet revolution is taking place. From the centuries-old International Cooperative Alliance (ICA) in Brussels, to Cooperation Vermont, to Cooperation Humboldt in California, to agricultural cooperatives in South African, to the NYC Network of Worker Cooperatives (NYC NOWC, which they pronounce "Nick-Knock"!), more and more organizations around the world promote cooperation. There is also a growing number of organizations helping to support cooperatives and businesses that want to become cooperatives. The International Organization of Industrial, Artisanal, and Service Producers' Co-operatives (CICOPA), for instance, is a global member-based organization that supports producer, worker, and social cooperatives around the world.[54] One of its core missions is promoting cooperation *among* cooperatives. CICOPA has a network of more than fifty members from thirty-five countries that it tries to link and assist. Those members include more than 65,000 enterprises that employ four million people across the world. To assist those members, it has three regional branches, CECOP (CICOPA Europe), CICOPA Américas, and CICOPA Asia-Pacific.

The Democracy at Work Institute at the United States Federation of Worker Cooperatives, led by Esteban Kelly, also actively supports worker cooperatives and seeks to increase cooperation.[55] Their mission, they explain, is to "expand the worker cooperative model to reach communities most directly affected by social and economic inequality, specifically people of color, recent immigrants, and low-wage workforces."[56] At a more local level, the Democracy Collaborative, founded at the University of Maryland, works to expand cooperatives and launch cooperative initiatives.[57] The *American Conservative* reports that it has been "at the forefront of a new model for Rust Belt cities struggling with growing poverty and unemployment, called the Cleveland Model from the city where it was first put into practice. The result, called the Evergreen Cooperative Initiative, was launched in 2008. Evergreen partnered with local educational, healthcare, and charitable organizations to start worker co-ops to provide some of the millions of dollars worth of goods and services they need every year."[58] The Democracy Collaborative, with funding from the Surdna Foundation, has also put in place a "Cooperative Growth Ecosystem" framework to encourage and engage people across public, private, financial and nonprofit sectors to catalyze worker cooperatives.[59]

In addition, the Platform Cooperativism Consortium at the New School in New York City promotes gig-worker platform cooperatives around the world; the Cooperative Development Foundation in Washington, DC, extends grants and loans to promote the development of cooperatives;[60] Co-opLaw provides legal analysis and resources for worker cooperatives; and the National Cooperative Business Association supports cooperative development in the United States. The Center for Cooperatives at the agricultural college at Ohio State University offers an online open-access course, Co-op Mastery: Beyond Cooperatives 101, that provides educational materials to understand every facet of the cooperative model, from formation to the legal, financial, and tax dimensions.[61] Even USAID supports overseas cooperative developments through U.S.-based cooperative development organizations.[62] USAID's Cooperative Development Program, in its own words, "invest(s) in cooperatives and credit unions around the world to build social cohesion, stabilize economies, and support local communities."[63]

The Community Wealth project maintains a long list of organizations that support cooperatives at the state and local level, including the Federation of Southern Cooperatives, the Cooperative Network, the California Center for Cooperative Development, the Food Co-op Initiative, the National Cooperative Grocers Association, the Northwest Cooperative Development Center, the Cooperative Teach-In, the Northcountry Cooperative Development Fund, and the Cooperative Fund of New England.[64] *Co-op News*, based in the United Kingdom, shares information about cooperation and the global cooperatives movement. A monthly magazine and a news website, it was established in 1871, is reader-owned, and is published by a cooperative society, Co-operative Press Ltd.[65] At the local level, NYC NOWC hosts free seminars on financing options for worker cooperatives. CooperationWorks!, a national U.S. network, also provides board training and business planning for new and ongoing cooperatives.

There is also a growing chorus of academics and public intellectuals advocating for cooperation and an increasing body of research and academic literature. Sara Horowitz, who founded the Freelancers Union and built a whole ecosystem around working freelancers, has developed a whole philosophy and practice of "mutualism" that promotes the objectives of cooperation. In her book, *Mutualism: Building the Next Economy from the Ground Up*, published in 2021, Horowitz charts a path for a mutualist economy, from the bottom up, one in which, in her words, "groups of like-minded people, yoked together by shared geography, a shared economic stake, or a shared belief, . . . come together to try to solve an intractable problem that government or markets either can't or won't solve for them."[66] E. G. Nadeau, who has been involved with cooperatives for more than fifty years since he served in the Peace Corps in Senegal in 1970, has written a series of books, including *The Cooperative Solution: How the*

United States Can Tame Recessions, Reduce Inequality, and Protect the Environment (2012) and, with Luc Nadeau, *The Cooperative Society: The Next Stage of Human History* (2016), building on earlier work with David Thompson in *Cooperation Works!: How People Are Using Cooperative Action to Rebuild Communities and Revitalize the Economy* (1996).[67] In his work, Nadeau argues that "humans may be on the threshold of a new historical stage, one characterized by cooperation, democracy, the equitable distribution of resources and a sustainable relationship with nature."[68] More recently, Nadeau published *Strengthening the Cooperative Community* (2021), in which he shares his experiences and personal stories and makes a full-throated argument for the cooperative approach.[69] Richard Wolff argues for self-directed worker enterprises in his book *Democracy at Work: A Cure for Capitalism*, published in 2012. Peter Ranis of the CUNY Graduate Center published *Cooperatives Confront Capitalism* in 2016; arguing for worker cooperatives in our post-Occupy digital economy, Ranis draws especially on lessons from the Argentinian cooperative context and argues for the use of eminent domain in the United States as a way to build more worker cooperatives and autonomy.[70] Catherine Mulder published *Transcending Capitalism Through Cooperative Practices* in 2015; in deep case studies, she explores democratic and cooperative alternatives to conventional shareholder companies, including not only conventional cooperatives like the New Era Window Cooperative and the Syracuse Cooperative Federal Credit Union but also the London Symphony Orchestra (musician-run and self-governing) and the Green Bay Packers (owned by the fans).[71]

There is a lot of new economics research on the cooperative economy and worker cooperatives by economists such as Francesco Caselli and Thomas Brzustowski at the London School of Economics, Ignacio Bretos at the University of Zaragoza, Roger A. McCain at Drexel University, Sonja Novkovic at St. Mary's University, Anu Puusa at the Finland Business School, Todd M. Schmit at Cornell University, and Spencer Thompson at the University of Cambridge, building on earlier economics research by Benjamin Ward and others, including John P. Bonin, Derek C. Jones, and Louis Putterman.[72] There are also new academic journals dedicated to the field, such as the *Journal of Co-operative Organization and Management*, which started in 2013; the *Journal of Cooperatives*, founded in 2007 with a focus on agribusiness and rural sectors, building on the *Journal of Agricultural Cooperation* (1986-1994); the *Journal of Cooperative Studies*, in print again since 2006; the *International Journal of Cooperative Studies*, founded in 2012; the *International Journal of*

Community and Cooperative Studies that began in 2014; and the *International Journal of Co-Operative Accounting and Management*, formed in 2018.[73]

Cooperation has prospered silently for years and now surrounds us: worker cooperatives for producing and manufacturing; credit unions for banking; housing cooperatives for living; mutuals for insuring; producer, retailer, and consumer cooperatives for commercial exchange; nonprofit organizations for good works and learning; mutual aid and community projects for living. It is time to take the next step.

TOWARD A POLITICAL, ECONOMIC, AND SOCIAL THEORY AND PRACTICE OF COÖPERISM

These pervasive and resilient initiatives reveal, at their core, a form of cooperation power that represents the surplus that is generated when cooperation produces more than the sum of its parts. Cooperation generates that extra element—that additional part beyond the sum of the parts—that we might call "coöpower." Coöpower derives from the strength of the values and principles at the heart of cooperation: participatory democracy, equity in the distribution of wealth, care for all the stakeholders, solidarity, sustainability, and concern for the working environment.

It is time to harvest and distill this coöpower and place it at the heart of a political, economic, and social paradigm. It is time to concentrate it and make it grow, almost like a fission chain reaction, off the productive interactions of these core values and principles. These ideals can build on one another, reinforce and empower one another, in a way that would amplify the quiet paradigm of cooperation. In effect, it is time to combine, leverage, and compound the most promising forms of cooperation.

There are today many cooperative forms that can serve as a basis for a larger society fueled by coöpower. But not all the instances of cooperation are perfect models. Some ESOPs, for instance, retain a very top-down managerial style. Some consumer cooperatives engage in unfavorable labor practices with their retail workers. Some retail cooperatives are primarily dedicated to reducing costs and increasing profitability. Some nonprofits have an autocratic management style, and some have a mission to undermine cooperation. In other words, not all cooperative enterprises fully promote the core values and principles—or all of them. Some cooperatives also go through de-cooperative phases and become

mixed or hybrid as they grow. Some get embroiled in disputes against unionization; others go through growing pains.

In order to make progress, then, we need to focus on the cooperative initiatives
that best promote the core values and principles of cooperation and find ways to
combine and concentrate them into an integrated framework—what we might call
"coöperism."[74] The idea of coöperism is not just to extend forms of cooperation to
other domains or increase the number of cooperative enterprises, although that
is part of it, but to *concentrate* forms of cooperation so that the more beneficial
forms aggregate and build on one another. The idea is to combine the most promising forms of cooperatives so that, for instance, a worker cooperative sells to a
consumer cooperative to enhance the amount of cooperation. Or a farmer cooperative sources a nonprofit community food service. The idea is to leverage forms
of cooperation so that, for example, a worker cooperative uses a credit union to
help employees become members. Or an insurance mutual supports the operation
of a producer cooperative. The effect is thus to *compound* cooperation and double
down on the forms that best promote the core principles, so that the benefits of
cooperation and coöpower are intensified and grow cumulatively.

Coöperism takes the most promising forms of cooperation, those that are
most true to the values and principles, and agglomerates them to create an integrated political, economic, and social whole that can displace existing frameworks, such as investor shareholder logics that extract capital from businesses or
the social paradigm of punishment and law-and-order that harms communities. It
represents a copious vision that spans the political, economic, and social domains.
It builds on the *political ideal* of participatory democracy, extending that model to
all the other realms of life—to the workplace, enabling workers to manage their
own environment and production through one-person-one-vote principles, and
to consumer cooperatives, insurance mutuals, and credit unions, transforming
the consumer, the insured, and the creditor or debtor into active agents rather
than passive objects. It offers an *economic model* of sustainability and ecology that
can displace the extractive logics of shareholder investment. Rather than individuals competing with one another for scarce resources or trying to reap all the
benefits, coöperism rests on the idea of benefiting all the stakeholders of an enterprise and respecting their environment. It provides a different *social framework* as
well. The logic of coöperism entails a different way of viewing the world. Rather
than relying on a paradigm of punishment, it paves the way for a social paradigm
of cooperation that puts in place the support and community mechanisms that

can address difficulties before they turn into harms. It allows for the circulation of a new form of power, coöpower, throughout society that, as it gains traction and momentum, can displace disciplinary power, biopower, expository power, and other forms of power.[75]

Coöperism will be more effective at dealing with our global crises than either of the two dominant paradigms. To be sure, it doesn't control major media outlets and may not lobby as well as the others. It doesn't wave a national flag. But it does not require a supermajority, just people working together and creating momentum. It's like a mole that persistently digs its tunnel, or the tortoise, constant and steady, that eventually leads the way. It promises to resolve the multiple crises we face in a far more effective manner.

In the face of global climate change, coöperism focuses on the environment as part of the collective well-being of consumers, producers, workers, and all the other stakeholders. As one of its core mandates, it centers the principle that cooperative enterprises strive toward sustainability and a healthy environment for communities.[76] Rather than competing so as to outlive others or gain higher ground, it seeks to improve the living conditions of all people. The goal of cooperation is not to maximize the extraction of profit but to support and maintain the stakeholders of the enterprise and to distribute well-being, which depends on an ecologically healthy environment. The logic, principles, and values of coöperism can serve to slow down our extractive societies headed into the climate abyss.

In the face of threats to democracy, it fosters social organization that strengthens and deepens our commitment to genuine participatory processes in which everyone has an equal vote. It expands the scope of full and fair electoral mechanisms. It trains us for widespread democratic participation infused with the values of solidarity, equality, and social justice, reflected in the "one vote principle" and nonhierarchical mutual relations.[77] In the face of new pandemics, it fosters collaboration, respect, and care for others, including those who are more vulnerable. In the face of growing inequality in society, it reverses the trend by distributing more equitably the benefits and wealth created by members of cooperative enterprises.

Coöperism shares family resemblances with other social movements and theoretical developments, which may also facilitate its growth. It resonates with community experiments in democratic decision making, what Charles Sabel, William Simon, and others call "democratic experimentalism"; with collaborative efforts and projects like Wikipedia and Linux, or what Yochai Benkler, Josh Lerner, Eben

Moglen, Jean Tirole, Mikhaïl Xifaras, and others refer to as the new open-source economics, free software projects, and creative commons; with Indigenous, environmental, and labor movements, like the Red Deal, or Canada's Leap Manifesto which advocates for an economy centered on "caring for one another and caring for the planet," as well as the Green New Deal; with steady-growth and degrowth movements in economics; with new theoretical writings on the craft and rituals of cooperation, such as Richard Sennett's book *Together*; as well as with older movements for worker autonomy such as the "operaismo" movements that Toni Negri and others made famous in Italy.[78] In fact, the word *cooperation* traces its etymology to the same root as *operaismo*: it comes from the Latin *operari*, "work," and *co-* or *com-*, "with, together." Coöperism comes from *co-operari*, "working together."

We have been led to believe that the political choice today is between individualism and government policy making—between patriotic liberty and government mandates. That choice is false. It is a deceit. It is, in truth, nothing more than a choice between regulation by shareholder investors and regulation by government policy makers who default to those equity holders. There is another more promising path: we can regulate ourselves through coöperism, in every facet of our lives, across all political, economic, and social domains—*we*, not the corporate investors for their own enrichment nor the government policy makers who end up enriching corporations and the superwealthy, but *ourselves*, through forms of distilled, leveraged, and compounded cooperation that place our well-being and the environment at the heart of the future. In the face of our newfound interdependence, this is an urgent choice to make.

Taken together, the political, economic, and social strands of coöperism form a new democratic theory that we might call "cooperation democracy." It includes a positive element that democratizes the many dimensions of our lives that today remain undemocratic—work and employment, finance, economics, social relations—but it also serves as a limiting principle to the idea of democracy itself. The fact is, not all forms of electoral democracy are of equal value. Some can be tyrannical, some racist, some can even tend toward fascism by majority vote. There must be substantive limits to the procedural conception of democracy. Cooperation democracy provides a measure for the quality of democracy to which we should aspire today.

A WORD ON LANGUAGE AND A ROAD MAP

I have chosen the word *coöperism*, with the suffix *-ism*, to communicate that these forms of cooperation amount to a political and economic regime in contrast to capitalism or communism. Other words could have been used—simply cooperation, for instance, or other variations on the word, such as cooperationism. By contrast to "cooperation" alone, though, the term *coöperism* is intended to capture the idea of a concentrated form of cooperation, one that leverages and compounds cooperation, one that enriches coöpower. The French economist and historian Charles Gide used the term *coopératisme*; he titled later editions of his book *Le Coopératisme*, beginning with the fifth in 1929. Earlier editions had used *coopération* in the title, but he opted to modify it to *coopératisme* not only to distinguish it from his other books with "cooperation" in the title but also, in his words, "because the word ending in *ism* better expresses the general idea that links all these chapters: to expose the characteristic traits of a social system that must be distinguished on the one hand from individualism and on the other from collectivism."[79]

A professor at the Collège de France, Gide spent his entire career and all his years of annual lectures at the Collège promoting cooperatives, particularly consumer cooperatives. Cofounder of the French cooperative philosophy, known as the École de Nîmes, and a proponent of cooperative federalism (which favored consumer over producer cooperatives), Gide published his numerous annual lectures at the Collège de France, including among others *Fourier, Precursor of Cooperation*; *Worker Cooperatives for Production*; *Cooperation in England and in Russia*; *The French Cooperatives During the War*, and *The Cooperatist Program*. His eventual embrace of the term *cooperatism* was an effort to systematize his lifelong research project and activism. For reasons that will become clear later, I did not want to follow in his footsteps.

The term *coöperism* serves better to show the broader political, economic, and social reach of cooperation: it represents a concentrated, integrated, systemic framework for promoting mutual welfare, health, and environment rather than maximizing profit. Hopefully, coöperism will begin to roll off the tongue the way that capitalism or communism did. As I explained in a footnote the first time I used the term, I have retained the use of the diaeresis on the second vowel (ö) not to sound pretentious, nor to resemble an issue of the *New Yorker*, but in order to distinguish the term from the urban slang and avoid the pronunciation "cooper-ism."[80] It should sound instead like "co-operism."

Second, I use the word *capital* extensively in this book. By capital, I mean equity, shares of stock, in essence the alienable financial stake in a corporation. Capital is the transferable equity interest in an ongoing publicly traded enterprise or, now increasingly for the superwealthy, investments in private equity or hedge funds that mimic stock market holdings. This differs from other possible definitions of the term. Thomas Piketty, in his book *Capital in the Twenty-First Century*, defines capital as any nonhuman asset. Capital, for Piketty, represents wealth.[81] In fact, he uses those two terms interchangeably, in his own words "as if they were perfectly synonymous." For Piketty, capital includes all assets (except human capital) that can be traded or exchanged on any kind of market. Piketty includes in his definition of capital all land and natural resources, as well as gold and other stores of value, and residential real estate. It includes patents and intellectual property, and other forms of immaterial capital reflected in stock value, for instance. In Piketty's words, "capital is defined as the sum total of nonhuman assets that can be owned and exchanged on some market. Capital includes all forms of real property as well as financial and professional capital (plants, infrastructure, machinery, patents, and so on) used by firms and government agencies." It is basically all wealth or assets that can be exchanged on markets. The one factor that Piketty excludes is human capital; so, by contrast to a thinker like Katharina Pistor, who includes human capital if it has been augmented, it does not include for Piketty any form of individual labor power, training, education, skills, or abilities. Piketty defines capital in this way because he is primarily interested in understanding the relationship between the portion of national income that is attributable to labor versus capital. In other words, he is primarily interested in measuring the wealth of nations, what he calls "national income," and understanding a country's domestic product as a relationship between capital and labor. So he writes, "all production must be distributed as income in one form or another, to either labor or capital: whether as wages, salaries, honoraria, bonuses, and so on (that is, as payments to workers and others who contributed labor to the process of production) or else as profits, dividends, interest, rent, royalties, and so on (that is, as payments to the owners of Capital used in the process of production)."[82] My interest here in capital is different: I am more focused on the logic of capital investment.

Katharina Pistor, in her book *The Code of Capital*, defines capital only as the limited set of assets that are legally privileged: assets become capital when lawyers bestow on them certain attributes of priority, durability, universality, and convertibility. Pistor offers a nice history and typology of the definition of capital in *The Code of Capital*. She refers to Fernand Braudel, who traced capital back to the thirteenth century as primarily "a fund of money, goods, or money rented out for interests, at least where this was permissible"; to Geoffrey Hodgson's book *Conceptualizing Capitalism*; and to other ways of conceiving of capital, whether as tangible, as a factor of production, or as an accounting variable. Disagreeing with both Karl Marx and Karl Polanyi, Pistor distinguishes capital from mere commodification. She writes: "Capitalism, it turns out, is more than just the exchange of goods in a market economy; it is a market economy in which some assets are placed on legal steroids."[83] The special feature of capital and capitalism, for Pistor, is the "asset prime" element. Karl Marx defined capital specifically as the money received from the sale of commodities that is then used as a mode of production to buy other commodities, equipment, or labor.[84] Although those other definitions may well have their place in empirical, legal, or economic analyses, I am using the term in a different way. For my purposes, capital is defined in its corporate-finance meaning: capital is transferrable ownership shares of publicly traded companies and contemporary substitutes like private equity or hedge fund investments. I am focused on the logic of what we (misleadingly) call capitalism. More on that later.

Third, in this book, I have not rehashed familiar arguments about the growing inequality in contemporary United States and other societies across the globe. Thomas Piketty and his fellow economists, Emmanuel Saez and others, have done this work more ably than I could. Their economic research, which has been subjected to the most intense scrutiny and peer review, establishes conclusively that the level of inequality has steadily grown, across the globe, since the decline of the welfare state in the mid-twentieth century. Their quantitative analyses have documented a U-curve in inequality that is rippling around the globe. I need not rehearse their arguments. Instead, I build on their foundation. Piketty's policy proposals focus mainly on redistributive taxation schemes and participatory socialism. "I am convinced," Piketty writes, "that capitalism and private property can be superseded and that a just society can be established on the basis of participatory socialism and social federalism."[85] Much of his analysis builds on practices from Nordic social democracies; but those of us in countries like the United States are far too removed from those Nordic practices to bridge the gap in time to deal with the looming crises. In addition, Piketty favors giving larger equity shareholders more voting power in cooperative enterprises, which goes against the central values and principles at the core of cooperation.[86] For reasons that will become clear in this book, I propose instead a different way of organizing economic and social exchange: coöperism. It is an approach that does not require mass collective action or convincing a supermajority. It starts instead with individual initiatives and small-group cooperation, and operates through a snowball effect to create social change. That snowball effect is crucial to its success. In that sense, this book offers a different vision for the future. It builds on Piketty, but orients us in another direction. You could read it as different concluding chapters to his two tomes.

Finally, I anchor the theory of coöperism in contemporary forms of cooperation that surround us today—from household names that we have come to cherish, including mutual insurance companies like State Farm, consumer cooperatives like R.E.I., and producer cooperatives like Land O'Lakes, to the many other more political and utopian experiments in cooperation, from Cooperation Jackson in Jackson, Mississippi, to Kingston Cheese Cooperative in Green Lake County, Wisconsin. Many of these companies and experiments have some weaknesses, and not every one is intended to be a perfect model. In fact, coöperism does not build on every one of them. But in laying the foundations, I am trying to privilege currently existing, ordinary household names of cooperation. They offer a different principle of economics: cooperation and mutualism, rather than shareholder profit and raw competition. My intention is to get at that essence. I will begin, then, with those well-known forms of cooperation to tease out, on their basis, a compounded theory of coöperism. I will also respond to potential criticisms. My ambition is to show how coöperism forms part of the larger democratic theory I call cooperation democracy and how it may have important implications for displacing the paradigm of punishment that operates in our punitive societies.

In terms of a road map, I will begin by exploring the omnipresence of cooperation throughout the world today to demonstrate how pervasive and often hidden it is (chapter 2). I will then expose the simplicity of cooperation by describing, in the most accessible terms possible, the corporate finance of cooperatives and mutuals. I will lift the hood and show the simple mechanisms that make cooperation function (chapter 3). Then, I will develop a political, economic, and social theory of coöperism (chapters 4, 5, and 6, respectively) as a concentrated form of cooperation that distills the core values and principles of cooperation into a unified and coherent political, economic, and social regime. I will argue that coöperism, as a leveraged form of cooperation, extends the political ideal of participatory democracy to every aspect of our lives, from consumption to housing to finance to daily living and mutual support (chapter 4); that it provides an economic alternative to the dominant economic regimes (misleadingly) called capitalism and communism (chapter 5); and that it offers an alternative social paradigm to the punishment paradigm in which we now live (chapter 6). I will then respond to the most powerful potential criticisms of the theory of coöperism from both the right and the left (chapter 7). Finally, I will articulate the larger framework of coöperism democracy—or what I call, for simplicity and for ease on the tongue, cooperation democracy—a framework that can save democratic theory in these times of crises and threats to democratic institutions (chapter 8).

An era of cooperation democracy is on our horizon. It heralds a transformation of our economy, our politics, and our society as significant as the revolution that replaced feudalism with capitalism. It augurs a coöperist society in which the well-being of everyone in society and the welfare of the environment are placed ahead of the profits of a few. It is now time, past time, to embrace and support this new horizon. The techniques and ways of cooperation have been refined and are simple. The legal forms have been developed. It is time to usher in the new age of coöperism. Its dawn could not be more pressing. With climate change, pandemics, nuclear proliferation, and other global threats, our human interdependence has never been greater or more urgent. Now is the time for an age of coöperism.

CHAPTER 2

The Ubiquity of Cooperation

I n 1888, a team of researchers under the direction of Herbert B. Adams and the auspices of the Johns Hopkins University fanned out across the United States to document every cooperative they encountered—hundreds of them scattered around the country, hidden in plain sight, from the deepest regions of the Deep South (the Coöperative Mining Company in Salisbury, Alabama, the Coöperative Underwear Factory in Richmond, Virginia, the Knights of Labor Coöperative Laundry in Fort Worth, Texas, among many others), to the uppermost reaches of the Northeast (the Somerset Coöperative Foundry, the East Templeton Coöperative Chair Company, the Middlesex Coöperative Boot and Shoe Company, and many more in Massachusetts, Vermont, and Maine).[1] In a 540-page, twelve-part, collaborative compilation, *History of Coöperation in the United States*, the team of five Johns Hopkins researchers surveyed and described every cooperative enterprise in New England, the Middle States, the Northwest, West, South, and Pacific Coast of the United States.[2] Adams's team recounted all the intricacies of each cooperative association, detailing their membership holdings and share value, the number of workers or stakeholders, their dates of incorporation, their profitability, and their internal organization. The researchers described everything from the creation of the Sociologic Society of America, organized in New York in 1882 by Imogene C. Fales to promote cooperation in that state, to the track record of growth and sustainability of cooperatives in the state of Massachusetts, which early on, in 1866, passed general laws for the incorporation of cooperative companies and retained official records of their assets and financial condition.[3]

Since that time, there have been detailed histories of different periods of cooperation, of different demographic groups cooperating, of different types and industries of cooperatives both in the United States and around the globe. W. E. B. Du Bois traced the history of African American cooperatives in his meticulous 1907 study, *Economic Co-operation Among Negro Americans*. Du Bois reached as far back as precolonial Africa, the West Indies, and the American colonies, before then tracing the history of cooperation during the antebellum period, especially surrounding the Underground Railroad. He broke down his analysis by type and sector of cooperation, discussing every form, from African American churches and schools to Black secret societies, insurance mutuals, and banks, to worker and producer cooperatives in the African American communities.[4] Du Bois's study had its origins in the Twelfth Conference for the Study of the Negro Problems held at Atlanta University in May 1907, which was entirely focused on the promise of cooperation. As part of the conference, the organizers, including Du Bois, Robert Page Sims, president of Bluefield State College in West Virginia, and Nils Olas Nelson, founder of the model cooperative company town in Leclaire, Illinois, pledged to support and promote cooperative efforts among African Americans: "We believe that every effort ought to be made to foster and emphasize present tendencies among Negroes toward co-operative effort and that the ideal of wide ownership of small capital and small accumulations among many rather than great riches among a few, should persistently be held before them."[5]

A hundred years later, Jessica Gordon Nembhard continued the history of African American cooperatives in her 2014 book, *Collective Courage: A History of African American Cooperative Economic Thought and Practice*. Nembhard recounts how Montgomery, Alabama, became the site of the founding of the Colored Merchants Association in 1925, a cooperative of African American grocery store owners; and New York City, the headquarters of the Young Negroes' Co-operative League, cofounded by Ella Jo Baker in 1930, with chapters across the country.[6] As Nembhard documents, cooperation in African American communities had deep Southern roots, was extensive, and spanned almost from the arrival of enslaved captured African men and women to the present. Cooperation Jackson today, in Jackson, Mississippi, continues that long tradition.[7] Alex Gourevitch traces the genealogy of how nineteenth-century "labor republicans," drawing on the classical tradition of republican thought, advocated for worker cooperatives, in his book *From Slavery to the Cooperative Commonwealth: Labor and Republican Liberty in the Nineteenth Century*.[8] Steve Leikin, in his account of *The Practical Utopians: American Workers and the Cooperative Movement in the Gilded Age*, covers the history of American worker cooperatives during the late nineteenth century. Leikin pays

particular attention to the relation between cooperatives and the labor movement and unionization, focusing on the history of the cooperatives associated
with the Knights of Labor, the Shoe Workers of Stoneham, and the Coopers
of Minneapolis.[9]

In terms of different types of cooperatives, Albert Sonnichsen surveyed the
early history of consumer cooperatives in the United States and internationally
in his 1919 book, *Consumers' Coöperation*.[10] Sonnichsen traced consumer cooperation in the United States from the early colonies through the Granger movement,
the Sovereigns of Industry, and Knights of Labor, to the cooperative societies
in southern Illinois, Seattle, Pennsylvania, Florida, and the Lower East Side of
New York City.[11] He offers a marvelous account of the tenacity and persistence
of Hyman Cohn, a Jewish salesman, who brought the idea of cooperatives to the
Lower East Side in the 1910s and was so dogged that he became known as Coöperative Cohn.[12] Cohn started the Coöperative League, which soon led to the opening of a cooperative hat store on Delancey Street and eventually the cooperative
production of hats. "The Coöperative League," Sonnichsen writes, "was undoubtedly the first *democratic* coöperative organization to carry on a general propa-
ganda in this country."[13] The longer historical arc is traced in Florence E. Parker's
A History of Distributive and Service Cooperation in the United States, 1829–1954.[14]

Joseph K. Knapp, who served as the administrator of the Farmer Cooperative
Service of the U.S. Department of Agriculture from 1953 to 1966, traced the history of farmer and agricultural cooperatives from the American colonies to the
mid-twentieth century in his two-volume work, *The Rise of American Cooperative
Enterprise 1620–1920* and *The Advance of American Cooperative Enterprise 1920–1945*.
He showed how economic adversity and recessions actually favored the expansion of the agricultural cooperative movement.[15] Robert Jackall and Henry M.
Levin recount the history of worker cooperatives, focusing mostly on the modern
period of the 1970s and 1980s in their book, *Worker Cooperatives in America*, published in 1984.[16]

More recently, John Curl's magisterial history of the cooperative movement
in the United States, *For All the People*, published in 2012—building on his earlier
book, *History of Work Cooperation in America* from 1980—traces the full history of
cooperation in this country.[17] Curl starts from indigenous traditions of cooperation and mutual aid, and the cooperative networks among enslaved Black persons in the antebellum South, to then recount the organizing by the Wobblies
and radical farmers of the Progressive Era in the early twentieth century, the

mutual aid projects following the Great Depression, the creation of the Cooperative League, and the emergence of modern cooperatives in the 1960s and '70s.[18] As John Curl shows, the United States has been a land of experimentation—from the Owenite cooperative experiment at New Harmony, Indiana, with more than nine hundred inhabitants and twenty thousand acres in 1825, to the myriad "Phalanxes" set up along the model of Charles Fourier's (some thirty-four of them from the North down to Mississippi between 1843 and 1850), to the communes of Icaria and Communia set up by French and German political refugees after 1848, to the abolitionist communities of Nashoba in Tennessee and all along the Underground Railroad, to the communes of the 1960s and 1970s.[19]

THE GLOBAL REACH OF COOPERATION

Today, there are millions of ongoing forms of cooperation around the world, hidden in plain view. More than 1.2 billion people are members of cooperative enterprises. In Italy alone, in 2008, there were more than 25,000 worker cooperatives, plus another 17,000 majority-employee-owned firms.[20]

Some forms of cooperation are very local, others international. Some are large consortiums, others small groupuscules. Some are fledgling, others centuries old. At the international level, the International Cooperative Alliance (ICA), now headquartered in Brussels, is perhaps one of the largest and oldest umbrella organizations to promote cooperation through associations and networks of cooperative members. The ICA was founded during the First Cooperative Congress held in London in August 1895, which was attended by representatives from cooperatives around the world, including Argentina, Australia, Belgium, Denmark, England, France, Germany, Holland, India, Italy, Serbia, Switzerland, and the United States.[21] The ICA has promoted the cooperative model around the world for decades now. It currently has 318 organization members from 112 countries, covering all sectors of the economy (industry, agriculture, services, goods, insurance, banking, etc.). In the United States, some of the organizations that belong to the ICA include the National Rural Electric Co-operative Association (NRECA) in Arlington, Virginia; the National Society of Accountants for Co-operatives (NSAC) in Dayton, Ohio; the Credit Union National Association, Inc. (CUNA) in Washington, DC; Land O'Lakes Venture37 and the National Co+op Grocers (NCG) in Minnesota; and the National Cooperative Bank (NCB) in Virginia.

At the local level, cooperation can emerge punctually, often in response to local-ized emergencies. The SolidarityNYC network developed after Hurricane Sandy hit New York City in 2012 and began coordinating relief networks and assistance. Shortly thereafter, a collective of academics, artists, community members, and organizers got together to learn about and share, through research and interviews, different facets of the solidarity economy that emerged in New York City in the wake of Sandy. With a team of volunteers who fanned out and interviewed people around the city, they worked with scholars and researchers, such as Olivia Geiger from the University of Massachusetts, Amherst, and Evan Casper-Flutterman from Rutgers University, to pull together a report compiling all the different fac-ets of cooperation in the city: *Growing a Resilient City: Collaboration in New York City's Solidarity Economy.*[22]

Some forms of cooperation become huge conglomerates, like the Mondragón consortium mentioned earlier, headquartered in the Basque province of Gipuz-koa, which manufactures automotive components, construction and industrial equipment, household equipment, and machine tools.[23] Mondragón began in the 1950s, with its first industrial cooperative created in 1956, Talleres Ulgor (now known as Fagor), producing heaters and kerosene stoves. The driving force behind Mondragón was a young Catholic praxis-oriented priest, José Mariá Arizmendiar-rieta, whose efforts to establish technical training schools, as well as cultural and educational associations, culminated in the opening of a number of cooperatives in the region, including agricultural, manufacturing, consumer, insurance, and banking cooperatives.[24] The cooperatives were integrated into one entity called the Mondragón Cooperative Group. Today it is composed of more than one hun-dred independent worker cooperatives. Including subsidiaries, it now employs more than 74,000 workers in about sixty-five countries.[25] The Mondragón con-sortium also includes a credit union called Caja Laboral Popular Cooperativa de Crédito. There is also now a Mondragón Cooperative University, operating since 1997.[26] The consortium recently brought in revenues of 12.5 billion euros.[27] It has gone through some difficult periods and crises, including strikes and strife, like most companies, and moments of refounding, but seventy years later it remains an exemplar of a large, industrial worker cooperative consortium—the seventh largest group in Spain.[28] The economist Spencer Thompson catalogues the stud-ies that have shown Mondragón to have a "high quality of management relative to conventional firms operating in the same sectors," "exceptional capacity for innovation," "deep-level cooperation," and "workers [who] reported greater levels of job control, participation, and work motivation; identified more strongly with their firm; and maintained higher-trust and more consensual relationships with their colleagues and managers than workers in capitalist firms with similar divisions of labour and management systems."[29]

Other forms of cooperation are targeted, focused on an economic sector or a single community or even a local garden. The Freelancers Union is a mutualist network based in New York City for freelance workers. Founded by Sara Horowitz on the basis of a nonprofit she established in 1995, Working Today, and in collaboration with Leyla Vural and others, the Freelancers Union established a mutualist insurance program and offers resources and legislative support to the ecosystem of freelance workers. The OSS (Outer Seed Shadow) Project in the Marble Hill community in the Bronx, started by community activist Jacki Fischer and artist Juanli Carrión in 2016, connects local communities in New York City with artists to create community gardens. Through community-led open calls, OSS creates collaborative gardens that promote healthy food, cultural pride, and community self-development. The OSS now supports three operating gardens and is part of the North West Bronx Food Justice Coalition.[30]

Other cooperation projects seek to transform the political economy of an entire region. Some have broad political ambitions. Cooperation Jackson, mentioned earlier, has as its mission, in its own words, "to transform Jackson's economy and social order by building a vibrant local social and solidarity economy anchored by worker and community owned enterprises that are grounded in sustainable practices of production, distribution, consumption and recycling/reuse."[31] It forms part of a long tradition in Jackson and, more broadly, in the tristate region of western Mississippi, eastern Louisiana, and southeastern Arkansas—the "Black Belt counties" along the Mississippi river—of trying to set up an autonomous territory based on principles of economic democracy and Black self-determination. Historically, it has antecedents going back to the Reconstruction era, when formerly enslaved Black men and women tried to establish independent areas in the western part of Mississippi; to the 1930s, when African American thinkers such as W. E. B. Du Bois were charting a path toward a separatist Black cooperative society; and to more recent efforts at Black self-determination.[32] It represents a copious vision of cooperation that extends to politics, education, training, manufacturing, health, and the welfare of the community and environment, with the goal of pushing all of these in a more democratic, ecologically regenerative, and self-determining direction.[33] With this aim in mind, Cooperation Jackson aspires to a range of institutions, including what it calls a "cooperative incubator," as well as a cooperative school and training center, a network of local cooperatives, and a cooperative credit union for banking.[34]

The more ambitious efforts at cooperation are attempting to create what people call a "solidarity economy." A solidarity economy is grounded in notions of democratic decision making, inclusiveness, cooperation, mutual aid, social justice, equity, and diversity. The term developed in the early twentieth century during the Spanish Civil War in Europe and in Latin America.[35] It was taken up again in the 1990s in Latin America under the rubric of the Social Solidarity Economy. It is now promoted as a way to extend more punctual cooperative arrangements into a larger economic network. As Ethan Miller of Bates College explains, the term *solidarity economy* is complex and carries several different meanings depending on who is using it. "It is, at once, a description of actually-existing cooperative economic practices; an articulation of shared values and transformative aspirations; a rallying point for connection between diverse activist efforts; a vision for what might emerge from such collaboration; and a loose theory of change that eschews singular, totalistic revolutionary models in favor of a more decentralized, experimental, emergent and plural approach."[36]

Solidarity-economy projects now span the world. Vishwas Satgar at the University of the Witwatersrand in Johannesburg, South Africa, has compiled case studies of solidarity-economy projects, growing out of a conference organized in 2011 through the Co-operative and Policy Alternative Center (COPAC) in Johannesburg, which Satgar cofounded and now chairs.[37] In his work on South African cooperatives, Satgar discusses promising cooperative projects originating from members, workers, and consumers. South Africa has had a robust governmental policy of promoting cooperatives since the end of apartheid; according to Satgar, those efforts have not produced as many viable member-driven organizations as expected, by contrast to the more successful bottom-up organizing.[38] The contrast here is important for proponents of the solidarity economy. Unlike "social economy" proposals that work within current logics and power structures, the solidarity-economy approach tries to develop a bottom-up member-based power structure and economic logic of self-determination. Scholars like Satgar, Michelle Williams, and others who are proponents of solidarity-economy approaches, stress the distinction. "Social economy approaches," Ethan Miller explains, "merely attempt to include people more equitably within an ultimately unchallenged capitalist power structure, while solidarity economy organizing is aimed at challenging and undoing that very structure."[39]

Mutual-aid projects are another form of cooperation and a growing phenomenon. Mutual aid embraces the notion of people building new social relations by taking matters into their own hands. Dean Spade, an advocate of mutual aid, has been involved in several projects, including one called the Big Door Brigade.[40] On its website, built by and maintained by Spade, the Big Door Brigade explains:

> Mutual aid is when people get together to meet each other's basic survival needs with a shared understanding that the systems we live under are not going to meet our needs and we can do it together RIGHT NOW! Mutual aid projects are a form of political participation in which people take responsibility for caring for one another and changing political conditions, not just through symbolic acts or putting pressure on their representatives in government, but by actually building new social relations that are more survivable. Most mutual aid projects are volunteer-based, with people jumping in to participate because they want to change what is going on right now, not wait to convince corporations or politicians to do the right thing.[41]

Mutual aid has a long, admirable history in the United States and around the world. It reaches back, in the United States, to early mutual aid among African Americans through organizations such as the African Methodist Church in Rhode Island, the Free African Society in the 1780s, or the Colored Farmers' National Alliance and Cooperative Union founded in 1886 in Texas, which ultimately opened chapters in every southern state and by 1891 had more than one million members, becoming the largest membership organization of its time.[42] Mutual aid today extends from volunteer groups who leave water in the desert for immigrants crossing the U.S.-Mexico border (the No More Deaths collective) to search-and-rescue NGOs in the central Mediterranean trying to save people migrating to Europe.[43] In fact, as Spade writes, mutual aid is a key ingredient of practically "every single social movement."[44] Mariame Kaba describes the practice of mutual aid as "prefiguring the world in which we want to live."[45] That was a central element in the Occupy Wall Street movement and in the critical theoretical work of Judith Butler on the concept of "assembly."[46]

COOPERATION IN CONVENTIONAL ECONOMIC DOMAINS

Cooperation also proliferates today in conventional economic settings and commerce, although here too it is often hidden or not known. It actually thrives, despite the fact that it is at a sharp disadvantage along fiscal, legal, and often ideological dimensions. The traditional corporate form and shareholding are favored through all kinds of incentives and preferences, such as lower tax rates on capital gains, government bailouts of "too-big-to-fail" corporations, the protection of the stock market, and the ideology of individualism. Yet despite all that, successful models of cooperatives and mutuals surround us.

There are numerous examples of cooperation in a range of industries. Not all of them may be blueprints for the ideal of coöperism (discussed in chapter 4), but the ubiquity of cooperation in conventional commerce demonstrates the potential for coordination and the realistic possibility of coöperism. To get a sense of the range and extent of cooperation hidden in plain sight, let's quickly take a whirlwind tour of some of these collaborations in the United States and elsewhere. These are household names in the United States and abroad, but most people do not even know that they are based on cooperation.

Mutual Insurance | State Farm

Insurance mutuals run by and for policyholders, not investors, are part of the very fabric of the founding of the United States. Benjamin Franklin helped start the Philadelphia Contributionship for the Insurance of Houses from Loss by Fire in 1752, which many consider the first recognized cooperative business in the United States and the oldest property insurance company in the country.[47] It continues to operate today as the Philadelphia Contributionship.[48]

Mutuals have a track record of longevity and resilience and represent a large portion of the insurance industry; as noted earlier, the five largest mutuals serve 25 percent of the market.[49] Not just in the United States, but across the globe, mutual insurance has proven to be especially effective at mitigating financial risk, particularly in the labor market.[50] Many mutuals arose among guild members as a way to reduce information asymmetries; those sharing the same profession were exposed to similar risks but could use the mutuals to even out the probability of those risks harming them.[51]

Since 2006, mutuals have been "the fastest growing part of the global insurance market, moving from a market share of 23.4 percent in 2007 to 27.3 percent in 2013."[52] Three of the top ten largest insurance companies in the world are mutuals: National Mutual Insurance Federation of Agricultural Co-operatives (Zenkyoren) in Japan and, in the United States, State Farm and the Kaiser Foundation.[53]

Membership in a mutual insurance company is typically based on holding a policy. Although that membership stake is not equivalent to an equity interest, since it cannot be freely sold or exchanged, it serves as the source of funding to operate the business. In effect, mutuals are funded either by the membership stake of current or prospective policyholders or by loans that are borrowed and paid off by operating profits. What is unique about the mutual insurance company, by contrast to capitalized insurance, is that the policyholder is "the sole focus" of a mutual insurance company.[54]

State Farm, the largest auto insurance company in the United States with 17 percent of the market, is a good illustration. Originally founded in 1922 as State Farm Mutual Automobile Insurance Company by George J. Mecherle, it began and grew as a way to capture a low-risk segment of the market. Mecherle was an Illinois farmer who became an insurance salesman and then decided to concentrate on selling automobile insurance to farmers at low rates.[55] Mecherle's working assumption was that rural and small-town drivers had lower accident rates than city dwellers or the nation as a whole, so together they could save money through lower rates in a mutual insurance company. The operation surpassed $1 million in revenue by 1928 and then opened an office in Berkeley. After auto insurance, State Farm went into life insurance in 1929 and fire insurance in 1935, reaching one million policies by 1944.[56]

Today, approximately one out of every five cars in the United States is insured through State Farm, and there are more than 16,000 agents across the country.[57] State Farm is one of the largest auto and home insurers in the country; as of its 2019 Annual Report, it had more than $178 billion in assets and a net income of $2.3 billion.[58]

At State Farm, member policyholders are the stakeholders. They elect the board of directors at an annual meeting that all members may attend. The first-named insured has a right to vote by proxy or in person.[59] The board decides on the vision and operations without any outside investor influence. Given the group's structure and principles, State Farm employees receive "ample group health, disability and dental plans" alongside traditional retirement plans and one-on-one financial planning; the company will provide $5,000 in assistance for any child adoption and a full workday off to help with schooling.[60]

According to Crain's Chicago Business, in a head-to-head comparison with a nonmutual like Allstate, the main difference in performance is due to cooperative ownership: "State Farm has more leeway to compete on price with the likes of Geico and Progressive, because its customer-owners benefit from any price cuts." By contrast, in an institution that is beholden to stockholders rather than policyholders, "every dime Allstate spends on claims or price cuts is one less dime for shareholders."[61] Since 2001, despite encroaching market entrants such as Geico and Progressive, "State Farm has an enviable position of being very over-capitalized and mutual status with no stockholder-earnings pressures."[62]

Credit Unions / Crédit Agricole, France

Credit unions and cooperative banks also have a long history dedicated to the welfare of their member account holders. They too share in a form of democratic governance and mutualism. Typically, any account holder may become a member, receives shares, and has one vote regardless of the number of shares they have. The ownership rights thus stem only from membership, not from the number of shares, which lowers the potential for takeovers. The bank's equity consists of those shares. The ambition of these unions is to promote the well-being of their members, rather than to maximize profit, since the business is not run for profit.[63]

Historically, there have been different models of cooperative banking, including cooperative banks, credit unions, and building societies. Cooperative banks started as a result of social movements during the 1850s, with many concentrated in Germany, and evolved along different lines.[64] One model, known as the Schulze-Delitzsch model of cooperative credit or a People's Bank, uses a general assembly as its main body for governance, allows for the election of executives and control entities, and pays members dividends derived from operating profits.[65] A second model, the Raiffeisen model, was adapted from the first model for more rural conditions and aimed to "render social co-living more harmonious."[66] Both models took on the form of credit unions in the United States and Canada. Building societies in the United Kingdom were initially meant to be terminating—they would serve to finance housing among a group of members and then dissolve—but these societies grew to be permanent, offering additional services to their customers. In the United States, building societies took the form of savings and loan associations. Today, savings and loans hold about $209 billion in assets and supplement the larger credit-union sector.[67]

In the United States, credit unions developed in the early twentieth century, with federal laws enabling their formation in 1934. They thrived in part by surviving the Great Depression and the financial crises of the 1980s, and they now have more than one hundred million members. By contrast to European credit unions, those in the United States tend to do business only with members and are focused on consumer lending.[68]

One of the reasons that cooperative banking is so robust is that it often works hand in hand with cooperative enterprises. International Raiffeisen Union estimates that more than nine hundred thousand cooperatives with more than five hundred million members in more than one hundred countries are using cooperative banking principles.[69] Rabobank in the Netherlands, for instance, the largest agricultural bank in the world, reaches 50 percent of Dutch citizens and is rated the world's third safest bank (as of 2009).[70]

The potential of credit unions is illustrated well by the Crédit Agricole Group in France, one of the country's leading banking institutions. The Crédit Agricole Group is composed of thirty-nine regional cooperative banks that together serve more than 21 million customers and 9.3 million member-clients.[71] In 2018, this represented 23.3 percent of French household deposits, or total assets of 1.7 trillion euros.[72]

Crédit Agricole began in 1885 as a local initiative, with the creation of the Société de Crédit Agricole de l'arrondissement de Poligny. The year before, the French government had passed the Act of 1884, legalizing farming cooperatives as authorized professional associations in response to farmers' having trouble accessing credit. A decade later, the Act of November 1894 allowed the creation of local agricultural banks by members of farm cooperatives. These ultimately "formed the foundation of the institutional 'pyramid' created by Crédit Agricole." The next layer, regional banks, was authorized by an Act in 1899 that helped enable the Banque de France to supply funds to farmer cooperatives. In the aftermath of World War I, another piece of legislation, the Act of August 1920, created the Caisse Nationale de Crédit Agricole (CNCA) (renamed as such in 1926) to act as a central clearing organization for the regional banks. Crédit Agricole became self-financing in 1963 after creating a dense nationwide network and raising funds through notes and long-term bonds. In 1988, Crédit Agricole Regional Banks bought the CNCA and transformed the entity into a limited liability company, completely independent of the state. The CNCA (the central clearinghouse) was listed on the stock exchange in 2001, resulting in a hybrid entity that now accompanies the thirty-nine fully cooperative banks.[73]

Today, after the public listing of the CNCA, the Crédit Agricole Group is a complex organization, but one that is essentially run by the thirty-nine regional cooperatives that have the majority stake in the total enterprise.[74] This hybrid model, in which the regional cooperatives own 54 percent of the entity, allows for the raising of some capital, while maintaining the credit union's ethical values as a cooperative. Crédit Agricole, for instance, has vowed not to sell its members' data and to "not operate in countries that do not exchange fiscal information to avoid tax evasion."[75] It does represent a form of decooperativization that may not be a good model for coöperism, the result of the fiscal and legal privileges and advantages of conventional corporate shareholding. As I discuss later, it would be better to make cooperation more advantageous, fiscally and legally, and thereby encourage more forms of cooperation rather than decooperativization.

Overall, credit unions differ from speculative banks and offer "real benefit for members who are represented in governance structures."[76] Because they are member owned, they can care less about profits and more about maintaining market share. In France, mutual banks comprise three-fifths of the banking market.[77]

Producer Cooperatives / Land O'Lakes

Producer cooperatives are especially prevalent in agriculture and farming, sectors in which many companies operating under cooperative principles have become household names, such as Land O'Lakes, Sunkist, and Ocean Spray.

Land O'Lakes, for instance, is a farmer-owned food and agricultural cooperative that is now a Fortune 200 and operates under several well-known trademarks, including Land O'Lakes, Purina Animal Nutrition, and WinField Solutions. Land O'Lakes classifies itself as a "farmer- and retail-owned cooperative" with a primary focus on "always supporting member-owners," as the company states in its Annual Report for 2019.[78] The organization spans horizontally across the agricultural field, from seed and crop inputs to B2B marketing to branded-good sales, and, of course, butter.[79]

Land O'Lakes originally started about one hundred years ago as the Minnesota Cooperative Creameries Association, the product of 320 dairy farmers meeting in St. Paul, Minnesota, with the purpose, in their own words, to "join together to effectively market and distribute members' dairy production across the country."[80] Land O'Lakes is now governed by a board of directors that is elected by its members; nearly half the directors are elected by the dairy producers and the other half by the agricultural members. The directors are elected to four-year terms at the organization's annual meetings by voting members. The board determines "policies and business objectives, controls financial policy, and hires the CEO."[81]

As of February 2020, Land O'Lakes consists of 1,711 dairy producers, 744 agricultural producers, and 989 agricultural retailers.[82] And it is doing extremely well. Land O'Lakes has net sales of $14 billion, net earnings of $207 million, and returns $187 million in cash to its members.

Consumer Cooperatives / REI

Consumer cooperatives also surround us, especially locally in the food and grocery sector, and they have weathered difficult economic times well. The sports apparel and equipment chain Recreational Equipment, Inc., better known as REI, is a good illustration. Founded in 1938 by a small group of Pacific Northwest mountaineers who were seeking out quality mountain-climbing equipment, REI is now one of the country's best-known specialty outdoor retail companies. And it operates fully as a consumer cooperative.[83]

REI began back in 1935 when a couple of Seattle-based outdoorspeople, Lloyd and Mary Anderson, were trying to buy quality ice axes and couldn't find them at the right price at local ski shops. They decided to buy directly from wholesalers in Austria at a price of $3.50 per ice axe, including postage, instead of about $20.[84] The Andersons started collecting money from friends who wanted to get in on their discovery, and they built up a wholesale purchasing operation. They officially formed the cooperative with the aid of a lawyer in 1938. The original mission statement from a bulletin published in 1938 reads as follows:

> Intent of the founders of this organization was to secure sufficient membership to make group buying possible; to distribute the goods with as little overheads expense as possible, using membership cooperation with the work as much as possible; to gradually build up a reserve of purchasing stock; to have the membership fee ($1.00) so that everyone interested will be financially able to join.[85]

REI was modeled in part on the Rochdale Pioneers Society of 1844 in England, which is considered one of the first successful consumer cooperatives. Rochdale "established the principles of linking voting rights to persons rather than shares" and first put in place a "dividend on purchases," basically a patronage refund.[86]

Membership in REI is open to all persons who pay the membership fee, which is a single-time fee of $20 for a lifetime membership with all voting rights in the affairs of REI, including electing its board of directors.[87] Members are entitled to dividends, relative to the amount of merchandise purchase from REI throughout the year, as well as to member-only discounts.[88] Members are sent candidate profiles for the board along with their annual dividend.[89] The board is ten to fourteen directors in size; each elected director serves for three years and can have a maximum of four consecutive terms.[90] Each REI member gets back 10 percent of the price paid on goods purchased through an annual dividend in March.[91]

REI is, again, a consumer cooperative, not a worker cooperative, and there has been some tension over the unionization of its retail-store workers. Some union organizers have accused the management of REI of union busting; however, there seems to be broad support among the membership for the unions. The retail workers in several REI stores have now voted to unionize or are headed that way, as in Soho in New York City and in California. Again, this may be an aspect that could be improved by broader embrace of coöperism, perhaps by joining consumer and worker cooperation.

Today, REI operates more than 160 retail stores throughout the United States. It has more than 19 million members.[92] It had net sales of over $3 billion, according to their last reported financial statements, year-end 2018.[93] According to a former CEO of REI, interviewed in the *Atlantic*, being a cooperative allows the management team—unlike the management of a publicly traded company whose earnings calls affect stock prices—to take a longer-term perspective and focus on growth over a five- or ten-year horizon.[94]

Worker Cooperatives | Isthmus Engineering and King Arthur Flour

Worker cooperatives have a long history of bringing democracy and equality to the workplace. They instantiate the values of solidarity and cooperation—and the principles of one person, one vote. In a worker cooperative, the workers are owners and have a vote and equal say to create a democratic workplace.[95] If there is one form of cooperation that instantiates the ideals of solidarity, mutuality, and social justice, it is the worker coop.

A lot of economic theory suggests that worker cooperatives will have a hard time operating because of the costs associated with collective decision making. John Hansmann's classic work on corporate organization, *The Ownership of Enterprise*, for instance, stipulates that firms are more successful when they are more efficient in reducing transaction costs—the costs to operate and generate profit—and that, given the smaller number of cooperatives than ordinary corporations, there must be a high transaction cost impediment that is offsetting the advantage of cooperatives.[96] The transaction costs in a cooperative model tend to be the demands of collective governance, since all the views of members must be considered. But those costs are offset by other factors, such as the enhanced labor incentive because of the vested stake that worker-owners have in the enterprise.[97] In many cases, the advantages trump. If our tax code and politics were transformed to favor cooperatives, there is no question they would thrive. They already do in many sectors.

A good illustration is the Isthmus Engineering & Manufacturing Co-Op (Isthmus Engineering, or IEM), based in Madison, Wisconsin, which builds robotic machines for industrial companies.[98] It has been used as a case study on successful worker cooperatives, especially noteworthy given that it operates in a high-technology environment that is often believed to be too competitive and difficult for cooperation.[99]

Isthmus Engineering started as a partnership of three mechanical engineers (who knew of each other through work with a family-owned business) and a bookkeeper. They performed contract engineering for nearby businesses and worked out of the home of one of the partners. New partners were brought in who had additional skills and required more flexibility in entry (and exit) than a limited liability partnership allowed. Two of the partners heard about the success of the Mondragón cooperative group at a conference, so they all decided to incorporate the partnership as a cooperative, using attorneys and advisers.[100] The cooperative now includes twenty-nine worker-owners, and membership in the cooperative is open to all employees.[101]

The decision to turn the partnership into a cooperative involved some personal financial risk for members of the cooperative because each one of them was underwriting a portion of the bank loan through cosigns.[102] But the enterprise proved successful. IEM has grown from two customers in the automotive industry in the early 1980s to a larger customer base with a skilled labor force. IEM now has annual revenues exceeding $15 million.

In the initial twelve years after incorporating as a cooperative in 1982, IEM grew from eight to fifty members. The membership fee was described as "the price of a small car."[103] The cooperative was structured into an administrative staff and five areas of "sales, controls (electrical) engineering, mechanical engineering, controls (electrical) assembly, mechanical assembly and machining."[104] Of the fifty employees, twenty-nine served on a board of directors that met biweekly to govern. IEM terminated some memberships in the 1990s and in the 2000s established a more rigorous membership process that remains open to every employee but "gives the board significant flexibility in considering applications."[105]

In order to become a member today, one has to have been a full-time employee for two years to apply. Unless an application is rejected by two-thirds of the membership, the applicant proceeds to board-member interviews and an invitation to join open and closed sessions of board meetings. Applicants can serve on board committees during this phase. One of the only limits is that only one applicant can be considered at a time. If the application is successful, meaning no more than three to five votes against it, the applicant is invited to join the cooperative conditional upon buying a share, priced around $20,000.[106] The principles of the cooperative are: "All owners must be workers, all owners serve on the Board, and all workers are eligible for ownership."[107]

In terms of income, almost all the workers (apart from the sales manager and general manager) receive hourly wages that are set on a scale from when the worker is first hired. The hourly wages do not change when a worker becomes an owner, but there is no longer a benefits package. Owners receive wages only if Isthmus Engineering is profitable. At the end of the year, owners "pay a certain percentage of their total earnings into common equity and receive a certain share as dividends."[108] When an employee-owner leaves the cooperative, their stock and equity are repurchased.

There are, of course, costs associated with being a worker cooperative. At times, to sustain growth and requests from customers, IEM has been forced to utilize contract workers or to offset a potential layoff by spreading the lack of work across multiple cooperative members (e.g., instead of getting rid of a forty-hour-a-week position, four workers are asked to work thirty-hour weeks until the work picks up).[109]

But there are many offsetting benefits. Mostly, given the lack of outside equity, the cooperative structure allows, even encourages, the group to focus on long-term strategies. There is little pressure to produce short-term profits at the expense of longevity.[110] Moreover, as worker-owners, line workers and those working on project teams are (or at least say they are) more self-motivated, in part because of the lack of hierarchy and the fact that they feel they have no one to answer to. There is also a certain amount of mutual monitoring that leads to a sense of empowerment and is a source of motivation to work. This reflects the absence of a manager-employee relationship, which apparently is felt positively by nonowning employees as well.[111] Even among the latter, apparently, there is a strong negative feeling about employees downplaying their work by invoking their status as "'only' an employee."[112] Similarly, there is a strong feeling that members should not leverage their ownership status.

Overall, the focus of Isthmus Engineering has been sustainability. In the words of one member: "Most companies would correlate profit margins with the size of the company. That's the last thing we do. Before profit, the first thing is sustainability."[113] And given its cooperative principle of "Concern for Community," Isthmus Engineering mobilized to produce and donate thousands of face shields to local clinics and cooperatives nationwide in the face of the COVID-19 crisis. It also helped the Medical College of Wisconsin create custom tooling to expedite production as part of the Milwaukee Million Mask Challenge (an effort by United Way to meet demand).[114]

Worker cooperatives come in varied forms and under different names. They can be structured as a partnership or a limited liability corporation, or even a corporation, so long as they abide by the principles of cooperatives, especially the "one vote principle" and nonhierarchy.[115] Another form of worker cooperative is called the "benefit corporation." Benefit corporations are traditional companies that take on a modified obligation toward accountability, transparency, and purpose, with a commitment to creating what is called "public benefit and sustainable value."[116] Some benefit corporations are legally required to consider and benefit all stakeholders, including workers. These too, even if they are not fully worker-owned cooperatives, can serve the goals of mutuality.

An example of a benefit corporation is King Arthur Flour, America's oldest flour company, founded in 1790. King Arthur is a certified B Corp (certified and evaluated as to social and environmental performance) and commits itself to a "triple bottom line" for "people, planet, and profit." It also is required to do a B Impact Assessment to show and certify its success toward these missions (independently done).[117]

Prior to 1996, King Arthur was a regular corporation run by Frank and Brinna Sands.[118] When the Sandses began thinking about retiring, they decided to sell their company to its employees through an employee stock ownership plan (ESOP). In an ESOP, a trust is formed as a legal entity to hold shares of stock on behalf of a company's employees. The ESOP trust is funded entirely by the company.[119] The trust gains cash through profit or loans and then uses that funding to acquire shares from the owner (the value is appraised independently). The trust then allocates the shares it has bought to employees. In effect, employees gain stock without a cash outlay.[120] The owner is paid over a period of time, often through a promissory note.[121] ESOPs function a lot like retirement plans such as 401(k)s, but there is one enormous difference: the company fully funds the ESOP and the employees do not contribute financially. For King Arthur specifically, "after the first year of employment, all workers who log more than 800 hours a year, including season and part-time laborers, are eligible for the employee stock ownership program."[122] According to Joseph Blasi of Rutgers University, coauthor of *The Citizen's Share: Reducing Inequality in the Twenty-First Century*, many family business owners are drawn to ESOPs to promote the best interests of their workers.[123]

This has proven successful for King Arthur, which has experienced major growth since transforming itself into an employee-owned business. It began distributing products outside of New England in the late 1990s and has now reached over $100 million in annual sales and sends more than two thousand King Arthur products to grocery stores.[124]

ESOPs are one of the major ways workers are becoming owner-operators in the United States.[125] Because of fiscal and legal disincentives, worker cooperatives have not flourished as much in the United States as in other countries such as Italy, France, or Spain. The Democracy at Work Institute conducted a survey in 2014 and found that there were 256 worker cooperatives in the United States with an estimated 6,300 workers and annual combined revenues of $367 million. That is relatively small compared, for instance, to just one large worker cooperative consortium, the Mondragón group, in Spain. But what is remarkable about the American sector is that it has doubled since the survey in 2014 and is dominated by women and persons of color. "Over 70 per cent of workers in co-operatives are women (versus 47 per cent in the general work force), and over 65 per cent are Latina/Latino or African American (versus 34 percent for U.S. workers generally)," Mark Kaswan reports.[126]

Retailer or Purchaser Cooperatives | Ace Hardware

Another form of cooperation consists of independent retailers working together through a cooperative arrangement to help each other and leverage their numbers. A good illustration is Ace Hardware. Ace began as a wholesale group in the

1920s. A number of Chicago hardware retailers banded together to pool their purchasing power and buy directly from manufacturers in order to avoid having to go through a middleman for their merchandise. The group formally incorporated its business as Ace Stores in 1928 and opened a warehouse in 1929. Membership expanded to forty-one retailers by 1934. By 1969, Ace had opened distribution centers in Georgia and California, expanding operations in the South and West.[127]

Originally, Ace Stores operated as a conventional wholesale group. When the cofounder and long-term president Richard Hesse retired in 1973, he sold the enterprise to its member-dealers to create a dealer-owned hardware cooperative, which is its current corporate structure.[128]

Today, Ace Hardware consists of hardware stores that are part of the cooperative in a franchiselike model, with Ace Hardware providing shared capabilities and brand recognition. Member retailers fall under one of two programs for Ace Hardware support: "Ace-branded" stores or "individually branded" stores. The former account for 91 percent of the national network, operating under the Ace brand and entitled to all services and benefits (including marketing). Individually branded stores represent about 9 percent of the national domestic network for Ace Hardware. They rely on Ace's product assortment and product pricing but do not participate in marketing programs (usually, they can leverage their brand name recognition in their local communities). Ace also now has a separate legal entity (AWH), formed in 2014, to sell to nonmember retailers.[129]

As a matter of corporate finance, Ace Hardware divides its membership structure into Class A and Class C stocks—Class A stock is $1,000 per share and Class C stock is $100 per share—with Class A stockholders having voting rights.[130] In order to be a member of Ace Hardware, a retailer must purchase stock and then receives patronage distributions based on the volume of merchandise purchased. Stock is sold only to approved retailers of hardware who apply for membership. Initial membership requires buying one share of Class A stock plus forty shares of Class C stock, for a total investment of $5,000. For each additional store location, members must purchase an additional fifty shares of Class C stock, but no additional Class A stock (as a way to limit dilution of voting parity between retailers within the cooperative).

As of year-end 2018, Ace Hardware reported $5.7 billion in annual revenues, with net income of $128 million. Ace Hardware had a total store count of 5,253. At this point, according to Ace, about three-quarters of American homes and businesses are "located within 15 minutes of speedy-sized Ace stores."[131]

Research suggests that, at a general level, many members of purchasing cooperatives find them to be a compelling strategy to manage supply-chain costs, often resulting in "2 to 5 percent cost savings." The competitive advantage of a cooperative as against other purchasing structures is that "a true purchasing cooperative can provide a monetary return to its members in the form of patronage dividends."[132] For Ace Hardware, the purchasing cooperative means that the member stores are its only shareholders, which gives them an advantage over "big box" retailers such as Lowe's and Home Depot.[133] Also, there tends to be high satisfaction among members. At Ace, apparently, the overall satisfaction of affiliates has been high: more than 90 percent surveyed "expressed strong pride in Ace," and 80 percent of retailers rated overall satisfaction as 8 or higher out of 10.[134]

THE RESILIENCE AND PRODUCTIVITY OF COOPERATION

Across these different economic sectors, cooperatives have proven resilient, especially during economic downturns and despite the favored treatment of capitalized corporations. A meta-statistical analysis of more than a hundred studies of worker-owned and cooperative enterprises found that on most key indicators of economic performance and productivity, businesses that engage in profit sharing outperform traditional corporations.[135] Worker-owners and those who share in profits are more likely to stay with their enterprise, have greater loyalty, and take greater pride in their work; they say they are willing to work hard, they make more suggestions about work and innovation, and they tend to have better work conditions.[136] Many studies also find that worker cooperatives have higher productivity.[137] The economist Spencer Thompson shows that worker cooperatives may also have an advantage in implementing complex divisions of labor, because they are better at achieving trust and loyalty among workers.[138] The best evidence suggests that cooperatives tend to have greater longevity, higher survival rates, and lower failure rates than traditional small businesses and corporations.[139]

In the financial sector, credit unions entered the financial crisis of 2007–2008 in stronger shape than their for-profit peers and came out of the recession stronger as well. Before 2007, cooperative financial institutions were reported to have "comparable or slightly higher earnings than investor-owned banks and achieved higher return on equity" and, in this sense, entered the crisis with a "stronger capital base than their competitors." In Europe, cooperative banks suffered only

7 percent of all banking industry asset write-downs and losses throughout the financial crisis, despite having 20 percent of the market. In large part, this was due to their limited exposure to subprime mortgages and investment activity. In the United Kingdom, mutual building societies suffered minimal losses.[140]

In fact, in the face of financial crises, financial cooperatives often see an increase in "almost every facet of their business." They see an increase in assets and deposits: for instance, 516 credit unions in Canada saw a six-month increase in assets in the second quarter of 2008; the Credit Union National Association in the United States saw deposits in credit unions increase by 10 percent in 2009; Rabobank in the Netherlands saw its share of loans increase to 42 percent of the total market. They see an increase in the volume of lending: for instance, loans by credit unions in the United States increased from $539 billion in 2007 to $575 billion in 2008, while 8,300 U.S. for-profit banks saw loans outstanding decrease from $7.91 trillion to $7.88 trillion. They see an increase in membership levels: for instance, in the United States, membership in credit unions rose to 90 million in 2008 from 85 million in 2004; Raiffeisen Switzerland had record growth in 2008 with 7.3 percent new members. And they offer better interest rates: in the United States, savings and credit cooperatives have better rates compared to their peers; favorable lending rates were also a major impetus for Brazilian owners and low-income families to form a savings and credit cooperative.[141]

Worker cooperatives have a record of actually growing during recessions. According to Johnston Birchall, author of "The Performance of Member-Owned Businesses Since the Financial Crisis of 2008," in *The Oxford Handbook of Mutual, Co-Operative, and Co-Owned Business*: "Since the late nineteenth century, in countries where there are strong worker co-operatives, these have tended to increase in number during recessions, both as new start-ups and takeovers of ailing businesses."[142] As evidence for this, Birchall notes that the worker cooperative sector in France grew by more than 263 cooperatives in 2013 (an increase of 17 percent since 2009) and had a survival rate of 77 percent versus 65 percent for conventional firms. In addition, the "level of indebtedness of worker co-ops was lower than that of comparable enterprises," and the job losses were less significant (e.g., in Spain, 6.4 percent versus 11.9 percent in other types of enterprises).[143] In the United States, in the decade after the 2008 financial crisis, the sheer number of worker-owned cooperatives almost doubled.[144]

The United Nations organization for cooperatives, the CICOPA (International Organization of Industrial, Artisanal, Service, and Producer Cooperatives), studied the question of resilience after the Great Recession of 2008 and concluded that cooperative enterprises have been more resilient than traditional for-profit companies: both the employment and enterprise survival rates were higher, which they attributed to the greater flexibility of worker cooperatives and their emphasis on maintaining jobs.[145] The CECOP-CICOPA Europe (International Organization of Industrial and Service Cooperatives, Europe) has conducted annual surveys that highlight the resilience of cooperatives by contrast to conventional enterprises. Cooperatives demonstrate lower job losses and failures: in Italy in 2011, for instance, 68 percent of cooperatives kept the same employment number, 18 percent grew, and only 13 percent contracted.[146] In France, the number of cooperatives increased throughout the 2008 crisis: in 2005, there were 1,612 worker cooperatives, and that number continued to rise through 2010, reaching a total of 1,822.[147] Bruno Roelants and his colleagues offer compelling hypotheses to explain the resilience of cooperationist enterprises, including the flexibility cooperatives have to weather temporary economic setbacks, their capacity to mobilize the participation of members and the wider community, the networks that develop among cooperatives, and their presence throughout substantial sectors of the economy.[148]

As the economist Virginie Pérotin concludes after reviewing all the evidence, worker cooperatives "survive as well as or better than conventional firms."[149] Similarly, the economists Thomas Brzustowski and Francesco Caselli at the London School of Economics, after surveying the recent large literature on worker cooperatives, conclude that "the evidence suggests that worker cooperatives tend to be (somewhat) more productive than conventional firms, to afford their workers greater job satisfaction, and to display comparable exit and investment rates."[150] There is every reason to believe this is true given the buy-in that cooperation affords.

Cooperation is pervasive in contemporary economy and society, often hidden in plain sight and unacknowledged. It operates in the shadows of advanced capitalist economies. Its omnipresence demonstrates the possibility and potential of an economic regime based on coöperism.

CHAPTER 3

The Simplicity of Cooperation

In the Mondragón consortium, each individual cooperative is fully worker owned. In each, the pay disparity between employees is capped, with the highest-paid directors earning a maximum of four-and-a-half times the salary of the lowest-paid worker.[1] The members of each individual cooperative decide at a general assembly how any surplus generated from the operations of the cooperative is distributed. The member cooperatives utilize the principle of "one worker one vote regardless of the share of capital owned."[2] The consortium maintains certain simple rules about the distribution of any surplus at member cooperatives: at least 10 percent goes to a social fund, at least 20 percent goes to the reserve fund, and a maximum of 70 percent is deposited directly to the members' individual accounts.[3] Within those maxi-min constraints, the members decide how much of the surplus is distributed or reinvested.

Today, the mechanisms of cooperation are simple and well understood, whether the enterprise involves consumer cooperatives; credit unions; insurance mutuals; producer, worker, or retailer cooperatives; nonprofit organizations; or mutual-aid projects. The basic principle is that, in member-owned enterprises, the capital of the entity is replaced by the aggregated membership stake in the ongoing business. In a consumer cooperative, all the customers are invited to become cooperative members for a small fee ($20 in the case of REI). Those membership fees accumulate, in the aggregate, to form the members' stake that effectively replaces equity capital. With seven million eligible voting members at REI as of December 31, 2019, the members' equity stood at $312 million.[4] Including retained earnings, the total members' equity surpassed $1 billion. In a worker cooperative, each worker-member is required over time to contribute the equivalent of a portion of their salary, which becomes their equity stake in the enterprise. At Mondragón, for example, each worker at a member cooperative must contribute one year's salary, which can also be borrowed at low interest from their credit union, Caja Laboral Popular Cooperativa de Crédito. A member opens an individual account at the credit union, which is then credited with yearly profits (or losses) from their cooperative. The account accrues interest similarly to a savings account.[5] The member contributions, aggregated, serve as the equity of the cooperative, which is then invested in equipment, machinery, research and design, etc.

By the twenty-first century, practically all the kinks of cooperation have been worked out. People know how to make cooperation work. It is simple and successful. Here I will break it down into its constituent parts, or basic building blocks, in order to explain, in the most comprehensible terms, the corporate finance of cooperation.

THE BASIC BUILDING BLOCKS

Material goods, land, real estate, homes and apartments, equipment, tools, machines, cars, trademarks, books—in short, all material interests—are subject to competing claims to use and enjoyment, whether temporary or long-lasting. Traditionally, we talk about these competing claims using the term *property*. But that term becomes easily confusing, and people rapidly make wild ideological claims about it. They talk about "private property" as if control over a piece of land or equipment is a unified coherent whole, or they talk about abolishing property as if it were possible to get rid of claims over material interests. The fact is, ownership and control of what we call property is not one single, unified thing. Someone may have ownership and possession of a material good but may have to allow others to use it. Someone may have a right to benefits from improvements they have made on someone else's property. And it is simply impossible to get rid of competing claims against others to do things with material interests; even in a regime of communal ownership, there will sometimes be competing claims to exercise control over material interests. As a result, it is important to be careful and precise about the terms we use. To be as clear as possible, I will use the term *material interests* rather than *property*.

There are almost always multiple claims to use or enjoy material interests. Those competing claims do not get resolved by themselves. Whoever or whatever institution ultimately resolves those competing claims—whether the state, a court, a majority vote of the people, a collective, an autocrat, a centralized party, any other decision-making entity—they will be the one allocating priority regarding those material interests. Whoever is allowed to collect dead timber on public or private land, maintain an agricultural field, build a shelter, consume fruits, hunt, or simply walk through a pasture is exercising some control over a material interest, and someone will decide whether they are allowed to do so when conflicts arise.

To think properly about economic organization, one must disambiguate the different dimensions of material interests, whether using Roman law and borrowing concepts like *usus*, *fructus*, and *abusus* or drawing on American legal realist thought and the notion of "bundles of property rights." Material interest is not a monolithic, unitary thing that is allocated or eviscerated as a whole. It is a complex bundle of possible interests that are almost always separated out and allocated in myriad ways, and hardly ever go away.[6] In addition, to understand material interests, it is important to focus on the actions that humans take. It involves verbs such as using, improving, alienating, or sharing interests such as goods, land, tools, workshops, or cars. Finally, it is important to recognize that someone or some entity ultimately and inexorably gets to have the final say on how those material interests are disambiguated and distributed and who gets to enjoy any part of them when there is conflict.

The challenge today is to promote a more equitable and just distribution of the enjoyment of material interests that protects the environment and makes possible sustainable economic exchange. This requires a detailed analysis, dissection, and understanding of material interests, and it connects directly to the question of who gets to reap or share the benefits of economic production, circulation, and consumption. Before beginning to articulate the different ways of distributing material interests, it is important first to articulate the subjects, objects, and possible actions associated with material interests.

The Subjects, Objects, and Actions of Material Interests

There is, first, a finite set of subjects who can be interest bearers—that is, who can exercise control over or be given the privilege to use or enjoy material interests. Interests can be allocated to:

- An individual person
- A family, however defined
- A partnership of two or more people

- A collection or group of people
- A legally chartered corporation
- A state (this generally corresponds to what we call "state ownership," "controlled economies," or "nationalization")
- A people (this often corresponds to what we refer to today as the "common," or in earlier times, as "the commons")

Notice that these different subjects or entities can be on either side of the relationship; for instance, a state could have title to land but allow an individual to use it, or an individual could have title to land but allow the state to use it.

Second, there are different objects of material interests. Most legal regimes throughout history have differentiated among:

- Immovable goods, such as land and buildings (real estate)
- Movable goods (commodities, supplies)
- Personal items (clothes, bedding, food)
- Intangible goods (intellectual property)
- Modes of production (equipment, tools)
- Financial goods (stocks, bonds, bank accounts)

There can be different regimes governing different objects of material interest, even within a coherent whole. So, for instance, title to land could be held by the state or a sovereign indigenous nation, while the buildings on the land could be built and used by private individuals, or built by private individuals for the use of a collectivity. Personal items could be assigned for use entirely to individuals, whereas modes of production could be assigned to a family or the collective.

Third, there is a wide set of actions that can be performed in relation to these material interests. Regarding land, for instance, there could be an assignment to different subjects for each of the following actions:

- Using the land for farming or just walking across it (use)
- Building something on the land, such as a barn or a home (construction)
- Getting revenue from the use of the land (enjoying the fruits)
- Improving or altering the land, as by removing rocks or leveling it (improvements)
- Exchanging the use or enjoyment of the land (alienation)

These three series—the subjects, objects, and actions surrounding material interests—are the elementary building blocks needed to understand distributions. Today, they are basic and well understood. Various thinkers have drawn up these lists and articulated these dimensions in slightly different ways. For instance, in their book *Common*, Dardot and Laval propose and discuss a similar list of possible material interests.[7] The American legal realists earlier showed us how these bundles of interests could be separated, related, and allocated.[8]

In addition, and importantly, there is the question of who gets to decide about how to interpret and resolve any disputes that arise. There are many potential conflicts over different combinations of material interests, leading to contestation and the need for a final resolution of any competing claims, such as how land can be used (zoning), how crops grown on the land are distributed (enjoying the fruits), who can improve or alter the land (improvements), who can reap the rewards of these improvements, or who has power to transfer, assign, or alienate any interests. Some person, group, or entity must have a final say over any dispute, and this can be organized in any number of ways:

- A single person decides (such as a judge)
- A panel of persons decides by majority (such as a court), by consensus, or by unanimity (such as a jury)
- A political party decides
- All citizens vote (as in a referendum)

Regardless of the entity, the final arbiter over any dispute is de facto the one who controls the allocation of material interests. If, for instance, the supreme court of a state has the final say over the allocation of zoning in that state, then that court is ultimately the arbiter of those relations, more so than the zoning board. If it is a people's council or open to popular democratic vote, then the council or all the citizens ultimately have control over the distribution of those material interests. In the end, the final decision maker in any dispute may have more control than the entity that purportedly has the authority to allocate (for instance, again, the zoning board of a township). This is why judicial review is such a potent tool for judges.

Allocating Material Interests

Once these different dimensions of material interests are clearly delineated, it is possible to allocate them in myriad ways based on different economic models without returning, on the one hand, to the illusion of private property or, on the other, to the fantasy of there being no property. I say "illusion of private property" because regimes of so-called private property are actually state-controlled allocations and enforcement of rights, privileges, duties, and obligations regarding materials interests, granting and favoring for the most part unlimited accumulation of use and alienation to private individuals and private entities like corporations. These are simply constructed regimes that favor the concentration of material interests in the hands of private individuals. On the other hand, I say "the fantasy of there being no property," because regimes that supposedly eliminate all property are actually state- or party-controlled allocations and enforcements of material interests that tend to favor party members, along with their families and friends, who have decision-making capacities. It is an illusion to believe that there could be no property. There are always multiple claims on material interests that affect how people can live.

When the goal is cooperation, the different dimensions of material interests are allocated according to a set of shared values and principles. Those values and principles are reflected, for instance, in those of the International Cooperative Alliance (ICA): the values of equal democratic participation, equitable distribution, openness, solidarity, social and environmental responsibility, and caring for others; and the principles of self-determination, with open, nondiscriminatory, voluntary membership that tends toward members contributing and benefiting equitably from the running of the cooperative projects and that strives toward the sustainable development of their environment and communities.[9] The overarching goal is to produce democratic participation, economic health, equity, a green environment, and social justice.

This is typically achieved in the following general manner: members pool their resources or borrow from credit unions in order to join and create a shared entity, the cooperative. The cooperative entity may then buy or produce goods, own equipment, or provide services. The members of the cooperative decide democratically how those objects of material interest are used and how the benefits or fruits of the actions on those material interests are shared among the members. The surpluses from the enterprise are generally distributed to the members based on their contributions and participation, but this is based again on democratic processes.

In a consumer cooperative, the consumers (what we usually call customers) join the cooperative by paying a membership fee that, in some cases, is considered a share of the enterprise. The cooperative leases or buys real estate, such as a store or warehouse, and buys, improves, or manufactures movable goods (commodities, for instance) that are held by the cooperative entity. The members, through their cooperative, have control over the movable goods or personal items like food. Members are allowed to shop at the store, for instance; sometimes nonmembers are allowed in, sometimes not. Members can purchase for their own account and take possession of the goods and use them, sometimes at a discounted price. At the end of the year, if the cooperative has made a surplus, it will be distributed to the members based on how much they have used the cooperative, or members will receive a further discount the following year, to be determined by the members through a democratic deliberative process. The entity that decides on the distribution of any surplus is the collection of members.

In a worker cooperative, the collective entity may own the modes of production (the equipment and tools). The members may decide, democratically, who will use the equipment and how, how much workers will be paid, and how the benefits of the cooperative enterprise will be shared by the members. The members are the primary subjects of material interests and govern the enterprise in a democratic fashion, by contrast to a conventional corporation in which managers are hired by the shareholders to run the enterprise. This reflects the members' interest in the cooperative as opposed to a shareholder's equity or stock ownership.

At the heart of the difference are questions of corporate finance. Let's go into this in more detail, focusing a bit more on the technical aspects of incorporating cooperative enterprises but still in a very accessible and understandable way.

THE CORPORATE FINANCE OF COOPERATION

Creating cooperation is as straightforward as realigning the different dimensions of material interests: the members, rather than outside investors, become the primary stakeholders. To understand this requires only a few fundamentals of corporate finance.

Under the conventional corporate model involving private capital, a commercial enterprise is started either by an individual, who buys tools and materials and starts making and selling goods or services, or by a partnership of individuals, who essentially do the same thing. They can incorporate and form a corporation or limited liability partnership, as a way to protect themselves from personal liability for the obligations of the company. They use the corporate form as a shield from personal liability, to keep their finances separate, to gain tax advantages, to get credit from a bank, and so on.

The Privately Held Company

A privately held company (whether individual owned, family owned, or a partnership) can buy and sell real estate, as well as goods, equipment, and intangibles, in its name. It owns all the assets (tools, inventory, goods, accounts receivable or payable, etc.) and is responsible for any debt. The owners of the privately held company can engage in myriad activities, using the incorporated form of the entity as the conduit for their actions. They can:

- Buy and own real estate and equipment
- Use their real estate and equipment in any legal way they want
- Sell, transact, exchange, and offer the goods or services that they produce
- Sell the company or any of its assets, or transform the structure of the company into something else such as an LLC or a B Corp
- Take out loans, pay off loans, increase or reduce their debt
- Pay themselves salaries
- Hire and pay employees (at or above minimum wage)
- Pay taxes on their profits
- Reinvest some of their profits into the enterprise
- Distribute monies to themselves, the owners, as distributed corporate profits

Essentially, the owners of a privately held company are the subjects of the material interests, and they can do practically anything with the objects of material interests. The one thing that they cannot do is raise equity on a public stock exchange, for which they would need to do an initial public offering (IPO) and become a publicly held company (with some minor exceptions, such as Regulation D in the United States, which allows privately held companies to sell a small, limited number of equity shares without registering with the Securities and Exchange Commission, or SEC). In a privately held company, as a result, the equity that the owners have in the company is not as liquid. In order to take their money out, the owners need to sell assets or distribute profits, pay themselves higher salaries, dissolve the company, or sell their equity in the company to someone else. This makes it slightly more difficult for a private company to raise major capital inflows.

The Publicly Traded Corporation

The major difference between the privately held company and the publicly held company is that, in the latter case, capital can flow in (or out) through the sale of equity shares on a public market. The fluctuating value of those publicly traded shares will change the total value of the firm and therefore the value of the equity stake of the shareholders. It will also affect the publicly traded corporation's ability to borrow money or raise more capital. The speculative nature of equity markets affects, positively and negatively, the ability of publicly traded companies to attract capital.

In order to become a publicly held company, a privately held company must go public through an IPO and raise equity capital from investors who become equity shareholders. One of the big differences between the private and public firm is all the disclosure regulations that surround the publicly traded company (all the SEC filings, quarterly statements, etc.). The shareholders, by contrast to the private owners, then become the primary subjects of the material interests of the enterprise. The collectivity of shareholders can do all the things that the private owners can do, listed earlier, plus raise more equity capital on the public markets. Some of the same things they can do as the private owners have different names. Their distribution of corporate profits, for instance, is called shareholder dividends. But the functionalities are similar in terms of the things they can do with the objects of material interest. In addition, publicly traded companies can buy back their equity shares by buying their own stock on the market, often enhancing the value of the remaining shares.

Distributing Wealth in the Case of Publicly Traded Corporations

In publicly traded corporations, the shareholders are usually passive investors who do not get involved in the actions regarding material interests. Usually, a board of shareholders hires managers to run the company and keep the shareholders satisfied, in good times through dividends (paying out profit) and increased equity value (rising stock price), which keep the investors holding onto the stock (or selling happily at a higher price) and thus increasing the company's equity value.

The equity shares represent the ownership stake in the enterprise. They represent the value of the enterprise. That value is or should be related to the current and expected profitability and cash flows of the company. On a double-entry accounting balance sheet, that value should reflect current assets, machinery, inventory, and goods owned, as well as the expected stream of incoming revenue, accounts payable, and likely future earnings, net of any debt or other obligations.

In addition to the equity shareholders, there are other stakeholders in the publicly traded corporation. There are, for instance, employees or workers who are paid by the corporation to do its work or provide its services; there may be consultants who provide services as well; there are suppliers who may provide essential goods or repair equipment. In both the private and publicly traded company, the owners or shareholders will determine how these other stakeholders relate to the material interests of the company. The shareholder investors, for instance, will determine, by delegation to their managers, the salaries of employees and their working conditions. In this sense, the shareholders are the deciders regarding the material interests of the employees.

The wealth generated by the enterprise is distributed to the different stakeholders of the company through salaries and benefits for the management and employees, contractual exchanges with customers or providers of goods and services, and distributions and benefits to the investor shareholders. All the wealth of the firm is distributed in these different ways. In theory, all the wealth generated by a publicly held corporation (over and above the servicing of debt obligations and the costs of operation) could be equitably distributed to workers, management, and outside affiliates such as consumers or suppliers. But those distributional decisions are controlled by the management, under the supervision of the board of directors, and ultimately by the shareholders. As a result, it is usually the shareholders and management who extract the most from the firm. This extraction of wealth by shareholders and management happens in a few ways. First, there are dividend distributions: the enterprise distributes part of its profits by means of a dividend on shares. Second, there is the value of the shareholding itself. If the firm is publicly traded, then that value can increase and be sold on the stock market at a profit. Management can find ways to affect stock prices (e.g., stock buyback programs) and thereby increase share value. By contrast to ordinary creditors (e.g., banks that loan to the enterprise or other bondholders), the shareholders assume more risk in return for the prospect of receiving a greater return. If things go badly, their equity stake may be wiped out. They have no guarantee of recouping their investment in case of bankruptcy, in contrast to a secured or primary creditor. If things go well, their return is not fixed by contract, as with debt obligations, but can exceed expectations.

For the most part, shareholder investors are primarily interested in the return on their investment. In most cases, they are distant from the enterprise and do not get involved in its management or decision-making process. Individuals and large institutional investors exert influence on the enterprise primarily through what Albert O. Hirshman called "exit": withdrawing from any engagement and selling their shares.[10] What the shareholder investors are most focused on is their prospective return on investment. And when they do vote on matters, there is no one-person-one-vote principle; instead, their votes are counted in proportion to the number of shares they own. So, in contrast to a worker cooperative where each of the members may have an equal say, investors with small numbers of shares (which is the largest pool of equity capital) have little input on any vote.[11] As a result, few shareholder investors vote or exercise their voice.

Because everything is focused on the return on investment, there is a gambling aspect to shareholder investing. It is primarily used as a vehicle to place savings and seek a high return. It is, for the most part, disengaged from the business. It is an elegant form of educated guessing and economic betting. Many of the early stock companies, like the West or East India trading companies, began as forms of gambling by the Dutch and British elite. At the time, they were gambling in part on the slave trade and on the value of human lives. Today, what is clear is that a logic of gambling undergirds practically all shareholder investment. Like the horse track or casino, betting on a commercial enterprise through stock acquisition is principally about making a profit. It pays little attention to, or at least has little incentive to care for, the welfare of the other stakeholders affiliated with the enterprise. In fact, they are generally a source of costs.

Today, with the rise of private equity and hedge funds, wealthy investors have found ingenious ways to mimic the publicly traded corporation without having to abide by all the regulations surrounding reporting, publicity, and public offerings. Functionally, though, they operate in the same way, insofar as investors can move their capital relatively easily and typically do not play a role in managing the enterprise, and the entities can raise capital from third parties. Private equity and hedge funds are in effect private, contracted, constructed replicas of publicly traded corporations. Here too, the model is a sophisticated form of gambling. To keep things simple, I will treat these simply as an artificial form of publicly traded corporations.

Cooperative Enterprises

As opposed to a gambling logic, cooperation operates more on a democratic, sustainable, and environmental logic of well-being for all the stakeholders. Its principal goal is the long-term welfare of its members, the stakeholders, and the environment. This changes the equation, even if the fundamentals of corporate finance are not vastly different.

The members of a cooperative (whether they are consumers, workers, producers, or bank account or insurance holders) acquire a share in the enterprise by purchasing that stake (a membership fee), by using the services of the enterprise (paying a premium or depositing money), by working for the enterprise for a certain amount of time, or by some other means. The members become the equivalent of the shareholders of the firm. They collectively retain the equity in the enterprise. Whatever the value of the enterprise is—again, in accounting terms, the assets and expected revenues minus the debt obligations—that value is effectively held by the members of the cooperative.

The cooperative enterprise, once incorporated, becomes the entity that effectively controls material interests (movable goods like commodities or modes of production like tools and equipment) on behalf of the members. The cooperative holds title to these material interests in the same way that a publicly held corporation holds title to land or goods. Decisions about the use or improvement of material interests are made by the members through a democratic process. Members may delegate ordinary decisions, by means of that participatory democratic process, to certain designated managers or supervisors. A cooperative may set up a trust to hold land or buildings for a community or the members and future members. Cooperation Jackson, for instance, has set up the Fannie Lou Hamer Community Land Trust (CLT) to purchase vacant lots, abandoned homes, and commercial facilities in the West Jackson neighborhood in order to remove them from market speculation and preserve them "for sustainable communal endeavors whether it be housing, playgrounds or corner stores." The land trust, they explain, provides a way to "steward land and housing and to provide housing that is permanently affordable. It puts control in the hands of a community to decide what it wants to develop on its collective land."[12]

As the cooperative enterprise creates wealth, the surplus generated can either be funneled back into the business or distributed to its members. At member cooperatives in the Mondragón consortium, you will recall, the distribution of any surplus is decided by a general assembly with a one-worker-one-vote rule and some general rules about the need to maintain a social fund and reserves.[13] The wealth of the cooperative, like that of a publicly traded corporation, is distributed by means of salaries to the employees, contractual exchanges with customers and providers of goods and services, and distributions and enhanced membership stakes for the members. As the ICA explains, members can allocate the surplus value that is created by the enterprise for the following purposes: "developing their cooperative, possibly by setting up reserves, part of which at least would be indivisible; benefiting members in proportion to their transactions with the cooperative; and supporting other activities approved by the membership."[14] The flows are similar to those in equity corporations, though the categories may have different names. Whereas distributions may be called dividends for the publicly traded corporation, they may be called patronage refunds in consumer cooperatives or patronage distributions in worker cooperatives. (Sometimes they are also called dividends in the cooperative context.)

With regard to worker cooperatives, I am using here the standard definition offered by the economist Virginie Pérotin: "a firm in which all or most of the capital is owned by employees in the firm, whether individually or collectively; where all employees have equal access to membership regardless of their occupational group; and where each member has one vote, regardless of the allocation of any individually owned capital in the firm." Worker cooperatives can have different financial structures and financial arrangements.[15] But if we take the basic structure of a worker-owned firm that follows the international cooperative principles, like those of the ICA, it is likely to look like this: workers acquire an interest in the firm and, as co-owners, then manage the enterprise in a democratic fashion. Material interests, such as equipment or commodities, are owned by the cooperative; their use, improvement, alienation, etc., are decided by the members. Any surpluses over the costs of production are either plowed back into the firm or distributed to the members based on their interest in the firm. There are no shareholder investors who vote in the management or have priority on the returns.

The Tax Court of the United States explained this well in their 1965 decision *Puget Sound Plywood, Inc. v. Commissioner of Internal Revenue*, which also defined cooperatives for purposes of the federal tax code.[16] In the process, the court clearly demarcated the differences with publicly traded corporations, offering a helpful and clear summary:

the basic and distinguishing feature of a workers cooperative association, as compared with a corporation-for-profit, is that in the case of a workers cooperative association the fruits and increases which the worker-members produce through their joint efforts are vested in and retained by the workers themselves, rather than in and by the association, as such, which functions only as an instrumentality for the benefit of the workers; and that these fruits and increases of the cooperative effort are then allocated among the active workers as patronage dividends, in proportion to their participation in producing the same. In the case of the corporation-for-profit, on the other hand, the fruits and increases of such organization belong to the corporate entity itself; and these increases (called net profits) are then either distributed or retained for the benefit of the equity owners, not in proportion to their personal efforts but rather in proportion to the amounts of capital which they supply. And also these same equity owners, acting either directly or indirectly, also select the management and control the functions and policies of their entity—not on a one-person one-vote basis without use of proxies, but rather through multiple voting in proportion to the number of shares of capital stock which they hold.[17]

In the United States, employee ownership often arises through a slightly different financial arrangement involving what is called an Employee Stock Ownership Plan (ESOP), as we saw earlier with King Arthur Flour. As Daniel Tischer and John Hoffmire explain, "since being established in 1973, Employee Stock Ownership Plans have been the most influential approach to transferring ownership to employees in the USA, partly because, with the company providing the collateral required through a trust, employees are not required to finance the purchase of shares themselves."[18] ESOPs have been popular and widespread in the United States. By the end of 2015, more than 9,300 companies had used ESOPs to transfer ownership stakes to employees, amounting to about $1 trillion in ownership equity distributed to around fifteen million employees. It is projected that a significant number of these ESOP transfers will lead to 100 percent employee ownership.[19]

I have focused primarily on consumer and worker cooperatives, but these principles of corporate finance apply as well to insurance mutuals, credit unions, and other cooperative enterprises. Much of the logic also applies to certain nonprofits, although the equity may not be owned by the people who work at the nonprofit, the stakeholders do not receive distributions, and typically they do not collectively own material interests. The nonprofit raises money predominantly through grants and charitable donations, and it distributes value through its operations and as salaries to its employees. It does not distribute any surplus to its stakeholders, as a cooperative could if it were operating at a surplus. Extra monies raised by the non-profit over and above its operating expenses go into an endowment as a reserve for future years, are invested in building and equipment, or are just saved for next year. Nonprofits do not have shareholder investors, and many of them promote the values and principles of cooperation. Apart from the equity and surplus, the flows are comparable in cooperatives and many nonprofit institutions.

THE CRUCIAL DIFFERENCE OF COOPERATION

There are, then, three major differences between the publicly held corporation and the cooperative enterprise. First, the cooperative organization (like the privately held corporation) has no liquid transferrable equity and cannot raise capital on the public markets. This places some constraints on its ability to grow. It means that the cooperative enterprise can only expand by bringing in more members (who often have less disposable cash than capital investors) or by borrowing or issuing obliga-tions. Naturally, this places some financial pressures on a growing cooperative. It makes it all the more important to cultivate symbiotic relations with credit unions and cooperative banks, as Mondragón has done with the Caja Laboral Popular.[20] Second, decision making at a cooperative is based on one-person-one-vote princi-ples, rather than in proportion to the equity stake as in publicly held corporations. This gives each member a greater voice in the management of the enterprise. Third, the decision makers in a cooperative are themselves members of the ongoing enter-prise and accountable to the other members, rather than to outside investors.

It is these latter distinctions that make all the difference. They mean that the member decision makers have a greater stake in the outcomes and care about the long-term sustainability of the enterprise, the welfare of its members, and their environment, rather than the immediate or short-term value of the corporation. It means that the member decision makers and those members in management positions have the members themselves, whether employees, consumers, or pro-ducers, and their working or consuming environment as their foremost interests. The cooperative exists for the welfare of its members, not the return on invest-ment to shareholders, as well as for the principles of democratic participation in the distribution of the wealth of the enterprise and the sustainable development of the environment and communities.

This has dramatic implications. It should not come as a surprise that at the member cooperatives of Mondragón, for instance, the disparity between the salary of the highest-paid directors and that of the lowest-paid workers cannot exceed 4.5 to 1.[21] When the members are the decision makers, the results are likely to be more equitable and just. Compare this to the average disparity in wages in enterprises in the United States today, expressed as the wage ratio between CEO pay and average worker pay. The average disparity in 2014 stood at 303 to 1.[22] At McDonald's, the wage ratio in 2018 was 3,101 to 1.[23]

"*Après moi, le déluge.*" After me, let it flood. Dardot and Laval refer to this as "the true 'spirit of capitalism.'"[24] Though somewhat dramatic, they are essentially right. The fact is, capital investors have little reason to care about the welfare of the company's employees while they are invested, and they have absolutely no reason to care about the company or its employees when they are selling their shareholdings. What this means, naturally, is that capital investors have no ongoing interest or incentive to pay attention to the long-term welfare of workers or employees, their working environment, or anyone else touched by the enterprise. The profit motive, the return on investment, is the only direct interest that the shareholder has.

This is a recipe for disaster. Shareholder investing has become a major source of today's problems precisely because of its extractive nature. Shareholding elevates selfish profit over human welfare. It detaches the owner of equity from any real investment in the lives of all those who work for or are associated with the enterprise. It turns the investor into a mere speculator on other people's lives. The ordinary stockholder really has only one primary interest: to maximize the return on their investment, to draw larger dividends, to sell their stock at a higher value. Their interest is to extract more from the enterprise via their equity stake; to squeeze out more from everyone who is associated with the enterprise; to eke out more from the workers; to manipulate share price through stock buybacks and other devices; to inflate future prospects—in effect, to make out like a bandit. The metaphor of extraction is important, as Saskia Sassen has emphasized.[25]

Most people who own stocks today, whether directly or indirectly, hold them as a form of speculation to increase the overall return on their savings and to increase their wealth—if possible, to increase their wealth more than others, and more than the market, since that is the only way to get richer, and richer than others. But this is nothing more than gambling on other people's livelihoods, more often than not, today, on other people's misery. It is nothing more than an effort to extract wealth from an enterprise, from its consumers or workers, from all the people whose livelihoods depend on the business. Shareholding has transformed ours into an extractive society. It is time to replace it with cooperation.

INCENTIVIZING COOPERATION

The benefits of cooperative arrangements should now be clear: they reduce social inequality by distributing the wealth created by the enterprise more equitably among the stakeholders and aim for the sustainable development of the environment and communities. They push against the ongoing threats to democracy by training citizens in all aspects of their lives to engage in participatory democratic decision making. They help combat climate change by prioritizing the sustainability of the environment. They foster a sense of solidarity that nurtures respect and caring for others in a way that favors collective responses to pandemics and other crises.

Many simple things can be done to promote cooperation. One key to incentivizing cooperation is to remove the privileged treatment of shareholder investment and instead make cooperative arrangements more financially and fiscally beneficial. That includes, first, getting rid of the more favorable tax treatment of capital gains on equity investments. In the United States, shareholder qualified dividends and long-term gains on investment are taxed at a capital gains rate, whereas cooperative distributions are taxed as income at a much higher rate. The federal tax rate on long-term capital gains ranges between 15 percent (for persons with taxable incomes between about $40,000 and $500,000) and 20 percent (for persons with larger taxable incomes). For most small investors, the rate is essentially 15 percent. In the case of private equity and hedge funds, the profits paid to managers are also taxed at the capital gains rate—what is known as the "carried interest loophole."[26] Again, the tax code treats those capital profits more favorably, with a top rate of 20 percent. By contrast, federal income tax rates reach up to 35 percent or 37 percent for persons with taxable incomes over about $200,000 or $500,000. This means it is far more advantageous, financially, to be investing capital in equity shares or private equity than earning patronage distributions from a cooperative.[27] The profit on an investment is worth more than the benefit of work. When you add state and city taxes in places like New York State and New York City, the differential is magnified even more.

Another way to incentivize cooperation is to invert the preferential treatment of shareholder investments for purposes of retirement accounts. Capital invested in institutional retirement accounts can often be contributed pretax (which effectively invests the amount that would have gone to the federal government in taxes), and the increased value over time is tax deferred (you do not pay any taxes until you take out the monies many years later). So, all of the gains are also cumulated on pretax dollars and pretax profits. The compounded advantage is enormous. Given the present value of money, this is another huge bonanza for shareholder investment. It creates a huge incentive to invest retirement monies in the stock market rather than in cooperative endeavors.

It is essential to replace these investor benefits with tax and financial incentives that would reward cooperation; for instance, we could simply use the long-term capital gains rates for cooperative distributions instead. There are many creative ways to make cooperation more financially attractive: allow members to use pretax earnings to buy their share of a cooperative; defer taxes on distributions until members sell their cooperative stake in the enterprise. Tax specialists can devise myriad ways to make any economic transaction lucrative and attractive. Right now, everything favors conventional equity shareholding and capital investment. That could easily be transformed.

When combined with tax changes, it would be easy to promote cooperation by spreading wealth and making cooperative membership more attractive and straightforward. One approach, purely hypothetical, builds on existing legal structures and represents a relatively small tweak of already existing institutions to help stimulate cooperation: (1) Change the rules of incorporation and taxation schemes to favor cooperatives, mutuals, unions, and nonprofits through tax incentives and benefits. This will ensure that business entities form as, or convert into, cooperatives rather than capitalized corporations. It will ensure that many more people begin to work in cooperative arrangements. (2) Raise money (perhaps by levying an inheritance tax) and ensure that the revenues are distributed to individuals in such a way that they can buy into cooperative enterprises. This approach is minimalist and, from a technical perspective, would only require a few budgetary fixes. At the other end, there are plenty of more maximalist approaches that would allow everyone to partake in cooperative arrangements.

In all of these scenarios, it would be helpful to institutionalize dispute resolution such that the final decision-making power to resolve any disputes over material interests would be allocated, say, to a committee consisting of seasoned members of cooperatives and mutualist organizations, elected by all the members of institutions of cooperation. The determinations of this body would be conclusive and binding on society. Naturally, this is simplifying matters, but the allocation of all the different material interests can be organized and distributed in myriad ways that would promote cooperation. Technically, it is easy. Making it happen would require a change in values—and that, I would argue, is occurring as cooperation is spreading around the world.

The imperative, then, is to redesign the economic and social landscape in such a way as to retain all the advantages of the cooperative framework—the emphasis on sustainability and prioritizing the welfare of consumers, workers, producers, affiliates, etc.—and to ensure economic health. We know how to do this. In fact, we can do it in a few easy steps. It is just a question of embracing cooperationist values. Now is the time to reconfigure and reimagine cooperation for the real, concrete, material world.

TOWARD COÖPERISM

The most important point is that it is extremely easy to design arrangements that favor cooperation. It is, in fact, as easy as tweaking the rules of incorporation and taxation. Designing cooperation, like designing capital, uses the basic toolkit of the lawyer, a toolkit that has been used and mastered for centuries. It is basic plumbing for the lawyer. As Katharina Pistor explains in her book *The Code of Capital*, corporate lawyers spend their time using the conventional, classic tools of legal practice to turn assets into capital.[28]

But it is just as simple to create cooperative enterprises. The methods of cooperation are as basic as those that code capital. They too use the core building blocks of the law school curriculum: contract law, property law, corporations, trusts and estates, bankruptcy. We can do the same work of coding basic assets—land, debt, knowledge, firms, institutions, intellectual property, digital assets—for cooperation. The way to code assets so that they are held in a mutual or credit union, the rules about surplus distributions, and the rules of incorporation, these too are the basic building blocks of lawyers. It is as simple to them as the use of a power drill is to the mechanic. We know how to incorporate cooperatives and mutuals. We know how to code cooperation. The question is not one of knowledge or expertise, but of will.

CHAPTER 4

The Political Theory of Coöperism

Historians and social theorists trace cooperation all the way back to prehistory and forward, in the modern period, to the guild system and chambers of merchants in the Italian city-states of the Middle Ages.[1] Many Western accounts of cooperatives begin toward the end of the eighteenth century with Robert Owen's opening of a model mill in New Lanark, Scotland, near Glasgow, in 1799, on principles of worker equity, or to the creation of the Rochdale Society of Equitable Pioneers, a consumer cooperative founded in 1844. The Rochdale Society, it is said, began when a few weavers and artisans came together and raised funds to sell food basics (butter, flour, oatmeal, sugar) in Rochdale, a small city outside Manchester in the county of Lancashire, England. It was founded on simple principles, including: "1) sale for cash at fixed prices; 2) end of the year rebate proportional to purchases; 3) freedom of purchasing (members were not required to shop only at the co-op); 4) minimum interest on loans; 5) democratic government (one head, one vote; women too could be voting members); and 6) ideological neutrality and tolerance."[2] By 1850, there were about six hundred members. The Rochdale Society continued to grow on those simple principles, adding a four-story headquarters building with many satellite outlets, as well as a library and a meeting hall (for men, I will come back to this); it also promoted education and public lectures. It became a model for the development of other consumer cooperatives in Manchester, elsewhere in England, and throughout Europe and the world.

Western histories of worker cooperatives usually begin with the formation of early associations of carpenters, woodworkers, millers, and other trades in early-nineteenth-century France and to the experiments of Louis Blanc with national worker-owned workshops, ultimately leading to national legislation in

1848 that provided for government funding and support of worker cooperatives. Credit unions and finance cooperatives are said to trace back to Germany in 1849, when Wilhelm Raiffeisen founded the first rural mutual bank in the Rhine Valley. Histories of farmer cooperative often begin in Scandinavia, particularly with dairy farming in Denmark.[3]

In the United States, histories of cooperation often begin with the practices of Indigenous peoples or of enslaved persons of African descent; or with the cod and whale fishing industries, where broad-based profit sharing was the norm and actually encouraged by early congressional legislation in 1792.[4] According to some historians, the development of cooperatives in the United States was tied to "the upheavals that characterized the Industrial Revolution in England during 1750–1850."[5] Others say cooperation was born in tandem with the republic. Benjamin Franklin started one of the first recognized mutuals in 1752. In 1810, the first recorded dairy and cheese cooperatives were organized, followed by cooperatives for other agricultural commodities.[6] Key historical moments in the emergence of cooperatives in the United States include the passage of a first credit union statute in Massachusetts in 1909; the establishment of the Cooperative League of the United States of America (CLUSA), intended to promote a broad cooperative agenda, in 1916; and the passage in 1922 of the Capper-Volstead Act in response to the Sherman Antitrust Act, allowing farmers to work together cooperatively, under certain circumstances, to process and market commodities.[7]

These origin stories reflect different historiographies of cooperation. Some are utopian; others are patriotic, even nationalistic; some are evolutionary; some are race-conscious, others not; some are Marxist; others are more conventional. Many are selective, predominantly focused on Western history; there would be far more to say at the global level, from South America to Africa and Asia. But the different historiographies are important because they reveal the central justifications that have been offered over time for cooperative enterprises. Embedded in those origin stories are different political theories of cooperation.

THE THREE TRADITIONAL JUSTIFICATIONS

These histories reveal three main justifications for cooperation: utopian, separatist self-determinist, and evolutionary. All three have distinct nineteenth- and twentieth-century roots. Let me review them here before proposing a contemporary political theory of coöperism better suited to our times of crises.

Utopianism

Many historians trace the origins of cooperatives back to early-nineteenth-century utopians: the Welsh industrialist Robert Owen (1771–1858), who refashioned his textile factory at New Lanark and, in 1825, created a social utopia at New Harmony, Indiana; the French merchant Charles Fourier (1772–1837), who imagined and promoted the *phalanstère* and an entirely new circulation of work and desire; Pierre-Joseph Proudhon (1809–1865), a self-proclaimed anarchist who is generally credited with developing a philosophy of mutualism; the French politician and historian Louis Blanc (1811–1882), who advocated for government-sponsored worker workshops. These were social visionaries focused on reorganizing modes of production in order to center the interests and welfare of the workers and their families, those who toiled in the factories and workshops of early industrialism. They were trying to develop a new organization of labor. Louis Blanc's most important tract, in fact, was called *The Organization of Labor*, published in 1839; it was one of the first texts to use the term *capitalist* in its modern meaning and to declare "from each according to his ability, to each according to his needs."[8] The emphasis was on reorganizing production for the benefit of workers and their families, limiting the hours of labor, improving living conditions, and promoting education.

Many people consider Robert Owen the father of the cooperative movement. Owen experimented in the early nineteenth century with enlightened factory workshops and towns that provided housing, education, and welfare for the workers; however, he was not experimenting with cooperatives so much as with top-down social-welfare arrangements at his factory in New Lanark and, later, the factory town in New Harmony, Indiana. Owen was more of a social reformer, along what we might today call social democratic lines, who believed strongly in government welfare programs. He argued for government provision of education and training for the poor. He advocated, throughout his life, for an eight-hour workday. In 1835, Owen formed the Association of All Classes of All Nations, which helped coin the term *socialism* and made it current in British terminology.

Owen set out his vision for society in a book, published in 1817, titled *A New View of Society: or, Essays on the Formation of the Human Character Preparatory to the Development of a Plan for Gradually Ameliorating the Condition of Mankind*, and in a report published in 1818 to the House of Commons Committee on the Poor Laws.[9] Owen decried the miserable conditions that, he argued, plagued three-fourths of the British population. Convinced that knowledge would produce action, he hoped to enlighten political leaders and the public. He explained that the education, training, and ethical formation of children would lead the disadvantaged away from lives of crime and vice toward more productive lives of labor; this would benefit not only the disadvantaged by relieving their poverty, but the privileged as well because they would be better able to enjoy their advantages.

Owen was convinced that, in his words, "man may by degrees be trained to live in any part of the world without poverty, without crime, and without punishment."[10] Insisting that what he was proposing could work not only in theory but also in practice, he spoke constantly of putting his "principles into practice."[11] And he did, in both Scotland and the United States, eventually losing all his wealth as he tried to construct more just microsocieties.

Owen was writing as an industrialist and a capitalist, interested in deriving profit from his reforms. He managed mills and tried to sustain himself on the revenues from his private enterprises. He employed "about five hundred children, who were procured chiefly from workhouses and charities in Edinburgh," ages 5 and 6, in the factory that he took over in 1784 at New Lanark.[12] Although he improved their work conditions, he was still motivated by the profit motive. Owen made this clear in various addresses, including this one to other industrialists at the beginning of the third essay in *A New View of Society*:

> Like you, I am a manufacturer for pecuniary profit. But having for many years acted on principles the reverse in many respects of those in which you have been instructed, and having found my procedure beneficial to others and to myself, even in a pecuniary point of view, I am anxious to explain such valuable principles, that you and those under influence may equally partake of their advantages.[13]

The profit motive is pervasive in Owen's writings. The programs he advanced, Owen writes in essay three, "will yet appear, upon a full minute investigation by minds equal to the comprehension of such a system, to combine a greater degree of substantial comfort to the individuals employed in the manufactory, and of pecuniary profit to the proprietors, than has hitherto been found attainable."[14] Owen appealed to the proprietors' keen sense of investment in machines and then draws the parallel to "vital machines," or workers.[15] He refers to "living machinery"—that is, workers as machines—anticipating Gary Becker's theory of human capital.[16] Tending to that living machinery, Owen argued, "will essentially add to your gains."[17]

In a strange way, this reflects Marx's critique of utopianism, which he described as "still stamped with the birthmarks of the old society from whose womb it emerges."[18] This does not undermine, by any means, the advances that Owen made possible in his time. He was years ahead of his peers in advocating for a social welfare state, for a national plan for education and ethical culture, for "the happiness of the community." "The end of government is to make the governed and the governors happy," Owen declared. "That government then is the best, which in practice produces the greatest happiness to the greatest number; including those who govern, and those who obey."[19] Thus, he was years ahead of his time in creating socially reformed workplaces, but he lived as an industrialist during a very different time, and some of his reasoning now feels anachronistic.

The same is true of Charles Fourier, whose quixotic work *The Theory of the Four Movements*, published in 1808, laid the foundation for a new vision of labor and desire based on his wildly imaginative *phalanstères*—self-sufficient, autonomous, utopian microcosms of 1,200 people designed for the benefit of workers and their families. Fourier was a brilliant and radical thinker, one of the founders of utopianism, and a feminist as well—in fact, it seems he used the term *feminist* first in 1837. He was also very forward looking on issues of sexuality. His writings on the libidinal motivations for labor inspired generations of thinkers at the intersection of cooperation and liberation, from Herbert Marcuse to André Breton, Roland Barthes, and Hakim Bey.[20]

Although Fourier put cooperation at the center of his enterprise, he was wedded to the idea of profit and the desire for luxury, which he placed at the emotional center of his project. The phalanxes would triumph, Fourier argued, because of human greed and desires. He wrote:

> The strongest passion of peasants, as of city-dwellers, is a love of profit. When they see an associative community yielding a profit (other things being equal) three times as large as that produced by a community of isolated families, as well as providing all its members with the most varied pleasures, they will forget all their rivalries and hasten to put association into practice. And no laws or coercion will be necessary for this to spread to every part of the world, because people everywhere are motivated by a desire for wealth and pleasure.[21]

As a result of this emphasis on profit and luxury, there are aspects of nineteenth-century utopianism that sit uncomfortably today. Its proponents often remained tied to conventional profit motives and industrial capitalism, imagining a future in terms of social welfare rather than fully self-sufficient and self-determining cooperation.

Even more, they were not sufficiently inclusive or attentive to intersectionality. In several cases, they were overtly prejudiced against minorities, especially Jews, and sexist. Fourier, for instance, had a number of such failings. He imagined a new family organization, but one that included domestic servants.[22] Fourier was also anti-Semitic. He believed that Jews, whom he associated with trade, were the source of evil and had to be forced to do farm work. In fact, he advocated for the return of Jews to Palestine.

Pierre-Joseph Proudhon is deeply problematic in this regard. Proudhon is credited with first articulating a mutualist philosophy. In *The System of Economic Contradictions, or the Philosophy of Poverty*, published in 1846, he argued for "a theory of mutuality" that would restore society to "the sincerity of its nature" and allow people "work, education, well-being, equality."[23] He came to his position from a unique perspective, a form of scientific absolutism that displaced the need for the state. He argued that there were rules of society that could be scientifically determined and that would supplant the need for a state or for any "governing by man." In this, Proudhon was deeply inspired by Claude Henri de Rouvroy, comte de Saint-Simon (1760–1825), who founded a political theory known as Saint-Simonianism that many people associate with utopianism. Saint-Simon believed so strongly in science that he thought humans could do away with the state, or at least limit it to minor functions such as promoting work and limiting idleness. A great admirer of Adam Smith, Saint-Simon favored a small government. Proudhon, who shared Saint-Simon's faith in science, believed we could do away with the state entirely and be governed completely by scientific principles.

Proudhon came to mutualism from a very different perspective than that of Owen or Fourier. He was one of the first persons to proclaim himself an anarchist, and to use that term. He did so in the final chapter of his 1840 book, *What Is Property?*, by way of a fictitious dialogue with his younger readers. There, he asserted that he was neither a republican, a monarchist, a democrat, a constitutionalist, nor a believer in mixed government. "I am an anarchist," he declared. He championed the abolition of all property.[24] In response to his infamous provocation in the title of that book, *What Is Property?*, Proudhon famously answered, "*Property Is Theft!*"[25] He advocated not for the equal or fair distribution of property but for its total abolition.[26] Instead, he proposed an economic regime based simply on possession. "Suppress property while maintaining possession, and by this simple modification of the principle, you will revolutionize the law, government, economy, and institutions," Proudhon declared, and "you will drive evil from the face of the earth."[27]

In terms of worker cooperatives, Proudhon imagined equitable workshops in which workers had full possession of the means of production. By contrast to Louis Blanc, who lobbied and got legislation passed for the French government to support worker workshops, Proudhon felt that any governmental intervention would undermine the cooperative project.[28] He was deeply critical of Blanc's proposals and argued that workshops could not be owned by the nation nor connected in any way to the state.[29] Instead, Proudhon advocated for an expansion of credit that would benefit workers and lead to the withering of the state.[30] At the same time, Proudhon was viscerally opposed to communism. He argued that communism essentially violates human nature: people want to give to others out of a sense of self, not obligation; plus, he said, communism puts laziness and industry on the same plane.[31] The only possible form of liberty, he argued, was anarchy. He also opposed revolution; on that, he was adamant. Instead of a proletarian uprising, Proudhon wanted to whittle away at property and the state slowly, through scientific knowledge, reason, and argument, to show the contradictions inherent in property relations, reveal scientifically that it is theft, or in his words, "burn property slowly with a small fire."[32] Workers needed science, not blood to drink. As he wrote in *What Is Property?*, "politics is a science and not a matter of stratagem, and the function of the legislator is reduced in the final analysis to the methodical search for truth."[33] In a letter to Marx, Proudhon insisted on the duty "to keep a critical and skeptical frame of mind" and "an almost absolute economic anti-dogmatism." He concluded the letter: "But for God's sake, after having demolished all *a priori* dogmatisms, let us not in turn dream of making our own, of indoctrinating the people."[34]

But although he articulated and in part gave birth to a mutualist philosophy and advocated for worker cooperatives, Proudhon himself was anti-Semitic and sexist. His famous confrontation with Marx was not purely intellectual; there was a deeply anti-Semitic dimension to it. This is what Proudhon wrote about

Jews (including Marx by name) in his private diaries in 1847, which were only published in the 1960s:

> December 26, 1847: Jews. Write an article against this race that poisons everything by sticking its nose into everything without ever mixing with any other people. Demand its expulsion from France with the exception of those individuals married to French women. Abolish synagogues and not admit them to any employment. Demand its expulsion. Finally, pursue the abolition of this religion. It's not without cause that the Christians called them deicides. The Jew is the enemy of humankind. They must be sent back to Asia or be exterminated. H. Heine, A. Weill, and others are nothing but secret spies; Rothschild, Crémieux, Marx, Fould, wicked, bilious, envious, bitter, etc. etc. beings who hate us. The Jew must disappear by steel or by fusion or by expulsion. Tolerate the elderly who no longer have children. Work to be done—What the peoples of the Middle Ages hated instinctively I hate upon reflection and irrevocably. The hatred of the Jew like the hatred of the English should be our first article of political faith. Moreover, the abolition of Judaism will come with the abolition of other religions. Begin by not allocating funds to the clergy and leaving this to religious offerings. —And then, a short while later, abolish the religion.[35]

It is hard to imagine drawing on Proudhon's ideas, whether on cooperation, anarchism, or the abolition of property, after reading this diatribe. Also a sexist, Proudhon wrote in his journals that women should be either courtesans or housekeepers and should be under the dominion of their masters.[36]

It is painful to read these utopian thinkers and come across passages that are so utterly unconscionable. It makes it difficult to ground a political theory of cooperation on their writings. It is not as if we are engaging in ontological philosophical theory and trying to set aside the fact that, for instance, Martin Heidegger was a member of the Nazi Party from 1933 till its demise in 1945—query whether we could even set that aside in his case. Here we are dealing with theorists of cooperation, of people working together, of solidarity and mutualism, who spout anti-Semitic, misogynistic, or otherwise hateful words. It is impossible to set that aside; it was threaded into the logic of their argument and cannot be disentangled.

It happens over and over. So, for instance, in Charles Gide's book *Le Coopératisme*, the reader comes to a chapter titled "The Enemies of Cooperation." It is a lecture

Gide delivered at the Congress of Cooperative Societies held at Grenoble, France, on October 15, 1893. Who are those "enemies of cooperation"? First and foremost, women. The first section of the chapter is titled simply "Les femmes" (women). The three other enemies are merchants, socialists, and internal enemies, so women even come before treasonous internal enemies as the worst threat to cooperation. Why? Gide's answer: "Throughout history, since Eve, women have liked the tempters," Gide writes. "And the merchant is the greatest tempter." Cooperation is apparently too austere for women, even repulsive, Gide explained. They do not like cooperatives, they prefer shiny, elegant shopping centers where they can "chit-chat without being pressed."[37] These passages are so offensive, it is impossible to return to these nineteenth- and early-twentieth-century texts. We cannot found cooperation on their tainted logic.

There must be something wrong with a utopian vision of cooperation that discriminates against women or Jews or that basks in the profit motives of industrialists or in the desire for luxury. There cannot be a true sense of solidarity in these visions; clearly, they are not up to the task of addressing our contemporary interdependence. People today must unite, not divide or harm each other. They must be inclusive and embracing of difference if they have any hope of genuinely working together, of genuinely *co-operari*.

More broadly, these utopian writings belong to an outdated discourse on political economy, one that was born in the late eighteenth century in Western Europe and predates the development of social research in politics, economics, and social theory. These writings were born of a different set of conversations than we are having today, conversations about natural law and human nature, theories of moral sentiment, arguments of raison d'état (reason of state). One can almost trace their emergence to the interval between Smith's *Theory of Moral Sentiments*, published in 1759, and his *Wealth of Nations*, published in 1776.[38] The latter work depended entirely, intellectually, on the former; the connection was not even made explicit but simply assumed. In that transition, we could say, political economy was born and would develop in the work of David Ricardo, Proudhon, Marx, and others.

But those taken-for-granted assumptions about human nature, natural law, and moral sentiment no longer hold today. They were displaced in the twentieth century by modern welfare economics, public-choice theories in political studies, critical theories more generally, and now, in the twenty-first century, by solidarity economics, ecological economics, and other greener forms of economic thinking.

To be sure, there are ways to interpret the subsequent debates between Keynes and Hayek, or the writings of Karl Polanyi and Joseph Schumpeter, as emanations of political economy and prolongations of that discourse. Contemporary economic writings are and can be placed in conversation with Smith and Marx. But those connections are more nostalgic than real, allusions rather than substance: contemporary thinkers refer back to Marx's "laws of capital," but they no longer really engage his theory of value or exchange. They do not seriously extend the debate over the difference between use and exchange value, for instance, which was at the heart of so many debates in political economy at the time.

Today, those nineteenth-century writings in political economy are primarily material for historians, especially economic historians, and nostalgic critical theorists. For those of us interested in praxis, we have learned far too much since then to be limited to those early debates and ideas. To be sure, the term *political economy* offers something that economics alone does not, emphasizing the necessarily political dimension of economic regimes. That is important. It is central to the project of cooperation. It allows us to see through the ideological discourse of capitalism, as I will discuss in the next chapter. It also nourishes useful concepts such as financialization, neoliberalism, and racial capitalism.[39] But that is not a reason to return to the exhausted discourse of the utopians. It is far better to make the affirmative argument in plain contemporary terms, without unearthing all the writings from the eighteenth and nineteenth centuries. Those writings introduce biases and errors, as well as prejudice.

For these reasons, it is crucial to reset the dial and not get caught in the quagmire of earlier historical debates. Our interdependence today in the face of global climate change could not have been imagined in the nineteenth century. We are past the point when wealthy industrialists like Robert Owen marshal philanthropic ideals to relieve the misery of five-year-old orphans working in their factories, or fanciful utopians like Charles Fourier, radical anarchists like Pierre-Joseph Proudhon, or even more elaborate cooperative philosophers and economic proponents of cooperative federalism like Charles Gide spout hateful diatribes. There is just no need to return there, nor to the type of top-down, state-sponsored forms of cooperative workshops envisaged in the mid-nineteenth century by someone like Louis Blanc. Blanc's model of legislating workshops differs from the model that needs to be developed today, in part because of the inevitable gridlock in liberal democracies. These times call for a horizontal, rhizomic, and inclusive intersectional vision of cooperation.

Separatist Self-Determination

W. E. B. Du Bois was an early scholar of cooperatives. You will recall his 1907 study, *Economic Co-operation Among Negro Americans*, which was a formative contribution to the field. In a subsequent short essay, published in 1935, Du Bois proposed a separatist Black society made up of cooperative associations exclusively for and by African Americans.[40] At the specific historical conjuncture, when African American families were doubly hit by the economic crisis of the Great Depression and discriminatory exclusion from the workforce and white unions, Du Bois returned to the idea of cooperatives as the most promising way to put African Americans on an equal footing with white Americans.

Du Bois anchored his vision of cooperation in existing models of cooperatives in the United States and abroad.[41] Du Bois had studied the history and trajectory of cooperative workshops and associations for the African American labor force. His was no pie-in-the-sky idealism or wild utopianism, but a realistic engagement based on the track record of successful cooperative initiatives. In his 1907 study, and also in his magnum opus *Black Reconstruction in America*, published in 1935, Du Bois discussed the movement toward worker cooperatives within the communities of freed Black men and women. He recounted the history of labor conventions, such as the one held in 1869 that called for the "establishment of cooperative workshops." Du Bois detailed the efforts of the Bureau of Labor, in 1870, to organize "Negro labor" and its call "to secure funds from bankers and capitalists for aid in establishing cooperative associations."[42] Du Bois was writing at a time of robust debate over the cooperative model of production and in the wake of a long history and a growing social movement for cooperatives in the United States. Peter Kropotkin's influential work *Mutual Aid: A Factor of Evolution*, which offered a more naturalist basis for cooperation, had appeared in essay form in the 1880s and was published in 1902.[43] The Cooperative League of the United States of America was founded in 1916, with the ambition of creating a "Cooperative Commonwealth." Focused on consumer cooperatives, predominantly for whites, the Cooperative League quickly won the support of the likes of John Dewey and Walter Lippmann.[44] That and other cooperative movements were on the rise, seen as viable alternatives to American capitalism modeled on competition. It was to those alternatives that Du Bois turned to in the 1930s.

In a speech delivered in June 1934 and in the essay published in 1935 in *Current History*, "A Negro Nation Within the Nation," Du Bois advocated for an

African American cooperative movement "separate from the national economy and mainstream labor."[45] Du Bois explicitly made the case for separatist Black cooperatives that would no longer depend on "the salvation of a white God" but instead "achieve a new economic solidarity." Du Bois began by noting the crises that Black workers faced, not just the economic downturn caused by the Great Depression but other forms of segregation, exclusion from the recovery efforts, and closed unions and union shops due to outright racism. Du Bois confronted what he diagnosed as insurmountable racism within the working class. The greatest problem facing the African American community, Du Bois argued, was white labor, which excluded, harassed, and terrorized the Black worker.[46] In the face of that racism, Du Bois advocated for separatist cooperation within the Black community, and specifically for the creation of a Black cooperative movement separate from white society.

Sympathetic to socialism, Du Bois nevertheless remained at arm's length from socialists because they did not acknowledge or promote the interests of African Americans. "The socialists still keep them in the background," Du Bois wrote. He was also deeply wary of unions, which were predominantly white and excluded African American workers, when they did not actively terrorize them. "Today it is white labor that keeps Negroes out of decent low-cost housing, that confines the protection of the best unions to 'white' men, that often will not sit in the same hall with black folk who already have joined the labor movement." Du Bois would not put his trust in unions. Nor did he embrace an internationalist or universalist vision. Yet Du Bois did believe in economic advancement, economic self-sufficiency, economic power. That was, in fact, the fundamental problem plaguing African American communities: "since emancipation he [the African American person] has never had an adequate economic foundation." For Du Bois, economic advancement within industrialized society was the necessary prerequisite for the social and political advancement of African Americans. So, Du Bois took the position that the only way for African Americans to protect themselves and advance to a position of equality was by gaining economic power: African Americans had "to begin planning for preservation through economic advancement." That translated into cooperation among African Americans: "letting Negro farmers feed Negro artisans, and Negro technicians guide Negro home industries, and Negro thinkers plan this integration of cooperation, while Negro artists dramatize and beautify the struggle."[47] This would lead to economic independence, which Du Bois described as "economic cooperation, organized self-defense and necessary self-confidence."[48]

Black separatism was intended to demonstrate the abilities of African Americans, ensure their economic advancement, and put them on an equal footing with whites within the current industrialized society.

Du Bois retained faith in the democratization of economic exchange. He believed that American industry was undergoing a democratic shift away from monopolization and concentration. He predicted inevitable and positive changes: "Greater democratic control of production and distribution is bound to replace existing autocratic and monopolistic methods."[49] Du Bois even believed that gradual transformations would favor the uplifting of African Americans. But change was not going to happen fast enough for Du Bois, or on its own. It depended on decision making rather than natural economic forces, what he called "human choice." It turned on people accepting African American workers. But that would only happen, Du Bois argued, if Black workers had more economic clout. Separatist cooperatives were the only way to demonstrate ability and achieve equal footing.

Du Bois took a stepwise approach: first, separatism as a way to achieve independence; second, cooperatives as a way to achieve economic growth; and third, all of this oriented to eventual integration and equality in a modern, more democratized society in which, ultimately, all race and class differences would be erased. Du Bois believed "in the ultimate uniting of mankind and in a unified American nation, with economic classes and racial barriers leveled"; but he believed that this could only happen through African American demonstration, not through white acceptance. It "is to be realized," he wrote, "only by such intensified class and race consciousness as will bring irresistible force rather than mere humanitarian appeals to bear on the motives and actions of men."[50] Racial prejudice had to be resolved first, and in order to do that, there needed to be cooperation among African Americans and isolation from whites. There needed to be an enclosed Black society of cooperation. But the ultimate objective was to level class and race differences.

Separatist self-determination was the key. "Negroes can develop in the United States an economic nation within a nation," Du Bois maintained, "able to work through inner cooperation, to found its own institutions, to educate its genius, and at the same time, without mob violence or extremes of race hatred, to keep in helpful touch and cooperate with the mass of the nation."[51] This would ultimately level classes and eliminate race distinctions. Du Bois said nothing about abolishing private property. In contrast to Marxists, Du Bois believed that classes could be leveled by means of cooperative organization. In this regard, Du Bois was making a unique and nuanced intervention in socialist debates: first, staying focused on race, which the socialists ignored; second, turning to cooperatives as a first step and end goal; and third, retaining faith in a more democratized cooperative economy that would eventually cast off race and class distinctions.

For Du Bois, cooperative arrangements were both a means and an end. Du Bois opposed the approach of Booker T. Washington, who sought to educate and train African American men and women to integrate them into white industry. Du Bois argued that there was sufficiently educated leadership. What was missing was the leadership itself. The need was not to fight segregation, as some activists and thinkers like James Weldon Johnson advocated, nor to wait for humanitarian benevolence from white people, but instead to separate and create a Black cooperative nation within the nation. Du Bois was willing to bear the burden of more segregation, and even more prejudice, in order to achieve this economic solidarity. He wrote:

> There exists today a chance for the Negroes to organize a cooperative State within their own group. By letting Negro farmers feed Negro artisans, and Negro technicians guide Negro home industries, and Negro thinkers plan this integration of cooperation, while Negro artists dramatize and beautify the struggle, economic independence can be achieved. To doubt this is possible is to doubt the essential humanity and the quality of brains of the American Negro.[52]

Du Bois's proposal was aimed at achieving, in the long run, a unified country without class or racial barriers. When the Black cooperative nation had been achieved, Du Bois believed, Black Americans would no longer be "refused fellowship and equality in the United States."[53]

Du Bois's writings form the backbone of a second justification for targeted forms of cooperation with a strong separatist and self-determinist element. The model has been taken up in a number of other contexts, including Cooperation Jackson in Mississippi and adjacent projects to create a separate region in the Black Belt counties of Mississippi, Louisiana, Arkansas, and Tennessee. But it is hard to imagine how it could form the basis for the kind of wide-scale cooperation that is called for today in the face of mounting crises like climate change and pandemics that call on us all to work together at the intersection of our identities. To be sure, there is a place for self-determination within groups. In the

United States, there is real value to traditionally Black colleges and institutions of higher learning, such as Morehouse College, Spellman College, Alabama State University, and many others. There is also value to all-women or all-men educational settings; there are many forms of cooperation that take place within those settings. A project like Cooperation Jackson has an extraordinary effect on the African American communities in the Jackson region, which have been historically neglected and openly, often violently, repressed. But our interdependence in the face of global crises creates an urgent need for everyone to work together. In this, I side with Richard Sennett, who urgently calls for cooperation across racial, ethnic, religious, economic, and other differences and throughout human exchange, from the street corner to online platforms.[54] In fact, I see this reflected in Cooperation Jackson now teaming up with Cooperation Vermont (which is not predominantly African American) to create a safer place in Vermont for climate refugees from Mississippi. This collaboration is proof of how crucial it is to increase the cooperation between groups.

At a conference called Jackson Rising intended to explore new economic models of cooperation, held at Jackson State University in May 2014, the members of Cooperation Jackson, as well as the mayor of Jackson, Chokwe Lumumba, encouraged and pledged to support other efforts at creating self-determining solidarity economies around the country. "We ask that you join us in this effort by organizing a Cooperation ___ wherever you live that is directly linked with grassroots efforts to build democratic people's power from the bottom-up and forming mutual bonds with us and formations like us throughout the US and the world," Kali Akuno declared. "This is how we will give birth to the new world waiting to be born."[55] As a result of the conference, new cooperative projects have been developed around the country, including Cooperation Vermont and Cooperation Humboldt in California. Cooperation Vermont was founded in 2021 with the help of Cooperation Jackson and now forms part of a larger consortium of cooperation called the People's Network for Land and Liberation, which also includes the Survivors Village/New Day Collective in the St. Bernard neighborhood of New Orleans and other cooperative initiatives. Cooperation Jackson is collaborating with Cooperation Vermont to provide institutional infrastructure and know-how, recently serving as the 501(c)(3) structure for the purchase of the Marshfield Village Store in Marshfield, Vermont, which is being converted into a community cooperative, owned by the workers and community members.[56] Part of the motivation is to provide links between Jackson and Vermont for the "climate refugees" being displaced from Mississippi by climate change. Kali Akuno himself has begun to move, with his family, to a farm operated by the Grassroots Center and Cooperation Vermont in Marshfield, Vermont.[57] Cooperation Humboldt, in Humboldt County on California's North Coast, aims to transform the area into "a regenerative community that can sustain life and future generations as we face climate crises and natural disasters," using the principles of cooperation, participatory democracy, equity, and solidarity.[58]

These intersectional developments, especially the effort to create cooperation networks for climate refugees, suggest that separatist self-determination may no longer be a viable response in the interdependent world in which we now live. The goal should be to increase cooperation inclusively and to nurture even more cooperation among cooperatives of different types and different demographic compositions, always staying attuned to the crucial need for equality between different groups. Du Bois's argument remains vital on the question of relative growth or inequality in growth and standards of living. It is essential, as Du Bois argued, that there not be inequalities between groups of different racial, ethnic, or for that matter gender or sexual, identities. There is no place for cooperation that does not contribute to the equalization of human welfare.

Evolutionary

At the turn of the twentieth century, the Russian polymath Pyotr Alexeyevich Kropotkin attempted to prove as a scientific matter that cooperation, rather than competition, was central to animal flourishing and evolution, including human evolution.[59] Although Kropotkin was not literally responding to Charles Darwin—he was actually responding more directly to an essay by Thomas Huxley, "The Struggle for Existence"[60]—Kropotkin was clearly making a scientific, evolutionary argument in the wake of Darwinian theory. His approach has spawned a larger literature on the evolutionary advantages of cooperation.

Kropotkin published his many writings on the topic in 1902 under the title *Mutual Aid: A Factor of Evolution*. There, he demonstrated that cooperation is a central practice in the lives of many animals, from swallows to marmots, and that it played a key role in human development, from the time of primitive hunter-gatherers to today. Kropotkin argued that cooperation was essential to the survival of our ancestors during medieval times and in nineteenth-century farming. Those earlier forms of cooperation had been undercut, he argued, by government institutions and the rise and accumulation of private property at the turn of the twentieth century, but cooperation remained basic to our existence and essential for our evolution. As Jia Tolentino notes, mutual aid for Kropotkin remained, in his words, "the necessary foundation of everyday life" and "the best guarantee of a still loftier evolution of our race."[61]

The anthropologist David Graeber considered Kropotkin's work on mutual aid more relevant than ever today.[62] Graeber too identified strands of mutual aid in varied projects around the globe, from the Democratic Federation of Northeast Syria (Rojava) to the global Occupy movement, the migrant solidarity mobilizations in Greece, the Zapatistas in Chiapas, and most recently, the solidarity aid projects that emerged during the COVID-19 pandemic. Like Kropotkin, Graeber self-identified as an anarchist. He penned with his coauthor, Andrej Grubačić, a new introduction to Kropotkin's book, *Mutual Aid*, which is being released in a new edition.[63] Graeber and Grubačić argue that although few young activists have read Kropotkin, their actions reflect his core idea of mutual aid, noting that "this book is being released in the belief that there is a new, radicalized generation, many of whom have never been exposed to these ideas directly, but who show all signs of being able to make a more clear-minded assessment of the global situation than their parents and grandparents, if only because they know that if they don't, the world in store for them will soon become an absolute hellscape." They explain:

> We write this introduction during a wave of global popular revolt against racism and state violence, as public authorities spew venom against "anarchists" in much the way they did in Kropotkin's time. It seems a peculiarly fitting moment to raise a glass to that old "despiser of law and private property" who changed the face of science in ways that continue to affect us today. Pyotr Kropotkin's scholarship was careful and colorful, insightful and revolutionary. It has also aged unusually well. Kropotkin's rejection of both capitalism and bureaucratic socialism, his predictions of where the latter might lead, have been vindicated time and time again. Looking back at most of the arguments that raged in his day, there's really no question about who was actually right.[64]

Kropotkin's work has received increasing attention, including in mainstream media, as a result of the pandemic and the flourishing of mutual-aid projects. The term *mutual aid* has been given new life. At the height of the pandemic in 2020, the lawyer and critical thinker Dean Spade authored a how-to manual titled *Mutual Aid: Building Solidarity During This Crisis (and the Next)*, influenced in many ways by Kropotkin.[65] Kropotkin is a central figure now for other thinkers, such as Simon Springer, who build on his work to ground their advocacy of mutual aid. Springer draws on Kropotkin's original concept of mutual aid, as opposed to hierarchical humanitarian approaches, to push back against the belief in forced scarcity and famine.[66]

The problem with the evolutionary arguments is that, frankly, few of us who care about cooperation are scientists with sufficient competence or training to judge these evolutionary contentions. As a scientific matter, I doubt that we could fully tranche the relative contribution of cooperation versus competition to human development and thriving. I am sure cooperation plays a major role in human life, and that it should play a greater role. That is the point of developing a theory of coöperism. I believe that cooperation is important for human flourishing. I know it is important for animals more generally; one need only watch a flock of birds, a herd of mammals, or a school of fish. But it is, scientifically, too complex for most of us to determine the relative weight of cooperation versus competition in human survival. It is too risky to base cooperation on evolutionary theory. It would be like returning to Proudhon or Saint-Simonianism and to their unfounded religious faith in science.

Modern variants of evolutionary theory are likewise not sufficiently developed to serve as a basis for cooperation in the real world. Game theorists adopted evolutionary logics in the 1980s to complexify more static game theories, and the field of evolutionary game theory became cutting edge in the 1990s. The research confirmed the idea that cooperation between reiterative players, learning the game and adapting, led to stable "Nash equilibria." A consensus developed that through the evolutionary process of players repeating games, getting to know how things work, and being able to adapt their strategies, cooperation between players increased. In other words, over time and with understanding of the games, players cooperate more, which benefits them. According to the economist Larry Samuelson, evolutionary game theory shows that "the dynamic processes shaping behavior in games lead to Nash equilibria."[67] This is true as well in the evolutionary biology game-theory context; as Alexander Stewart and Joshua Plotkin explain in the *Proceedings of the National Academy of Sciences*, "a consensus has emerged that, in an evolving population, cooperation tends to triumph over cheating—through reciprocity and generosity."[68] As the players accumulate experience with games and start adapting, the dynamic process shapes individual behaviors and leads to stable outcomes. Thus, cooperation happens in an evolutionary way through a dynamic process and brings about favorable outcomes.[69]

However, evolutionary game theory reached a plateau and then petered out. It was "initially surrounded by a great deal of excitement," Samuelson notes, and "for a while (approximately the 1990s) lay at the center of game theory as well as perhaps economic theory more generally. . . . More recently, it has receded into the background."[70] In part, this reflects a broader trend: research on cooperative games fell out of favor and receives little attention today, in contrast to game-theory research on noncooperative games. The difference should be intuitive, but just to be clear: "Noncooperative game theory assumes that players act independently, with the central question being whether a player can gain from a unilateral deviation. Cooperative game theory assumes that players can form coalitions, with the central question being whether a collection of players can find a (binding) allocation of the payoffs available to the coalition that would allow them all to gain from forming the coalition."[71]

In cooperative game theory, players can sign binding contracts and find other ways to cooperate. At the inception of the field of game theory, this received a lot of attention from some of its giants like John von Neumann, Oskar Morgenstern, John Nash, Lloyd Shapley, Gerard Debreu, and Herbert Scarf. In fact, the origins of game theory were from a cooperative game theory perspective, assuming that players could form coalitions that would make them better off than if they acted independently.[72] This approach proved to be very promising. As the economist Eric Maskin explains, game theory models with cooperation are characterized as more robust because the discontinuities in noncooperative models do not occur. There is also less emphasis on players' strategies and only payoffs matter.[73]

Most of the attention in the field then focused on noncooperative games. In fact, all the Nobel prizes that have been awarded in game theory have been for research exclusively on the noncooperative game theory front. "Despite its auspicious beginnings," Maskin writes, "cooperative game theory has been used far less than noncooperative theory as a predictive tool in economics."[74] Today, as Samuelson observes, "cooperative game theory appears to have disappeared from economics. First-year graduate theory courses routinely cover the basics of noncooperative game theory, but may not even mention the [cooperative notion of the] core. The classic texts that shepherded game theory into widespread use in economics, Fudenberg and Tiróle (1991) and Myerson (1991), are weighted toward the discussion of noncooperative game theory."[75]

This reflects, I believe, a slight bias against cooperation among economists and game theorists, which I attribute to the methodological preference in economics for individualism—namely, the idea that research hypotheses and explanations of social behavior should start from individual action at the player level and be grounded in the study of individual behavior (whether of an individual player, an individual firm, or an individual nation).[76] The result, I would argue, is a tendency to discount findings of cooperation. As Samuelson notes, if an archetypal prisoner's dilemma leads to cooperation, game theorists will conclude that the game chosen to approximate reality must be incorrect.[77] In a "true" prisoner's dilemma, cooperation would never be the rational choice, and the dominant strategy—the Nash equilibrium—would necessitate mutual defection. A bias toward noncooperation is often baked into game theory logic.

There has been some game theory work done specifically on cooperatives—as distinct from cooperative game theory[78]—and this tends to show that producer and worker cooperatives can achieve advantageous equilibria and mitigate the problems of monopolies and overaccumulation of capital.[79] In an early seminal game theory paper on purchasing cooperatives in agriculture, Richard Sexton found that the inner workings of cooperatives can lead to equilibria and that cooperatives may play a role "to mitigate the excesses of monopoly power."[80]

Here again, there is not enough reliable work to really tranche the issues or to found a theory of coöperism. Overall, Samuelson calls for "new work in cooperative game theory," which is undoubtedly right.[81] Cooperative, as opposed to noncooperative, game theory is still understudied. Until that changes, with positive results, it makes little sense to rest a real-world social theory on game theory foundations.

GROUNDING A POLITICAL THEORY OF COÖPERISM

We must reimagine cooperation for our times in a way that is neither utopian, nor separatist, nor evolutionary—and especially not exclusionary, but rather inclusive and open. Given our newfound interdependence, we need a praxis of cooperation built on the foundations of already existing and successful cooperative legal forms. Instead of going back to nineteenth-century political economy, to separatist or evolutionary theory, it is better to return to the tried-and-true values of cooperation and imagine a new theory of coöperism for these times.

We are in a different place today than Kropotkin was, writing in the late nineteenth century. We are in a world that has been irreversibly changed and is on a precipice. Our natural environment has been altered in such radical ways that our survival as a species is now far more dependent on our policies and decisions, on our choices. The climate crisis has effectively changed the equation. We humans are now interdependent in a way that neither Owen, nor Fourier, nor Du Bois, nor Kropotkin could have imagined. This means that we need to choose cooperation, not as a matter of natural selection or a question of utopian vision, not as something dictated by economic laws of capital or accumulation, but as our existential choice and only viable path forward to sustainability.

The way forward is to combine, leverage, and compound cooperation into a political, economic, and social theory of coöperism: to distill the power of cooperation and concentrate it into an integrated structure that extends and augments cooperation. The place to begin is with a theory that focuses on the process of cooperation, rather than on individuals or on entities such as the state. A processual theory similar to Andrew Abbott's "processual sociology," coöperism centers the processes of cooperation rather placing the individual person or the administrative state at the heart of the analysis.[82] The processual better reflects our human condition. It corresponds, as Abbott suggests, to the idea "that everything in the social world is continuously in the process of making, remaking, and unmaking itself (and other things), instant by instant."[83] It privileges the actions humans take in their interactions, just as the theory of material interests (see chapter 3) privileges actions and verbs over static objects. The theory of coöperism, rather than starting from the two entities at the extreme poles of the political debate (individuals and the administrative state), privileges the actions humans take together, their cooperative praxis.[84]

Beginning with the processes of cooperation, we see that certain of forms of cooperation are more beneficial than others. Worker cooperation, for example, is particularly formidable at reducing inequality. But some forms can be even more powerful when they are combined with other modes of cooperation such as consumer cooperatives, or leveraged by means of a connected credit union, or compounded by doubling down on the core principles of democratic participation and sustainability. Coöperism, then, is grounded in three core principles: it is concentrated and compounded; it is deliberate and chosen; it is open and inclusive.

CONCENTRATED AND COMPOUNDED

A political theory of coöperism seeks, first, to extend existing forms of cooperation to other dimensions of our lives, but second, and perhaps more important, to concentrate cooperation. Coöperism starts from the recognition that although all forms of cooperation are beneficial, some instantiations of cooperation are more faithful to the core values and principles of cooperation than others. Coöperism privileges and promotes those forms of cooperation that are most beneficial and combines them to create an integrated network of cooperation. These include worker cooperatives that are genuinely dedicated to the goals of democratic participation, equitable distribution of wealth, and respect for a sustainable environment. (Not all ESOPs, for instance, are equally dedicated to participatory governance, and some retain top-down management styles; not all worker cooperatives are equally focused on environmental issues.) They include consumer and producer cooperatives that truly respect the relationship between consumption and the environment, or that aim to reduce consumption or improve working conditions. They might include some, but not all, retail cooperatives. (Not all retail cooperatives contribute as much as others to the mission of cooperation; some are more focused on the profitability of member retailers.) Similarly, they may include some nonprofit organizations that aspire to the principles of cooperatives. (Not all do. Some are effectively run as rigid hierarchies and do not give the people who work there a say in the management or direction of the nonprofit. This is true even of small nonprofits that may be run top-down by an executive director). The point is to ensure that coöperism encourages the initiatives that best promote the core principles.

The central idea of compounding cooperation, then, is to double down on the values and principles of cooperation as follows:

Combine cooperation. Conjoin cooperative enterprises so that, for instance, a worker cooperative that produces goods distributes through a consumer cooperative and, conversely, a consumer cooperative buys its products from a worker cooperative. Even more ambitiously, think about joining a consumer cooperative with a retail-worker cooperative. This avoids the problem of a consumer cooperative exploiting its labor force or fighting against fair wages or unionization. In many cases, consumer cooperatives begin to produce goods, and they certainly hire employees to sell their goods; that production needs to be part of the mission of cooperation. At the same time, these combinations can multiply the number of forms of cooperation in which people participate so that, for instance, a member of a farmer cooperative may also become a member of its related consumer cooperative or mutual.

Leverage cooperation: Link cooperative enterprises so that, for instance, a worker cooperative uses a credit union to help workers borrow the funds necessary to join the cooperative. We see this in the case of Mondragón setting up the Caja Laboral Popular Cooperativa de Crédito as a vehicle, in part, to assist members in financing their participation in the cooperative. There can also be ways to leverage an insurance mutual so that it assists a farmer cooperative in its operations. The idea is that different forms of cooperation can work together to make possible even more cooperation.

Compound cooperation: Grow cooperation on top of cooperation in order to push cooperative enterprises even further. So, for instance, nonprofit organizations could be encouraged to embrace the principle of democratic participation to turn employees more into cooperative members. Worker cooperatives could be pushed to extend the principle of looking out for the welfare of all stakeholders, not just the members, by treating everyone in their supply chain with greater respect.[85] Tax rules could be tweaked to allow cooperative members to use pretax dollars to pay for membership or to allow patronage distributions to be reinvested in cooperation tax-free.

The idea is to distill, concentrate, and amplify cooperation: to find ways to increase the benefits of cooperation in the same way that interest can compound; to extend the enhanced forms of cooperation to more domains; and to compound the political model of participatory democracy, respect for the environment, and caring for all the stakeholders.

In all this, it is important to distinguish discrete instances of cooperation or mutual aid from the broader theory of coöperism. Specific cooperatives or mutual-aid projects will represent one style of cooperation alongside others. Each one will have its own unique features and dominant traits, and some weaknesses. Some mutual-aid projects represent only temporary remedies that depend on other people having enough money, time, and resources to volunteer and shop for others. By themselves, they may not appear very useful in addressing the broader crises we face. But by compounding them with others, combining and linking them into a theory of coöperism, isolated cooperative initiatives can form part of a greater whole.

Coöperism draws on the existing values and principles that have been developed for cooperatives and other solidarity economies. It need not reinvent the wheel regarding basic values and principles. At its heart is participatory democratic decision making applied not just to the political realm but to every other facet of our lives: consumption, labor, production, education, finance, insurance, mutual aid. Coöperism builds on the principles that favor equal voice and shared well-being, both of which are essential to creating a more sustainable environment. Under all of the charters, from the United Nations to the ICA guidelines, the principles that define the cooperative enterprise include democratic member control of the enterprise and participation in the enterprise; open, inclusive, and voluntary membership; caring for all the stakeholders and a sustainable environment; autonomy and independence.[86] These mirror the core principles of cooperatives that have emerged in experiments throughout history, which also include each member having substantially equal control and ownership and an equal say in matters; each member having a functional role in the enterprise; and a primary focus on the well-being of all the stakeholders and the working environment.[87] What characterizes the cooperative versus other forms of business structures is the notion of one-member, one-vote and the idea that the primary purpose of a cooperative is not profit maximization or short-term growth but the well-being of all stakeholders.[88] Those guiding principles are precisely what will promote a more sustainable living environment.

These are the values and principles that need to be distilled, rather than diluted. In his important work *Capital and Ideology*, Thomas Piketty suggests that the voting structure of cooperatives could be relaxed in some cases and individuals who supply more capital given more votes.[89] Piketty offers a set of provisos: workers would still be represented in assemblies; a ceiling might be set on the number of votes; different classes of voting rights might be created. That, however, is precisely the wrong direction to go in. Rather than dilute the power of cooperation, coöperism seeks to distill coöpower and multiply it through forms of combination and leverage. What is so powerful about cooperative values and principles is precisely making sure that equals—consumers, workers, debtors, creditors—have equal say in the operations of the joint enterprise. It is the people who are equals, not the capital.

Coöperism draws as well on the ideals of a solidarity economy. RIPESS, the Intercontinental Network for the Promotion of the Social Solidarity Economy, states in its charter from 2008 that its values include, among others, democracy, solidarity, inclusiveness, diversity, sustainable development, equality, equity, and justice for all. Its vision is:

> a way of economic organization that determines what is productive from the standpoint of the human person and the respect for ecological limits. This implies an economy that makes it possible that all the people have access to the material, intellectual and spiritual resources that guarantee their dignity; that promotes the respect for individual, social and economic rights; that stimulates democratic participation in economic decision making and citizen control of the operation of the markets and the intervention of the State; that push for the adoption of environmental and social responsibility criteria in production, distribution and consumption; and finally, that strives for social and gender equity in wealth distribution.[90]

Coöperism embraces these values and seeks to magnify them, not reinvent them. Similarly, the Network of Alternative and Solidarity Economy Networks (REAS, for Red de redes de economía alternativa y solidaria) lists in its charter of principles from May 2011 six foundational principles including equity, environmental sustainability, and non-profit-making.[91] It describes the principle of cooperation as follows:

> We intend to build collectively a model of society based on harmonious local development, fair commercial relations, equality, trust, co-responsibility, transparency, respect. We assume that the Solidarity Economy is based on a participatory and democratic ethic, that wants to promote learning and cooperative work among people and organizations, through processes of collaboration, joint decision making, shared assumption of responsibilities and duties, which guarantee the maximum horizontality possible while respecting the autonomy of each one, without generating dependencies. We believe that these cooperation processes should be extended to all levels: local, regional or autonomous, state and international and should normally be articulated in Networks where these values are lived and promoted.[92]

These are the values and principles that coöperism seeks to leverage. Participatory democracy is at the heart of all this; the key is to extend our democratic ideals into all social realms, including economics, production, consumption, and social life.

Richard D. Wolff emphasizes the democratic nature of worker cooperatives: the application of democratic values and principles within the workplace.[93] The workplace, Wolff argues, is the last bastion of feudalism and monarchy, a place where strict hierarchy governs. Wolff draws a parallel between the workplace and the political sphere, arguing that only in the workplace do the old models of despotism apply. The one place that democratic theory has not reached is the workplace—which is the place where many of us spend the most time. Coöperism builds on this. It does not reinvent the values or principles; it tries to leverage, compound, and concentrate them.

Coöperism respects individual initiative while recognizing the need for social organization. The impetus and force of mutual aid, cooperatives, and mutuals will often be individual members coming together and launching an enterprise. In this sense, the more successful initiatives are bottom-up or grassroots. But that does not mean there is no need for organizational mechanisms or regulatory frameworks to ensure the smooth functioning of these initiatives. Forms of cooperation may appear to require little regulation, but that is only because the regulation is often hidden. In the example of Invisible Hands, discussed earlier, the groceries where the mutual-aid volunteers shopped (Fairway Markets) are regulated for food safety, worker health and safety, etc. These regulations differ from those that are needed for credit unions or insurance mutuals, but they remain essential to the functioning of a solidaristic society. Coöperism will help bring about an equitable form of social organization.

DELIBERATE AND CHOSEN

By contrast to nineteenth-century theories of human nature or evolution, and to economic theories that articulate "laws" of capital or accumulation, coöperism is a matter of deliberate intentional human choice. Cooperation cannot be assumed to be inherent in our nature or dictated by the survival of the fittest. Coöperism must be deliberately chosen and constructed. In this regard, the political theory of coöperism builds on the work of Thomas Piketty, Katharina Pistor, and others who underscore the constructed nature of economic organization.

As you will recall, Thomas Piketty and his colleagues meticulously documented what had been the general consensus in the historiography of capitalism: a "Golden Age" of capitalism from the late 1940s to the 1970s marked by welfarist commitments to full employment, expanding opportunities, and stable well-distributed growth, followed by a period of "unleashed" capitalism and neoliberalism, associated with the rise of Ronald Reagan and Margaret Thatcher, which undid many of those favorable trends.[94] There is a general consensus that the first period lessened disparities in income and wealth through more progressive taxation schemes and more generous social welfare programs, but that the second period saw increased inequality as a result of the dismantling of the regulatory structures intended to distribute wealth more equitably. If anything, the fall of the Berlin Wall and collapse of Soviet communism facilitated an even more aggressive unleashing of capitalism. Piketty and his colleagues' research confirms all of this.[95]

But Piketty's work demonstrates another crucial point, which has been amplified by the work of other thinkers such as my Columbia colleague Katharina Pistor: the current forms of economic organization are human made and constructed. Lawyers "code capital," in Pistor's words, and thereby create and protect wealth. Similarly, policy makers choose legal and fiscal systems that shape societal distributions and, through justificatory discourses and ideologies, people rationalize and entrench the resulting inequalities. In short, as Piketty's work also demonstrates, the economic organization of society is chosen.

Piketty shows that social inequalities are created and maintained through a combination of public policy and ideological justifications, which is why he followed up his earlier book *Capital in the Twenty-First Century* with a sequel, *Capital and Ideology*. His thesis is that public policies create inequalities, and shared ideologies justify and perpetuate those inequalities, so that social inequalities are in fact chosen. The justificatory ideologies are autonomous, not superstructural; they do not merely derive from economic principles. As such, they facilitate the policies that perpetuate inequality. Though they vary over time, they consistently enable and entrench social hierarchy.

Piketty uses a positivist and descriptive definition of ideology to describe the shared beliefs within society that perpetuate forms of inequality. "I use 'ideology' in a positive and constructive sense," he writes, "to refer to a set of a priori plausible ideas and discourses describing how society should be structured."[96] Piketty is careful to eschew the pejorative use of the term, but he does use it in a critical manner, in that he is critical of those justifications of inequality. He is not valorizing the notion of ideology as have others, especially Destutt de Tracy, who coined the term to describe the science of ideas in 1796, and other French Enlightenment thinkers who embraced the label "ideologues"; nor does he disparage it as did others, famously Napoleon Bonaparte after the 18th of Brumaire when he attacked the ideologues, and Marx and Engels in their critique of the young Hegelians Bruno Bauer and Max Stirner, and Ludwig Feuerbach, in their 1846 manuscript *The German Ideology*.[97] Piketty also is not using the term pejoratively to connote class consciousness, false consciousness, or ideological state apparatuses in the tradition of critical thinkers such as Lukács, Gramsci, Horkheimer, and Althusser.[98] If anything, Piketty is closer in his usage to the more sociological approach that Karl Mannheim developed in *Ideology and Utopia*.[99] As an example of ideology, Piketty discusses proprietarian ideologies during the French Revolution, which suggested that redistribution of property would open a Pandora's box and cause political instability and permanent chaos.[100] He also cites more contemporary discourses justifying inequality, such as the following: "modern inequality is . . . just because it is the result of a freely chosen process in which everyone enjoys equal access to the market and to property and automatically benefits from the wealth accumulated by the wealthiest individuals, who are also the most enterprising, deserving, and useful. Hence modern inequality is said to be diametrically opposed to the kind of inequality found in premodern societies, which was based on rigid, arbitrary, and often despotic differences of status."[101] This represents, Piketty argues, a dominant ideological justification for wealth inequality in the West today.

On the basis of this notion of ideology, Piketty argues that social inequality is constructed by public policy and justified by autonomous ideational formations. Ideologies have real effects. "Evolving ideas are nothing unless they lead to institutional experiments and practical demonstrations," Piketty writes.[102] The point is that inequality is essentially *chosen*, by public policies and ideologies, and that we could choose a different economic path forward. In this sense, Piketty is a constructivist. He believes that we choose our inequality deliberately, and that we could just as easily choose more equitable distributions. He argues for more equitable rules, such as progressive taxes, inheritance taxes, and power sharing within firms, to "make ownership of capital temporary" and promote "permanent circulation of property."[103] Piketty espouses, ultimately, what he calls a participatory socialist framework, and a spirit of cooperation.[104]

A theory of coöperism must embrace Piketty's constructivism, even if not his exact solutions. The greatest contribution of his work is that it documents and proves the deliberate mechanisms of inequality. It rebuts the idea, held by so many, that there is something baked into capital, or that there are laws of capital accumulation. There is nothing mysterious, no godly forces; it is all chosen. As Piketty writes:

> Inequality is neither economic nor technological; it is ideological and political. . . . In other words, the market and competition, profits and wages, capital and debt, skilled and unskilled workers, natives and aliens, tax havens and competitiveness—none of these things exist as such. All are social and historical constructs, which depend entirely on the legal, fiscal, educational, and political systems that people choose to adopt and the conceptual definitions they choose to work with. These choices are shaped by each society's conception of social justice and economic fairness and by the relative political and ideological power of contending groups and discourses. Importantly, this relative power is not exclusively material; it is also intellectual and ideological. In other words, ideas and ideologies count in history. They enable us to imagine new worlds and different types of society. Many paths are possible."[105]

This is arguably a simplification. There are some stubborn political realities to deal with, including the extreme polarization today that makes it practically impossible to imagine convincing a supermajority of voters. It is important to acknowledge that Piketty is an economist, a modeler, and the whole point of modeling is to simplify. I might put more emphasis on entrenched relations of power in society. Piketty does note "the relative political and ideological power of contending groups and discourses" and that "this relative power is not exclusively material; it is also intellectual and ideological." He is cognizant of power dynamics. I would emphasize those more, incorporating the Frankfurt School theories of ideology and Foucaultian theories of regimes of truth to show how thick, pervasive, and long lasting these illusions are, and how hard they are to change.[106] They are constitutive of our way of seeing and knowing the world, which is why the snowball effect of coöperism is so much more promising in a country like the United States than the collective action required to either dismantle or strengthen the state. It is precisely for this reason that coöperism is a better path forward than rugged individualism or the type of participatory socialism that Piketty advocates for.[107]

Putting that aside, Piketty is correct that economic policies are a matter of existential choice. They are tools, instruments. Legislators and policy makers deploy these tools to increase or decrease inequality in society, as do lawyers.

As Katharina Pistor explains in *The Code of Capital*, lawyers contribute by coding capital, using a basic toolkit that has been used for centuries. Pistor demonstrates how lawyers, deploying the conventional tools of legal practice and relying on the enforcement powers of the state, turn ordinary assets into capital, thereby protecting wealth.[108] Pistor emphasizes the legal dimension over the political, the fiscal, and others. Piketty focuses more on those other factors, specifically on the "fiscal, educational, and political systems that people choose to adopt and the conceptual definitions they choose to work with."[109] Pistor's analysis focuses on the legal side, however, in part because she is a legal theorist.

Pistor defines capital, for purposes of her discussion, as an asset with advantageous properties for its owner. These advantageous properties render an asset more valuable by giving it a competitive advantage over other assets. It may be protected from taxation; it may have priority claims as against other credit holders; it may survive an economic downturn better than other assets or less well coded capital. Historically, the class of assets that could be coded as capital—that is, transformed into capital by lawyers—has changed over time. Whereas before it was primarily landed property and immovable goods, over time it has come to include ideas and know-how (intellectual property, trademarks, and patents) as well as digital assets such as computer code. But the notion of an asset is very simple: it consists of anything that can be owned. The methods of coding capital are simple and basic as well, as Pistor demonstrates. They use the classic building blocks of the law school curriculum: contract law, property law, corporations, trusts and estates, and bankruptcy. These are all basic tools of the lawyer, even if they can be used in innovative ways to create unheard-of capital forms, such as the complex derivatives and mortgage-backed securities that were responsible for the 2007 recession.

What turns assets into capital, Pistor demonstrates, is the combination of legal code and state enforcement. Its two elements, then, are law and government. Regarding the law, Pistor could not be clearer: it is lawyers who convert assets into capital, through simple legal acts and transformations. Pistor is talking about the "*legal* coding of capital." As she emphasizes, "observers treat law as a side show when in fact it is the very cloth from which capital is cut." At the same time, she is equally clear about the centrality of the state. Without the state's protection and enforcement of the legal code, it could not operate. As she writes, "accumulating wealth over long stretches of time requires additional fortification that only a code backed by the coercive powers of the state can offer." Together, lawyers and the state can provide and enforce "the code of capital" that serves to give the capital holder an advantage over others. Together they provide "the legal privileging of some assets, which gives their holders a comparative advantage in accumulating wealth over others."[110] She concludes: "In short, capital is inextricably linked to law and state power."[111]

The most important point of Pistor's work is to show how simple the plumbing is. First, we are dealing with very basic, common, straightforward assets. These include land, debt, knowledge, firms or institutions, intellectual property, and digital assets like code. "Ordinary assets are just that," Pistor writes, "a plot of land, a promise to be paid in the future, the pooled resources from friends and family to set up a new business, or individual skills and know-how." Second, the tools of the trade, those of the attorney, are also basic. They are the core elements of private law, most of which are taught in the first year of law school, such as contract law and property law, along with second-year courses in corporations, trusts and estates, bankruptcy law, and secured transactions. Third, the transformation of assets into capital is a simple enhancement that gives some assets merely "a comparative advantage over others." Those advantages are also simple and can be reduced to four main ones: priority, or the idea that the capital owner has a higher claim to an asset than others; durability, which means that the ownership extends in time; universality, which means that it extends spatially; and convertibility, which means the capability to convert the asset into liquid money.[112] "Law is code," summarizes Pistor; "it turns a simple asset into a capital asset by bestowing the attributes of priority, durability, universality, and convertibility on it."[113] Fourth and finally, the entire scheme rests on two basic instincts or practices common throughout history:

> For centuries, private attorneys have molded and adapted these legal modules to a changing roster of assets and have thereby enhanced their clients' wealth. And states have supported the coding of capital by offering their coercive law powers to enforce the legal rights that have been bestowed on capital.[114]

This has been understood by thinkers on all points along the political spectrum for years. The simplicity of structuring competition or cooperation has been studied for decades. It was well understood by early liberals in the twentieth century, referred to as "ordoliberals," those who favored order and liberal markets. This was, in fact, their "singularity," as some commentators have remarked:

the recognition of the central role of legal regulation in structuring a market society. At the Walter Lippmann colloquium held in France in August 1938, Louis
Rougier, the organizer, placed basic legal regulation at the core of market society,
anticipating the idea of coding capital or cooperation. Rougier explained:

> The liberal regime is not just the result of a spontaneous natural order as
> the many authors of the Natural codes declared in the eighteenth century; it
> is also the result of a legal order that presupposes juridical intervention by the
> state. Economic life takes place [in fact] within a juridical framework which
> fixes the regime of property, contracts, patents, bankruptcy, the status of pro-
> fessional associations and commercial societies, the currency, and banking,
> none of which are given by nature, like the laws of economic equilibrium, but
> are contingent creations of legislation.[115]

This is a striking passage that prefigures our discussion of the legal coding of
economic organization. It means that the economic and juridical are fully integrated: the relationship between law and economics is not one of superstructure
and infrastructure, but of co-constituency. The model is not Marx, but Weber.

All this work, especially Katharina Pistor's, makes plain that competition or
cooperation is easily constructed using the basic tools of the lawyer, enforced by
government. The code of cooperation is just as simple as the code of capital. In
fact, cooperation is already being coded throughout the world. Many countries
have codified in their laws the principles and operating structure of cooperatives.
Some national constitutions include provisions conferring special status on cooperatives.[116] There is a cooperative law code that varies somewhat by nation and
state but that crisscrosses the globe. Some scholars, notably Henry Hansmann and
Reinier Kraakman, argue that there is no need for a distinct legal code for cooperatives; however, many countries have developed such codes.[117] These include
consumer cooperative legislation in Japan; cooperative laws in Norway and Por-
tugal; social enterprise laws in the UK, Finland, and Italy; social and solidarity
economy laws in France, Spain, and Ecuador; and other cooperation codes in
Argentina, Australia, Austria, Belgium, Brazil, Canada, Chile, China, Colombia,
Germany, Hungary, India, Ireland, Mexico, the Netherlands, Peru, Poland, Korea,
Russia, South Africa, Turkey, and Uruguay.[118] Approximately half the states in
the United States have incorporation statutes for cooperatives, including specific
worker cooperative, consumer cooperative, and/or general cooperative statutes

that can be used for incorporation. In those states that do not have specific legislation for incorporating cooperatives, a range of other options can mimic the cooperative legal form, from benefit corporations to partnerships and LLCs (limited liability corporations) all the way to more ordinary S or C corporations.[119]

In sum, coöperism can easily be constructed using a legal code of cooperation. Coöperism should be understood as deliberate, chosen, constructed, not a product of natural selection nor of any economic laws. There is an existential dimension to coöperism that is inescapable and foundational.

OPEN AND INCLUSIVE

The third core principle of coöperism is that it must be inclusive, nondiscriminatory, and open to everyone, with equal respect and concern. This should always have been an ethical mandate, but our interdependence has increased the stakes. This needs little further discussion, just constant vigilance and attention to the question that Du Bois underscored about inequalities in stages of growth. Coöperism demands a constant effort to ensure that there are no disparities in the level of well-being of all different groups.

At the heart of it all is a political theory of coöperism, in that the animating spirit is to extend the political theory of participatory democracy to the social, economic, and other aspects of our lives. Coöperism brings together the different strands of cooperation—consumer, producer, and worker cooperatives, insurance mutuals, credit unions, nonprofit institutions, mutual-aid projects, cooperation hubs or cities, and the broader ideal of a solidarity economy—in order to deliberately leverage their coöpower and create a coordinated response for our interdependent world. This implicates as well an economic theory, discussed in the next chapter.

CHAPTER 5

The Economic Theory of Coöperism

In the fifth edition of his *Principles of Political Economy* published in the early 1860s, John Stuart Mill surveyed the landscape of worker cooperatives in England and France.[1] In a section of the treatise titled "Examples of the Association of Labourers Among Themselves," Mill detailed, and praised, the internal operation of worker cooperatives. He discussed the association of tailors in Clichy and of carpenters and furnituremakers in the faubourg Saint-Antoine of Paris, as well as the Leeds Flour Mill, the Rochdale Society, and the Corn-Mill Society, among others, in England. Mill concluded that cooperatives represented the hope for the future:

> The form of association, which if mankind continue to improve, must be expected in the end to predominate, is not that which can exist between a capitalist as chief and workpeople without a voice in the management, but the association of the labourers themselves on terms of equality, collectively owning the capital with which they carry on their operations, and working under managers elected and removable by themselves.[2]

Mill was not alone in these hopes and belief. Throughout the ages, there have been prophets of cooperatives. The Cooperative League of the United States of America, founded in 1916, actually imagined creating a Cooperative Commonwealth.[3]

Cooperatives, credit unions, mutuals, nonprofits, and mutual aid certainly have the potential that Mill and others attribute to them. But as I mentioned in the last chapter, some instantiations of cooperation are more effective than others in promoting the core values and principles. The ambition of coöperism is not just to expand the reach of cooperation but, more than that, to distill, concentrate, and amplify the most promising forms of cooperation, those that are truest to the values and principles at its core, in order to create an integrated and coordinated economic system powered by coöpower.

In this sense, coöperism represents an economic theory, not just a political theory. It proposes an integrated, unified, and coherent economic system that can serve to displace the two dominant regimes that have defined recent history, somewhat misleadingly called capitalism and communism. The two dominant regimes actually have more in common than we tend to ascribe to them. They offer only one alternative: top-down enforcement of economic regulations that favor either the wealthy or party elites. Coöperism is a far better alternative, one that favors the rest of the people.

THE WHIGGISH HISTORY OF CAPITALISM'S TRIUMPH

Ever since the fall of the Berlin Wall in 1989 and the collapse of Soviet communism, many if not most people in the West believe that capitalism triumphed and showed itself to be superior to communal forms of economic organization. There is a widely shared view that the United States and the USSR were two competing models, capitalism versus communism, and that the American model prevailed. It is certainly true that Russia, in the post-Soviet era, has turned to hypercapitalist, oligopolistic economic methods; that China and other communist countries like Vietnam have embraced a new form of state capitalism; and that collectivism elsewhere across the world has encountered difficulties, as in Venezuela or Cuba. Most Americans believe this history proves capitalism triumphant. For some, economic history has reached an end point: in the notorious words of the American political scientist Francis Fukuyama, the "end of history as such: that is, the end point of mankind's ideological evolution and the universalization of Western liberal democracy as the final form of human government."[4]

The problem with this Whiggish consensus is that it is based on an outdated Cold War mentality built on two grand illusions: "capitalism" and "communism." Both terms, it turns out, are deeply misleading. There never was a competition between two different economic regimes. Both rested on a similar model, which I call "dirigisme," a mode of economic organization in which a centralized body plays a dominant directive role. The capitalist model rests on the illusion of a free market, when in truth capitalism is made possible only by robust state interventions and guarantees.[5] The idea of communism rests on the illusion of a common, when in fact it too is made possible only by a large centralized state. Both have in common a top-down, centralized form of economic structure; the balance of power simply shifts, in one or the other, from wealthy investors to party members. Both of these models historically are types of dirigisme that benefit elites, whether the wealthy or party elites or both at the same time. Coöperism, by contrast, centers the other people—the consumers, producers, workers, debtors, insured, and members of mutualist projects—and the environment. Coöperism turns the economy over to those who create, invent, produce, make, work, labor, aid, and serve others. It privileges the welfare of all stakeholders, not just those who are well connected such as investors or party members, and the sustainability of the cooperative enterprises and the living environment.

It is essential that we set aside the misleading Cold War debates about capitalism versus communism and understand that those terms are deeply deceptive. American capitalism may look and feel as if it were all about free markets and private enterprise, but in fact the entire system rests wholly on the government's promise, and track record, of rescuing large corporations in case of economic and financial collapse. Without the federal government backstop, without that promise and the reality of bailing out big business during depressions, recessions, and pandemics, the fragile and deeply indebted structure of American capitalism would collapse in a minute. Among other things, foreign investors would withdraw their capital and the treasury market would implode. The ideology of American capitalism serves to mask the fact that the entire system is a house of cards that ultimately funnels wealth to the richest and most privileged Americans. American capitalism must be understood as a top-down form of economic redistribution. Real-world communism is also pure ideology. It claims to place everything in common, when in fact it monopolizes ownership in the hands of a centralized state apparatus; all allocations and distributions of goods and wealth become, essentially, the magnanimous (more often self-serving) decisions of a centralized bureaucracy or autocracy.

The centuries-old debate between capitalism and communism rests on imagined ideal types that are misleading and pure illusions. They mask the actual allocation and real distributions of material interests. They need to be unmasked and then relegated to the twentieth century. To move forward with the economic theory of coöperism, the most important first step is to leave behind these misleading labels and illusory terms.

THE MISLEADING LABEL *CAPITALISM*

The label *capitalism* was always a misnomer, coined paradoxically by its critics in the nineteenth century. The term misleadingly suggests that there is such a thing as capital that inherently functions in certain ways and is governed by stable economic laws of its own. That, however, is an illusion.[6] Capital is just an artifact shaped by law and politics, constructed and enforced by the state. Its code is entirely human made, as Katharina Pistor shows. There are no "laws" of capital. People in the West today do not live in a system in which capital or "free enterprise" dictates their economic circumstances.

The use of the term *capitalism* dates to the early nineteenth century, and should have remained there. The notion of capitalism as an economic system grounded in capital investments traces to that period, in both the French and English languages. The first use of the term *capitalism* in English traces to 1833 in the *Standard*; earlier uses in other languages included the French term *capitalisme* (possession of capital, 1753) and the German term *Kapitalismus* (also possession of capital, 1787 or earlier, well before Marx coined the term for the economic system in 1863).[7] The term *capitalist*, with a *t*, had an earlier provenance, also related to the term *capital*, which itself was in usage in the thirteenth and fourteenth centuries. Its etymology traces to the French *capitaliste*, a person subject to a capital tax, an investor, someone engaged in investing capital. Along these lines, in English, the term *capitalist* was used beginning in 1774, referring to the Dutch wealthy subject and to "capitation," a tax on wealth. Its date stamp in English is related to the German term *Capitalist*, investor, moneylender (1673), or rich person (1687).[8]

For its more political economic meaning, though, we must turn to the mid-nineteenth century and, for the most part, to the socialist critics of capitalism, especially Marx and Engels. This is ironic, since it is in this usage of the term that capitalism became reified and naturalized—as if capital, as a thing, functions through autonomous economic laws when in fact it is nothing more than a code and set of crystalized government rules of economic redistribution. Capitalism, paradoxically, was turned into a naturalized object by its critics. But so-called capitalism is not primarily about the object "capital." Rather, it is about government privileging returns on capital investment with more favorable tax rates, government protecting capital investors by bailing them out during financial crises, and government encouraging and underwriting the stock markets. In this sense, capitalism is really about the state's control over the distribution of material interests.

Capitalism as an economic regime then, is the product of government and elite control of the mechanisms of redistribution: bailouts during crises that allow managers to enrich themselves during good times without holding reserves or taking risk into account because they are bailed out during bad times; rules of capital accumulation that make it easy for those with wealth to hoard more than others and pass it on to their heirs; wide-ranging actions, from judicial decisions to intelligence shared by top officials with elites to selective club admissions, that give those with capital the knowledge and ability to capitalize on their wealth. Especially by bailing them out during crises, the government allows capital holders to extract wealth in good times and be rescued in bad times.

One of the greatest problems with retaining the term *capitalism* is that it suggests that capital and private enterprise are governed by certain economic laws, that they function naturally in certain ways. Even Marx naturalized capital too much, paying insufficient attention to the political dimension of bailouts and handouts. This was facilitated by the very nomenclature of capitalism. This type of economic regime should no longer be called capitalist, but rather by a term that has government and elite control and redistribution at its heart. It is closer to the "state capitalism" that people attribute to China; but again, the term *capitalism* in state capitalism is a red herring. All the terms that quickly come to mind are lacking: *corporate welfarism* does not afford enough attention to the centrality of this welfare system, as if welfare were just something in addition, when in fact it is the whole system; *cronyism* gets at the corruption of it all and its elitism, but is too demeaning; *profiteering*, like the pirates of past, captures something about booty and stolen profit and has an interesting relationship to state sanction and complicity, but the relationship to the state is reversed, in that it was the pirates who were in charge and only later licensed.

I propose instead that we simply call it *dirigisme* to capture the element of state control and the way in which the state distributes the spoils. In the United States, people live in a type of state-directed tournament or gladiator system where political leaders bestow spoils on those with the greatest wealth and privilege, a form of "tournament dirigisme" that is all about the extraction of wealth and its redistribution to the wealthiest and most privileged. The best model for understanding this may be Steven Levitt and Sudhir Venkatesh's work on gang finances, drawing on the tournament model of Edward Lazear and Sherwin

Rosen from 1981 to explain the extraction of capital at the top of a social pyramid.[9] This form of tournament dirigisme offers hugely disproportionate rewards to those wealthy elites with the most capital and connections. It seeks to extract as much wealth as possible from the enterprise for the shareholders, venture capitalists, and equity investors.[10] The capital investors have one guiding interest: to extract profit. They are not concerned about growth and equity, nor about other persons affiliated with the enterprise. They want a good return on their investment. Another metaphor here is gold mining, or mining more generally. Tournament dirigisme is an extractive process that seeks to extract capital as wealth and leave behind the detritus. It then abandons the space of extraction, like an old mine, and does not look back. All it wants is the profit.

There is, of course, a spectrum of extraction. At the most extreme end are the vulture capitalists who buy failing enterprises because they are worth more sold as assets than they are as ongoing enterprises. That is pure extraction. Investors like T. Boone Pickens or Carl Icahn, who used to be referred to as takeover artists or corporate raiders, often pursued a strategy of buying companies literally to extract capital, more capital than they paid, by breaking up the company and selling its assets. But even in less extreme forms, extraction is at the heart of the capitalist enterprise: to mine a higher return on investment than others, or than the market, by working others to the bone. Otherwise, there is no comparative enrichment.

Marx's critique of capitalist modes of production focused so much on labor and the exploitation of workers that it did not sufficiently account for the central role of the state in directing distributions in favor of capital holders. Marx also had a fetish for capital, for surplus value, and for the commodity that is our labor. He replicated that objectification and turned it into the idea of an economic regime of capitalism. "It is often said," as Foucault reminds us in his lectures on the *Birth of Biopolitics*, "that there is no theory of power in Marx, that the theory of the state is inadequate, and that it really is time to produce it."[11] This is correct, or mostly so, I would argue. Perhaps Marx did not need one at the time. Perhaps he had sufficient work to do to understand the political economy of industrial production. But we certainly need such a theory today, because so-called capitalism is now nothing more than tournament dirigisme.

The problem, to be honest, goes back further. Adam Smith set out to analyze the economic well-being of a nation or of society as a whole, the wealth of a nation. But he developed instead a magical theory in which economic development and the division of labor ultimately benefited the workers, even the lowest on the social order. For Smith, the wealth of nations lifted every boat. Marx was right to call this bourgeois economics. And while Marx took an opposing viewpoint, that of the factory worker or tradesman, he may well have focused too much on labor, as Max Horkheimer, Axel Honneth, and others later argued.[12] Marx also gave too much autonomy to capital. Neither Smith nor Marx, paradoxically, paid sufficient attention to the dirigisme. With the New Deal, but certainly with the bailouts of the Great Recession of 2008 and the COVID-19 pandemic, we live in a more transparent age in which we can see the key central role of the state.

The Reality of American Dirigisme

To get a sense of what we are really dealing with when we talk about capitalism, it is worth taking a look at the 2020 government bailout passed in response to the pandemic. In the immediate aftermath of the COVID-19 outbreak and the resulting economic crash, Republican President Donald Trump signed on March 27, 2020, a $2.2 trillion package titled the Coronavirus Aid, Relief, and Economic Security Act, or CARES Act. The legislation flew through both a Republican Senate and a majority Democratic House of Representatives and was passed without an impact assessment by the Congressional Budget Office (CBO). It was hailed by Republicans, who favor small or no government, and Democrats alike as landmark legislation.

To give an idea of the scale of the package, the total national debt of the United States stood at $23,535,039,888,496.42, essentially $23.5 trillion, on the day the president signed the CARES Act.[13] Thus the bailout represented almost 10 percent of America's enormous national debt. Even that underestimates the size of the measure because the national debt had grown so fast in the past decades. The total national debt stood at only $5 trillion in 1996. It doubled to about $10 trillion by 2008, and then doubled again to about $20 trillion in 2017. With such a high national debt today, the CARES Act may seem to add a relatively small contribution to the country's indebtedness, but that is merely an artifact of the colossal size of the national debt itself.

To give a better idea, the size of the CARES Act was about 2.5 times the federal government's financial deficit for the entire fiscal year 2019. The federal deficit for 2019 was approximately $984 billion, or almost a trillion dollars, up from $779 billion for 2018 and $666 billion for 2017.[14] Alternatively, the CARES Act was about half the size of the entire federal budget for fiscal 2019 (October 1, 2018 to September 30, 2019), which reached $4.45 trillion. As another comparative measure, the 2008 bailout was about $800 billion, only about a third of the CARES Act. In other words, we are talking about a gigantic bailout in 2020.

The main components of the CARES Act included:

- $500 billion in government support to corporations (of which $25 billion went to passenger airlines, $4 billion to cargo airlines, and $17 billion to companies related to national security) (Title IV)[15]
- $350 billion in government support to small businesses for loans to cover worker payroll and other expenses (Title I),[16] loans that can be forgiven[17]
- Another $350 billion in government support to small businesses,[18] plus another about $40 billion for special loans[19]
- $150 billion in government support to states, tribal governments, and local governments (Title V)[20]
- $100 billion in government support to hospitals
- $45 billion for a disaster relief fund[21]
- $32 billion in government support to airline workers for wages and benefits
- $10 billion in government grants-in-aid to airports[22]
- $3.5 billion in government support to states to support child-care facilities and to universities to support federal work-study jobs for students

In addition, the CARES Act provided $500 billion in government support to low-income households, which was distributed through a $1,200 stimulus check with a signed letter from Donald Trump. There were also lots of smaller grants in the Act, including "$100 million for additional rural broadband and $150 million for arts and humanities grants to bring cultural programming to Americans stuck at home," "$425 million to deal with mental health and substance abuse disorders related to the pandemic," and $400 million "to protect and expand voting for the 2020 election cycle."[23]

For present purposes, let's focus on the first item, the $500 billion in government loans to corporations, with a special focus on the airline industry. The treatment of airline companies is particularly telling.

The Airline Bailouts First, Title IV of the CARES Act is titled the "Coronavirus Economic Stabilization Act of 2020" and provides for $500 billion in loans and investments to American corporations. Of that sum, the Act provides that "$25,000,000,000 shall be available to make loans and loan guarantees for passenger air carriers," and another $4 billion for cargo air carriers.[24] The loans are not to exceed five years and will impose certain restrictions on the corporations, including limitations on dividend payments and other capital distributions with respect to the common stock and restrictions on reducing their employment levels by more than 10 percent.[25] For any of these loans or loan guarantees, the government must also receive, for publicly traded corporations, a warrant or equity interest and, for non-publicly traded corporations, a warrant, equity interest, or senior debt instrument.[26]

Second, Subtitle B of Title IV, titled "Air Carrier Worker Support," provides another $32 billion dollars to the airline industry by way of direct payments to workers in the industry. This is broken down, specifically, into $25 billion for passenger airline companies, $4 billion for cargo airline companies, and $3 billion for airline industry contractors, such as catering, baggage handling, ticketing, and aircraft cleaning. More specifically, the Act provides:

> To preserve aviation jobs and compensate air carrier industry workers, the Secretary [of the Treasury] shall provide financial assistance that shall exclusively be used for the continuation of payment of employee wages, salaries, and benefits to—

(1)   passenger air carriers, in an aggregate amount up to $25,000,000,000;

(2)   cargo air carriers, in the aggregate amount up to $4,000,000,000; and

(3)   contractors, in an aggregate amount up to $3,000,000,000.[27]

Here too there are some temporary strings attached. Airlines may not furlough workers during the grant, and there are some restrictions on executive pay. Moreover, to "protect taxpayers," the Treasury Department may seek equity in the companies. According to the Act, "The Secretary may receive warrants, options, preferred stock, debt securities, notes, or other financial instruments issued by recipients of financial assistance under this subtitle which, in the sole determination of the Secretary, provide appropriate compensation to the Federal Government for the provision of the financial assistance."[28]

So, for airlines, these provisions amount to $29 billion in loans and $29 billion in direct payments to workers (eliminating that cost for the airlines), for a total of $58 billion. On April 14, 2020, the Treasury Department and several airlines reached agreement on the terms of the bailout. The department indicated that the following airlines would participate in the payroll-support program (the grants from the federal government to pay airline workers): Alaska Airlines, Allegiant Air, American Airlines, Delta Air Lines, Frontier Airlines, Hawaiian Airlines, JetBlue Airways, United Airlines, SkyWest Airlines, and Southwest Airlines.

According to the *New York Times*, "American Airlines said it would receive $5.8 billion as part of the deal, with more than $4 billion in grants and the remaining $1.7 billion as a low-interest loan. The funds are intended to be used to pay employees, and the airlines that take them are prohibited from major staffing or pay cuts through September. American Airlines plans to separately apply for a nearly $4.8 billion loan from the department as well."[29] Southwest Airlines said it would seek $2.2 billion in grant money and $1 billion in a low-interest loan.

As soon as the government and the airlines began negotiating the associated warrants (in essence, equity collateral), it became clear that the airlines had little intention of repaying the loans or securing them. With regard to the $1 billion loan to Southwest, the Treasury Department was expected to get only $2.6 million in warrants, which could be used to buy an equity stake. The *Times* reported:

> The administration had spent weeks haggling with the airlines over the terms of the bailout, with Mr. Mnuchin pushing the airlines to agree to repay 30 percent of the money over a period of five years. The Treasury Department also has been seeking warrants to purchase stock in the companies that take money. Airlines have complained that Treasury was effectively turning the grants into loans by requiring repayment.
>
> Last week, the Treasury Department said that it would not require airlines that receive up to $100 million in bailout money to give the government equity stakes or other compensation. The government had received over 200 applications from American airlines seeking payroll support and Treasury said that the majority of those were asking for less than $10 million.[30]

So, the corporations were resisting repaying any of the grants and trying to get out from under the equity stakes by asking for grants in multiple lower-level denomination applications. The corporations were getting significant amounts of money compared to their profits years earlier, and any restrictions were temporary. As soon as the grant period was over, the corporations would begin laying off their employees. American Airlines threatened to lay off 19,000 workers at the end of August 2020.[31]

Let's continue with American Airlines. American made profits of $7.6 billion in 2015, up from about $500 million in 2007 and less than $250 million the previous year. As my Columbia colleague Tim Wu argued in the *New York Times*, it used most of those profits to shore up its stock price. "From 2014 to 2020, in an attempt to increase its earnings per share," Wu explained, "American spent more than $15 billion buying back its own stock."[32] American Airlines was not the only one; this was an industrywide phenomenon. The airline industry as a whole "collectively spent more than $45 billion on stock buybacks over the past eight years." Other industries also engaged in these types of buybacks, even when the conditions looked risky. "As recently as March 3 of this year, with the crisis already beginning, the Hilton hotel chain put $2 billion into a stock buyback."[33]

So, while American Airlines was getting bailed out, it had spent its profits earlier buying back stock as a way to increase the capital shareholders' value. In other words, the airline was extracting value during good times and getting bailed out by the federal government, or the public's tax dollars, during bad times.

It is not just the airlines that were extracting profit from the pandemic. Of the other $454 billion earmarked for the Federal Reserve Board of Governors, those funds could be used not just for loans and loan guarantees but also for "other investments." These included the following:

> "to make loans and loan guarantees to, and other investments in, programs or facilities established by the Board of Governors of the Federal Reserve System for the purpose of providing liquidity to the financial system that supports lending to eligible businesses, States, or municipalities by—

(A)   purchasing obligations or other interests directly from issuers of such obligations or other interests;
(B)   purchasing obligations or other interests in secondary markets or otherwise; or
(C)   making loans, including loans or other advances secured by collateral.[34]

This represented a huge amount of money that could be invested directly into publicly traded corporations to protect shareholder value.

Hidden Jackpots in the CARES Act   There were hidden treasures for the wealthy in the bailout legislation, as so often happens when a bill like this runs through

Congress with lightning speed, allowing the majority, in this case the Republican majority in the Senate, to sneak into the bill beneficial tax changes for the wealthy that they had previously been trying to get passed.

One such provision temporarily suspends a limitation, passed in 2017 as part of the massive Republican tax code revisions, on the amount of deductions to nonbusiness income (e.g., capital gains) that owners of businesses established as "pass-through" entities can claim as a way to reduce their taxes owed.[35] The provision effectively amended section 172(a) of the Internal Revenue Code, which deals with "net operating loss deductions" for all kinds of entities, including farmers, insurance companies, businesses, and taxpayers other than corporations.[36] The section that effectuates these changes is innocuous and imperceptible, using language that no lay person would suspect of having much impact. It is the kind of language that starts:

> (1) IN GENERAL.—The first sentence of section 172(a) of the Internal Revenue Code of 1986 is amended by striking "an amount equal to" and all that follows and inserting "an amount equal to—

"(1) in the case of a taxable year beginning before January 1, 2021, the aggregate of the net operating loss carryovers to such year, plus the net operating loss carrybacks to such year, and

"(2) in the case of a taxable year beginning after December 31, 2020, the sum of—
"(A) the aggregate amount of net operating losses arising in taxable years beginning before January 1, 2018, carried to such taxable year, plus
"(B) the lesser of—
   "(i) the aggregate amount of net operating losses arising in taxable years beginning after December 31, 2017, carried to such taxable year, or
   "(ii) 80 percent of the excess (if any) of—
       "(I) taxable income computed without regard to the deductions under this section and sections 199A and 250, over
       "(II) the amount determined under subparagraph (A)."[37]

A nonpartisan congressional body, the Joint Committee on Taxation (JCT), headed by Senator Chuck Grassley (R-Iowa) and Representative Richard Neal (D-Mass.), issued a report on March 26, 2020, estimating some of the revenue effects of these tax provisions included in the CARES Act.[38] It estimated that the amendment to section 172(a) of the IRC, as it affects taxpayers other than corporations, would reduce tax revenues by $74.3 billion in 2020, with continued reductions over the next decade resulting in total revenue losses over the period 2020–2030 of $169.6 billion. In addition, the "Modifications for net operating losses ('NOLs')" was estimated to generate $80 billion in lost tax revenue in 2020.[39]

In a subsequent letter dated April 9, 2020, responding to an informational request from Senator Sheldon Whitehouse (D-R.I.) and Representative Lloyd Doggett (D-Tex.), the JTC broke down the likely distributional effect of the tax change by income category, revealing that the tax reductions would disproportionately benefit the wealthy.[40] In its table, the JCT documented that 81.8 percent of the total reduction in tax liability of $86 billion in 2020 (in other words, $70.3 billion in reduced tax revenues) would likely benefit those with an income over $1 million. The table also revealed that approximately 43,000 returns will be filed by taxpayers with income over $1 million.

This suggests that taxpayers in the highest tax bracket (over $1 million in income) will receive on average a tax bonanza of $1.63 million.[41] This represents, as Senator Whitehouse and Representative Doggett state, "a massive windfall for a small group of wealthy taxpayers from a Republican provision in the coronavirus relief bill." In fact, 95 percent of those who will likely benefit from the tax change make over $200,000. Representative Doggett put it in these terms: "For those earning $1 million annually, a tax break buried in the recent coronavirus relief legislation is so generous that its total cost is more than total new funding for all hospitals in America and more than the total provided to all state and local governments. Someone wrongly seized on this health emergency to reward ultrarich beneficiaries, likely including the Trump family, with a tax loophole not available to middle class families."[42]

All in all, this minor tax provision hidden in the CARES Act will reduce tax revenues, and increase the wealth of the wealthy, by an estimated total of $195 billion over ten years, according to the JCT.[43] That far outweighs much of the benefits of the CARES Act for those ordinary citizens getting a $1,200 check.

The Reality of Contemporary "Capitalism"

One need look no further than the CARES Act, or the earlier bailout of 2008, to realize that all the talk about the American system of free markets is a smoke screen for a system of state control that funnels wealth primarily to the wealthiest and most privileged shareholder investors.

There is no better demonstration of this than the behavior of the American stock markets in the six months following the outbreak of the COVID-19 pandemic. The economic news could not have been worse. Unemployment reached depression levels. Economic growth dropped precipitously. Yet the stock markets hit record highs for months. In March and April 2020, more than thirty million Americans filed first-time unemployment claims, pushing unemployment to its highest levels since the Great Depression. Despite that, the U.S. stock markets recorded in April their best month since 1987.[44] After an initial shock, the markets rallied steadily, rising more than 30 percent since their lows in late March 2020. Dire economic news continued to pound the country for the following four months. In the second quarter of 2020, the American economy lost a third of its steam, with quarterly economic growth (GDP) declining at an annual rate of 32.9 percent—the worst quarter in at least 145 years.[45] Yet in August 2020, the S&P had its best month since 1986 and the NASDAQ its best since 2000.[46] In September 2020, the Dow Jones rose above 29,000 to reach record highs from before the pandemic.[47]

Most economists were puzzled and offered fanciful daily explanations.[48] Even Paul Krugman had little to say, suggesting that "investors are buying stocks in part because they have nowhere else to go."[49] But there is no wonder the markets defied the economic crash. The reason is obvious: the pandemic was a boon for capital extraction. For the markets, there is nothing like a good crisis when the right people are in power. A crisis provides the perfect opportunity for more capital extraction. Philip Mirowski wrote tellingly about this during the financial meltdown of 2008, under the title *Never Let a Serious Crisis Go to Waste*.[50] Now, too, the Faustian logic is clear.

First, President Trump and the majority Republican Senate made it crystal clear that they had the backs of the large-capital corporations no matter how bad things got.[51] By strengthening the largest corporations, the CARES Act helped them weed out their smaller competitors and facilitated monopolistic practices later. After the crisis, the large-capital corporations were poised to reap extractive profits while many small businesses and mom-and-pop stores went out of business.

Second, the sunset provisions on the bailout restrictions would allow shareholders and managers to enrich themselves when an economic recovery eventually happened, again without ever needing to build reserves, because they know they will be bailed out next time as well. As Tim Wu details, these recurring bailouts have allowed wealthy managers to pillage in good times, through stock buybacks and exorbitant executive pay, and get rescued in bad.[52] This too enhances market value while extracting capital for the wealthy.

Third, Trump sapped any momentum toward universal health care by promising financial exceptions for coronavirus-related health-care costs. These COVID-19 carve-outs protected the Republicans from greater backlash in the November 2020 elections. Eventually, the less fortunate will continue to be ravaged by ordinary cancers and poverty-related diseases without any coverage, their health issues likely exacerbated by COVID effects, to the financial benefit of private insurance and corporate and wealthier taxpayers who did not have to deal with more universal health care.[53]

Fourth, the pandemic disproportionately decimated the most vulnerable populations: the elderly, the poor, the uninsured, the incarcerated, and persons of color. The racial imbalance was unconscionable: the coronavirus mortality rate for African Americans was almost three times higher than the mortality rate for whites in the first few months.[54] The rates of infection in prisons and jails were also horrifying.[55] The populations at risk were disproportionately older and poorer, so on Medicare and Medicaid. Some refer to this as "culling the herd."[56] Market investors could expect that social security would be less of a drag on the economy in the future.

Fifth, the Republicans were able to secret into the bailouts tax bonanzas for millionaires. The tax provisions discussed earlier disproportionately benefited about 43,000 taxpayers in the highest tax bracket (over $1 million in income) who would receive an average windfall of $1.63 million per filer.[57]

The stock markets have become the mirror of an ugly truth of capital extraction. Foucault presciently observed, back in 1979, that markets are the touchstone of truth in neoliberal times.[58] The ugly truth that they reveal today is that the pandemic was a gold mine for large-capital corporations, institutional investors, and the wealthiest. I once overheard a New York real estate tycoon talking about the land grab in the Adirondacks in the 1930s and commenting "Wasn't the Great Depression grand!" Institutional investors felt the same way about the COVID-19 pandemic.

None of this is limited to the Republican Party. Democratic administrations are also beholden to Wall Street and wealthy donors. The most recent ones—those of Bill Clinton, Barack Obama, and Joe Biden—avidly embraced neoliberal policies such as workfare for the unemployed and welfare for the corporate elite.

The Paulson and Geithner bailouts of 2008 were the model for the CARES Act. The Biden climate and energy bill, the Inflation Reduction Act—though absolutely necessary to help slow climate change given the gridlock in Washington—is another financial bonanza for corporations, especially fossil fuel and energy companies, alternative energy companies, and electric car companies, because the legislation works primarily through tax breaks and incentives for corporations.

The CARES Act replicates fully the experience of 2008. As Mirowski demonstrates, neoliberalism was strengthened rather than weakened by the 2007–2008 crisis. Its proponents persevered, redoubled their efforts to capture the economics profession, and came through with policy proposals and responses that outflanked the left-leaning neoclassical economists. In the process, they extracted even more capital from the economy. As Mirowski writes, "The tenacity of neoliberal doctrines that might have otherwise been refuted at every turn since 2008 has to be rooted in the extent to which a kind of 'folk' or 'everyday' neoliberalism has sunk so deeply into the cultural unconscious that even a few rude shocks can't begin to bring it to the surface long enough to provoke discomfort."[59]

Time and again, we have witnessed extractive capitalism exploit crises. "They know what it means to never let a serious crisis go to waste," as Mirowski says.[60] It is past time to stop talking about capitalism, or even neoliberalism, and refer instead to a system of tournament dirigisme. The only way forward now is a genuine transformation that replaces our existing dirigiste regime with coöperism, an economic regime that concentrates cooperative, mutualist, and nonprofit ways of living, working, and saving the environment.

•

THE PROBLEM WITH THE LABEL *COMMUNISM*

The term *communism* is no less misleading. Derived from the root *common*, communism suggests the abolition of private property and the creation of a common shared by all. But in communist regimes, there has never been such a common; there is, instead, a centralized state- or party-driven allocation of material interests. Here too the nomenclature is entirely deceiving.

The term *communism* traces to the same period as *capitalism*, the early nineteenth century. Understood as the political and economic system that abolishes private property, the term *communism* was first used in the *New York Spectator* in August 1840. The term *Communism* with a capital *C*, associated with Marx and the proletarian overthrow of the bourgeois class, came into use in English in about 1850.[61] Regarding its French usage, the *Oxford English Dictionary* notes:

> The coinage of the French term has been variously attributed to Charles Augustin Sainte-Beuve (1804–69), French poet, novelist, and critic (in a letter of 3rd August 1840: see C. A. Sainte-Beuve *Correspondance générale* III. 332), Étienne Cabet (1788–1856), French philosopher (E. Cabet *Histoire populaire de la révolution française* IV. (1840) 331), and Théophile Thoré (1807–69), French art critic (T. Thoré *La verité sur le parti démocratique* (1840) 27). All three seem to have arrived at the term independently in 1840.[62]

The term *communist* in English, with a *t* at the end, has a similar time stamp, around 1840, with or without the capital *C*. The term was used previously, in the late eighteenth century in France, with different connotations, but its current usage there also traces to the mid-nineteenth:

> French *communiste* was used earlier (1769) with reference to participants in the collective possession of land (mortmain). The French term was also used for other kinds of collective ownership in the late 18th cent., e.g. with reference to the right of pasturing animals on common land (1789). It was also used from at least the 1830s to refer to adherents of François-Noël Babeuf (1760–97), militant French revolutionary. Coinage of the term in the sense 'advocate or adherent of the theory of communism' has been variously attributed to Pierre-Joseph Proudhon (1809–65), French editor, politician, and social theorist (P.-J. Proudhon *Qu'est-ce que la propriété?* (1840) 326) and Étienne Cabet (1788–1856), French philosopher (É. Cabet *Comment je suis communiste* (1840)). Both seem to have arrived at the term independently in 1840.[63]

Despite the ambition, the animating ideal of collective or communal ownership of property, the abolition of private property in favor of the common, has never been realized at a national level other than through state nationalization of the modes of production, which means essentially a state-run operation. The laudable ideal of living together in common has worked at the level of the commune but does not scale up to the level of a large economy like the United States. As soon as the communal body grows beyond the size of the commune, the governing mechanisms get crystalized into an elite party or centralized state apparatus that inevitably becomes autocratic. The abolition of private property in favor of communal ownership inescapably requires a governing mechanism and institutions of dispute resolution. Proponents of the common often speak of the need for democratic governance of the common by the people, but that is nothing more than an abstract ideal that must be concretized in legal form. In practice, that legal form takes the shape of a decision-making body (such as a Communist Party leadership) and juridical rules. That is why communalism has never truly existed at a national level. Every experiment has rapidly devolved into another form of state dirigisme: an autocracy of an elite party or a centralized state apparatus. Instead of using the term *communism*, we should call it too *dirigisme*, perhaps qualifying it as *party* or *state* dirigisme. The fundamental problem is that the concept of common ownership is far too blunt an instrument to describe accurately how material interests are distributed and used in society.[64]

On the Common

This last point calls for much longer and sustained debate with Michael Hardt and Toni Negri, or with Pierre Dardot and Christian Laval, all of whom have reimagined the concept of the common for today.[65] For Dardot and Laval, but not for Hardt and Negri, the argument for the common rejects the traditional notion of communism. Dardot and Laval work hard to distinguish themselves from the type of state communism that, they believe, has plagued the term *common*. They refer to "the communist burden," the way that real-world communist regimes have distorted the concept of the common. Their main effort is to liberate the concept of the common from the state:

> In other words, it [the common] is a term that helps us turn our back on the strategy of state communism once and for all. By appropriating and operating the means of production in its entirety, the communist state methodically destroyed the prospects for real socialism, which "has always been conceived of as a deepening—not a rejection—of political democracy." For those dissatisfied with the neoliberal version of "freedom," the common is thus a means of opening up a new path. It is precisely this context that explains the thematic emergence of the common in the 1990s. It was a shared political demand that could be found in the most local and concrete struggles, as well as within the largest national and international political mobilizations.[66]

At practically every juncture, Dardot and Laval try to distinguish their concept of the common from what has come before. They even distinguish their concept from the notion of "the commons" tied to the antiglobalization struggles of the 1990s. Those movements constructed their interpretation of the world in terms of a second "enclosure": not the early enclosure of lands in the seventeenth and eighteenth centuries, but rather a renewed global enclosure of property, associated with privatization and neoliberalism, that took away common space from the people. The struggle in the 1990s was to reclaim "the commons," in the plural, consisting of water and land that were being privatized. By contrast to these antiglobalist movements, which they characterize as trying to develop the commons as small isolated pockets outside of capitalism, Dardot and Laval propose a more radical path.[67] They reject any approach to changing the world that does not involve taking power. They also reject the Marxist logic of getting beyond capitalism from within. Dardot and Laval call for a revolutionary concept of the common as a new way forward, one that will destroy and replace neoliberalism.[68] They do not believe that piecemeal reform will do any good, or that the creation of pockets of common goods will save us from ecological peril. Instead, they call for a radical transformation, a revolution, "profoundly transforming the economy and the society *by overthrowing the system of norms* that now directly threatens nature and humanity itself."[69]

Dardot and Laval are careful to attribute the concept of the *common*, in the singular, to Hardt and Negri, arguing that this is a decisive and radical achievement: not to think of the commons as something that effectively preceded capitalism but rather as a new development to get past capitalism.

> For us, the common is the philosophical principle that makes it possible to conceive of a future beyond neoliberalism, and for Hardt and Negri the common is the only possible path toward a non-capitalist future. The common is also a category tasked with undermining any residual nostalgia for state socialism, particularly in terms of the state's monopolization of a bureaucratized public service. In other words, the common is a category that transcends public and private.[70]

Dardot and Laval place their concept of the common in the practical lineage of the environmental and ecological movements and the alter-globalization movements of the 1990s. They trace the intellectual lineage directly back not only to the writings of Hardt and Negri, but to the empirical work done by and following Elinor Ostrom and the emergence of what they refer to as the field of "common studies." They emphasize the shift from the plural to the singular, from "the commons" to "the common," reflecting the more abstract and substantial concept of the common, as opposed to the traditional or historical examples of the commons. "In short, we are living in a moment in which the 'common' is a term that designates a regime of practices, struggles, institutions, and research all dedicated to realizing a non-capitalist future."[71]

Many of the specific projects that Dardot and Laval support—especially in the context of technological innovation and the new virtual commons, the "knowledge commons" that other critical thinkers, such as Yochai Benkler, Eben Moglen, Mikhaïl Xifaras, and Hardt and Negri, embrace—have family resemblances with forms of cooperation.[72] This is especially true in the developing sectors of information technology and digital creation. The invention and collective nonprofit work on open-source operating systems like Linux, open-access software like LibreOffice, and open-source platforms like Wikipedia are good examples of cooperative endeavors, often discussed by proponents of "open-source economics."[73]

What is particularly powerful about coöperism is that it can build on these efforts in an incremental way and does not require massive collective action to transform property relations or create a common. Coöperism uses a snowball effect to spur more and more cooperation. It allows for a virtuous circle of growth of cooperation. It does not require seizing power, which immediately creates collective-action problems in this increasingly polarized world. Each and every one of us can start working on coöperism right now and contribute to its proliferation.

GETTING BEYOND THE COLD WAR

In any event, I agree with Dardot and Laval that we desperately need to get beyond the terms *capitalism* and *communism* and the crude debates of the Cold War. Historically, neither term was accurate. What was really at play was some other confrontation between Western tournament dirigisme and state- or party-centralized control of material interests. The former is a system of spoils directed by the government for the benefit of those at the top of the wealth pyramid; the latter is a system of spoils directed, most often, by a central party apparatus that increasingly resembles what we call capitalism.

It is imperative to imagine an alternative economic regime of coöperism based on people working together as opposed to these two dominant forms of dirigisme. It is imperative to imagine a new form of distilled and compounded cooperation as an economic model in itself and to get beyond the illusory debate between Hayek and Marx. The former rests on the fabricated myth of individualism, as if individuals alone take responsibility for and achieve economic success, when in fact their success has depended entirely on state bailouts. Too many people are still entranced by the myth of individualism: the idea that we can go it alone, inventing, creating, and building things by ourselves and reaping all the benefits. It is so ingrained in the public imagination, tied to the image of the pioneer gold prospector and the shiny rewards of solitary hard work. This ideology undergirds the logic of capital extraction. But for the most part, we invent, create, and produce through mutual support and collaboration, what Richard Sennett calls the craft of cooperation.[74] It is these forms of cooperation that must ground a postpandemic economy.

The Ravages of the Red Scare

In order to move forward, then, it is essential to leave behind these Cold War ideologies. They have been especially debilitating to the movement for cooperation. In the United States, McCarthyism distorted the trajectory of the American cooperative movement. The Red Scare knocked the momentum for cooperation off its path, in a direction that undermined its full potential.

This is evident, for instance, in the historical trajectory of the Cooperative League. James Peter Warbasse, the New York doctor who founded the Cooperative League in 1916, grounded his own vision of cooperation in evolutionary theory and human nature, essentially in biology. Warbasse stated that "the forces which promote co-operation are the natural human instincts, the inherent animal tendency toward mutual aid, which has existed as a biological necessity since animals began, and without which the race would perish."[75] One can hear Kropotkin in these words. In fact, Warbasse cited Kropotkin's work in his manifesto of 1923, *Co-operative Democracy*.[76] There were other influences as well, and his writings sometimes reflect an eclectic mix that by now should be familiar to the reader. As Clarke Chambers explains:

> His theory of consumers cooperation . . . was drawn primarily from two
> French theorists, Charles Gide and Ernest Poisson. He borrowed both from

Marxian socialism and Kropotkin's mutual associationalism. Good nineteenth century secular and religious humanitarianism obviously infused his whole approach to life. He may not have been a careful student of either William James or John Dewey, but pragmatism came naturally to influence his beliefs. For all this eclecticism his system was surprisingly logical, coherent, and persuasive.[77]

Despite this eclectic origin, Warbasse and the Cooperative League had to veer right in order to sidestep McCarthyism. Warbasse began in opposition to both capitalism and socialism.[78] In fact, his original position was close to coöperism. At an early stage, Warbasse coined the term *co-operative democracy*, which he imaged as a third way, an alternative to both capitalism and socialism. Warbasse positioned himself politically as opposed to both because they both tended toward statism. As Chambers explains:

> Capitalism was doomed; but its declared alternative, the socialist state, was equally to be feared. Co-operation offered the only valid way to win a new world. The need was for the application of "constructive social engineering" to usher in, by evolutionary steps, a cooperative society. Both capitalism and socialism tended toward statism. . . . The paternal state, welfare capitalist or socialist, corroded the self-reliance of the people, destroyed their initiative, usurped their liberties. The paternal state led to insolence and arrogance on the one hand, and indifference and submission on the other.[79]

In the postwar period, the Cooperative League became increasingly conservative, especially as the Cold War got hot. In 1946, a designated language committee of the League "recommended that there be no more 'indiscriminate' criticism of capitalism, for that merely aroused hostility and misunderstanding," Chambers recounts. The language committee wrote that "Indiscriminate attacks on 'capitalism' may cause the speaker to be classified as a communist or fascist . . . Many who are alienated by an attack on 'capitalism' will heartily support opposition to monopoly." The committee also urged members to avoid use of the term "Cooperative Commonwealth," because it suggested that "all enterprise should be taken over by cooperatives 'which is neither true nor possible.'"[80]

Today, the Cooperative League is part of the National Cooperative Business Association, one of the largest American networks for cooperation.[81] The pendulum swings reflect all the geopolitical shifts of the twentieth century. The Russian Revolution, the Great Depression, the Cold War, and McCarthyism pushed and pulled cooperative movements in different directions and distorted their discourse. They also sucked the momentum out of the movement. We should not follow those vicissitudes today.

COÖPERISM ECONOMICS

Coöperism, as a coherent, deliberate, chosen form of concentrated cooperation powered by coöpower, serves as a better model, economic regime, and alternative to existing forms of dirigiste economics. In order to move forward and truly instantiate an economic system based on coöperism—on concentrated, combined, leveraged forms of cooperation that distill coöpower—it is essential to reconcile the different strands of cooperative economics, especially the tensions between those who privilege consumer cooperatives (favored by cooperative federalists) versus worker/producer cooperatives (favored by cooperative individualists).

The terms *cooperative federalism* and *cooperative individualism* were popularized in the late nineteenth century by the English economist and sociologist Martha Beatrice Webb (1858-1943), one of the founders of the London School of Economics, in her book *The Cooperative Movement in Great Britain*, published in 1891. Webb defined the two terms in a footnote:

> The term Individualist has been used within the Cooperative movement for the last twenty years to denote that school of Co-operators who insist that each separate manufacturing establishment shall be governed (and if possible owned) by those who work therein; the profits being divided among these working proprietors. Hence the cry 'the mine for the miners,' 'the land for the labourers' (I do not know whether they would add the school for the schoolmasters, or the sewers for the sewer-cleaners). Those Co-operators who, on the other hand, advocate the democratic administration of industry (after the model of political democracy) are usually styled Federalist.[82]

The potential difference between the two models arose as early as the Rochdale Society, when the members had to decide what to do with any surpluses generated at the store. As Webb explained, there were three groups to whom the surplus could be distributed: the consumers, the workers at the cooperative, or the owners of capital. In the case of the Rochdale Society, the consumers and the workers would have been the same people, although the amount of effort expended by the working members could have affected the distribution of the surplus based on purchases alone; each member at the time was required to work in equitable amounts, but the amount of their purchases surely differed. At Rochdale, the owners of capital would have been the original twenty-eight founders.

Webb argued in favor of the first choice, the consumers, suggesting that it realized "the Owenite ideal" and eliminated any "profit on price."[83] This was the route the Rochdale Society had chosen. Webb was a cooperative federalist and argued against worker cooperatives on the ground that few of them had succeeded. She argued that the internal contradictions were likely to defeat cooperation. Consumer cooperatives not only functioned better, she argued, but they also led to other benefits for society:

> It was the government by the customers (that is, by the community, or such of the community as chose to take part) that forced the officials of different societies to arrive at the best methods of book-keeping, auditing, and stock-taking through discussions at the district conferences, as well as to secure by combined action in wholesale trading and manufacture the best quality and the lowest price in goods supplied. A society governed by a close body of workers of shareholders absorbing all profits arising out of transactions with the outside public would be more than human if they instructed their competitors in the art of buying and selling. But with the government of the store by the customers each society is as willing to teach as it is anxious to learn.[84]

Other famous cooperative federalists included Charles Gide, discussed earlier, and later, the Belgian economist Paul Lambert (1912–1977). Lambert wrote extensively on the subject in his book *La Doctrine coopérative*.[85] He argued that consumer control is the most effective way to control prices in the face of monopolistic practices.

Christian Socialists in England were prominent promoters of cooperative individualism, highly influenced by the French Catholic thinker and politician

Philippe-Joseph-Benjamin Buchez (1796–1865), who is often referred to as the father of the French worker cooperative movement.[86] In 1831, Buchez founded an association of cabinet makers in Paris and outlined five key principles of cooperative individualism:

- First, [the workers] would elect democratically one or two workers to "hold the signature of the company."
- Secondly, the method of payment would be based upon skill and the traditional rates paid for the particular craft.
- Thirdly, the profits of the company would be divided equally, and 20 per cent would be used "as relief or distributed among the associates proportionately to their work."
- Buchez's fourth principle was that the cooperative's capital could not be removed by individual members even if the cooperative were to be dissolved.
- Finally, workers in the cooperative would have to become members by the end of their first year of employment.[87]

Much of the ensuing debate during the early twentieth century rehearsed the themes that I set aside in the previous chapter. The federalists tended to accuse the individualists of being greedy protocapitalists who did not always promote the public interest. The Christian Socialists were drawn to producer cooperatives in part because they could be a conservative force against drastic changes in society and property, a "bulwark against revolution," and also because they promoted and regenerated Christian morals. "Consumption is primarily the animal element," they wrote, "production the divine. [Man] shares the former with the meanest of creatures; the latter with his Maker." The Christian Socialists claimed that producer cooperatives were "the true outcome of the Christian religion . . . a new manifestation of the Counsels of God for the redemption of man out of the slavery of the flesh to the freedom of the spirit."[88]

The debates mixed religious, evolutionary, and scientistic discourse and included a lot of statements about human nature. Proponents argued over the moral and religious advantages of the different cooperative forms and over which least replicated the logics of capitalism.

Ultimately, some of the participants tried to bridge the divide. Although Lambert favored federalism, he softened the edges of Gide's positions and tried to reconcile the differences. Lambert argued that producers' interests were also important and that one could not have a nation just of consumers.

> The power of the consumers cannot be absolute. It is impossible to neglect the legitimate interest of the producers; besides, some place must be left for the producers' democracy; on a more general level, the economic policy (the choice between free trade and protection, for instance) cannot exclusively take into account the consumers' interest. This is the weakness of the principle. But here is its strength: the consumer must be present at all the stages of economic decision; if he is not to have all the supremacy, he must have some share of it—a share that in the strategical points of economy, must never be inferior to the producers.[89]

These debates did not extend much into the late twentieth century and have almost evaporated in the twenty-first. They have been superseded by more promising theories of solidarity economics and ecological economics, discussed earlier.

Coöperism economics, which draws on solidarity and ecological economics, overcomes the competition between cooperative federalists and individualists by keeping all eyes on the prize: the core values and principles of cooperation. The goal is not to privilege one type of cooperation over another but rather to privilege, and then concentrate and leverage, those cooperative enterprises that best promote those core values and principles. Coöperism seeks to compound those experiments in cooperation that most distill and augment coöpower.

It does not make sense to argue that one form of cooperation is inherently more in tune with the values and principles of cooperation than another. Instead, judgments need to be made so as to encourage and leverage those experiments with cooperation that are truest to the values of participatory democracy, equity, and care of the environment. Consumer cooperatives that are particularly attentive to environmental matters, to their carbon footprint, to how and where they source, and to how they serve their members and relate to their workers should be included. They may contribute as much as worker cooperatives that equally focus on their footprint and impact on the climate and on their relationships to suppliers. There are ways to combine these efforts so that the best consumer cooperatives are sourcing from the better producer cooperatives. Those forms of cooperation can work together, as well as with other forms such as credit unions and mutual aid. We have seen those symbioses in action. There is nothing inherent in one form of cooperation, or in the human nature of members of any particular cooperative form, that should favor one style over another. It all turns on how faithful the cooperative enterprise is to the values and principles at the core of cooperation.

To be sure, there may be empirical differences between different forms of cooperatives that exist today. A study conducted in 1984 comparing worker and consumer cooperatives in northern California and Oregon found that members of producer cooperatives tend to be more politically oriented and activist. On average, they found that "the most important motives for members of [consumer] cooperatives were price savings, better quality goods and services, and convenience"; by contrast, "for those in [worker] collectives, the most important considerations were greater control over the operation, support for co-op values, better quality goods and services, and new learning." As a result, the members of worker cooperatives appeared more concerned about political and social change.[90] But that is an artifact of not holding constant, or evaluating, the most important variable: the extent to which the individual cooperatives studied were faithful to the core values and principles of cooperation.

The key to coöperism is to favor those cooperative enterprises that most promote those values and principles, to incentivize cooperation through the methods discussed earlier (see "Incentivizing Cooperation" in chapter 3), and to combine, leverage, and compound them into an integrated economic system.

A FINAL THOUGHT ON GROWTH

There are varying opinions today in the field of economics on the benefits and disadvantages of privileging growth as an economic goal. It is important to underscore that not everyone who favors cooperation follows the mainstream economic position that growth, or a continually rising GDP, is necessary for political stability. Most challenge the metric of GDP to measure growth, and there are different views within the cooperative movement about growth itself. Some people remain focused on growth, or what is called "green growth," others embrace a no-growth economy, and some argue for degrowth.[91] Given the threat of global climate change, it may well be that for many jurisdictions, a steady-state economy or degrowth may be more adapted to our times.

Some heterodox economists, such as Joan Martinez Alier, Herman Daly, Tim Jackson, and Kate Raworth, have argued the benefits of foregoing growth in favor of sustainable economic and environmental equilibria.[92] These economists, proponents of "steady-state economics," or sometimes "ecological economics," challenge the conventional measure of economic well-being, namely GDP growth. They argue that GDP as a metric does not include costs associated with growth, and that it is therefore necessary to be more nuanced about economic well-being and standards of living. Bigger is not always better: it may come with costs that are detrimental to net well-being. Given the reality of limited resources on Earth and the need for ecosystems to survive, these economists argue for sustainability rather than growth.

There are other heterodox economists who go further and argue for degrowth, antigrowth, or declining-state strategies. These include economists such as Nicholas Georgescu-Roegen in the United States, Baptiste Mylondo and Serge Latouche in France, Giorgios Kallis in Greece, and Christian Kerschner in Austria.[93] Kallis explains, in his manifesto titled *Degrowth*, that it is possible to vastly shrink consumption and resource depletion on Earth without sacrificing well-being. "It is possible to have meaningful employment and secure well-being with much less through-put and output than is found in wealthy countries today," Kallis writes.[94] The degrowth movement, which began in France in the 1970s, does not simply seek to end consumerism for the sake of the environment but also emphasizes the need for radical redistribution of resources and a shift in values. The problems they identify include both the excessive use of resources and their unjust distribution.[95] Matthias Schmelzer, Aaron Vansintjan, and Andrea Vetter have recently published a new manifesto on degrowth, *The Future Is Degrowth: A Guide to a World Beyond Capitalism*, which emphasizes the ecological problems with growth models, as well as the historical and social rationale for degrowth as a response to colonialism and fossil-fueled industrialization.[96] These visions of degrowth are put in practice in political-ecology cooperative projects such as the Longo Maï cooperative network in Costa Rica, France, Germany, Switzerland, and Ukraine started in 1973 or the TERA eco-village projects in southwestern France begun in 2014.

Coöperism does not favor growth at all costs; it embraces a more wholistic definition of growth that takes sustainability and the environment into account. There is room within coöperism for healthy debate on the question, though it leans toward a location-specific analysis. Rather than focusing on GDP, it focuses on GPS. What might best fit one wealthy industrialized country may not be appropriate for another less privileged country; even within a jurisdiction, there may be room for degrowth in certain communities and green growth in others in order to equalize the distribution of resources and well-being. So the resolution of this question will likely depend on location-specific considerations at the national, regional, departmental, or even municipal level, focused primarily on comparative levels of economic development. For this reason, coöperism need not tranche the question universally at this time, but rather encourage more research and healthy debate.

CHAPTER 6

The Social Theory of Coöperism

I n a series of lectures pronounced at the Collège de France in 1973 titled *The Punitive Society*, the French philosopher Michel Foucault painted a haunting picture of Western society. He delivered his portrait at a time of heightened repression in France in the aftermath of the May 1968 revolution. It was the exact moment that racialized mass incarceration would skyrocket on the other side of the Atlantic, where Foucault had just visited Attica Prison. In the United States, imprisonment began climbing exponentially starting in 1973, rising to more than 2.3 million incarcerated people by 2008. A full 1 percent of the adult population in the United States was behind bars. One out of every thirty-one adults, or 7.3 million people, were under criminal supervision, including parole and probation. The situation was far worse for persons of color. One in nine African American men between the ages of twenty and thirty-four—more than 10 percent—were behind bars by 2008.[1]

Like inequality in society, the public policies that created this travesty were chosen and deliberate. There were no natural laws of detention or evolutionary principles at play.[2] It was all constructed and enforced by legislators, sentencing judges, prosecutors, and corrections officials. The human-made exponential curve shown in figure 6.1 hides the devastating toll on human lives.

What Foucault showed, in those lectures on *The Punitive Society* and two years later in his book *Discipline and Punish*, is that some modern Western societies govern by means of a punishment paradigm. Punishment is not so much a response to crime as it is the mechanism through which these societies create and maintain their social order. Governments impose punishment with the stated intention of combating criminality, but in reality the punishments serve more to shape and structure social hierarchies—in the United States, a social and racial order. Foucault's lectures on the

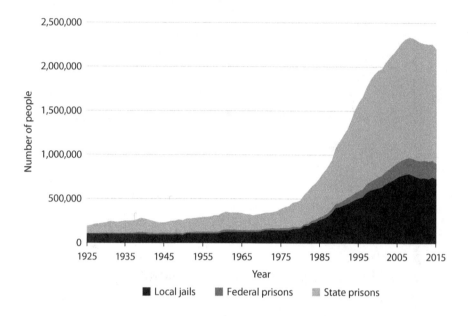

Figure 6.1 Populations of federal prisons, state prisons, and local jails (1925–2015)

Source: Prison Policy Initiative.

The data used for this figure were obtained from the Prison Policy Initiative's "State prisons, local jails and federal prisons, incarceration rates and counts, 1925–2020" data set, which can be found on the Prison Policy Initiative's Data Toolbox page. "Data Toolbox," Prison Policy Initiative, accessed September 4, 2022, https://www.prisonpolicy.org/data/. Local jails' population data were available for the years 1940, 1950, 1960, 1970, 1978, 1980, and every year 1983 and after. For this figure, local jails' populations for the years prior to 1940 were estimated to be equal to the jail population of 1940. In the years following 1940 for which no data are available, the mean of the closest available data points before and after the year in question was used.

punitive society were prescient of what was to come. They were also deeply insightful in exposing the punishment paradigm in modern society.

In many liberal democracies, individuals are left to fend for themselves, with relatively little direction or support, until the moment they do something that is perceived to be wrong, and then they are punished, often severely. That is certainly the case in the United States. In America, we don't spend too much on public education or skills training. We don't have very good public-health or mental-health systems, or accessible drug-treatment programs. Pretty much everything is privatized—the better schools, the fancy treatment facilities, the counseling. The main public institutions for mental health are now county jails. America's largest mental hospital, in fact, is the Cook County Jail.[3] We let people figure things out for themselves, pay for it on their own, get in debt with student loans; basically, we leave them alone and let them find their way. But the minute they are accused of wrongdoing, then we go after them with everything we've got. We'll spend all the money in the world to punish. In New York City, we'll lock someone up pretrial, before they have even been found guilty of a crime, at a cost of $556,539 per person per year.[4] We'll spend more than half a million dollars per person to punish them if we think they've gotten out of line, or fit the profile. But we won't spend a dime on them until that time. If you don't believe me, let me take you to a public drug-treatment facility off the Van Wyck Expressway in Queens and show you what I mean. To be honest, matters are even worse because the people we punish in America are disproportionately poor and of color.

There is a punishment paradigm that dominates in many liberal democracies and serves to create a particular social order of racial, class, and gender hierarchy. Many of us have been searching for an alternative to this punishment paradigm for years. Many have debated and discussed an education paradigm, or a justice-and-education paradigm, restorative justice programs, and now a transformative justice paradigm, all of which are promising. But these alternatives, I believe, fit better as part of a cooperation paradigm.

In addition to a political and economic theory, coöperism represents a social theory that can replace the punishment paradigm with a cooperation paradigm, creating a more just social order based on equal citizenship, equity, and respect and care for others and for the environment. Coöperism allows us to transcend the punishment paradigm of the punitive society and achieve a new society based on cooperation. It seeks to put in place the mechanisms of mutual support that will allow people to thrive. It cares about people from the start, rather than investing in them only through prison construction and guard labor. We need to replace today's punishment paradigm with coöperism.

A SOCIAL THEORY OF CRIME AND PUNISHMENT

The timing could not be more propitious. Today, there is a swelling movement in the United States and around the world arguing for the abolition of punitive practices and institutions, including the police, jails and prisons, child protective services, immigration detention, and border policing—in effect, for the abolition of the punitive society. The new abolitionists ("new" in relation to the earlier movement for the abolition of chattel slavery) have fueled national debates over whether to reform or abolish the central institutions of the criminal legal process. In the United States especially, their writings are flourishing and reaching increasingly large audiences. Mariame Kaba's collection of essays, *We Do This 'Til We Free Us*, published in March 2021, appeared on the *New York Times* paperback nonfiction bestseller list. Dorothy Roberts wrote the foreword to the *Harvard Law Review*'s esteemed annual constitutional law survey for 2019 under the title "Abolition Constitutionalism." Ruth Wilson Gilmore's work has been profiled in the pages of the *New York Times Magazine*. Derecka Purnell's book *Becoming Abolitionists* has been received to acclaim, as has a new book by Angela Davis, Gina Dent, Erica Meiners, and Beth Richie, *Abolition. Feminism. Now.* And a wave of abolitionist writings are being published in scholarly journals and news outlets by thought leaders and organizers, including Amna Akbar, Che Gossett, Alexis Hoag, Allegra McLeod, Barbara Ransby, Andrea Ritchie, Dylan Rodriguez, Omavi Shukur, Keeanga-Yamahtta Taylor, and Harsha Walia, nourishing a national debate over abolition.[5] These writings along with abolitionist organizing have, in Akbar's words, "catapulted abolition into the mainstream and, in the process, unsettled the intellectual foundations of . . . reform discourse."[6] Not just in the United States but globally, they have sparked a worldwide movement for Black lives and for abolition.[7] They have also significantly affected public opinion. At the height of the George Floyd protests in July 2020, a Gallup poll found that 33 percent of respondents between the ages of eighteen and thirty-four, and almost a quarter of all nonwhite Americans, supported the idea of abolishing police departments.[8]

Many people are skeptical, though. Many, including many progressive thinkers, doubt we will ever get beyond the punishment paradigm. Most progressives consider the emerging debate over abolition to be a nuisance or, worse, something that is driving a wedge among progressives. Many argue that the movement for abolition of the police is counterproductive to the shared goals of reformers and abolitionists. Former president Barack Obama expressed this sentiment in his critique of the idea of "defunding" the police. "You lost a big audience the minute you say it, which makes it a lot less likely that you're actually going to get the changes you want done," President Obama said on a political talk show in December 2020. "The key is deciding, do you want to actually get something done, or do you want to feel good among the people you already agree with?"[9] Many progressives agree with this sentiment. They fear that the new movements for abolition will only backfire and push the country in a more conservative direction, away from productive social reforms. Meanwhile, on the far right, Marjorie Taylor Greene has embraced the "defund" language, selling T-shirts that say "Defund the FBI"; but many Republicans also view that as a counterproductive strategy.[10] Some radical thinkers also resist the calls for abolition, viewing them as a form of identitarianism. Slavoj Žižek questions the prospects of intersectional-identitarian movements, arguing that they fail to appreciate the centrality of class struggle.[11] For Žižek, class, rather than gender, sexuality, race, or ethnicity, represents the only true form of pure antagonism; class struggle alone, he argues, aims to abolish a dominating class completely, whereas race or gender struggles seek "forms of reconciliation."[12] Class, for Žižek, represents the principal contradiction that traverses all particular contradictions (i.e., the localized and situated conflicts over race or gender); on this view, the focus needs to remain on class struggle.

But far from a nuisance or distraction as many progressives and conservatives suggest, and far from a subsidiary or subordinate phenomenon as some Marxists might suggest, the new movements to abolish prisons and police build on a long history of critical thought that challenges the punishment paradigm and, as a result, is an extremely promising development. They have also been a galvanizing force, along with the movement for Black lives, which has helped bring about the largest and most diverse protest in American history. They are a powerful force for social change, perhaps the force with the greatest political momentum today, sparking "a global movement for racial and economic equality."[13]

The new abolitionist movements force us to address a central challenge to contemporary liberalism: whether the institutions, practices, and agents of law enforcement (the punishment paradigm) function to redress the harms associated with illegal behavior or, instead, serve primarily to impose a social and racial order on society. This question goes to the heart of whether the punishment paradigm is a response to crime and to deviations of law or constitutes a mode of governing that produces racial, ethnic, gender, and other hierarchies. In its most concrete form, this poses the question whether there is a legitimate relationship between "crime and punishment" or whether punishment does its own work, independent of crime.

The challenge takes aim at a central premise of contemporary legal and political liberalism: that law and legal rights are neutral devices that serve merely as hedges to allow each individual to pursue their own vision of the good life without imposing their values on others.[14] It proposes instead that the punitive paradigm serves primarily to impose racial, gender, and other forms of perverse hierarchies on society. The law does not simply redress the claimed injury caused when an individual crosses a legal hedge; rather, it contributes to entrenching forms of discrimination and oppression against persons of color and other marginalized groups. It reproduces racial, caste, and class structures.[15]

This challenge is at the very core of the new movements for abolition. So, for instance, when contemporary abolitionist scholars and practitioners such as Amna Akbar, Brandon Hasbrouk, Mariame Kaba, Derecka Purnell, and Alex Vitale demonstrate how contemporary American policing practices trace back to slave patrols and are continuous, historically, with the enforcement of chattel slavery and fugitive slave laws;[16] or when abolitionist historians and legal scholars like Dennis Childs or Dorothy Roberts trace racialized mass incarceration to its antecedents in the convict-leasing practices and plantation prisons that arose during Reconstruction, or demonstrate that the modern death penalty and legal executions grow out of practices of Southern lynching at the turn of the twentieth century;[17] or, more generally, when abolitionist thinkers and activists, from Angela Davis to Ruth Wilson Gilmore, argue that there are historical links from slavery to Jim Crow, the urban ghetto, resistance to the civil rights movement, and our racialized punitive society today[18]—all of these thinkers show that the criminal law and its enforcement are instruments of social ordering predominantly deployed to keep African Americans and other persons of color in a condition of second-class citizenship.

Critical social theorists had posed this challenge for more than a century, but to little avail. Like a tree falling in a forest unheard, no one paid attention. Most liberal thinkers, including many progressive thinkers, were able to dodge the challenge by taking reasonable-sounding positions that essentially swept the issue under the rug. "Of course the law shapes society," they responded, "but it must be enforced to address the harms of violent crime, and there are ways to make it less racially discriminatory." In this way, even progressives were able to avoid the heart of the challenge. Meanwhile, Marxist thinkers paid relatively little attention to law and legal structures, believing that they were superstructural and obviously instrumentalized in furtherance of class oppression. To make matters worse, many of the critical theorists who actually challenged legal liberalism, such as W. E. B. Du Bois and members of the Frankfurt School, were either intentionally marginalized for political reasons or had to tone down their critique in order to assimilate into liberal institutions of higher education.[19]

Only now, as a result of the newfound debate over abolition, are people beginning to take seriously, or at least debate, the challenge to the punishment paradigm.

Addressing the challenge carefully and honestly will help us identify an alternative paradigm of cooperation that properly reflects our interdependence, not only as humans, but also with life on Earth. Coöperism offers a new paradigm for society.

Let me emphasize, the critique of the punishment paradigm is a deep challenge to the neutrality of the law. It is a direct attack on the idea that, in a liberal democracy, it is proper to leave people alone but then punish them when they violate the law; that the enforcement of law is not itself political but simply maintains society; that, in a liberal democracy, in contrast to autocracies, we value freedom and individual autonomy and are governed by the rule of law, not of men. Through the punishment paradigm, this translates into the idea that there is a necessary link between crime and punishment: illegal activity is what triggers punishment, and punishment is limited to preventing or remedying crime. The legitimacy of that relationship founds the liberal state. It grounds the philosophical, literary, and juridical discourse of "crime and punishment," from Hobbes and Locke, through Cesare Beccaria and Dostoyevsky, to John Stuart Mill and John Rawls. A foundational premise of liberal democracy is that that there should be as much freedom as possible, limited and enforced by the criminal law; that there should be freedom except where there is force or fraud; that people should only be punished for committing illegal acts that harm others. This is the central foundational premise of Western liberal democracy, and it rests firmly on the conceptual pillars of legal neutrality and the rule of law.

But for more than a century now, critical thinkers have documented, historically and theoretically, how the enforcement of criminal law serves instead, and primarily, as a political device deployed by coalitions in power to reproduce and entrench social and racial hierarchies. Rather than maintaining a neutral framework intended to benefit all citizens, the law and its enforcement shape the racial, sexual, and class order in society. Punishment is not merely a response to crime; it is a principal tool, weapon, tactic, or technique deployed to reproduce racial and social hierarchies. This critique of liberal democracy went unheard for decades. The challenge to the punishment paradigm has finally propelled this critical insight into mainstream debate.

W. E .B. Du Bois, Black Reconstruction in America (1935)

W. E. B. Du Bois was at the fountainhead of this critical tradition. In his pathbreaking book *Black Reconstruction in America: 1860–1880*, published in 1935, Du Bois demonstrated that the enforcement of penal law was used as one of the main devices to re-enslave freed Black women and men after Emancipation. Through the implementation of Black Codes in the former Confederate states, which imposed severe punishments and labor restrictions on African American men and women, new punitive practices of convict leasing and plantation prisons emerged that gave birth to new forms of slavery. "The whole criminal system," Du Bois wrote, "came to be used as a method of keeping Negroes at work and intimidating them."[20]

The enforcement of the criminal law practically replaced property law as the principal stratagem to perpetuate white supremacy. The penal law served not to redress instances of criminal harm but rather to enforce a racial hierarchy that had been unsettled during Reconstruction. It served to impose the social order of white supremacy. Du Bois made this explicit: "In no part of the modern world has there been so open and conscious a traffic in crime for deliberate social degradation and private profit as in the South since slavery," Du Bois emphasized. "Since 1876 Negroes have been arrested on the slightest provocation and given long sentences or fines which they were compelled to work out. The resulting peonage of criminals extended into every Southern state and led to the most revolting situations."[21] In tandem, the enforcement of penal law was widely used to disenfranchise Black men and women of their civil and political rights.[22]

Du Bois traced the continuity from chattel slavery to criminal punishment in the 1930s, well before modern mass incarceration of African Americans. And he exposed as well the deeper economic logic motivating that continuity: "The horrid system of convict leasing gave to the state *a profit in crime*, not to mention the vast profits which came to the private contractors," Du Bois showed.[23] Through new punishment practices, the criminal law served to transform American slavery into a new system of peonage that, in many cases, exceeded the horrors of the antebellum period.

In many respects, Du Bois was far ahead of more orthodox Marxist analyses, which in their more classical formulations often resorted, in a somewhat reactionary way, to notions of the "criminal element" or what they called the *lumpenproletariat*. Du Bois's engagement with critical thought—which, as Cedric Robinson shows in *Black Marxism*, represented a critique, an advance, and an alternative—was especially productive for students of crime and punishment.[24]

Rusche and Kirchheimer, Punishment and Social Structure (1939)

Writing at about the same time, a group of critical thinkers, members of the Frankfurt School then in exile at Columbia University, also set out to challenge the link between crime and punishment. In their pioneering book *Punishment and Social Structure*, published in 1939, Georg Rusche and Otto Kirchheimer reviewed the history of Western punishment practices since the seventeenth century and demonstrated their inextricable interconnection with the labor needs of those in power. Rusche and Kirchheimer documented how punishment practices served primarily to bolster economic regimes: modes of punishment are shaped, predominantly, by the need for labor.

Rusche and Kirchheimer unearthed evidence, for instance, showing how punishments such as transportation and the galleys served primarily to uphold the *ancien régime*. The evidence was hidden in plain view, in letters and official correspondence between the monarchy and the judges and prosecutors. "Since His Majesty urgently needs more men to strengthen His rowing crews," the King's administrators wrote to the public prosecutor of Paris by letter dated February 21, 1676, "He wishes you to take the necessary steps in His name in order to have the criminals judged quickly." In response to such a request, the public prosecutor at Bordeaux wrote back: "You will be gratified to learn that this Court has twenty prisoners who will be chained together this morning and sent off."[25] Rusche and Kirchheimer went on to meticulously trace how imprisonment and prison labor were used, after the Industrial Revolution, to help negotiate the fluctuating supply and demand for workers. They demonstrated how the prison became the chief form of punishment when industrial changes eliminated the need for houses of corrections and how transportation was later used to deal with excess labor and the needs of the new colonies.[26] Thorsten Sellin summarized their overarching argument: "Fundamentally, then, the aim of all punishment is the protection of those social values which the dominant social group of a state regard as good for 'society.'"[27]

Rusche and Kirchheimer explicitly took aim at the purported relationship between crime and punishment. Their aim, they wrote, was to "strip" the "ideological veils and juristic appearance and to describe it in its real relationships." They declared:

> The bond, transparent or not, that is supposed to exist between crime and punishment prevents any insight into the independent significance of the history of penal systems. It must be broken. Punishment is neither a simple consequence of crime, nor the reverse side of crime, nor a mere means which is determined by the end to be achieved. Punishment must be understood as a social phenomenon freed from both its juristic concept and its social ends.[28]

Rusche and Kirchheimer focused primarily on the relationship between punishment practices and the supply of labor. Their work spawned a wealth of scientific studies testing whether and how punishments are shaped by systems of economic production, which became known in the literature as the Rusche-Kirchheimer hypothesis.[29] The crux of their hypothesis targeted the supposed link between crime and punishment.

Angela Davis, "Political Prisoners, Prisons, and Black Liberation" (1971)

It is that link between crime and punishment that Angela Davis explicitly set out to "pull apart," beginning even before her fugitivity in 1971. In her brilliant book *Are Prisons Obsolete?*, Davis underscored the need to "do the ideological work of pulling apart the conceptual link between crime and punishment." If we did that, Davis wrote, "we would recognize that 'punishment' does not follow from 'crime' in the neat and logical sequence offered by discourses that insist on the justice of imprisonment, but rather punishment—primarily through imprisonment (and sometimes death)—is linked to the agendas of politicians, the profit drive of corporations, and media representations of crime."[30] Punishment has its own logic and functions separate from crime reduction, Davis argued. Punishment constructs our social and racial hierarchy.

Angela Davis's theoretical intervention—pulling apart the purported link between crime and punishment—was nourished by her own lived experience as a fugitive from the law and a political prisoner, as well as by the experiences of other members of the Black Panther and Black liberation movements, of the Soledad Brothers, and of other political prisoners. In 1971, incarcerated in the Marin County Jail, Davis documented the political nature of criminal law enforcement in America. In her May 1971 letter from jail, she wrote: "The prison is a key component of the state's coercive apparatus. . . . The prison has actually operated as an instrument of class domination, a means of prohibiting the have-nots from encroaching upon the haves."[31]

Davis emphasized how the enforcement of the criminal law was used as a tool of repression and a form of counterrevolution, specifically identifying the "system of 'preventive fascism,' as Marcuse has termed it, in which the role of the judicial and penal systems loom large." Davis portrayed policing as social ordering, the courts as an enabler, the prison as the main tool or device, and the prison "frame-up" as the final act of elimination. She noted the increasing awareness of this among Black and Latinx prisoners themselves: "Prisoners—especially blacks, Chicanos and Puerto Ricans—are increasingly advancing the proposition that they are *political* prisoners. They contend that they are political prisoners in the sense that they are largely the victims of an oppressive politico-economic order, swiftly becoming conscious of the causes underlying their victimization."[32]

The writings and speeches of George Jackson, Eldridge Cleaver, Bobby Seale, and other movement leaders at the time confirmed the political nature of law enforcement. Jackson was clear that the definitions of crimes were tied directly to maintaining an economic order and property relations, and that criminal law enforcement was intended to repress any form of resistance to racial and economic hierarchies.[33] Jackson combined, in his critique, the racial and the economic dimensions: the enforcement of the criminal law and the "chief repressive institutions," such as the police and prison, served to impose a racial capitalist order that both subjugated persons of color and quashed political resistance.[34]

Frantz Fanon had developed a similar thesis regarding the role of policing as a political weapon to control populations living under colonial rule. In the French colonies, Fanon noted, and others agreed, the police and prisons served "as the linchpin" of French imperialism.[35] Angela Davis, writing from her cell in Marin County jail, highlighted the parallel: "Fanon's analysis of the role of colonial police is an appropriate description of the function of the police in America's ghettos."[36] Meanwhile, James Baldwin compared Davis's plight—detained, chained, isolated in jail—to that of "the Jewish housewife in the boxcar headed to Dachau, or as any one of our ancestors, chained together in the name of Jesus, headed for a Christian land."[37] Baldwin situated the prison and the enforcement of criminal law in the register of politics and warfare. He referred to the women and men in prison as "the numberless prisoners in our concentration camps—for that is what they are."[38]

Michel Foucault, Penal Theories and Institutions *(1972) and* The Punitive Society *(1973)*

At about the same time, across the Atlantic, Catharine von Bülow, Daniel Defert, Michel Foucault, Jean Genet, and others were challenging the neutrality of punishment.

"The death of George Jackson is not a prison accident. It is a political assassination."[39] Thus opens the tract *Intolerance Inquiry: The Assassination of George Jackson*, by members of the Prison Information Group, published November 10, 1971, concerning the shooting death of George Jackson at San Quentin on August 21, 1971. In an essay titled "The Masked Assassination," Bülow, Defert, and Foucault treat punishment as political warfare—not the consequence of crime, but rather a form of civil war. They too deconstruct the purported relationship between crime and punishment:

> What is happening in the prisons is war, a war having other fronts in the black ghettos, the army, and the courts. . . . Today, the imprisoned revolutionary militants and the common law prisoners, who became revolutionaries specifically during their detention, paved the way for the war front to extend inside prisons. . . . At this stage, the ruling power is left with one resort: assassination.[40]

Writing of Jackson's plight—serving more than ten years in prison before being gunned down by a prison guard—Bülow, Defert, and Foucault denounced the penal system as warfare: "Ten years in prison for seventy dollars is a political experience—an experience of hostage, of a concentration camp, of class warfare, an experience of the colonized." With reference to Jackson's brother, Jonathan Jackson, they wrote: "This same justice system, with its white judges and its white jurors, consigned hundreds of thousands of African Americans to the bloodthirsty guards of concentration camps."[41]

In his lectures on *Penal Theories and Institutions* a few months later, Foucault developed what he called a political theory of criminal law.[42] Beginning in January 1972, Foucault minutely demonstrated over the course of seven lectures how Cardinal Richelieu and his emissary, Chancellor Séguier, repressed the *Nu-pieds* (barefoot) rebellion in Normandy in 1639 through a strategic interlacing of the penal sanction and military force.

"Penality is political from top to bottom," Foucault declared on March 1, 1972.[43] His political theory of criminal law had several elements, the first and most important of which called for a rigid deconstruction of the assumed relation between crime and punishment. Criminal law enforcement, Foucault argued, is not a consequence of criminality. It is not a reaction to delinquency or crime, which are themselves fabricated by criminal law enforcement during a process of social struggle. The enforcement of criminal law is instead a response and reaction to that political struggle. As he explained in his lecture of January 26, 1972, "all the major phases of the evolution of the penal system, of the repressive system, are ways of responding to forms of popular struggles."[44] Crime had to be understood as a threat, as an attack on the state's power. "Crime is always, in at least one of its dimensions," he said, "an attack on the public power, a struggle against it, the provisional suspension of its laws."[45] Thus, criminal law enforcement could only be properly understood within the framework of social struggle as a weapon, tactic, or strategy in relations of power being waged within society.[46] This led Foucault to his concept of the "punitive society," the topic of his lectures the following year, 1973.[47]

Two years later, Foucault published his famous book on the birth of the prison, *Discipline and Punish* (1975), which built on this theoretical foundation, as well as on his own militant encounters with prison.[48] Of greatest importance here, Foucault's stated aim was to eradicate the purported relationship between crime and punishment in order to expose all the work that disciplinary practices achieve in modern society:

> We must first rid ourselves of the illusion that punishment is above all (if not exclusively) a means of reducing crime and that, in this role, according to the social forms, the political systems or beliefs, it may be severe or lenient, tend toward expiation or instead toward obtaining reparation, applied in pursuit of individuals or for the attribution of collective responsibility.[49]

In other words, Foucault argued, we must sever the supposed link between crime and punishment, stop distracting ourselves with theories of just punishment, and focus instead on what economic and social forms punishments achieve in society. In this, Foucault explicitly built on Rusche and Kirschheimer. He emphasized that their work—in his words, their *"grand livre"*—provided a number of "essential reference points."[50] First and foremost was the need to break the link between crime and punishment.

In the 1970s, these arguments were taking root in many countries, including Scandinavia and northern Europe, and especially in Latin America. In 1974, the Norwegian sociologist Thomas Mathiesen published a groundbreaking work of critical criminology, *The Politics of Abolition*. Mathiesen explored Scandinavian penal reforms and called for the abolition of prisons. His work became influential in countries such as the Netherlands and Argentina.[51]

Dorothy Roberts, Ruth Wilson Gilmore, and the 2000s

Since the turn of the twenty-first century, abolitionist scholars have built on these foundations to highlight the political nature of law enforcement and to deconstruct the supposed relation between crime and punishment.

Dorothy Roberts, in one of the earliest law review articles offering an abolitionist framework, in 2007, begins from this premise: what we call the "criminal justice system" is not about redressing crime, but about imposing a racial order.[52] "The U.S criminal justice system has always functioned, in coordination with other institutions and social policy, to subordinate black people and maintain the racial caste system." Roberts argues that every aspect of criminal law is tied up with imposing a racial order: it is "engrained in the very construction of the system and implicated in its every aspect—how crimes are defined, how suspects are identified, how charging decisions are made, how trials are conducted, and how punishments are imposed."[53]

Roberts traces the history of the key institutions of the criminal law back to the enslavement and control of African Americans: "The pillars of the U.S. criminal justice system—mass imprisonment, capital punishment, and police terror— can all be traced to the enslavement of Africans." More generally, and in direct conversation with the work of Rusche and Kirschheimer, Roberts notes, "Penal institutions have historically been key components of social policy aimed at governing marginal social groups."[54] Roberts traces the death penalty back to the lethal punishment of enslaved Africans, the Black Codes during and after slavery, the lynching of freed Black persons after Emancipation, and the racialized use of public executions.[55] Roberts ties coercive interrogation in this country back to the lynching era as well.[56] In sum, Roberts writes,

> I argue that these immoral practices [mass incarceration, capital punishment, and police terror] have flourished in the United States in order to impose a racist order. Understanding their racial origins and function helps to explain their endurance and the need to abolish them.[57]

In her 2007 book *Golden Gulag: Prisons, Surplus, Crisis, and Opposition in Globalizing California*, Ruth Wilson Gilmore documented the political economy of the California prison-industrial complex (PIC), demonstrating how political and economic forces, surplus finance capital, and labor issues, rather than crime, were what brought about the massive prison expansion.[58] Michelle Alexander, in her 2010 book *The New Jim Crow: Mass Incarceration in the Age of Colorblindness*, demonstrated how mass incarceration functions as a form of racial segregation and oppression similar to post-Reconstruction Jim Crow laws.[59] The very title of Alexander's book deconstructs the crime-and-punishment nexus and demonstrates the political dimensions of punishment practices: mass incarceration is not the product of criminality but a new form of the old social regime of Jim Crow. The same is true of Jonathan Simon's *Governing Through Crime* (2007)—again, the very title expresses the deconstruction of crime and punishment—and Katherine Beckett's *Making Crime Pay* (1997).

Loïc Wacquant's 2000 study of what he called the "structural and functional homologies" among the "four peculiar institutions"—slavery, Jim Crow, urban ghettoization, and racialized mass incarceration—made the point as well.[60] Punishment is just the last of these peculiar institutions that impose racial hierarchy. Wacquant is explicit about the need to sever the connection between crime and punishment. To understand Black hypercarceration, he writes, "we first need to break out of the narrow 'crime and punishment' paradigm and examine the broader role of the penal system as an *instrument for managing dispossessed and dishonored groups*." In a footnote, Wacquant traces this explicitly back to Rusche and Kirchheimer: "In this, I follow Georg Rusche: 'Punishment must be understood as a social phenomenon freed from both its juristic concept and its social ends,' that is, its official mission of crime control, so that it may be replaced in the complete system of strategies, including social policies, aimed at regulating the poor."[61]

Similarly, in their work on capital punishment, Carol Steiker and Jordan Steiker demonstrate how the intricate Eighth Amendment jurisprudence surrounding the death penalty is best understood not as addressing questions of crime and deterrence but instead as serving to legitimize the death penalty. It makes little sense to evaluate the criminal law within the conventional framework, because the legal enforcement serves other purposes. As they cunningly remark, "You can't know that a thing is not being done well until you know what it is that is being done."[62]

Contemporary New and Feminist Abolitionism

The more recent abolitionist writings build on this intellectual tradition but push it further. Spurred by the documentation of police killings and the movements for Black lives, these writings further deconstruct the crime and punishment nexus.[63] They offer a more radical vision of abolition that seeks not only to break the link between crime and punishment and get rid of the PIC institutions and practices but, further, to undo the world that makes those possible.

For Mariame Kaba, breaking the link between crime and punishment is a fundamental starting point. "*What work do prisons and policing actually do?*" Kaba asks. "Most people assume that incarceration helps to reduce violence and crime," she writes, but "facts and history tell a different story." Kaba pulls apart the crime and punishment nexus:

> Increasing rates of incarceration have a minimal impact on crimes rates. Research and common sense suggest that economic precarity is correlated with higher crime rates. Moreover, crime and harm are not synonymous. All that is criminalized isn't harmful, and all harm isn't necessarily criminalized. For example, wage theft by employers isn't generally criminalized, but it is definitely harmful.[64]

In the debate over policing, the new abolitionists demonstrate that the police function is tied to maintaining the racial order, not to combating crime. "Policing is among the vestiges of slavery, colonialism, and genocide," Derecka Purnell writes, "tailored in America to suppress slave revolts, catch runaways, and repress labor organizing."[65] Contemporary policing practices, Purnell and others argue, trace back to slave patrols in the South and to the control of freed persons and labor in the North; they emphasize the legacy of police violence against African American and Latinx communities.[66] Brandon Hasbrouck shows how modern policing reflects the badges and incidents of slavery, originally intended to be abolished by the Thirteenth Amendment.[67] Chenjerai Kumanyika argues that policing evolved as a form of labor control: the control of enslaved persons in the South, and of labor in the North, such that the "institution of policing is very much connected to the enactment of violence against strikers and union-breaking."[68] In the debate over prisons, Dorothy Roberts emphasizes that racialized mass incarceration is the legacy of slavery and serves to maintain a racial, gender, and class hierarchy.[69] In the debate over the death penalty, the new abolitionists connect the modern history of executions back to the history of lynching in the South.[70] In *Slaves of the State*, Dennis Childs documents how slavery was transformed into institutions of punishment: "the convict lease camp, the chain-gang camp, the county farm, the peonage camp, the prison plantation, and the 'modern' penitentiary." This is the continuity of "neoslavery from the chain gang to the prison-industrial complex."[71]

In her extraordinary historical research on convict leasing, chain gangs, and the Milledgeville State Prison Farm in Georgia during the late nineteenth and

early twentieth centuries, Sarah Haley meticulously unveils the ideological construction of our punitive society by focusing on the forms of punishment meted
out to Black women at the turn of the twentieth century in the state of Georgia.[72]
Haley shows us the ideological groundwork that founds our contemporary
understanding and prejudices regarding the human condition. She writes that
she is trying to explain "the necessity of violence against black women's bodies
in the maintenance of white supremacy as an ideological, economic and political
order during a period of rapid historical transition." Haley's work exposes the
depth of the hegemonic structures of belief that entrench ideologies of antiblack-
ness and heteropatriarchy. Her work not only underscores the urgency of abolitionist feminism but also highlights how difficult the task is, given the long-term
pervasive ideological constructs that have produced contemporary society. Her
research amplifies the interlocking systems of state and interpersonal violence
by exposing the ideological construction, gendered and racialized, of our present
reality. Haley offers a "history of ideology" and shows in minute detail, through
the archives of punishment, how those punitive forms contributed to "the construction of racially determined and defined gendered subject positions during
the long historical era in which segregation took hold."[73]

Almost one hundred years ago, W. E. B. Du Bois referred to punitive practices
postbellum as "a new form of servitude."[74] Few listened. But today the challenges
to the punishment paradigm are finally reaching larger and larger audiences, and
establishing what for so many decades was marginalized and ignored: that the
enforcement of criminal law is not so much a response to harmful activity as it is
an instrument for social and racial ordering, and that rather than redressing the
individual and social harms associated with crime, the enforcement of law in the
United States serves to perpetuate racial subordination.

THE IMPLICATIONS FOR THE NOTION OF HARM

Many progressive thinkers today still manage to sidestep these challenges to the
punishment paradigm. For the most part, they do so by taking what appears to
be a reasonable middle ground: the truth must lie somewhere in between, as it
always does. The penal law surely enforces a social order, but it also addresses
harms associated with crimes. Law enforcement tries to remedy the individual
and collective harms of criminality and, in the process, inevitably imposes a

particular vision of society that affects gender, racial, class, and other relations. So, for instance, the elimination of the marital rape exception, challenges to stand-your-own-ground laws, changes to heat-of-passion defenses, and the elimination of the homosexual advance defense all address the harms of crime while simultaneously shaping racial, gender, and other relations of power in society. It is not an "either-or," many progressives respond, but a "both-and."

According to this view, it is possible to bracket the broader political issues, recognize and try to address racism and sexism, even systemic racism, but stay focused on the enforcement of law to address social harms. Progressive reformers thus continue to offer ways to fix the law and propose new ways to address the harms of society without creating racist outcomes. Violent crime and disorder cause individual and systemic harms that need to be addressed, the argument goes; through careful, reformed practice, progressive actors can get back to enforcing law as a just response to harm. It's better not to get too political, on this view, because there will never be universal agreement about social ordering and anyway it is best to leave that to democratic politics. In the meantime, progressive thinkers can find better ways to address social harms. This may mean incremental reform measures or more ambitious reform, such as a turn to restorative justice or other more holistic approaches, to address the harm caused by crime and deviance from the law.

But far from being more reasonable, this progressive reform position is entirely unstable, because the existing social and racial order shapes the very conceptions of harms and violence that lie at the heart of law enforcement. In other words, the perception of harm and violence associated with illegality is determined by race, gender, class, and other relations of power in society. It is not possible to talk about social harms in a vacuum. Those "harms" are themselves artifacts of the present social condition and racial hierarchies.

This is not just a chicken-and-egg problem. One cannot simply respond, "Well, all these problems are co-constitutive, so we might as well just start somewhere." They are not equally co-constitutive. To be sure, there is feedback. The fact, for instance, that we sentence to death and execute more Black men convicted of white-victim homicides fuels a perception of Black criminality that then reinforces racial subjugation in this country; and the tragic effects of "Black criminality" are well documented.[75] Still, it is not the case that the penal law is wholly, or primarily, or even equally responsible for systemic racism in American society, a society that was based on slavery and the genocide of indigenous peoples.

No, there is some directionality: a systematically racist society uses the penal law as one tool among others to maintain, perpetuate, and augment racial domination. What this means is that we have to be far more nuanced about how the social order shapes and uses penal law as a tool of domination.[76] Returning to racial disparities in capital punishment, the fact that the death penalty is enforced more in homicide cases involving white victims reflects the fact that white life is valued more than the lives of persons of color. It reveals that the harm of white-victim homicides is perceived, at least by most of the principals in the criminal legal ordeal, as greater than the harm of Black-victim homicides.[77] Relations of racial power in American society shape those racialized conceptions of value and harms. In other words, social forces shape perceived harms.

I have written at length elsewhere about the malleability of harm (*The Collapse of the Harm Principle*) and the limits of the liberal understanding of harm and violence (several chapters in *Critique and Praxis*).[78] Others as well have discussed the constructed nature of the conception of violence in criminal law.[79] Suffice it to say here that the notions of harm and violence are inextricably linked to the social context within which they are situated. There are no universals here, and any attempt to reduce these concepts to their core or their reasonable meaning is nothing more than an imposition of a minority position on the whole; it is an imperialist project. We cannot start from a universal or common core to harm; we have to start from the social context.

Many people believe, instinctively, that there are universal harms that traverse human history, such as murder, rape, and theft. They argue that these harms have been prohibited throughout history, from the earliest tablets and commandments to Napoleonic and modern penal codes. "Thou shalt not kill" represents a universal maxim, many would argue. But that is far too simplistic. What matters are not the broad abstract categories of, say, murder or rape, but the way in which those prohibitions are interpreted and shaped by the social order. The different ways that rape was defined—how the *harm* of rape was defined—utterly transforms the prohibition: at common law, rape was limited to violent stranger rape where a woman physically resisted to her utmost; marital rape was not considered rape; nonconsent was not considered rape. It was a very different harm, shaped by patriarchal norms, than what we consider to be rape today. The fact that patricide was one of the most egregious offenses under the Napoleonic Code, or the changing definitions of justified police killings of civilians, give homicide and its associated harms very different meanings. To speak of murder as a universal harm but ignore the social and historical ways in which it is defined and prosecuted is to miss the most important dimension.

We need to pay far more attention to the ways in which social and racial forces shape the harms that the law aims to address. When we do, it becomes clear that for the vast majority of contemporary law enforcement, the perceived harms associated with illegal behavior (drugs, disorderly conduct, resisting arrest, prostitution, theft, quality-of-life offenses, even justifiable homicide) are shaped, or rather distorted, by the existing social and racial hierarchy, not just race, but gender, sexuality, class, poverty, patriarchy, and more. We tend to enforce street crime, public crimes, and crimes of poverty because, given the way our society is racially structured, we view them as more harmful than white-collar crimes, even if white-collar crimes may far outweigh the former in terms of true social costs. We do that because we are enforcing a social and racial order. Most of what we police and enforce, we do because we perceive the harm to be greatest, but that harm perception is shaped by the existing social order.[80]

It is a Sisyphean task to discuss harms divorced from the social and racial ordering. Something is perceived as harmful, calling for law enforcement, only within the normative framework of a social hierarchy. Theft of private property is only perceived as harmful in a social order that rests on private property; prostitution only causes cognizable harm where the moral order privileges noncommercial consensual sexual relations. These are truisms, but they have crucial implications that we constantly sweep under the rug: the normative social and racial order determines our conceptions of harm for purposes of law enforcement, meaning that we simply cannot bracket the social ordering.[81]

Given that social forces shape perceptions of harm, it makes no sense to say "Let's just hold off on the politics, deal with that separately, but keep enforcing the law in an even-handed way to prevent harms," because the very notion of harm at the heart of law enforcement, the very measure of "an even-handed way," is inflected by the normative structure of the existing social and racial order.

Once we take seriously the challenge to the punishment paradigm and realize that our present notions of harm and violence are inextricably linked to the current social and racial order, the question becomes what the world would look like if it were not disfigured by racial, gender, class, and other forms of injustice.

Pragmatic thinkers will resist this invitation as overly utopian.[82] Rather than imagine a just social order, the pragmatist will respond that we should extract racism, even systemic racism, from current practices and institutions and enforce the law on a race-neutral basis. This might be accomplished by means of a positivist legal approach, just enforcing the penal code in a neutral way, or by addressing social harms holding race constant. That, however, is impossible because society without social and racial hierarchy would be an entirely different society and, as a result, the harms would be different.

That is what coöperism reveals: it shows the potential of cooperation and participatory democracy across all aspects of our lives. What would a world of cooperation, without systemic racism, look like? It would be an entirely different world, one in which everyone treats all others with equal dignity, true respect, and humanity, where everyone regards others as truly equals, as their own, as people to care about. What makes it possible for us all to allow the inequality that surrounds us, as well as the racial, gender and sexuality hierarchies and other forms of domination along lines of poverty and class, is not just evil intent, although there is plenty of that, but a disregard for the lives of others, for the humanity of others. What makes it possible to tolerate walking by a homeless person lying on the ground, bundled up in winter, is that they are not our child, our brother, our loved one, our friend; they are not our equal; they do not command the respect or dignity we would afford someone we know. We turn our eyes away because they are not of us, not our own, not fully human, because we are not working or eating or sharing cooperatively with them.

Just imagine, for a moment, what coöperism would look like: a world where people cooperate in all dimensions of consumption, work, housing, aid, and support, regardless of race or ethnicity as well as gender, sexuality, poverty, or class. This would be a world without racial segregation and deep inequality in housing and education, where there would not be elite white suburban public schools and struggling Black urban public schools, where access to good health care would not be different in the South Bronx than on the Upper East Side, where the parks on the South Side of Chicago would look like Millennium Park in the Loop, where there would not be hollowed out Black neighborhoods or "million dollar blocks,"[83] where urban public housing would not be predominantly for people of color, where our courts would not be filled almost exclusively with Black and Latinx defendants, where young Mexican and Asian men would not be relegated to driving e-bikes into the wee hours of the morning in subfreezing temperatures delivering Uber Eats to wealthy white college students and families, where young Mexican women would have other options than cleaning the homes of wealthy mostly white families for cash or manning the grocery checkout, where young Black men would be more likely to be employed than incarcerated, where Pakistanis and Haitians would not be driving cabs but sitting on corporate boards, where all the most menial jobs in society would not be relegated to women and minorities. This would *not* be the same world that we live in today merely stripped of race and ethnicity. It would *not* be a society like ours today with the single exception that the color of our skins would be randomly distributed across occupations, neighborhoods, classrooms, and professions.

Coöperism would entail a different society from the punitive society we live in today. In that different society, what would harm consist of? Harm also would be completely different. Our values would be different, and so would our conceptions of harm. Harm might mean not helping the person who is struggling and homeless. It might mean not finding work for the young man who is panhandling in front of the grocery store. It might mean not providing an apprenticeship to someone without work. It might mean not volunteering at a child-care center in order to help working mothers. Just imagine how different our notions of harm would be in a world that truly addressed relations of race and power. It is, in fact, practically unimaginable what society would value. Our values and conceptions of harm would be completely different.

The task, then, must be to inquire what coöperism would look like and how that would affect our conception of harm. We need to address questions in reverse order.[84] It is essential to start in the right place and ask the right question: What would robust cooperation look like? And what would harm amount to there? As Mariame Kaba writes in *We Do This 'Til We Free Us*, the proper inquiry must begin "not with the question 'What do we have now, and how can we make it better?' Instead, let's ask, 'What can we imagine for ourselves and the world?' If we do that, then boundless possibilities of a more just world await us."[85]

Coöperism, by contrast to other progressive efforts, contains the only seeds of a just transformation of society. Reformist achievements, such as the passage and survival of Obamacare, tend to be compromised policies that satisfy few and achieve little.[86] It is important to recognize this and to work toward a coöperist future. Instead of impeding the efforts, we need to work with and toward abolition and a new society based on cooperation.

As for the critiques from the left, they are simply outdated. It does not make sense to think of class as the principal contradiction and other social, racial, gender, and sexuality conflicts as the particular contradiction, as Žižek proposes. If anything, it makes more sense to conceptualize the movement for Black lives as the contemporary instantiation of class struggle. As Barbara Ransby argues in her essay "The Class Politics of Black Lives Matter," the movements for Black lives embrace demands for economic justice, rest on a conception of racial capitalism, and seek to uplift the lives of the most marginalized populations.[87] They represent the current embodiment of what would formerly have been called "class struggle," even if they do not center the working class and especially not the white working class. Žižek may refer to class struggle as the only form of "pure" antagonism, or the principal antagonism, but today it is the challenge to the punishment paradigm that represents the radical form of contradiction.

In the end, the effort to imagine coöperism is an exercise in what Harsha Walia refers to, in the context of borders and migration, as an exercise in "worldmaking."[88] In arguing for a world without borders between nations, Walia draws on the Arendtian notion of worldmaking as a process of "homemaking"; she closes her discussion with a passage from Toni Morrison's essay "Home" from the collection *The House That Race Built*:

> In this new space one can imagine safety without walls, can iterate difference that is prized but unprivileged, and can conceive of a third, if you will pardon the expression, world 'already made for me, both snug and wide open, with a doorway never needing to be closed.' Home.[89]

In an interview from 1976, Foucault said that "there can be no reform of the prison without the search for a new society." He added that, when trying to imagine what punishment would look like in that new society, one should not ask what form of punishment would be "more gentle, acceptable, or efficient," but instead raise a more fundamental and difficult question: "Can one in effect conceptualize a society in which power has no need for illegalities?"[90] That is the proper place to start.

SOME MODELS FOR THE PARADIGM OF COÖPERISM

A new paradigm of a society based on cooperation is emerging, one that may lead us beyond the punitive society we now live in. This vision fundamentally changes the questions we ask. It reformulates the problems we must address. And it represents the most promising path forward to address our current crises.

One source of skepticism regarding cooperation is whether it would be possible to imagine a society without punishment. Is it possible to imagine a large-scale society that does not punish as ours does? What role would there be for the enforcement of law in a world that is not marked by racial and ethnic hierarchy, by gender domination, by class conflict? What would be considered harmful and call for enforcement? What role would there be for punishment to address those new harms?

There are no easy responses because so much of what we identify today as criminal activity is itself the product of systemic racism and sexism. Domestic violence is mostly gender violence that would not exist if there were more cooperation and systemic sexism did not traverse our society. Much of the street policing of drugs and minor disorder are the product of poverty and racism that, again, would not be the case if a cooperation paradigm governed. Even white-collar crimes—cornering markets, insider trading, consumer fraud—would not exist if we had a society based on cooperation, collaboration, and mutual respect.

In other words, the conceptions of harms would be entirely different in a cooperative society that was not riven with racism and sexism; so would the definitions of crimes and our conception of how to address norm violations. We would be living in a world of cooperation, respect, and dignity, of treating others as one would want to be treated oneself. Under those circumstances, we would not treat norm deviation by caging people in disgusting environments where they are more likely to get raped than educated. Even restorative justice would have to be reimagined because the notions of harm underlying restorative approaches would change so much.

In fact, we would need to build beyond restorative justice, or reimagine it, because it remains today too wedded to the existing understandings of harm shaped by our current society. At present, restorative justice takes those conceptions of harm as its starting point and seeks to include all the parties who have been affected by a crime, including the persons who claim to have been harmed, those who allegedly committed the harm, and often their respective families and communities, in a process of collective resolution that allows all parties to be heard, to be understood, and to participate in the formulation of a redress of the harm.[91] In practice, restorative justice often involves conferencing methods that bring the parties together to discuss and find ways forward. Restorative justice, of course, comes in many variations and can also serve as an umbrella term to cover other innovative developments, such as therapeutic jurisprudence or positive criminology.[92] But most of these practices assume current definitions of crime and of harm. They have not yet been reimagined for a society without racism and sexism.

Restorative justice tends to be a form of alternative dispute resolution within the existing criminal legal ordeal.[93] It remains nested within the traditional framework of crime and punishment; it displaces punishment to a substantial degree but is consistent with punishment as an alternative. John Braithwaite, a proponent of restorative justice, recognizes this: "Basically, we should try restorative justice, perhaps again and again; when restorative justice fails, try deterrence, and when deterrence fails, try incapacitation."[94] In this sense, restorative justice is best understood as a form of punishment that traces back to a form of compensation as punishment.[95] It is an effort at compensation and making whole, but it assumes current ideas of harm. This approach is too limited to the crime-and-punishment model.

Instead, we might look for guidance in the new experiments in transformative justice. Mariame Kaba discusses transformative justice principles at length in her 2021 book, and she and others, such as Allegra McLeod, detail some of its practices and experiments.[96] Kaba describes the ambition of transformative justice as the effort to address violence and harm in such a way as not to increase violence or harm (terms that we would need to reexamine in a just world). "It's asking us to respond in ways that don't rely on the state or social services," Kaba explains. "Transformative justice is militantly against the dichotomies between victims and perpetrators, because the world is more complex than that."[97]

One such experiment involved the response to an allegation of sexual assault where both the person victimized and the person accused were members of the Chicago organization Black Youth Project 100 (BYP100). In that case, the organization deliberately did not turn to the police or criminal law enforcement and instead created a process of its own to address the allegation, convening what it called a "community accountability process," or what McLeod calls "a transformative justice process to come to terms with the harm done."[98] It began with about fifteen months' worth of work, each party working with a separate support team, and then led to a convening.[99] The process brought together both parties, along with transformative justice facilitators, in an effort to address the harm alleged without implicating law enforcement. McLeod refers to this, citing Harsha Walia, as an effort "to realize critical commitments at a local scale as a politics of prefiguration in which participants seek through their own choices and relationships to prefigure the sort of world in which they wish to live."[100] The organization produced, in addition, new ways of dealing with future incidents, including creating a Healing and Safety Council that would convene whenever there was an allegation of misconduct. According to McLeod, "the Council is composed of two squads, one focused on prevention and one on intervention, and both collaborate to respond to harm in the organization's chapters and to foster a culture of 'healing praxis.'" They also created a manual, *Stay Woke Stay Whole: Black Activist Manual*, to help prevent and address future harms.[101]

Kaba and McLeod elsewhere detail other alternative efforts at achieving justice outside the criminal law framework in response to police brutality and torture.[102] In Chicago, in the wake of serial torture by the infamous police commander Jon Burge, local activists put in place efforts to document and memorialize the incidents, to bear witness to history. They created testimonial evidence and records of what happened, sharing these with international organizations dedicated to human rights, including the Inter-American Commission for Human Rights and the United Nations Committee Against Torture. Activists created the Chicago Torture Justice Memorials (CTJM) project to memorialize the police torture. They also sought reparations through legislation and the creation of institutions to "offer rehabilitative support and treatment, community education, and vocational assistance."[103] McLeod describes other initiatives in Chicago, New York, and elsewhere to take over traditional police spaces (like the neighborhood adjacent to the Chicago Police Department's infamous Homan Square headquarters) and replace them with the kinds of institutions and practices associated with abolition democracy, such as public educational workshops and clothing and meal programs.[104]

There are numerous ongoing experiments with transformative justice, ranging from the narrow area of intimate-partner violence to broader violence-interruption programs.[105] A collective of organizers and critical thinkers, including Alisa Bierria, Hyejin Shim, Mariame Kaba, and Stacy Suh, have developed a model called "Survived and Punished" that seeks to protect survivors of domestic and sexual violence from the criminal law and includes a mutual-aid manual that treats "Survivor Defense as Abolitionist Praxis."[106] This forms part of a broader effort to acknowledge harm and victimization and the needs of survivors without deflecting the call for abolition.[107] A number of violence-interruption programs have been developed as well in cities around the country. The model, originally conceived on the basis of a public-health paradigm, has evolved through community engagement.

Violence-interrupter programs now locate their interventions within the broader context of community mobilization, public education campaigns, and the provision of services such as GED programs, counseling, and health treatment.[108] These and other programs seek forms of reconciliation and repair.[109]

THE END OF THE PUNISHMENT PARADIGM

Challenging the link between crime and punishment pushes us to realize the larger implications of a world of mutual respect and cooperation, one that would fundamentally change the way we think about harm, victimization, crime, and how to address deviations from the norms. An ethic of care and cooperation would displace the punitive paradigm. It would render obsolete the notion of enforcing the criminal law. Instead of punishment, there would be a panoply of measures of care, well-being, education, and support to help individuals work through problems. These measures would take us beyond punishment practices.

In a society based on coöperism, when someone deviates from the norm, others would likely interpret that as a call for care and assistance. In the same way a partner or parent tries to understand what their loved one is going through and what their needs are, people in a cooperative society would try to understand what brought about the norm violation and how best to address the needs. They would try to help the person understand their actions and what they need to do in order to try to achieve their goals. When our loved ones lash out, we often rightly say that they may be calling out for attention. I believe that is how we would treat people when they engage in norm-violating behavior under conditions of cooperation and equity, as if they were essentially asking for help, knowingly or unwittingly. People would intervene to help the individual understand their situation better, work with the individual to identify the problems that led them to act that way, and work to address those problems. We would be committed to working with people to put their lives back on track. Naturally, we would do the same with the persons affected by those actions. We would try to help everyone heal. This pushes hard on the definition of crime. We know that legal definitions of violence and violent crime are themselves a function of political choices.[110] But to push this one step further, we may need to get rid of the conception of crime entirely: the concept of crime may be the wrong way to understand norm deviation in a cooperative, egalitarian, respectful society.

What becomes clear from all this is that it takes an incredible investment in and commitment to mutual care, support, enrichment, and cooperation to enact a society of coöperism. We would all need to dedicate parts of our days, every day, to serving and helping others. It would be like participating in a cooperative, where we each have to give part of our time and energy each day to taking care of others and serving others. In a caring and cooperative society, we would need to invest in one another, care for one another, and treat one another with equal humanity and dignity. This would certainly call for what Seyla Benhabib refers to as a foundational social transformation. Those have occurred. With Hobbes and modern political theory, Benhabib reminds us, "A momentous transformation in the Western philosophical tradition took place when 'the good life' was no longer viewed as the life of doing 'just and noble deeds,' as it was for Aristotle, or as the life of Christian virtue and devotion, as it was for St. Augustine, but rather, when the good life became defined as the life of individual satisfaction and consumption."[111] Benhabib is referring to the way modern science and political theory gave rise to a new, more individualistic way of thinking. A new view of science allowed moderns to reduce human experience to fear of death and then justify an authoritarian political regime. In a similar way, the life of care, mutuality, and cooperation would require a foundational change in political vision and action, in our very way of being.

In many societies today, people have embraced a logic of punishment, a form of individualism in which the principal role of government is to punish. Coöperism would displace that with a logic of cooperation. It aims to transcend our punitive society and to put in its place a social order marked by cooperative arrangements throughout every aspect of our lives, including education, training, work, apprenticeship, housing, food, health, finance, leisure, aid, and support. Coöperism can displace the punishment paradigm and replace it with a cooperation paradigm.

CHAPTER 7

A Defense of Coöperism

The idea of coöperism likely will provoke many objections, as the concept of cooperation has for decades, even centuries. There will be questions about its feasibility, its comparative disadvantages, its utopianism. There will be critics at both ends of the political spectrum. On the right, people will argue that capital markets are here to stay and that capital has a higher return than any other form of investment. They will argue that competition is more effective and that cooperatives will underperform in the long run. They will ridicule the idea of doing away with punishment. On the left, critics will claim that coöperism would undermine unionization, syndicalism, socialism, and other forms of class struggle. They will argue that we need not less but more centralized forms of coordination—or, for the anarchists, no state at all. Some will say I have drawn straw figures of capitalism and communism, that there are socially responsible forms of capitalism or, at the other end, cooperative forms of socialism.

Many of these challenges have already been addressed. Cooperatives do compete and thrive even in traditional sectors, as evidenced by the Mondragón group, Land O'Lakes, and Crédit Agricole. The best evidence suggests they are more resilient than traditional firms, especially during economic downturns. They can also flourish with unionization, as we are seeing in a number of cases now. They constitute a solidarity politics. As for the straw-man critique, there are of course many new trends in corporate social responsibility and in ESG-conscious (environment, social, and governance) investing. I support those initiatives; I do not mean to impugn them. But they are so marginal to capital markets that they are unlikely to have any real effect. They are generating a lot of compliance and new managerial jobs for ecofriendly corporate employees, but they run counter to the core logic of shareholder investing and for that reason are unlikely to have substantial traction.

Coöperism, by contrast, builds on a logic of concentrated cooperation and ecologically sustainable economics that points in one unified direction and, as a result, will gain momentum. There is no inherent contradiction or friction, as in the case of responsible investing where investors chase the greatest returns while tying one hand (or finger, or less) behind their back. To be sure, there are other promising political platforms, such as the DSA (Democratic Socialists of America) and new twists on socialism. As I write, my colleague Derecka Purnell along with Ruth Wilson Gilmore, Kali Akuno, and others are gathering at the Socialism 2022: Change Everything conference in Chicago to think through new visions of socialism and abolitionism. I am sure they will develop promising proposals. But the fact that socialism would require an electoral majority means that, in the United States at least, it is an unlikely path forward, at least in the foreseeable future. Cooperation, by contrast, is already here. Each of us, individually and together, can make coöperism flourish right now. It can grow incrementally through a snowball effect. Coöperism is a theory that we all can put into action at this very moment.

I have already addressed many of these challenges. But let me respond here to a few pointed critiques, first from the right and then from the left.

ON CAPITAL MARKETS

The total value of the equity markets in the United States, as of December 31, 2019, was $37.7 trillion, consisting of (1) the New York Stock Exchange, which lists about 2,400 companies and had a total equity value of about $21 trillion; (2) the NASDAQ, which lists about 3,800 companies and had a total equity value of about $11 trillion; and (3) the OTC (over the counter, officially the OTCQX U.S. Market), which trades about ten thousand securities, including foreign companies, multinationals, and other quirky entities.[1] In addition, there is a growing market of private equity and hedge funds that are mimicking these public markets. Where would all that capital go? After all, capital represents money that individuals ultimately own and place in the markets, either directly through brokerage accounts, mutual funds, or retirement accounts or indirectly through pensions or savings accounts that are invested in the market (or loaned out for investment purposes) by banks. What would happen to it all?

The answer is actually pretty simple. First, a substantial portion of it would be converted into membership contributions that would be placed in the cooperative enterprises and accrue wealth for the consumers, workers, or other cooperative members. Many more people would get involved in producer, worker, and consumer cooperatives, including finding creative ways to cooperate. Recently, for instance, in the context of solar power, people who cannot put panels on their homes because they have low exposure are getting together to place panels on a commercial structure or warehouse roof and sharing the solar energy that is produced. Those kinds of innovative cooperative initiatives would increase dramatically under coöperism, throughout all sectors of the economy, including in worker cooperatives.

Second, another substantial portion could be lent to cooperative and mutualist enterprises as ordinary debt (bond obligations) to support expansion of the enterprises (to buy equipment and facilities for manufacturing, goods and commodities for consumption, etc.). With the right kind of ingenuity and incentives, people could start lending directly to cooperative enterprises. In other words, rather than investing in the stock market, they could support cooperatives by lending them money, basically creating debt obligations rather than capital investments. There could be creative ways for the government to support and secure this lending and make it doubly attractive to people through tax incentives and credits.

As for the rest, this may be surprising, but it is basically borrowed wealth that does not amount to that much. Well over two-thirds of it in the United States is, in effect, canceled out by national debt. At the end of June 2020, the U.S. national debt exceeded $26 trillion and was mounting at a stunning clip, up more than $3 trillion in the first six months of 2020. In total, that is about $212,000 in debt per American taxpayer, or $80,000 per citizen.[2] Our capital prosperity in this country is a figment of our national debt. If we think about capital accumulation holistically, the equity in private hands in the United States is offset by the collective debt Americans owe as a nation. In effect, our prosperity, concentrated in the hands of the few, is nothing more than borrowed wealth.

At the global level, the total value of all stocks around the world stood at about $90 trillion in 2019.[3] This capital, invested in the stock markets, consists either of savings (retirement accounts, brokerage accounts, bank accounts that are invested by banks, etc.) or monies borrowed on margin. Total margin debt (individual and institutional) in the United States stood at around $600 billion in 2019, equal to about 1.6 percent of the market capitalization of the stock markets, so a small fraction.[4] The total market capitalization, then, essentially represents disposable savings as investments. The $37.7 trillion in the United States represent mostly monies that individuals ultimately own, either directly through retirement accounts, brokerage accounts, or mutual funds, or indirectly through savings accounts that are then invested in the market (or loaned out) by banks, or doubly indirectly by corporations (ultimately owned by shareholders) that invest in the markets themselves.

Surprisingly, though, these numbers are not that big. First, on a per capita basis (given a U.S. population of 329.6 million),[5] the market capitalization is about $114,381 per person (if only Americans, and not foreigners, held the capital). Second, in the aggregate, they are not that big either. To put them in perspective, it is worth emphasizing that:

- The U.S. national debt stood at about $25 trillion on May 8, 2020
- The U.S. GDP stood at about $21 trillion on May 8, 2020[6]

Plus, the national debt is skyrocketing. It already exceeded $26 trillion by the end of June 2020, up more than $3 trillion in the first six months of 2020. By October 9, 2022, it stood above $31 trillion. As a result of the COVID-19 bailouts, the national debt now stands at 98 percent of the economy, and is projected to outsize the nation's entire annual economy imminently—a situation that the country has not experienced since World War II. According to the Congressional Budget Office, "Federal debt, as a share of the economy, is now on track to smash America's World War II–era record by 2023."[7] On a per capita basis, again, that's about $212,000 in debt per American taxpayer, or $80,000 per citizen.

This almost wipes out the aggregate U.S. market capitalization. So all the talk about the importance of market capital is empty: it is pretty much borrowed money at the national level. Market capitalization in this country is now in essence a figment of our imagination.

Even so, if the corporate landscape were reconfigured to favor cooperation, a significant portion of the money that is now market capitalization would be reinvested into cooperative and mutual enterprises as membership equity. First, capital investors would use their savings instead to invest in themselves and their ongoing enterprises. Workers and employees would put portions of their savings into the enterprises to form cooperatives. Producers and consumers as well would invest in cooperation. Much of the existing capital would be placed in our own ongoing businesses. Second, capital investors could lend their monies to cooperative enterprises. Thus, another big portion of the existing capital markets would be reinvested in the debt obligations of cooperatives. This could be incentivized by the government, by offering favorable tax treatment, assuring a certain level of return on the debt obligations of cooperatives, and securing those loans, which would make it even more attractive for those with capital to place their savings in cooperative enterprises. Third, and most important, there would be a gradual redistribution and evening of wealth over the longer term that would effectively displace the kind of hoarding of wealth that produces so much of today's market capitalization. A more equalized distribution of wealth would mean that a portion of the capital would be used instead as consumption: employees and workers would have more money to spend on their homes, vehicles, household goods, and other goods and services. The invested capital, in part, would be funneled back into the economy as consumption and circulation.

The redesign and creation of a coöperist economy will reduce the amount of wealth that is extracted as capital and returned into investment speculation. Any surpluses that the cooperative enterprises make (after paying taxes and reinvesting a certain amount in the enterprise) will be distributed to their members. The return on members' equity may be lower than one would expect from extractive capitalism, primarily because salaries may be higher for most workers and more equitable. But as more equitable wealth begins to permeate the economy, it will be transformed into consumption and economic circulation.

ON THE RETURN ON CAPITAL

Defenders of capital markets will respond that equity investments funnel resources to the most productive and efficient economic producers, thus ensuring enhanced economic growth and prosperity for all. If wealth is properly directed to the better-performing enterprises, they argue, it will create more jobs and will spread out the benefits of economic production. The rising tide will lift all boats: the increased return on capital will be spent as consumption, fueling the economy, creating jobs, and spreading the wealth.

But these arguments are purely ideological. They have no empirical basis. If anything, they are belied by social reality, and by the research of Piketty and his colleagues. The condition of the average American worker, the shrinking middle class, and the growing impoverished majority in the United States utterly betray the ideological claims of capital. The best empirical evidence shows mounting levels of inequality within the postindustrial Western capitalist societies and growing indebtedness within the major economies, to the point that many of the supposedly wealthiest countries have effectively hocked their common.[8] The idea that capital investment is magically lifting all boats is fantasy. The reality of the COVID-19 economic crash and its stark inequalities based on race, class, and poverty show the lie of the claims of capital.

Even so, some will argue that the return on capital invested in the stock market has always exceeded the return on obligations, and would likely exceed the return on cooperative membership. As a result, capital wealth would just flee the jurisdiction and find other countries in which to invest. There would be a flight of capital and no way to funnel that capital into cooperative enterprises. The coöperist economy, in effect, would collapse.

It is of course true that capital investment has historically outperformed investment in Treasury, state, municipal, or corporate bonds. We tend to explain that based on the risk-reward equation: the return on U.S. Treasuries, for instance, has historically been lower than the return on stocks because there is little or no risk. The spread between the (long-term) return on Treasury bonds and stock markets supposedly reflects this natural risk-reward equation. To be sure, it is a particularly strange time to compare Treasuries and the stock market because the United States is devouring debt, which first pushed government fixed-income returns to historic lows—in fact, even negative returns for a split moment—and inflated the S&P 500; and then, with a period of high inflation in spring 2022 due to the pandemic and rising interest rates, pushed rates back up. But the historical data are nevertheless consistent. For $100 invested at the start of 1928, you would have had in 2019:

- $502,417.21 if you had placed it in the S&P 500
- $48,668.87 if you had placed it in BAA corporate bonds
- $8,012.89 if you had placed it in U.S. Treasury bonds
- $2,079.94 if you had placed it in three-month Treasury bills[9]

There is, of course, greater risk if one speculates on individual stocks, especially if one does not maintain a diversified portfolio. But assuming you kept the money in a market index and did not speculate further—if, for instance, you just had an S&P 500 Index over the long term—the returns for the four asset classes over the past two decades are shown in table 7.1.

TABLE 7.1 Historical Returns on Stocks, Bonds, and Bills

Year	S&P 500 (includes dividends)	Three-month Treasury bill	U.S. Treasury bond	BAA corporate bond
1999	20.89%	4.64%	–8.25%	0.84%
2000	–9.03%	5.82%	16.66%	9.33%
2001	–11.85%	3.39%	5.57%	7.82%
2002	–21.97%	1.60%	15.12%	12.18%
2003	28.36%	1.01%	0.38%	13.53%
2004	10.74%	1.37%	4.49%	9.89%
2005	4.83%	3.15%	2.87%	4.92%
2006	15.61%	4.73%	1.96%	7.05%
2007	5.48%	4.35%	10.21%	3.15%
2008	–36.55%	1.37%	20.10%	–5.07%
2009	25.94%	0.15%	–11.12%	23.33%
2010	14.82%	0.14%	8.46%	8.35%
2011	2.10%	0.05%	16.04%	12.58%
2012	15.89%	0.09%	2.97%	10.12%
2013	32.15%	0.06%	–9.10%	–1.06%
2014	13.52%	0.03%	10.75%	10.38%
2015	1.38%	0.05%	1.28%	–0.70%
2016	11.77%	0.32%	0.69%	10.37%
2017	21.61%	0.93%	2.80%	9.72%
2018	–4.23%	1.94%	–0.02%	–2.76%
2019	31.22%	1.55%	9.64%	15.33%

Source: Aswath Damodaran, "Historical Returns on Stocks, Bonds and Bills: 1928–2021," https://pages.stern.nyu.edu/~adamodar/New_Home_Page/datafile/histretSP.html

The fact is, historically, average returns have been sharply different: over the period 1928–2019, the investment return for the S&P 500 averaged 9.5 percent per year, for Treasury bonds 4.8 percent, and for Treasury bills 3.4 percent.[10] From a financial perspective, the compounded difference in interest of about 5 percent over ninety years results in a huge difference in wealth. In the short term, people may prefer to avoid risk, but over the long term, the differential is staggering. Though hard to believe, this is mathematically correct. If you use the compound interest calculator on the website of the U.S. government, for instance, and you compare 4.8 percent and 9.5 percent compounded annually, you get a striking difference.[11]

Part of this differential, especially with compounding, is reduced as a result of tax rates. Most of us are familiar with the basic tax rules in the United States: dividends from stock holdings (which are paid with after-tax corporate dollars), are taxable at the federal, state, and local level, but at a lower rate equal to 15 percent or a maximum rate of 20 percent at the federal level for qualified dividends; returns on capital (capital gains) will depend on whether they are short or long term; long-term capital gains are taxed at a lower rate (up to 15 percent or 20 percent federal maximum, depending on tax bracket); interest income is fully taxable at ordinary income tax rates, which can easily reach almost 50 percent in high tax brackets when federal, state, and municipal taxes are included; interest on U.S. Treasuries are taxed at the federal income tax rate, but exempt from state and local taxes; and interest on municipal bonds is triple tax-free.

So, making some back-of-the-envelope calculations, it is fair to say that the difference in the net return on the different investment portfolios is less stark when we account for taxes and their compounding effect. In simple terms, we might expect the following:

1. On a Treasury bond annual return of 4.8 percent, there should be about a 35 percent tax rate for the highest federal tax bracket, and no state and local taxes, so that return would reduce to about 3.12 percent.
2. On the equity return of 9.5 percent, there should be about 20 percent federal tax rate at the highest tax bracket, plus another 8.82 percent for, say, New York State, plus New York City taxes of about 3.8 percent, for a total of about 32.62 percent tax rate, which would lower the net return to about 6.4 percent.

That means, in effect, a slightly smaller net disparity. Originally, the differential was 4.7 percent; with the tax load, it would be 3.28 percent. There is still a difference if you compound annually, but the differential between 3.12 percent and 6.4 percent is much smaller: $2,159.19 versus $49,449.60 if you use a one-hundred-year time frame and the same compound interest calculator on the website of the U.S. government. Of course, tax shelters and tax planning could help increase the net differential.

In any event, the remaining differential is precisely what makes the proponents of capital investment so sure of their argument that everyone would prefer investing in the stock markets, or even that the federal government should replace Social Security with individual stock market accounts. This is the strongest argument against coöperism and for capital investment: the long-term returns over the twentieth century demonstrate that capital investment is the most advantageous thing to do with your savings. In all likelihood, returns on mutual and cooperative equity would look more like returns on bond obligations; therefore, coöperism is a nonstarter.

The problem with this argument is that these differentials are entirely human-made. They are created, principally, by the tax code, but also by the American government's promise to bail out big business, by the extraction of capital by shareholders, and by geopolitics. They are fabricated by the favorable treatment of capital in general and, more specifically, by all the legal and tax rules regarding the deduction of generous business expenses, the amortization of real estate, the favorable treatment of capital gains, the tax deferment of retirement accounts, etc. All the rules favor capital investment and wealth extraction for equity holders. The result, as many have shown, is that return on capital is typically greater than economic growth, which precisely reflects the extraction of capital from the corporate enterprise.[12]

In real economic terms, the surplus is the product of managerial choice combined with the legal and tax rules favoring capital. It is not inherent to capital investment. It is the by-product of a legal-political-economic regime that favors the capital investor. It is an artifact of the shared belief that the U.S. government will rescue the big corporations. Add to that the reality that most major public corporations finesse the tax rules in such a way as to actually glean tax revenues from the federal government. So, for instance, in 2015, American Airlines made profits of more than $4.6 billion but received a tax refund of almost $3 billion. From 2001 to 2014, Boeing made profits of $52.5 billion yet received a net federal tax refund of $757 million and an additional $55 million in state tax refunds.[13]

There are, then, several artificial dimensions to the purportedly natural higher return on capital investments. First, the Treasury can attract investors by means of security and safety and, as a result, does not need to reward them with rates of return equal to corporate equity. That, of course, is a factor of the United States' geopolitical position and recent history of stability. It is a political artifact and would change dramatically if, for instance, large sovereign investors such as China sold their Treasuries or decided to stop buying them. It is entirely related to how much debt the country has and its political track record of honoring its debt. The situation is clearly very different for a country like Venezuela.

Second, capital returns are artificially inflated by the general exploitation of labor: by not paying workers adequately, by perpetuating huge disparities with management compensation, by not distributing profits to the workers, and by relying on the federal government and states to support workers. For instance, because Walmart does not pay a living wage, many of its employees rely on Medicaid for health insurance, food stamps to feed their families, and government-subsidized housing for their shelter. As a result, American taxpayers support Walmart employees, and therefore underwrite Walmart itself, to the tune of about $6.2 billion each year. Meanwhile, Walmart made almost $15 billion in profits in 2015. In the fast-food industry, again because of unacceptably low wages, American taxpayers spend about $7 billion a year subsidizing companies like McDonald's, Burger King, and Wendy's.[14]

Third, the differential is inflated because the managers of public companies extract and hoard the profits for capital investors. They distribute profits entirely to the shareholders and themselves, paying out dividends and buying back stock, gearing everything toward profiting the shareholder and not the other persons affiliated with their commerce.

Fourth, and most important, the differential is the product of state dirigisme that favors capital investors: bailouts in bad times, tax loopholes for capital investors, tax breaks for capital gains, etc. If these were eliminated, the rates of return on capital investments would decline because the profits would be distributed more evenly and there would not be the hoarding or state-sanctioned profiteering. The higher return on capital, again, is entirely human-made.

Those differentials are fabricated. They can be reengineered to favor coöperism. The laws of incorporation, the tax code, and the government bailouts can all be reconfigured to privilege mutuals and cooperatives so that consumers, workers, and producers can receive the benefit of economic growth. It is simply a question of will. Coöperism can be made to be more profitable. This is not to suggest that it would be easy to create that will. No, it will be difficult to reduce the benefits of capital investment, especially given how many people imagine or fantasize themselves to be wealthy one day. Coöperism will not be easily achieved precisely because of the ideology of capital investment. But there is far more cooperation around us than we acknowledge, and it is growing. Its time has come.

ON HISTORICAL CRITICISMS FROM THE LEFT

There are also strong criticisms of cooperatives and mutuals from the left. Here, the critique is mainly that cooperatives undermine the efforts at unionization, syndicalism, and revolutionary socialism—in other words, they undercut class struggle.

Perhaps most prominently, Karl Marx and Friedrich Engels criticized cooperatives and philosophies of mutualism such as that of Pierre-Joseph Proudhon. To Proudhon's book *The Philosophy of Poverty*, in which he spells out his ideas about mutualism and worker cooperatives, Marx responded with a book titled *The Poverty of Philosophy: Answer to the* Philosophy of Poverty *by M. Proudhon*, a searing critique of both Proudhon's economics and his philosophy.[15] Marx famously opened his book, written in Brussels in 1847, with this public slapdown: "M. Proudhon has the misfortune of being peculiarly misunderstood in Europe. In France, he has the right to be a bad economist, because he is reputed to be a good German philosopher. In Germany, he has the right to be a bad philosopher, because he is reputed to be one of the ablest French economists. Being both German and economist at the same time, we desire to protest against this double error."[16]

For Marx, worker cooperatives and mutualist associations represented a tainted form of economic evolution. According to Marx's historical account, worker cooperatives were defective because they still bore the imprint of private property relations and self-interest: workers in cooperatives were still oriented toward the profitability of their own workshops and burdened by a regime of competition. He wrote in volume 3 of *Capital*:

> The cooperative factories run by workers themselves are, within the old form, the first examples of the emergence of a new form, even though they naturally reproduce in all cases, in their present organization, all the defects of the existing system, and must reproduce them.

Thus, worker cooperatives could only be "viewed as transition forms from the capitalist mode of production to the associated one . . . in a positive way."[17]

In his *Critique of the Gotha Program* (1875), Marx characterized worker cooperatives as a stage of economic development "in every respect, economically, morally, and intellectually, still stamped with the birthmarks of the old society from whose womb it emerges." They represented a step forward perhaps but were nevertheless tainted by "defects," which "are inevitable in the first phase of communist society as it is when it has just emerged after prolonged birth pangs from capitalist society." They must give place, Marx argued, to a more wholesome transformation of the economy. As he famously wrote:

> In a higher phase of communist society, after the enslaving subordination of the individual to the division of labor, and therewith also the antithesis

between mental and physical labor, has vanished; after labor has become not only a means of life but life's prime want; after the productive forces have also increased with the all-around development of the individual, and all the springs of co-operative wealth flow more abundantly—only then can the narrow horizon of bourgeois right be crossed in its entirety and society inscribe on its banners: From each according to his ability, to each according to his needs!

Cooperatives played, at most, an instrumental role. That was also true, in part, of Du Bois's vision of cooperation, but in contrast to Du Bois, cooperatives played no part in Marx's final vision for a just society. For Marx, cooperatives were at best a temporary vehicle to lift workers and create the possibility of movement toward a truly just society, a stepping stone toward the final, revolutionary stage of society. And even then, not all cooperatives qualified. Marx stressed that worker cooperatives were useful only when they were created by the workers themselves: "as far as the present co-operative societies are concerned, they are of value *only* in so far as they are the independent creations of the workers and not protégés either of the government or of the bourgeois."[18]

Instead of abolishing all property, as Proudhon had proposed, Marx and Engels argued for the abolition of *private* property, the "expropriation of the expropriators," and the withering of the state. In the *Communist Manifesto*, they described the final stage and their radical demands in numbered bullet points: abolition of property in land, abolition of inheritance, centralization of credit and all means of communication and transport, and full confiscation of all capital from the bourgeoisie.[19] Their ultimate vision was a radical, revolutionary program spelled out in detail for all to see and hear. In this vision, there was really no place for cooperatives.

These critiques have continued over time. Other radical thinkers, such as Louis Auguste Blanqui, favored proposals such as a commune or state ownership of the means of production but were equally skeptical of cooperatives. The Paris Commune in 1871 brought many of these debates and disagreements to the fore. Although the Commune reflected many aspects of cooperation and saw the creation of many cooperatives and worker workshops, it was also the fulcrum of political contestation over these questions. Attacks on cooperatives have continued to the present, leading to friction even within the cooperative movement, such as regarding the unionization of workers or syndicalism. There are still critiques today that cooperatives undermine class struggle, as in Sharryn Kasmir's *The Myth of Mondragón*.[20] Kasmir concludes her empirical analysis of Mondragón: "In evaluating the cooperative system, we should, therefore, think in ideological terms, including imagining what it would be like if workers were active in larger political movements and if, in this age of flexible accumulation, we could build organizations that truly transferred power to workers and genuinely created more just workplaces."[21] In a short foreword to the book, the late CUNY anthropologist June C. Nash underscores that "the very ideological stance of the cooperatives as harmoniously integrated worker-management teams mitigates the expression of antagonism based on structural opposition that persists in these settings."[22] In plain language, it mitigates class conflict.

Marx was adamant about not deceiving anyone or hiding his agenda. "The Communists disdain to conceal their views and aims," Marx and Engels wrote. They were open about overthrowing the bourgeoisie through revolution and striking fear in their opponents. "Let the ruling class tremble at a Communist revolution," Marx and Engels declared. "In a word, you reproach us with intending to do away with your property. Precisely so; that is just what we intend."[23]

I too believe in honesty and not hiding any agenda. The fact is, these far-fetched visions of proletarian revolution and the withering of the state are, at this point in history, delusions. First, the working class as a revolutionary potential barely exists anymore in the West. In a country like the United States, Ronald Reagan and the Chicago School neoliberals succeeded in killing off the already declining unions. Syndicalism is a pipe dream at this point in the United States. Although there are some encouraging signs, such as at Amazon, REI, or even Columbia University, with the unionization of graduate student workers, the overall rate of unionization in the United States has plummeted. In 2021, the rate of wage and salary workers belonging to unions was down to 10.3 percent, from 20.1 percent in 1983, the first year for comparable union data.[24] White blue-collar workers are now flocking to white supremacist authoritarians in the Donald Trump mold (such as Ron DeSantis, Josh Hawley, Ted Cruz, and Marjorie Taylor Greene), mostly on identitarian bases. Most white working men, regardless of their socioeconomic position, fear that their lifelong privileges and immunities are slipping. Today, there is hardly any remaining shared class consciousness between the white working-class man in rural America and his African American counterpart in urban America. Cultural and identitarian cleavages trump class allegiance. This is also true in other Western countries, such as France, where the traditional working-class former communist strongholds in the outer urban areas have turned toward Marie Le Pen's reactionary party, the National Rally.[25] The Occupy Wall Street movement in 2011 had a class dimension, reflected in the slogan "the 99 percent"; however, even there, the 99 percent included more of the disadvantaged population (what classic Marxists would have referred to as the *lumpenproletariat*) and a lot of what would have been called the "bourgeoisie," as opposed to the traditional proletariat. Meanwhile, the #BLM uprisings in summer 2020 and beyond transcend class struggle, even if there are socioeconomic factors at play.[26] Class conflict is a very different animal today.

Second, the problems of scalability are practically insurmountable. The idea of communalism, rather than cooperation, may work at a retail level, in a commune or kibbutz; however, it does not scale well to the aggregate, municipal, or national level, by contrast to the cooperative form which, as we have seen, can lead to huge conglomerates. The vision of communalism is admirable, but it is unmanageable at this point. If history is any guide, it cannot be scaled up without a centralized state that too often tilts toward authoritarianism. By contrast, the cooperative form can be scaled up and grow with a snowball effect.

Third, there is no need to speculate over a future beyond coöperism. I do not believe in the end of history. I suspect that, once coöperism is established, there will be new questions to ask and problems to solve. Who knows where that will take us? It would be such a radically different experience to live in a more just world built on coöperism that we can leave what comes after to a later time.[27] There is no final stage for a just society; it is always in construction. We first need to experience robust coöperism; there is no point speculating what will come after. Nor is there any point in returning to the nineteenth-century debates about the withering of the state. The internal debates between Proudhon and Marx on property, or between Proudhon and Louis Blanc on the organization of worker workshops and the role of the state, are theoretically rich and informative.[28] But again, we have learned so much since then, and cooperation has evolved so significantly since the nineteenth century, that there is little point in returning to those ideological debates. The ground needs to be cleared, especially today when the reality and practice of mutuals and cooperative enterprises, from worker cooperatives to credit unions, have proven to be so effective, even more resilient than traditional private corporations.

In the end, perhaps it is Lenin's critique of Marx that is more persuasive. Lenin engaged Marx on the question of cooperatives in the context of his own critique of utopians such as Robert Owen in two articles "On Cooperation."[29] The articles serve as a broad rehabilitation of cooperative societies, which Lenin, following Marx, had earlier disparaged, or at least not paid sufficient attention to. Returning to the question in 1923, Lenin revises his view and proposes that cooperative societies could operate as the primary mechanism to bring the mass of agricultural workers into the fold of social justice.

In the context of that argument, Lenin critiques the utopians (the "old cooperators") as "ridiculously fantastic," "romantic," "even banal." He suggests that utopians such as Robert Owen were "fantastic" because they failed to account for class struggle. They aspired to a peaceful transition to a cooperative society without ever recognizing, as Marx had, that it would be necessary first to have a class correction, to level the social field. Without first clearing the ground of class conflict, class struggle would infuse and corrupt any new forms of economic exchange based on cooperation. Lenin spells this out in the second article, dated January 6, 1923:

> Why were the plans of the old cooperators, from Robert Owen onwards, fantastic? Because they dreamed of peacefully remodeling contemporary society into socialism without taking account of such fundamental questions as the class struggle, the capture of political power by the working-class, the overthrow of the rule of the exploiting class. That is why we are right in regarding as entirely fantastic this "cooperative" socialism, and as romantic, and even banal, the dream of transforming class enemies into class collaborators and class war into class peace (so-called class truce) by merely organizing the population in cooperative societies.[30]

Lenin argued there first needed to be a political and social revolution; only after that could there be a shift toward cooperation. The transition to a cooperative society would take several steps. The first was the overthrow of the ruling class and the seizing of the means of production, because it created a neutral environment that rid subsequent transformations of resurgent class conflict. The eradication of class conflict was a prerequisite, according to Lenin: "socialism cannot be established without a class struggle for the political power and a state." This had neither been achieved by the time of, nor was it in the blueprint of, say, Robert Owen's *A New View of Society* (1813). But it had been achieved in Russia by 1923, and this made all the difference. It is what allowed Lenin to push forward to the next stage: cooperatives. Political change made possible cultural transformation, or what Lenin referred to as "a cultural revolution." He explained:

> The radical modification is this; formerly we placed, and had to place, the main emphasis on the political struggle, on revolution, on winning political power, etc. Now the emphasis is changing and shifting to peaceful, organizational, "cultural" work. I should say that emphasis is shifting to educational work, were it not for our international relations, were it not for the fact that we have to fight for our position on a worldscale. If we leave that aside, however, and confine ourselves to internal economic relations, the emphasis in our work is certainly shifting to education.

That shift toward education, Lenin argued, was necessary to render agricultural workers literate and to organize them in cooperative societies: "the economic object of this educational work among the peasants is to organize the latter in cooperative societies."[31]

In the end, Lenin rehabilitated cooperatives from a Marxist perspective. C. L. R. James also embraced this argument for cooperatives in his analysis of the situation in Ghana at the time of Kwame Nkrumah, drawing on Lenin's writings as a model.[32] This approach was also reflected in the work of other African leaders, as in Julius Nyerere's Arusha Declaration on the African idea of cooperation, or *ujamaa*. Seeing what was happening with cooperation in Tanzania, James concluded in 1977: "I remain now, as I was then, more than ever convinced that once again something new had come out of Africa, pointing out the road not only for Africa and Africans but for all those seeking to lift ourselves from the parlous conditions of our collapsing century."[33]

The passage of time has changed things. It has created a new form of complete and utter human interdependence. It has also revealed the omnipresence of cooperation. With a growing movement for cooperatives, solidarity and ecological economics, and new forms of mutualism, it has become clear that we can now envisage a cooperative society without the radical political revolution that Lenin and others called for. There has been an inversion of the cultural and the political, or perhaps an embeddedness, which means that we can now achieve coöperism through our deliberate choices. We do not need to wait for a revolution. We can choose coöperism now.

ON THE CHALLENGE OF UTOPIANISM

Many people will object that the idea of coöperism replacing the punishment paradigm with a cooperation paradigm is outlandishly utopian. Skeptics will argue that the idea of a society of cooperation without punishment is unrealistic. How is it even possible to imagine a modern, postindustrial society that does not punish?

Before you dismiss the argument out of hand, it is worth considering a few things that, taken together, make clear that the distance between our present punitive society and one that punishes justly is perhaps as far, if not further, than that between our present society and one based on cooperation. In other words, there is probably more work to be done to realize a society that comes close to just punishment, however defined, than one that does not punish. In the end, it is probably less utopian to aspire to a world of cooperation.

First, as a factual matter, the vast majority of victims of crime in the United States do not see their victimizer punished.[34] Fewer than one out of three property victimizations and four out of ten crimes of violence are even reported to police.[35] Of those, only a fraction result in investigation and arrest. Clearance rates for reported crimes, meaning only that someone was arrested for the offense, are minimal: 17.2 percent for all reported property crimes in 2019, 30.5 percent for reported robberies, 32.9 percent for reported rapes, and 45.5 percent for all reported violent crime.[36] This means that less than 20 percent of violent victimization results in an arrest. And typically, only about two-thirds of those arrests for violent crimes result in prosecution.[37] In other words, the vast majority of persons who are victims of crime, even violent crime, do not experience the satisfaction of punishment. For most crimes, the forms of coercion and fraud that surround us today, there is no punishment. We don't punish; we scapegoat. We find one or two people—or two million—and punish them brutally. We put them in cages for twenty-six years or more; we place them in solitary confinement for decades.[38] As to all the other offending, for the most part we don't even blink an eye; we let it go. That is a reality that is unlikely to change anytime soon.

Second, punishment in the United States is not only horrific, but it is also meted out in a demonstrably racist fashion.[39] At every step of the criminal legal ordeal, persons of color are stopped, arrested, detained, prosecuted, sentenced, imprisoned, and even executed, disproportionately not only to their share of the general population but to their share of criminal activity.[40] From the most extreme to the most minor forms of punishment, across practically every metric and dimension, punishment is exercised in a racist manner. The death penalty in the United States, for instance, is grossly disproportionately administered in homicide cases involving white victims, holding constant all other likely covariates.[41] The racial problem with the death penalty, in fact, reaches deeper than just race to the specific skin tone and stereotypically Black facial features of accused persons.[42] At the other extreme, police stop-and-frisks in a city like New York are disproportionately targeted at persons of color.[43]

Third, both theoretically and empirically, the traditional justifications for punishment are not well founded. There is, for instance, no reliable social-scientific evidence of a deterrent effect to punishment.[44] Selective incapacitation as well is more myth than reality; in large part, it has simply fueled mass incarceration, which it was intended to eliminate. Utilitarian theories of punishment are, for the most part, only theories. Moreover, there is no honest way to tranche the religious or deontological justifications for punishment—that is, to adjudicate whether a Judeo-Christian principle of an eye for an eye or a Kantian principle of *jus talionis* is right or wrong. It would require a treatise for me to establish this, and I cannot do it justice in the confines of this book, but the truth is, there is simply no way for society at large to agree on a set of truth conditions that would allow us to determine whether retributive justifications for punishment are correct. Religious arguments for punishment require a leap of faith; similarly, deontological arguments for punishment require a leap of reason. So, the traditional justifications for punishment fall short.

Fourth, there are a number of good reasons to be skeptical about punishment in general. So, for instance, when it comes to our children, our partners, our family members, our peers, and our colleagues, we tend to strive as much as possible to *avoid* punishment. For the most part, we do everything we can to avoid punishing our children, our loved ones, and those we respect and treat with equal dignity. In other words, when we are dealing with people whom we treat with dignity and respect, we try to avoid punishing them. In addition, we do not allow private citizens to punish. We consider that to be vigilantism or mere revenge, and we reserve punishment for the state. In fact, we define the state in terms of the power to punish and the legitimate monopoly on violence. We do so despite the fact that the American state has shown itself to be uniquely bad at the task. This should, at the very least, raise a doubt in our minds about punishment (also about the obligations of the state: rather than a monopoly on violence, why do we not define the state in terms of an obligation to ensure our well-being?) Moreover, from a utilitarian perspective, punishment is a bad thing. As Bentham stated most clearly, punishment is the intentional infliction of pain, and pain is quintessentially a disutility. Bentham could not have been clearer on this: "All punishment is mischief: all punishment in itself is evil."[45] Punishment is justified from a utilitarian perspective only if it increases overall social welfare. This means that a proponent of punishment would have a lot of empirical work to do to establish that American punishment practices are actually making the world a better place.

When you put all these points together, the burden on the proponents of just punishment is far greater than that on those who want to transcend the punishment paradigm.[46] We are much further from a society that punishes justly than we are from a society that does not punish. The chaos and turmoil that we experience in American society today is more likely the effect of a deficiency of just punishment than of a lack of punishment. In the end, it is far more unrealistic to believe in the possibility of just punishment than to imagine a society without punishment.

ON THE REFORMIST ALTERNATIVE

Finally, many progressives will argue for reformist measures on punishment rather than wholesale replacement of the punishment paradigm. Even some abolitionists are willing to consider what they call "nonreformist reforms," reforms that genuinely pursue or contribute to an abolitionist agenda. Ruth Wilson Gilmore refers to these reforms as "changes that, at the end of the day, unravel rather than widen the net of social control through criminalization."[47] As Dan Berger, Mariame Kaba, and David Stein observe, "Central to abolitionist work are the many fights for non-reformist reforms—those measures that reduce the power of an oppressive system while illuminating the system's inability to solve the crises it creates." They add:

> abolitionists have insisted on reforms that reduce rather than strengthen the scale and scope of policing, imprisonment, and surveillance.
> . . . The history of the American carceral state is one in which reforms have often grown the state's capacity to punish: reforms of indeterminate sentencing led to mandatory minimums, the death penalty to life without parole, sexual

violence against gender-nonconforming people gave rise to "gender-respon-
sive" prisons. Instead of pushing to adopt the Finnish model of incarceration—
itself a far-fetched enterprise—abolitionists have engaged these contradictions
by pursuing reforms that shrink the state's capacity for violence.[48]

For abolitionists, the idea of nonreformist reforms is that they are ultimately
oriented toward ending the punishment paradigm. As Amna Akbar writes,
"Rather than aiming to improve police through better regulation and more
resources, reform rooted in an abolitionist horizon aims to contest and then to
shrink the role of police, ultimately seeking to transform our political, economic,
and social order to achieve broader social provision for human needs."[49] Jocelyn
Simonson notes, "The relationship between abolition (as the goal) and reform (as
a means to an end) remains a live debate. Many continue to endorse what Wilson
Gilmore calls 'non-reformist reforms'—in other words, reforms that shrink the
carceral system and thus continue to move us incrementally, in the words of abolitionist organizer Mariame Kaba, 'toward the horizon of abolition.'"[50]

Simonson catalogues the types of nonreformist reforms that most progressives can agree on: "abolishing solitary confinement and capital punishment;
moratoriums on prison construction or expansion; freeing survivors of physical
and sexual violence, the elderly, infirm, juveniles, and all political prisoners; sentencing reform; ending cash bail; abolishing electronic monitoring, broken win-
dows policing, and the criminalization of poverty; and a federal jobs and homes
guarantee for the formerly incarcerated."[51] Kaba, for instance, in a New York Times
op-ed "Yes, We Mean Literally Abolish the Police," includes a paragraph proposing a 50 percent cut in police funding, short of complete abolition.[52] Dorothy
Roberts further distinguishes between those reforms that "correct problems perceived as aberrational flaws in the system," which "only help to legitimize and
strengthen its operation," and those reforms that "reduce the power of an oppressive system while illuminating the system's inability to solve the crises it creates,"
adding, in relation to her own project, "Abolition constitutionalism could support many of the nonreformist reforms in which prison abolitionists and other
activists are already engaged."[53]

But not all abolitionists agree. Some believe that even nonreformist reforms
risk being appropriated by those invested in the punitive society. Máximo Langer
reminds us of Thomas Mathiesen's critique of the notion of "non-reformist
reforms" in Mathiesen's 1974 book, The Politics of Abolition. Mathiesen conceded

that such an idea was "theoretically interesting" but, in contrast to others, maintained that even nonreformist reforms are not truly safe from being appropriated by those interested in perpetuating the status quo.[54]

In my opinion, the concept of "nonreformist reforms" merely allows us to skirt the inherent contradictions and tensions in abolitionism and, for that reason, should be avoided. It does not resolve anything, it just brushes the contradictions under the rug. Better to face them, embrace them, and take uncomfortable positions recognizing that there are inevitable friction in our politics.

Reform of the punishment paradigm is too fraught. The reason is that reform efforts were born in tandem with the punishment paradigm itself, with the prison, and with the punitive society. In fact, many of the central institutions and practices of punishment today constitute reforms of earlier forms of punishment. The penitentiary itself was born as a reformation of corporal punishment and torture, and the current institutions have only survived because they are constantly viewed as needing reform and being reformed. Angela Davis opened her book *Are Prisons Obsolete?* on this theme:

> It is ironic that the prison itself was a product of concerted efforts by reformers to create a better system of punishment. If the words "prison reform" so easily slip from our lips, it is because "prison" and "reform" have been inextricably linked since the beginning of the use of imprisonment as the main means of punishing those who violate social norms.

In her epigraph, she points the reader to a passage from Foucault's *Discipline and Punish*:

> One should recall that the movement for reforming the prisons, for controlling their functioning is not a recent phenomenon. It does not even seem to have originated in a recognition of failure. Prison "reform" is virtually contemporary with the prison itself: it constitutes, as it were, its programme.[55]

In *Discipline and Punish*, Foucault went on to say:

> From the outset, the prison was caught up in a series of accompanying mechanisms, whose purpose was apparently to correct it, but which seem to form part of its very functioning, so closely have they been bound up with its

existence throughout its long history. . . . There were inquiries. . . . There were
societies for supervising the functioning of the prisons and for suggesting
improvements. . . . There were programmes drawn up to improve the functioning of the machine-prison . . . [and] publications that sprang more or less
directly from the prison and were drawn up either by philanthropists . . . or a
little later by "specialists" . . . or, again, by former prisoners . . .

The prison should not be seen as an inert institution, shaken at intervals
by reform movements. The "theory of the prison" was its constant set of oper-
ational instructions rather than its incidental criticism—one of its conditions
of functioning.[56]

The prison has lasted and survived primarily because it is considered a reform
institution constantly in need of reform and of being reformed—in effect, because
it never seems to achieve its objective and thus always needs to be rethought and
reformed. How long should we continue to play that game?

The same is true of the police function. Abolitionist writers recount the dis-
illusioning history of wave upon wave of police reform commissions and reform
projects that have been implemented with great hopes but have led nowhere.[57]
The history goes back at least to 1894 with the Lexow Committee that inves-
tigated police misconduct in New York City; it runs through the well-known
Wickersham Commission in 1931, the Kerner Commission in 1967, and most
recently, President Obama's Task Force on Twenty-First-Century Policing. As
Mariame Kaba emphasizes, "These commissions didn't stop the violence; they
just served as a kind of counterinsurgent function each time police violence led
to protests." The most recent Obama Task Force, Kaba argues, recommended
piecemeal reforms in the wake of the police killings of Michael Brown and Eric
Garner, "procedural tweaks like implicit-bias training, police-community listen-
ing sessions, slight alterations of use-of-force policies and systems to identify
potentially problematic officers early on."[58] But they had little or no effect. Many
policing reforms had been implemented in Minneapolis, Kaba emphasizes, but
none of that stopped the ghastly killing of George Floyd.

In light of this history, I would argue that the concept of nonreformist reforms
simply avoids the real question: whether the criminal law and its enforcement
serves to redress harms or imposes a social and racial order. The turn to nonreformist reforms dodges the central challenge to the punishment paradigm, in
much the same way as the "truth must lie somewhere in between, as it always

does" response. It avoids it by finding the political and policy overlap in the Venn diagram of the progressive and abolitionist agendas. Finding the overlap can be useful, pragmatically, but it does nothing to solve the inherent contradictions or resolve the fundamental question of criminal law and its enforcement. Reaching consensus by finding an overlap simply allows the two ships to pass silently in the night. In any event, regardless of one's position on nonreformist reforms, they should not be allowed to get in the way of coöperism.

CHAPTER 8

Cooperation Democracy

More democracies are failing today and veering into autocracy than at any point in the past century. According to the Varieties of Democracy Institute at the University of Gothenburg in Sweden, the number of liberal democracies in the world is steadily declining. It now stands at thirty-four nations representing about 13 percent of the global population, the lowest level in over a quarter century, down from forty-two countries at its peak in 2012. The number of closed autocracies has increased from twenty-five to thirty since 2011, now representing 26 percent of the world's population. Countries with electoral autocracies represent 44 percent of the world's population, or about 3.4 billion people. In addition, toxic polarization is rising around the globe. Toxic polarization—defined as declining respect for counterarguments, opposition, and pluralism—got more severe in thirty-two countries in 2021, compared to only five countries in 2011.[1]

We are experiencing a democratic crisis around the world. In the United States, the situation is critical. When Donald Trump was elected in 2016, many Democrats believed that the Russians had helped get him elected and questioned the legitimacy of his mandate. Four years later, when Joe Biden was elected, Trump, his advisers, and a mass of his supporters challenged the peaceful transition of the presidency. The January 6th insurrection was an armed and violent uprising intended to keep Trump in power despite his electoral loss. On the right, many Republicans continue to believe Trump's unfounded claims of a stolen election. There is growing anxiety about the fragility of American democracy. The *New York Times* carried an extensive and probing series of opinion pieces following January 6th, including essays by former President Jimmy Carter ("I Fear for Our

Democracy"), my colleague and friend Jedediah Britton-Purdy ("The Republican Party Is Succeeding Because We Are Not a True Democracy"), well-known political essayists Rebecca Solnit and Francis Fukuyama, and other thinkers across the political spectrum, decrying the threat to democracy.[2] The editorial board of the *Times* ran its own opinion piece under the title "Every Day Is Jan. 6 Now," arguing that the country faces an ongoing daily threat to its democratic institutions: "the Republic faces an existential threat from a movement that is openly contemptuous of democracy and has shown that it is willing to use violence to achieve its ends," the board wrote. "No self-governing society can survive such a threat by denying that it exists."[3] Many argued for the urgency of strengthening existing democratic institutions. "The sooner we do," the *New York Times* editorial board concluded, "the sooner we might hope to salvage a democracy that is in grave danger."[4]

Some of the rhetoric was overblown, and some of it is misleading. The United States is not a 250-year-old democracy at the brink of failure. It is a young and fledgling democracy that just barely withstood a stress test in 2021. The United States was founded as a republic, to be exact a representative aristocracy, not a democracy. It was not a democracy during the antebellum period when Black people were enslaved and Indigenous peoples were displaced and killed. It was not a democracy before women acquired national suffrage in 1920 or prior to the Voting Rights Act of 1965 that sought to lift Jim Crow restrictions on Black voters. For most of its history, the United States has been a representative republic with limited franchise, not a democracy. And still today, with voter suppression, political gerrymandering, unlimited corporate spending on elections, low (55-62 percent) voter turnout in the most important national presidential elections, the United States is a young, limping democracy at best. The problem is not just the counter-majoritarian dimensions of American democratic institutions, such as the Electoral College and the U.S. Senate, which are not democratically representative and undermine fair and equal democratic representation; there are many ongoing challenges to full and fair elections and one-person-one-vote principles in the United States.

But even if we set all that aside, there remains a problem with all the discourse about the threats to democracy, a problem that is reflected in the recent global findings by the Varieties of Democracy Institute, namely that we often focus too much on the *form* of democracy and not sufficiently on the *quality* of democracy.

Electoral democracy is not something to be valued in and of itself. Democratic elections are not a be-all and end-all, especially if they lead to authoritarian forms of governing. There must be certain *substantive* limits to the notion of democracy, above and beyond the procedural definitions.

THE PARADOX OF DEMOCRATIC THEORY

This raises a central paradox in democratic theory regarding the relationship between the procedural and substantive dimensions of democracies. Democracy is generally defined along procedural lines. It is a political decision-making process that privileges the general public, rather than an elite aristocratic group or a single autocrat. General definitions of democracy are heavily weighted toward the procedural dimension. For a political system to be considered minimally democratic (what some call an electoral democracy), there needs to be at a minimum fair and open elections with universal suffrage and some freedom of expression and assembly. In defining liberal democracy, most people add to fair and open elections a respect for individual rights, functioning courts, the rule of law, and some constraints on the executive.[5] But the root and core of all definitions of democracy is fair elections open to all citizens. The form that a democracy can take may vary, from representational democracy to direct democracy, but throughout all definitions of democracy, there is a strong procedural element. We identify a democracy when we believe that the people have a say in political decisions or that all citizens participate in the decision-making process through fair and open elections.

This creates a tension between form and substance: the trouble is that even when there are fair and open elections, and other guarantees such as a free press, the outcomes of democratic decision making are not always worthy. Democratic processes can produce discrimination against minorities, despite counter-majoritarian safeguards. In the United States, for instance, the racially discriminatory and exponential increase in incarceration discussed in chapter 6, resulting in one in nine, or more than 10 percent, of African-American men between the ages of twenty and thirty-four being caged behind bars, occurred through a democratic process involving democratically elected Democratic and Republican administrations. None of the safeguards prevents the possibility that a democracy may reach terrible decisions.[6] They can sometimes lead to very nondemocratic outcomes. In fact, they can even result in the election of authoritarian leaders. Even high-participation democracy may not prevent dreadful outcomes.[7] At those moments, the tension between form and substance is at its most acute. Most defenders of democracy will defend democracy up to a point, but not where the outcomes are unacceptable. That's when substantive checks on democratic decision making become necessary.

This is where the notion of coöperist democracy, or "cooperation democracy" to make it easier on the tongue, is so powerful and helpful. The point is, not all democracies are worth fighting for, only those that are imbued with coöperism. Cooperation democracy can define substantive limits to democratic theory along the lines of coöperism, understood as the practices and institutions that promote the core values and principles of cooperation and extend them throughout every aspect of our lives.

Anyone invested in politics is not going to settle for a democracy that functions formally but legitimately goes off the rails. We do not want a democracy that merely functions; we want a democracy that functions well. The difficulty is how to identify a substantive check that does not simply impose outcomes nondemocratically—in other words, how to place substantive limits on a democracy that do not end up being undemocratic. Cooperation democracy does that by extending the practice of genuine participatory democracy and one-person-one-vote principles throughout every aspect of our lives, including work, consumption, production, and mutual support. Cooperation democracy is not undemocratic. To the contrary, it enshrines as its first core value and principle full participatory democracy across the board. In other words, it is a substantive limit to democratic theory that has at its heart a principle of democracy.

Cooperation democracy injects a substantive democratic limiting principle right into the center of democratic theory. It privileges only those democratic regimes that promote concentrated forms of cooperation: those that place all citizens on an equal footing, that give everyone a full participatory role in all aspects of their lives, that promote the values and principles of self-determination, solidarity, sustainability, and mutualism at the heart of coöperism. What cooperation democracy offers, then, is a vision of democracy that is fully democratic both procedurally and substantively, tying the notion of democratic decision making to institutions and practices that truly make possible one-person-one-vote, equal citizenship, solidarity, and sustainability. The ambition is to put all the people, including those who have traditionally been disadvantaged, in a position such that they can and do fully exercise their democratic rights. Cooperation democracy, I would argue, is a truly democratic ideal worth fighting for.

THE RELATIONSHIP TO ABOLITION DEMOCRACY

There are precursors to the notion of cooperation democracy. In the early twentieth century, you will recall, the Cooperative League of the United States of America spoke of creating a "Cooperative Commonwealth."[8] Recall also that James Peter Warbasse, discussed in chapter 5, titled his 1923 manifesto *Co-operative Democracy*.[9] There have been many proposals to anchor democracy in cooperation. Perhaps one of the most relevant here is W. E. B. Du Bois's notion of "abolition democracy," at least as it is interpreted by Angela Davis, Eduardo Mendieta, and others. Let me focus on this last concept.

The term *abolition democracy* is a complicated one in Du Bois's writings, because he uses it in several different ways. I will use it here to speak specifically about a notion of democracy that is "abolitionist," in the sense that it seeks to get rid of practices and institutions like slavery and its afterlife, including convict leasing, plantation prisons, and racialized mass incarceration, that undermine the equal humanity of all citizens. It seeks to put in place instead institutions that could found a society based on equality and democratic participation. As Robin D. G. Kelley notes, there were other precursors to the idea of abolition democracy, including T. Thomas Fortune's book *Black and White: Land, Labor, and Politics in the South*, in which he specifically called on the South to "spend less money on penitentiaries and more money on schools." But for reasons that Kelley and Seth Moglen detail, including Fortune's complex alliance with Booker T. Washington, the focus has remained on Du Bois, who coined the term *abolition democracy*.[10]

W. E. B. Du Bois on Abolition Democracy

In *Black Reconstruction in America*, Du Bois argued that the reconstructive work necessary to achieve the ambition of a racially just society, begun with Emancipation, was abandoned when Reconstruction was brutally aborted in 1877. As a result, the abolition of slavery was accomplished only in the narrow sense that chattel slavery was ended, but the true ambition, the creation of a racially just society, was never realized. It required the construction of new institutions, new practices, and new social relations that would have afforded freed Black persons the economic, political, and social capital to live as equal members of society.

That ambition, as Du Bois documents in *Black Reconstruction*, was thwarted by White resistance and terror during the decade following the end of the Civil War and ultimately abandoned with the political compromise of 1876–77, which resulted in the negotiated election of President Rutherford B. Hayes and the withdrawal of federal troops from the South. It was thwarted by a reign of White terrorism, accentuated in, but not limited to, the South. After the Civil War, as Du Bois wrote, the South "looked backward toward slavery," with the passage of Black Codes and the rise of the Klan.[11] Mississippi, for instance, "simply reenacted her slave code and made it operative so far as punishments were concerned."[12] The period after the war was truly a reign of terror: the formerly enslaved were held back by brute force, terrorized, killed, and dispossessed. As Du Bois observed, "war may go on more secretly, more spasmodically, and yet as truly as before the peace. This was the case in the South after Lee's surrender."[13]

In the more aspirational passages of the book, Du Bois offered a vision of what a racially just society might look like and of the work necessary to achieve a just society. He placed this under the name *abolition democracy*: "Abolition-democracy demands for Negroes physical freedom, civil rights, economic opportunity and education and the right to vote, as a matter of sheer human justice and right."[14] It required establishing new institutions in society that would pave the way for equality. For Du Bois, it meant public education, jobs, and equal civil and political rights. These are the more visionary passages of Du Bois's book. In these aspirational passages, abolition democracy is described as an enlightened, righteous, just ambition, "based on freedom, intelligence and power for all men."[15]

In other passages, though, the notion of abolition democracy is tethered more to a historical interest analysis. In those passages, it is portrayed as an economically motivated, self-interested project of small capitalists and the labor movement, united in faith in individualism, on the one hand, and on the other hand, Northern industrialist capitalists who were opposed to slavery for profit motives and wanted to enlist Black labor for purposes of industrialization.[16] My colleague Derecka Purnell does a brilliant job of distinguishing between these two historical conceptions of abolition democracy in Du Bois's writings in her book *Becoming Abolitionists*.[17]

There are, then, in Du Bois's text several different battling conceptions of abolition democracy: the first, a more forward looking and aspirational ideal;[18] the other two more historical, at times the product of an alliance between laborers and small capitalists, at other times reflecting the interests of Northern industrialists, both of them far closer to Derrick Bell's theory of interest convergence.[19] These different conceptions of abolition democracy correspond, in effect, to an ideal vision for the future, on the one hand, and to the historical reality of what blocked it, on the other.[20] As Du Bois documents, many in the North were torn between them: "the one was abolition-democracy based on freedom, intelligence and power for all men; the other was industry for private profit directed by an autocracy determined at any price to amass wealth and power. The uncomprehending resistance of the South, and the pressure of black folk, made these two thoughts uneasy and temporary allies."[21]

The first, the ideal vision, was tied to the discourse of staunch abolitionists, such as Senator Charles Sumner and his inspiring speeches in 1866 that, in Du Bois's words, "laid down a Magna Charta of democracy in America."[22] It led to a moment of glory for the ideal of abolition democracy during Reconstruction: "Here for the first time there was established between the white and black of this country a contact on terms of essential social equality and mutual respect . . . on the whole, the result was one of the most astonishing successes in new and sudden human contacts." This ideal offered the possibility of "endowed Negro education, legal civil rights, and eventually even votes for Negroes to offset the Southern threat of economic attack." It was tied to a vision of federal government intervention through civil rather than military means. "The abolition-democracy," Du Bois explained, "advocated Federal control to guide and direct the rise of the Negro, but they desired this control to be civil rather than military."[23]

The second, the historical reality, was associated at times with a momentary alliance of smaller capitalists and workers, aiming to bring Black persons into the workforce and to protect against Southern backlash. "The abolition-democracy was the liberal movement among both laborers and small capitalists," Du Bois explained, "who united in the American Assumption [the myth of individualism and the self-made man], but saw the danger of slavery to both capital and labor." Along these lines, there was a historical potential, ultimately unrealized, for labor to unite. As Du Bois suggested, this historical articulation of abolition democracy "pushed towards the conception of a dictatorship of labor, although few of its advocates wholly grasped the fact that this necessarily involved dictatorship by labor over capital and industry."[24] At other times, Du Bois describes the historical discourse of abolition democracy as Northern industrialists opposing slavery with the ambition of tapping a new source of labor, Black workers, for their own benefit up North.

It is possible to untangle these battling conceptions of abolition democracy, as the philosopher Robert Gooding-Williams does, by distinguishing between an ideal of abolition democracy, on the one hand, and the actual historical movements for abolition democracy, on the other.[25] This leaves us, then, with the possibility of an ideal vision of abolition democracy different from its historical manifestations. Gooding-Williams reminds us of what ultimately emerged in American history: rather than abolition democracy, the country veered toward what Du Bois called democratic despotism and a new imperialism.[26] Du Bois did not sugarcoat the situation; he called it out in no uncertain terms.[27] He wrote: "[Northern industry] began in 1876 an exploitation which was built on much the same sort of slavery which it helped to overthrow in 1863. It murdered democracy in the United States so completely that the world does not recognize its corpse."[28]

Angela Davis on Abolition Democracy

Angela Davis built on the first, ideal vision of abolition democracy in Du Bois's work and turned it into a broader ambition to abolish not just the direct legacies of slavery but the punitive society more broadly. Her vision was tied to a transformation of our political economy, one with more of a socialist ambition. There are several steps to her argument.

To begin with, Davis and members of Critical Resistance tied the idea of abolition democracy to the larger goal of abolishing what they called the "prison industrial complex" (PIC), a term intended to highlight the way the prison (standing in for the broader punitive state) was inextricably linked to industrialized advanced capitalism. As with slavery, simply reforming or even abolishing the prison, Davis explained, would only result in new institutions of systemic racism. Prison abolition had to be accompanied by "the creation of an array of social institutions that would begin to solve the social problems that set people on the track to prison."[29] As Davis argues in her book *Are Prisons Obsolete?*, these new institutions would not replicate the prison, using similar practices and institutions, but replace it:

> We would not be looking for prisonlike substitutes for the prison, such as house arrest safeguarded by electronic surveillance bracelets. Rather, positing decarceration as our overarching strategy, we would try to envision a continuum of alternatives to imprisonment—demilitarization of schools, revitalization of education at all levels, a health system that provides free physical and mental care to all, and a justice system based on reparation and reconciliation rather than retribution and vengeance.[30]

These alternatives include "job and living wage programs, alternatives to the disestablished welfare program, community-based recreation, and many more."[31] As Dorothy Roberts argues as well, in her 2007 article "Constructing a Criminal Justice System Free of Racial Bias: An Abolitionist Framework":

> Abolishing these institutions [mass incarceration, capital punishment, and police terror] should be accompanied by a redirection of criminal justice spending to rebuild the neighborhoods that they have devastated. There should be a massive infusion of resources to poor and low-income neighborhoods to help residents build local institutions, support social networks, and create social citizenship.[32]

Davis was always clear that her vision for a just society, like Du Bois's, requires economic and institutional transformation, not just abolition.[33] It requires, in the words of Ruth Wilson Gilmore, "campaigns that both create solid organizations and foster robust coalitions among already existing organizations."[34] Derecka Purnell and others continue to emphasize this today: the struggle for abolition is part of a larger struggle for "self-determination, an end to capitalism, the return of Indigenous land, the redistribution of land for newly freed Black people, and for autonomous regions where communities could test their independence."[35] It aims also to address the crises of ableism, transphobia, and sexual violence through an abolitionist paradigm.[36]

Many abolitionists, including Davis, Purnell, Gilmore, and others, are oriented more toward socialist visions. Purnell writes, "For me and many of my peers, our abolitionist fight and future is committed to decolonization, disability justice, Earth justice, and socialism."[37] Davis explains:

> I'm convinced that the ultimate eradication of racism is going to require us to move toward a more socialist organization of our economies, of our other institutions. I think we have a long way to go before we can begin to talk about an economic system that is not based on exploitation and the super exploitation of Black people, Latinx people, other racialized populations. But I do think that we now have the conceptual means to engage in discussions—popular discussions—about capitalism. Occupy, it was new language. The notion of the prison industrial complex requires us to understand the globalization of capitalism. Anticapitalist consciousness helps us to understand the predicament of immigrants, who are barred from the US by the wall that has

been created by the current occupant. These conditions have been created by global capitalism. This is a period during which we need to begin a process of popular education, which will allow people to understand the interconnections of racism, hetero-patriarchy, capitalism.[38]

The reason, for Davis, is clear: it is possible to abolish one specific form of property (chattel slavery or prison labor), but without transforming property relations writ large, racial oppression will be reestablished. If the relations of production and exchange are not transformed, the same forms of racial exploitation will take place.

New Abolitionism and an Ethic of Care

The swelling abolitionist movement, discussed in chapter 6, has taken the baton, drawing in part on Du Bois's and Davis's discussion of abolition democracy, arguing for the abolition of the police, prisons, juvenile detention facilities, immigration detention, and border policing and proposing new forms of cooperation instead.[39] It is the culmination of a long historical trajectory dating back to the first abolitionist movements and including, more recently, liberation movements from the 1960s, prison revolts from the 1970s, and the founding in the late 1980s and 1990s of Critical Resistance by Angela Davis, Rose Braz, Rachel Herzing, and others.[40] This second wave of abolitionism targets not only the prison and police but, more broadly, the social and economic structures that legitimize prisons and produce a punitive society.[41] Its ambition, in the words of Fred Moten and Stefano Harney, is "not so much the abolition of prisons, but the abolition of a society that could have prisons, that could have slavery, that could have the wage, and therefore not abolition as the elimination of anything but abolition as the founding of a new society."[42]

In their book *Abolition. Feminism. Now.*, Angela Davis, Gina Dent, Erica Meiners, and Beth Richie emphasize how their vision is inextricably linked to antiracism and anticapitalism and, in that sense, is tied to the longer arc of Black feminism that goes back to the Combahee River Collective statement of 1977.[43] They embrace a robust conception of abolition that is not limited to the negative task of abolishing certain institutions but also includes the positive task of reconstruction. At the same time, they highlight the need to assure the safety of women and nonbinary, queer, and transgender persons from violence and harm. Abolitionist feminism underscores the dual tasks of ensuring the welfare and safety of women and others harmed by patriarchy while, at the same time, not reverting to the punitive mechanisms of the state. As they explain, the struggle to end violence against women took on a carceral turn toward criminal law enforcement (mandatory arrest and no-drop policies, for instance) during the latter part of the twentieth century. Abolitionist feminist activism aims to end violence against women without recourse to the police or prisons, to find a different paradigm than the criminal justice system as a way to end violence against women. It embraces instead movements and organizations like INCITE! and others that oppose carceral feminism. This coming together of antiviolence and anticarceral creates a unique form of activism that is inextricably linked to a broader anticapitalist effort. This comes through, for instance, in the authors' criticism of Michelle Alexander and Ava DuVernay, in which they emphasize that the problems of racialized mass incarceration cannot be solved "by conventional and domestic civil rights activism" but will necessarily entail "disturbing larger global frameworks of power such as capitalism and heteropatriarchy."[44]

In its most robust expressions, the new abolitionist movement advocates for a society based on an ethic of care, mutual aid, and cooperation. Many of the practitioners place care at the core of their bold and audacious imaginations about a world without race or class oppression. They are not alone. A growing body of theory and practice of care has built on the foundations of the idea of an "ethic of care" developed in the works of Carol Gilligan, Nel Noddings, and others in the 1980s, in Joan Tronto's pathbreaking book *Caring Democracy*, and in other engagements with the politics of care, including *The Care Manifesto* of the Care Collective.[45] These ideals are tied to community building, social transformation, solidarity, and love.[46] Dean Spade speaks about "scaling up" mutual-aid work "to a point where everyone has what they need."[47] Bryan Stevenson focuses attention on the relationship among care, health, and well-being. In an interview on "How America Can Heal," Stevenson remarks: "We're going to have to talk about ending crime in a meaningful way and that's not more police, and more prisons, and more punishment. It is actually interventions rooted in care [and] a belief in what can happen when people recover from the things that have burdened them."[48] Patrisse Cullors adds:

> Abolition is about how we treat each other. It is about how we show up in relationships. Abolition is about how we respond to harm caused and how we respond when we cause harm. . . . We need to be committed to building a culture that is rooted in care, dignity, and accountability.[49]

Cooperation is also at the heart of it, as Mariame Kaba suggests in *We Do This 'Til We Free Us*:

> People like me who want to abolish prisons and police, however, have a vision of a different society, built on cooperation instead of individualism, on mutual aid instead of self-preservation. What would the country look like if it had billions of extra dollars to spend on housing, food and education for all? This change in society wouldn't happen immediately, but the protests show that many people are ready to embrace a different vision of safety and justice.[50]

Somewhat like Du Bois's ideal of abolition democracy, the new abolitionists articulate a robust vision that has, on my reading, a tripartite structure. It includes, first, the negative task of abolishing the institutions of domination and punishment; second, the positive task of creating new social institutions for housing, jobs, food, health, and education; and third, the radical task of transforming our political economy. The third task can take different forms depending on the author: social democratic, socialist, anarchist, left libertarian, or other. For Derecka Purnell, it takes the form of "robust movements for socialism, decolonization, disability justice, and Earth justice" and an ideal of a socialist world where "everyone would have a decent place to live, enough food to eat, clean water to drink, clean air to breathe, medical attention when they need it, warm clothes for the cold weather, a good education, and the ability to develop to their fullest potential."[51] That is, indeed, an inspiring vision.

TOWARD COOPERATION DEMOCRACY

Cooperation democracy has a similar tripartite structure. In emphasizing participatory democracy and the core values and principles of cooperation, it puts the first emphasis on the third element: establishing an integrated theory and practice of coöperism. It starts by combining and leveraging the most promising forms of cooperatives, mutuals, nonprofits, mutual-aid projects, and other support networks, those that most embody the core values and principles of cooperation and that, together, form an integrated political theory and practice. It then builds on that integrated economic regime to develop even more institutions that will displace the reality of tournament or state dirigisme. And, on the basis of this political and economic framework, it makes possible the replacement of the punishment paradigm with a social theory and practice of cooperation, a cooperation paradigm. In a sense, it inverts the logic, and the temporality, of the tripartite structure.

With participatory democratic decision making as one of its core values and principles, cooperation democracy provides a limiting principle for democratic theory; in this way, it can save democratic theory. Cooperation democracy envisages a society in which people work together to create better work environments and training, education, and apprenticeships that make possible collaboration on an equal footing, an equal say in the management of enterprises, and respect for the working and living environment. Apprenticeships could form a key dimension, drawing on the Swiss apprenticeship model that has proven so successful as integrating younger people into the economy, but modifying it to promote the values and principles of cooperation.[52] Nonprofits and community organizations can help create supportive living environments, greener spaces, and the values of solidarity and caring for others; worker and consumer cooperatives can promote the fifth core principle of cooperatives, education and training. Cooperation democracy aims for a society in which everyone will achieve their full potential.

Coöperism places a limit on democracy. It has as its goal democratic participation throughout all aspects of our lives. In the end, there is no reason to support just any form of majoritarian decision making. A majority vote, even with freedoms and counter-majoritarian checks, does not guarantee favorable outcomes. It does not ensure equity and nondiscrimination, and neither do the conventional counter-majoritarian devices like courts, especially when those are subject to political appointment. What is urgently needed today is a limiting principle on democracy that is substantive, not just procedural. That is what coöperism provides and makes possible. Cooperation democracy offers a new democratic theory worth fighting for.

THE AGE OF COÖPERISM

This is the dawning of an age of coöperism. A future of integrated cooperative projects and mutual collaborations is on the horizon. They will augur a more sustainable, equitable, democratic, and caring society that operates on the paradigm of cooperation. There is no need to wait to realize this ambition. There is no need to convince a majority of other people. No need to seize power, nor to dismantle the state. Each of us can determine, or continue, to work together to concentrate, leverage, and compound cooperation and watch coöperism grow like a snowball rolling down a hill. The models of cooperation are at hand. The core values and principles are crystal clear. We can do this together now.

Rather than conclude these reflections, which are intended instead to be an opening, I will attempt in these final pages to recap as succinctly as possible the ground covered in order to lay a clear foundation for the trajectory ahead.

Global climate change has created, for humans, a form of extreme interdependence that could never have been imagined before. Humans have become symbiotic, codependent to an unprecedented degree. This is the result of a long history of unrestrained competition and extraction of wealth that took the form, in the recent past, of imperialism, colonialism, slavery, apartheid, and exploitation—in sum, unconscionable and unlimited grabs for resources. The effects on our natural and social environment are now causing crises that are rippling through liberal democracies around the world. The dominant two responses are forms of either individualism or statism, but both are blocked and have become dead ends. Both require a supermajority to either shrink or empower the government. As the endless tug-of-war stretches on, polarization is rising; threats to democracy and the danger of civil strife are increasing. As the poles get further apart, there is more paralysis and gridlock: liberal democratic governments are increasingly unable to effectively pass or uphold their regulations, but their temporary mandates and interventions impede those who are trying to go it alone.

There is, however, another path that receives less attention because it does not depend on electoral politics. It is more promising, and realistic, because it draws on actually existing and successful practices—cooperatives, mutuals, credit unions, nonprofits, mutual aid. It can move forward on its own because it does not depend on widescale coordination, nor on the dismantling of the state. It is the path of cooperation based on the long-standing values and principles of cooperatives: democratic participation, equity, solidarity, respect for others and the environment. It operates on well-established principles of one-person-one-vote, the equitable distribution of wealth, caring for the welfare of all stakeholders and the Earth, sustainability, mutual aid and assistance, sharing, and being attentive to communal well-being. It is the paradigm of people working together, cooperating, and extending the ideal of participatory democracy to all the other areas of their lives, from consumer cooperatives to credit unions, from worker cooperatives to insurance mutuals, from nonprofits to mutual aid.

It turns out that these forms of cooperation surround us and that there is a growing movement toward cooperation in countries around the world: consumers who work together to coordinate consumption to support each other and the environment; producers who combine their harvest or farmers who share their equipment; workers who get together to form an owner-operated cooperative and share in the equitable distribution of their labor; residents who come together to comanage their living quarters and conditions; educators or lawyers who get together to work for the public interest in nonprofits and community organizations; citizens around the world who engage in mutual aid in times of crises. These forms of cooperation are flourishing in all corners of the world based on a unique logic, a logic of democratic participation and attention to the well-being of others and the environment.

The theory of coöperism builds on this momentum. It seeks to extend these forms of cooperation more widely, on the understanding that all forms of cooperation are beneficial but, even more, to concentrate and leverage the instances of cooperation that are most true to the core values and principles. Not all instances of cooperation are equally effective in addressing the global climate crisis and the other crises humans face, including growing inequalities within societies and threats to democracy. Some cooperative enterprises are not sufficiently attentive to worker welfare and may oppose worker unionization. Some ESOPs, community groups, and nonprofits retain hierarchical structures and management. Some retail cooperatives remain too focused on conventional profit motives. The ubiquity of cooperative enterprises demonstrates the real possibility of extending cooperation, but some instantiations of cooperation could be privileged and reinforced over others.

Coöperism is, first, a political theory and practice grounded in deliberate choice in the face of our newfound interdependence. Coöperism identifies and then integrates, leverages, and compounds the most promising cooperative initiatives. It seeks to distill the power of cooperation, the power that is generated by people working together, by the fact that the whole is greater than the sum of the parts. That greater element is precisely what I have called coöpower. The core idea of coöperism is to deploy and leverage that coöpower through forms of combination: to *combine* cooperation so that, for instance, worker cooperative distribute through consumer cooperatives; to *leverage* cooperation so that members of a worker cooperative, for example, obtain the credit they need to join the cooperative from a credit union, or get insurance from a mutual; to *concentrate* cooperation by doubling down on the core values and principles so that, for instance, the respect for all stakeholders extends further to all suppliers in the chain. Coöperism takes the most promising forms of cooperation and integrates them into a coordinated framework that extends the political notion of democratic participation to all aspects of life and promotes respect for the human environment, care for human well-being, equity, and solidarity.

Coöperism forms, second, an economic theory and practice that can displace existing economic regimes of dirigisme, what we conventionally call capitalism and communism (both misnomers). Capitalist economies, we were led to believe, were governed by the economic laws of capital: both the strongest proponents of capitalism (the free market economists of the Chicago School) and its staunchest opponents (Marxists and anarchists) held that capital had inherent traits that produced good (or bad) outcomes—that capital, in effect, has a force of its own. But capital does not exist as an autonomous thing. It is not alive. It is not governed by natural laws. It is purely a creature of the human-made laws surrounding incorporation, taxation, corporate finance, bankruptcy, etc. It can be privileged or disfavored. The term communism is equally misleading. The valiant idea of living together in common and sharing means of production most often results in a centralized state apparatus that tends toward authoritarianism. The model may possibly work under certain conditions for a small commune, but it does not scale up well to the level of a large economy. Instead, it too produces a form of dirigisme. It is time to end our various experiments in dirigisme and embrace a new economic regime of coöperism.

Coöperism provides, third, a social theory that would replace the punishment paradigm with a paradigm of cooperation. It proposes an alternative to the punitive society so pervasive in Western liberal democracies. Rather than leave people to their own devices and then punish them severely when they are accused of wrongdoing, coöperism begins by fostering education, job and skills training, mental health, counseling, and therapy through a deep investment in the core values of cooperation and a wide array of community nonprofit organizations, cooperatives, and mutual-aid projects.

Coöperism is the most promising way to address our urgent crises today. Worker cooperatives are focused on the working environment, not just profitability. Harmful emissions and carbon footprints are not just an externality for them, as they are for a distant shareholder of a publicly traded corporation intent on maximizing profits. Those environmental consequences affect the living and working environment for workers. Farmer cooperatives better utilize farm equipment and machinery, resulting in less consumption and waste, and a reduction of the carbon footprint of agriculture. Consumer cooperatives are oriented to servicing the needs of their members, including their health, welfare, and environment, and do not have as their goal, like many conventional stores, increased sales or consumption. The values and principles of cooperation place the environment at the heart of the enterprise.

By drawing on the core values of cooperation and mutualism, on the coöpower generated by people working together, on the political, economic, and social theory and practice of coöperism, a new world of cooperation democracy is within our grasp. I have no doubt that when the modern history of humankind is written in the next century or thereafter—assuming we make the right choices on global climate change—it will be a story of the transformation from feudal coercion to capitalist competition to cooperation democracy.

Acknowledgments

What if indeed, it is impossible in all ages, indeed in any age of human communities, of the human race as a global community, not to ask, "What more are we
to do?"

—Biodun Jeyifo, 2021[1]

In my last book, *Critique and Praxis*, I reformulated the question "What
is to be done?" and directed it at myself only. "What more am *I* to do?"
I asked. I did so to guard against speaking for anyone else. I had my dear
colleague Gayatri Chakravorty Spivak's admonition in mind—namely, that "ven-
triloquism" can so easily become the "intellectual's stock-in-trade."[2]

The critic Biodun Jeyifo took me to task. He acknowledged that reorienting
the question had some benefits. It served, in his words, as "a radical and honorable rejection of all forms of vanguardism and myths of the inevitability of the
triumph of revolutions in critique and praxis."[3] Nevertheless, he argued, it leaves
out a vital dimension: our collective work together. So, Biodun Jeyifo proposed
that we augment the revised formulation to address the question "What more are
we to do?"

I thank Biodun Jeyifo for that reformulation and have sought to address it in
this book. I acknowledge that all of my work has always been the collaborative
product of working arm in arm with my longtime partner, Mia Ruyter, and our
children, Isadora and Léonard; my longtime friends and colleagues; and now my
new teammates at the Initiative for a Just Society (IJS) Lisette Bamenga, Ken-
yatta Emmanuel, Che Gossett, Marissa Gutierrez-Vicario, Alexis Hoag, Derecka
Purnell, Fonda Shen, and Omavi Shukur; my brilliant research assistants Fonda

Shen again, Tanveer Singh, Alexis Marin, and Julia Udell; and my friends and coworkers Adebambo Adesanya, Anna Krauthamer, and Ghislaine Pagès. This book *is* the collaborative product of so many conversations, and sharing of ideas and practices, with friends and colleagues such as Amna Akbar, Amy Allen, Étienne Balibar, Leonard Benardo, Steve Bright, Tom Durkin, François Ewald, Jeremy Kessler, Daniele Lorenzini, Karuna Mantena, Martha Minow, Eben Moglen, Antonio Pele, David Pozen, Dorothy Roberts, Gayatri Chakravorty Spivak, Bryan Stevenson, Ann Stoler, Brandon Terry, Kendall Thomas, Jesús Velasco, Cornel West, Bruce Western, and so many more. I am in their debt, and in solidarity. I also want to thank my extraordinary editor, Eric Schwartz, for his encouragement, guidance, and fidelity; Lowell Frye at Columbia University Press for shepherding this book through to publication; and Jennifer Crewe for her constant support and leadership.

With humility, then—without in any way embracing any form of vanguardism—and with deep gratitude to all my working partners, I dedicate this book to them and to the question *What more are we to do together*?

Bernard E. Harcourt
New York City
November 10, 2022

Notes

GETTING STARTED

1. See *Special Report on Global Warming of 1.5°C* (SR15) (Geneva: Intergovernmental Panel on Climate Change [IPCC], October 8, 2018); Mark Lynas, Benjamin Z. Houlton, and Simon Perry, "Greater Than 99 Percent Consensus on Human Caused Climate Change in the Peer-Reviewed Scientific Literature," *Environmental Research Letters* 16, no. 11 (2021), https://doi.org/10.1088/1748-9326/ac2966; NASA Earth Observatory, "World of Change: Global Temperatures," https://earthobservatory.nasa.gov/world-of-change/global-temperatures.

2. See *Special Report on Global Warming of 1.5°C* (SR15); Lynas, Houlton, and Perry, "Greater Than 99 Percent Consensus on Human Caused Climate Change in the Peer-Reviewed Scientific Literature."

1. THE URGENCY OF COOPERATION

1. See Vanessa A. Boese, Nazifa Alizada, Martin Lundstedt, Kelly Morrison, Natalia Natsika, Yuko Sato, Hugo Tai, and Staffan I. Lindberg, *Democracy Report 2022: Autocratization Changing Nature?* (Gothenburg, Sweden: Varieties of Democracy Institute, 2022), https://v-dem.net/media/publications/dr_2022.pdf.

2. See, for example, Benoit Berthelot, "Billionaire 'French Murdoch' Is Building His Own Right-Wing Media Empire," *Bloomberg News*, July 21, 2022, https://www.bloomberg.com/news/articles/2022-07-21/the-rupert-murdoch-of-france-has-a-12-billion-plan-to-take-on-netflix-disney.

3. I place "deregulation" in quotes here to emphasize the term that is deployed by its advocates. I could use the term "reregulation" to underscore that it is not producing less regulation but different regulatory mechanisms. I would argue that there are no "deregulated" economic spaces and that any "deregulation" results in other forms and equal amounts of other regulatory mechanisms. See Bernard E. Harcourt, *The Illusion of Free Markets* (Cambridge, MA: Harvard University Press, 2011). In order not to distract the reader, I will try to use the term *federal deregulation* so as not to have to put quotes all the time around "deregulation" or "deregulate."

4. Many people on the political left would argue that the Democratic Party is more centrist than leftist, and that is surely the case from a broader international perspective. However, I am describing here the dominant models within the spectrum of the United States.

5.   As Ira Katznelson, Reinhold Martin, and others have shown, FDR's southern strategy regarding the New Deal reinforced segregation and racial inequality in this country. Ira Katznelson, *Fear Itself: The New Deal and the Origins of Our Time* (New York: Norton, 2013); Reinhold Martin, "Abolish Oil," *Places Journal*, June 2020, https://placesjournal.org/article /abolish-oil/. It is also interesting to note that the modern New Deal administrative state eclipsed other efforts at fair trade, including associationalist initiatives by trade associations of independent proprietors seeking to tame competition. See Laura Phillips Sawyer, *American Fair Trade: Proprietary Capitalism, Corporatism, and the "New Competition," 1890–1940* (Cambridge: Cambridge University Press, 2018).

6.   See Bernard E. Harcourt, *Critique and Praxis* (New York: Columbia University Press, 2020), 246–49.

7.   *West Virginia v. EPA*, 597 U.S. __ (2022), slip opinion, 18.

8.   *West Virginia v. EPA*, 597 U.S. __ (2022) (GORSUCH, L., concurring), slip opinion, 5–6.

9.   Charlie Savage, "E.P.A. Ruling Is Milestone," *New York Times*, June 30, 2022.

10.   Philip Hamburger, *Is Administrative Law Unlawful?* (Chicago: University of Chicago Press, 2014); and Philip Hamburger, *The Administrative Threat* (New York: Encounter, 2017). My Columbia colleague Thomas W. Merrill has also written on the topic, challenging what is known as the *Chevron* doctrine, under which federal courts defer to agency interpretations of unclear laws. See Thomas W. Merrill, *The* Chevron *Doctrine: Its Rise and Fall, and the Future of the Administrative State* (Cambridge, MA: Harvard University Press, 2022). Merrill takes a more nuanced view and is not as radical as Philip Hamburger. Merrill rejects the idea of discarding the administrative state and instead argues for a better allocation of responsibilities between courts and agencies.

11.   *West Virginia v. EPA*, 597 U.S. __ (2022) (GORSUCH, J., concurring), slip opinion, 4.

12.   *Dobbs v. Jackson Women's Health Organization*, 597 U.S.__ (2022).

13.   Tony Romm, "Senate Approves Inflation Reduction Act, Clinching Long-Delayed Health and Climate Bill," *Washington Post*, August 7, 2022, https://www.washingtonpost.com /us-policy/2022/08/07/senate-inflation-reduction-act-climate/.

14.   See, for example, Ben Lefebvre, Kelsey Tamborrino, and Josh Siegel, "Historic Climate Bill to Supercharge Clean Energy Industry," *Politico*, August 7, 2022, https://www.politico.com /news/2022/08/07/inflation-reduction-act-climate-biden-00050230.

15.   Isabella Isaacs-Thomas, "What the Inflation Reduction Act Does for Green Energy," *PBS NewsHour*, August 11, 2022, https://www.pbs.org/newshour/science/what-the-inflation -reduction-act-does-for-green-energy.

16.   The saga undoubtedly will go on. As I send this manuscript off to Columbia University Press, the Democrats in Congress have managed to slip into the budget reconciliation measure (thus avoiding a filibuster) language defining the emissions in the *West Virginia v. EPA* case (carbon dioxide produced by burning fossil fuels) as pollution (more technically an "air pollutant"), thus giving the EPA legislative authority to regulate greenhouse gases. Apparently, Senate Republicans objected to the language and to the fact that it appears in a budget bill. See Lisa Friedman, "Democrats Designed the Climate Law to Be a Game Changer. Here's How," *New York Times*, August 22, 2022, https://www.nytimes .com/2022/08/22/climate/epa-supreme-court-pollution.html. We will have to see how the federal courts rule when the next challenge is brought.

17. *West Virginia v. EPA*, 597 U.S. __ (2022), slip opinion, 18, 17, 19.

18. *West Virginia v. EPA*, 597 U.S. __ (2022), slip opinion, 20 (my emphasis).

19. *West Virginia v. EPA*, 597 U.S. __ (2022), slip opinion, 31 (my emphasis).

20. See, for example, Colin Lalley, "Health Insurance Companies Are Thriving in the Age of Obamacare," *Policygenius*, May 26, 2017, https://www.policygenius.com/health-insurance /news/obamacare-health-insurance-company-stock-prices/.

21. Noah Kirsch, "The Three Richest Americans Hold More Wealth Than Bottom 50 Percent of the Country, Study Finds," *Forbes*, November 9, 2017, https://www.forbes.com/sites /noahkirsch/2017/11/09/the-3-richest-americans-hold-more-wealth-than-bottom-50-of -country-study-finds/.

22. "Eight Billionaires Own as Much as Poorest Half of Global Population," *Philanthropy News Digest*, January 18, 2017, https://philanthropynewsdigest.org/news/eight-billionaires -own-as-much-as-poorest-half-of-global-population.

23. Thomas Piketty, *Capital in the Twenty-First Century* (Cambridge, MA: Harvard University Press, 2014); Thomas Piketty, *Capital and Ideology* (Cambridge, MA: Harvard University Press, 2020); Lucas Chancel, Thomas Piketty, Emmanuel Saez, and Gabriel Zucman, *World Inequality Report 2022*, World Inequality Lab, https://wir2022.wid.world/www-site/uploads /2022/03/0098-21_WIL_RIM_RAPPORT_A4.pdf.

24. Piketty's descriptive analysis regarding increasing inequality has withstood review and critiques; by contrast, his explanation regarding the relationship between capital return and growth (often conceptualized as "r > g")—which I do not rely on in this book and from which Piketty himself has retreated—has been cast in doubt. But for the overwhelming majority of critics, including economists such as Daron Acemoglu, James Robinson, Lawrence Blume, Steven Durlauf, and Lawrence Summers, Piketty's descriptive empirical claims stand. For an excellent review and discussion that links to the secondary literature on Piketty's work, see generally Marshall Steinbaum, "Why Are Economists Giving Piketty the Cold Shoulder?," *Boston Review*, May 12, 2017, https://bostonreview.net /articles/marshall-steinbaum-beyond-piketty/.

25. International Cooperative Alliance (ICA), "Cooperative Identity, Values and Principles," https://www.ica.coop/en/whats-co-op/co-operative-identity-values-principles.

26. ICA, "Cooperative Identity, Values and Principles."

27. *Puget Sound Plywood, Inc. v. Commissioner of Internal Revenue*, 44 T.C. 305 (U.S.T.C., 1965).

28. Jan Shepel, "Kingston Cheese Cooperative Emerges from Pandemic with New Vibrancy," *Wisconsin State Farmer*, https://www.wisfarmer.com/story/news/2022/06/21/kingston-cheese -cooperative-emerges-pandemic-new-vibrancy/7685133001/.

29. Kali Akuno and Ajamu Nangwaya, *Jackson Rising: The Struggle for Economic Democracy and Black Self-Determination in Jackson, Mississippi* (Wakefield, Quebec: Daraja, 2017), 20–21, 29, 32; Cooperation Jackson, "Sustainable Communities Initiative," https://cooperationjackson .org/sustainable-communities-initiative.

30. U.S. Solidarity Network, "Our Story," https://ussen.org.

31. Ethan Miller, *Reimagining Livelihoods: Life Beyond Economy, Society, and Environment* (Minneapolis: University of Minnesota Press, 2019).

32. Devi Ruia and Prerna Jagadeesh, "Voters Strongly Support Worker Cooperatives," *Data for Progress*, August 31, 2021, https://www.dataforprogress.org/blog/2021/8/31/voters-strongly

-support-worker-cooperatives. The methodology of the survey was as follows: "From June 11 to 14, 2021, Data for Progress conducted a survey of 1,175 likely voters nationally using web panel respondents. The sample was weighted to be representative of likely voters by age, gender, education, race, and voting history. The survey was conducted in English. The margin of error is ±3 percentage points. N=1175 unless otherwise specified." See also Benjamin Gillies, "Worker Cooperatives: A Bipartisan Solution to America's Growing Income Inequality," *Kennedy School Review* (blog), June 15, 2016, https://ksr.hkspublications .org/2016/06/15/worker-cooperatives-a-bipartisan-solution-to-americas-growing-income -inequality/ (pointing to bipartisan support post-2008 for worker cooperatives in areas such as Reading, Pennsylvania, and Austin, Texas).

33.   Matthew Robare, "Can Cooperative Businesses Save Communities?," *American Conservative*, August 25, 2016, https://www.theamericanconservative.com/can-cooperative-businesses -save-communities/.

34.   Quoted in Gillies, "Worker Cooperatives."

35.   Land O'Lakes, https://www.landolakesinc.com/; Sunkist, https://www.sunkist.com/about -us/; Ocean Spray, https://www.oceanspray.com/; State Farm, https://www.statefarm .com/; Liberty Mutual, https://www.libertymutual.com/; REI, https://www.rei.com/; Ace Hardware, https://www.acehardware.com/about-us; Isthmus Engineering and Manufac- turing, https://www.isthmuseng.com/; Cooperative Home Care Associates, http://www .chcany.org/; Daphne Berry, "The Worker Co-operative Form in the Home Care Industry in the USA," in *The Oxford Handbook of Mutual, Co-operative, and Co-owned Business*, ed. Jonathan Michie, Joseph R. Blasi, and Carlo Borzaga (Oxford: Oxford University Press, 2017), 386–397; King Arthur Flour, *King Arthur Flour: Benefit Corporation Annual Report 2018* (King Arthur Flour, 2019), https://www.kingarthurbaking.com/sites/default/files/2019 -06/2018-bcorp-report.pdf; AK Press, https://www.akpress.org/; Navy Credit Union, September 5, 2020, https://www.navyfederal.org/.

36.   Lynn Pitman, "History of Cooperatives in the United States: An Overview," University of Wisconsin Center for Cooperatives, Madison, Wisconsin, revised December 2018, https://resources.uwcc.wisc.edu/History_of_Cooperatives.pdf, 2.

37.   National Association of Mutual Insurance Companies, "About Mutual Insurance," https:// web.archive.org/web/20210124082153/https://www.namic.org/about/mutuals.

38.   Brian Van Slyke, "Pandemic Crash Shows Worker Co-Ops Are More Resilient Than Tra- ditional Business," *Truthout*, May 8, 2020, https://truthout.org/articles/pandemic-crash -shows-worker-co-ops-are-more-resilient-than-traditional-business/.

39.   Silvio Goglio and Panu Kalmi, "Credit Unions and Co-Operative Banks Across the World," in *The Oxford Handbook of Mutual, Co-operative, and Co-owned Business*, ed. Jonathan Michie, Joseph R. Blasi, and Carlo Borzaga (Oxford: Oxford University Press, 2017), 148.

40.   Crédit Agricole Group, "Crédit Agricole," https://www.credit-agricole.com/en/business -lines-and-brands/all-brands/credit-agricole.

41.   Anca Voinea, "How Does Crédit Agricole Stay Local While Operating Multinationally?," *Co-Operative News* (blog), September 5, 2018, https://www.thenews.coop/131687/sector /banking-and-insurance/credit-agricole-stay-local-operating-multinationally/.

42.   Mondragón Corporation, "About Us," https://www.mondragon-corporation.com/en/about -us/; Xabier Barandiaran and Javier Lezaun, "The Mondragón Experience," in *The Oxford*

Handbook of Mutual, Co-operative, and Co-owned Business, ed. Jonathan Michie, Joseph R. Blasi, and Carlo Borzaga (Oxford: Oxford University Press, 2017), 279; Erik Olin Wright, *Envisioning Real Utopias* (London: Verso, 2010), 240–46; see also Sharryn Kasmir, *The Myth of Mondragón: Cooperatives, Politics, and Working-Class Life in a Basque Town* (Albany: State University of New York Press, 1996).

43. Swann-Morton, "Swann-Morton History," https://www.swann-morton.com/pages/history .php. Estimated revenues from "Swann-Morton's Competitors, Revenue, Number of Employees, Funding and Acquisitions," Owler, https://www.owler.com/company/swann -morton.

44. Justice Cream (website), http://justicecream.org.

45. Jia Tolentino, "Can I Help You? The Meaning of Mutual Aid During a Pandemic," *New Yorker*, May 18, 2020, 24–29.

46. Dean Spade, *Mutual Aid: Building Solidarity During This Crisis (and the Next)* (New York: Verso, 2020); Dean Spade, "Solidarity Not Charity: Mutual Aid for Mobilization and Survival," *Social Text 142* 38, no. 1 (March 2020): 131–51.

47. Jonathan Michie, Joseph R. Blasi, and Carlo Borzaga, "Introduction and Overview," in *The Oxford Handbook of Mutual, Co-operative, and Co-owned Business*, ed. Jonathan Michie, Joseph R. Blasi, and Carlo Borzaga (Oxford: Oxford University Press, 2017), xxiv; John Curl, *For All the People: Uncovering the Hidden History of Cooperation, Cooperative Movements, and Communalism in America*, 2nd ed. (Oakland, CA: PM, 2012), v.

48. See ICA, "International Cooperative Alliance," https://www.ica.coop/en/about-us /international-cooperative-alliance; Dave Grace and Associates, *Measuring the Size and Scope of the Cooperative Economy: Results of the 2014 Global Census on Co-operatives* (Madison, WI: United Nation's Secretariat Department of Economic and Social Affairs Division for Social Policy and Development, 2014), https://www.un.org/esa/socdev/documents /2014/coopsegm/grace.pdf.

49. Vera Zamagni, "A Worldwide Historical Perspective on Co-operatives and Their Evolution," in *The Oxford Handbook of Mutual, Co-operative, and Co-owned Business*, ed. Jonathan Michie, Joseph R. Blasi, and Carlo Borzaga (Oxford: Oxford University Press, 2017), 99.

50. See "About Co-op News," *Co-op News*, https://www.thenews.coop/about/.

51. Donald A. Frederick, "Income Tax Treatment of Cooperatives," Cooperative Information Report, Business and Cooperative Services, United States Department of Agriculture (Washington, DC: USDA Rural Development, 2013), 3–5 (tally from National Cooperative Business Association), https://www.rd.usda.gov/files/cir44-1.pdf.

52. Rebecca Harvey, "What Has Caused the Number of US Worker Co-ops to Nearly Double?," *Co-op News*, August 7, 2018, https://www.thenews.coop/130862/sector/worker-coops /caused-number-us-worker-co-ops-nearly-double/.

53. Daphne Berry, "The Worker Co-operative Form in the Home Care Industry in the USA," in *The Oxford Handbook of Mutual, Co-operative, and Co-owned Business*, ed. Jonathan Michie, Joseph R. Blasi, and Carlo Borzaga (Oxford: Oxford University Press, 2017), 387, 394; Frank Thomas, "The Emergence of Multi-Stakeholder Co-operatives in the Movement of Farm Machinery Co-operatives (CUMAs) in France," in *The Oxford Handbook of Mutual, Co-operative, and Co-owned Business*, ed. Jonathan Michie, Joseph R. Blasi, and Carlo Borzaga (Oxford: Oxford University Press, 2017), 499–500.

54.   See CICOPA, "Mission and Values," CICOPA, https://www.cicopa.coop/about/our-values/.

55.   Mark J. Kaswan, "US Worker Co-operatives," in *The Oxford Handbook of Mutual, Co-operative, and Co-owned Business*, ed. Jonathan Michie, Joseph R. Blasi, and Carlo Borzaga (Oxford: Oxford University Press, 2017), 537.

56.   See Democracy at Work Institute, "Mission and Vision," https://institute.coop/about-dawi/mission-vision.

57.   Democracy Collaborative, "Expanding Democratic Ownership," https://democracycollaborative.org/expanding-democratic-ownership.

58.   Robare, "Can Cooperative Businesses Save Communities?"

59.   See Melissa Hoover and Hilary Abell, *The Cooperative Growth Ecosystem: Inclusive Economic Development in Action*, Democracy at Work Institute and Project Equity, n.d., https://institute.coop/sites/default/files/resources/Ecosystem%20Report.pdf.

60.   See generally CooperationWorks!, "About Us," https://cooperationworks.coop/about/; Cooperative Development Foundation, "About CDF," https://www.cdf.coop/about.

61.   "Co-Op Mastery: Beyond Cooperatives 101," Ohio State University College of Food, Agricultural, and Environmental Sciences, https://u.osu.edu/coopmastery/.

62.   Platform Cooperativism Consortium (website), https://platform.coop; Cooperative Development Foundation (website), https://www.cdf.coop; Co-opLaw.org (website), https://www.co-oplaw.org/; National Cooperative Business Association CLUSA International (website), https://ncbaclusa.coop; USAID, "Cooperative Development Program," https://www.usaid.gov/local-faith-and-transformative-partnerships/cooperative-development-program.

63.   USAID, "Cooperative Development Program."

64.   Community-Wealth.org, "Support Organizations: Cooperatives," https://community-wealth.org/strategies/panel/coops/support.html.

65.   See generally "About Co-op News."

66.   Sara Horowitz, with Andy Kifer, *Mutualism: Building the Next Economy from the Ground Up* (New York: Random House, 2021), 16.

67.   E. G. Nadeau, *The Cooperative Solution: How the United States Can Tame Recessions, Reduce Inequality, and Protect the Environment* (n.p.: CreateSpace Independent Publishing Platform, 2012); E. G. Nadeau and Luc Nadeau, *The Cooperative Society: The Next Stage of Human History* (Madison, WI: Emile G. Nadeau, 2016); E. G. Nadeau and David Thompson, *Cooperation Works!: How People Are Using Cooperative Action to Rebuild Communities and Revitalize the Economy* (Rochester, MN: Lone Oak, 1996).

68.   Nadeau and Nadeau, *The Cooperative Society*, 1.

69.   E. G. Nadeau, *Strengthening the Cooperative Community* (Madison, WI: Emile G. Nadeau, 2021).

70.   Peter Ranis, *Cooperatives Confront Capitalism: Challenging the Neoliberal Economy* (London: Zed, 2016); see also the collection of articles on the promising economics of worker cooperatives in John H. Pencavel, ed., *The Economics of Worker Cooperatives* (Cheltenham, UK: Edward Elgar, 2013). There is a longer tradition of this in economics as well, along a spectrum that includes Martin L. Weitzman, *The Share Economy* (Cambridge, MA: Harvard University Press, 1986); and Stephen Resnick and Richard Wolff, *Knowledge and Class* (Chicago: University of Chicago Press, 1987); for a discussion, see Thomas Brzustowski

and Francesco Caselli, "Economic Growth in a Cooperative Economy," *IDEAS Working Paper Series from RePEc*, 2021, https://www.proquest.com/working-papers/economic-growth -cooperative-economy/docview/2587466273/se-2, 4.

71. On the Packers, see generally Dave Zirin, "Those Nonprofit Packers," *New Yorker*, January 25, 2011, https://www.newyorker.com/sports/sporting-scene/those-non-profit-packers.

72. See, for example, Brzustowski and Caselli, "Economic Growth in a Cooperative Economy"; John P. Bonin and Louis Putterman, *Economics of Cooperation and the Labour-Managed Economy* (London: Routledge, 2013); Roger A. McCain, "Cooperation and Effort, Reciprocity and Mutual Supervision in Worker Cooperatives," in *Cooperative Firms in Global Markets*, ed. S. Novkovic and V. Sena (Bingley, UK: Emerald Group, 2007), https://doi .org/10.1016/S0885-3339(06)10007-1; Benjamin Ward, "The Firm in Illyria: Market Syndicalism," *American Economic Review* 48, no. 4 (1958): 566–89; and John P. Bonin, Derek C. Jones, and Louis Putterman, "Theoretical and Empirical Studies of Producer Cooperatives: Will Ever the Twain Meet?," *Journal of Economic Literature* 31, no. 3 (1993): 1290–1320.

73. "Aims and Scope," *Journal of Co-operative Organization and Management*, https://www .sciencedirect.com/journal/journal-of-co-operative-organization-and-management/about /aims-and-scope (This journal "provide[s] the primary forum for advancement and dissemination of scientific knowledge on co-operative organizations and their management."); "Aims and Scope," *Journal of Cooperatives*, https://accc.k-state.edu/ncera210 /jocpdfs/guidelines/JOCAimandScope.pdf ("The emphasis of the journal is on cooperatives in the agribusiness and rural sectors and for cooperatively related research with a strong economic or business focus."); "Journal of Cooperatives Library," *Journal of Cooperatives*, https://accc.k-state.edu/ncera210/; *Journal of Cooperative Studies*, https://www .ukscs.coop/pages/journal-of-co-operative-studies ("The editors welcome contributions on co-operative education, management, governance and leadership, and related subject areas of relevance to the co-operative sector.); "About the Journal," *International Journal of Cooperative Studies*, https://www.worldscholars.org/index.php/ijcs/about (This journal "aims to generate theoretical knowledge as well as promoting research and innovation within the cooperative sector." It ceased publication in 2019.); *International Journal of Community and Cooperative Studies*, European-American Journals, https://www.eajournals.org /journals/international-journal-of-community-and-cooperative-studies-ijccs/ (This journal "promotes research and innovation in the areas of rural and community development, geography and regional planning, rural cooperatives, community health; capacity building, social work, community empowerment, sustainable development, human resource development, social capital, economic development, urban studies. Cooperative sectors covers [sic] rural, agriculture, consumer, housing, worker, social, credit and other related areas."); *International Journal of Co-Operative Accounting and Management*, https://www .smu.ca/academics/sobey/ijcam.html (This new journal combined two original journals. "The International Journal of Co-operative Management (IJCM) was published from 2003–2015, editor Dr. Peter Davis, University of Leicester. In January 2018, IJCM merged with the Journal of Co-operative Accounting and Reporting (JCAR) to form a new journal, the International Journal of Co-operative Accounting and Management (IJCAM).")

74. I am adding the diaeresis on the second vowel here, not only to conform to the more traditional two-vowel rule but also to distinguish "coöperism" from the urban slang that

has developed around the term "cooperism," meaning being hurtful or mean or making a mockery of anyone called Cooper. See "Cooperism," *Urban Dictionary*, https://www.urbandictionary.com/define.php?term=Cooperism. I prefer to retain the diaeresis in the book to harken back to movements throughout history that promoted "coöperation" in all different languages that used the diaeresis—*coöpérative, coöperatie*, etc. Incidentally, the little national museum that has been set up in Schriedam, outside Rotterdam, to preserve the history of the Dutch movement for cooperatives, the Nationaal Coöperatie Museum, is a darling space, definitely worth the visit; see Nationaal Coöperatie Museum (website), https://www.cooperatie-museum.nl.

75. On disciplinary power, see Michel Foucault, *Discipline and Punish: The Birth of the Prison*, trans. Alan Sheridan (New York: Vintage, 1975), 26–28; on biopower, see Michel Foucault, "Part 5: Right of Death and Power Over Life," in *The History of Sexuality*, vol. 1: *An Introduction*, trans. Robert Hurley (New York: Pantheon, 1978), 133–159; on expository power, see Bernard E. Harcourt, *Exposed: Desire and Disobedience in the Digital Age* (Cambridge, MA: Harvard University Press, 2015), 89–92; on infopower, see Colin Koopman, *How We Became Our Data* (Chicago: University of Chicago Press, 2019); on spectacular power, see Guy Debord, *Society of the Spectacle*, trans. Ken Knabb (London: Rebel, 2002). For a radical theory of power, see Steven Lukes, *Power: A Radical View*, 3rd ed. (New York: Bloomsbury, 2021); see also Bernard E. Harcourt, "Radical Thought from Marx, Nietzsche, and Freud, Through Foucault, to the Present: Comments on Steven Lukes's *In Defense of 'False Consciousness,'*" *Chicago Unbound* (2011): 29–51.

76. ICA, "Cooperative Identity, Values and Principles."

77. Janelle Orsi, William Lisa, and Sushil Jacob, *Legal Guide to Cooperative Conversions: A Business Owner's Legal Guide to Cooperative Conversion Including Conversion Models, Case Studies, and Sample Documents* (Sustainable Economies Law Center, n.d.), 38; see also "Business Structures 101: Co-Op Mastery," Ohio State University College of Food, Agricultural, and Environmental Sciences, https://u.osu.edu/coopmastery/legal/alternative-business-structures/.

78. See, for example, Charles Frederick Sabel and William H. Simon, "Democratic Experimentalism," in *Searching for Contemporary Legal Thought*, ed. Justin Desautels-Stein and Christopher Tomlins (New York: Cambridge University Press, 2017); Mikhaïl Xifaras, "The Role of Law in Critical Theory," *Praxis 13/13* (blog), December 2, 2018, https://blogs.law.columbia.edu/praxis1313/mikhail-xifaras-the-role-of-the-law-in-critical-theory-the-role-of-property-in-the-commons/; Josh Lerner and Jean Tirole, "Some Simple Economics of Open Source," *Journal of Industrial Economics* 50, no. 2 (June 2002): 197–234; Yochai Benkler, "Peer Production, the Commons, and the Future of the Firm," *Strategic Organization* 15, no. 2 (2017): 264–274; Eben Moglen, "Anarchism Triumphant: Free Software and the Death of Copyright," *First Monday*, August 2, 1999, http://firstmonday.org/ojs/index.php/fm/article/view/684/594; Richard Sennett, *Together: The Rituals, Pleasures and Politics of Cooperation* (New Haven, CT: Yale University Press, 2013); Red Nation, *The Red Deal: Indigenous Action to Save Our Earth* (Common Notions, 2021); Kate Aronoff, Alyssa Battistoni, Daniel Aldana Cohen, and Thea Riofrancos, *A Planet to Win: Why We Need a Green New Deal* (New York: Verso, 2019); Alyssa Battistoni, "Living, Not Just Surviving," *Jacobin*, August 15, 2015, https://jacobinmag.com/2017/08/living-not-just-surviving/; on steady-state and degrowth

economics, see chapter 5, *infra*, notes 91–96; Sylvère Lotringer and Christian Marazzi, eds., *Autonomia: Post-Political Politics* (New York: Semiotext(e), 2007); Antonio Negri, *From the Factory to the Metropolis*, trans. Ed Emery (Cambridge: Polity, 2018).

79. Charles Gide, "Avant-propos," in *Le Coopératisme: Conférences de propagande*, 5th ed. (Paris: Librairie du Recueil Sirey, 1929), v.

80. See "Cooperism," *Urban Dictionary*, https://www.urbandictionary.com/define.php?term =Cooperism.

81. Piketty, *Capital in the Twenty-First Century*, 45.

82. Piketty, *Capital in the Twenty-First Century*, 45–46.

83. Katharina Pistor, *The Code of Capital* (Princeton, NJ: Princeton University Press, 2019), 183, 9–11.

84. Karl Marx, *Capital* (New York: Vintage, 1976), 1:247–248, 709. For a general discussion of the divergence in definitions of capital between Marx's work and Piketty's writings, see David Campbell, "The Fetishism of Divergence: A Critique of Piketty," *Journal of Corporate Law Studies* 15, no. 1 (April 2015): 183.

85. Piketty, *Capital and Ideology*, 1036; see also 966–1034.

86. Piketty, *Capital and Ideology*, 511. Piketty does refer to his vision as "a cooperative and ideal (not to say idyllic) scenario." Piketty, *Capital and Ideology*, 1031 (my emphasis). So he does share a lot with the vision of cooperation; but overall the proposals are very different, even if sympathetic.

2. THE UBIQUITY OF COOPERATION

1. Herbert B. Adams, *History of Coöperation in the United States* (Baltimore: Johns Hopkins University Press, 1888), 501, 78–80.

2. Adams, *History of Coöperation in the United States*.

3. Adams, *History of Coöperation in the United States*, 10–103, 105.

4. W. E. B. Du Bois, *Economic Co-operation Among Negro Americans: Report of a Social Study Made by Atlanta University, Under the Patronage of the Carnegie Institution of Washington, D.C., Together with the Proceedings of the Twelfth Conference for the Study of the Negro Problems, Held at Atlanta University, on Tuesday, May the 28th, 1907* (Atlanta: Atlanta University Press, 1907).

5. Du Bois, *Economic Co-operation Among Negro Americans*, "Resolutions of the Conference."

6. Jessica Gordon Nembhard, *Collective Courage: A History of African American Cooperative Economic Thought and Practice* (University Park: Pennsylvania State University Press, 2014), 116.

7. See generally Jessica Gordon Nembhard, "A Long and Strong History with Southern Roots," in *Jackson Rising: The Struggle for Economic Democracy and Black Self-Determination in Jackson, Mississippi*, by Kali Akuno and Ajamu Nangwaya (Wakefield, Quebec: Daraja, 2017), 171–181.

8. Alex Gourevitch, *From Slavery to the Cooperative Commonwealth: Labor and Republican Liberty in the Nineteenth Century* (New York: Cambridge University Press, 2014).

9. Steven Bernard Leikin, *The Practical Utopians: American Workers and the Cooperative Movement in the Gilded Age* (Detroit, MI: Wayne State University Press, 2005).

10. Albert Sonnichsen, *Consumers' Coöperation* (New York: Macmillan, 1919).

11. Sonnichsen, *Consumers' Coöperation*, 145–170.

12. Sonnichsen, *Consumers' Coöperation*, 152.

13. Sonnichsen, *Consumers' Coöperation*, 155.

14. Florence E. Parker, *The First 125 Years: A History of Distributive and Service Cooperation in the United States, 1829–1954* (Superior, WI: Cooperative League, 1956).

15. Joseph G. Knapp, *The Rise of American Cooperative Enterprise 1620–1920* (Danville, IL: Interstate, 1969); Joseph G. Knapp, *The Advance of American Cooperative Enterprise 1920–1945* (Danville, IL: Interstate, 1973).

16. Robert Jackall and Henry M. Levin, *Worker Cooperatives in America* (Berkeley: University of California Press, 1984); for this period, 1960s and '70s, see also John Case and Rosemary C. R. Taylor, eds., *Co-ops, Communes and Collectives: Experiments in Social Change in the 1960s and 1970s* (New York: Pantheon, 1979).

17. John Curl, *For All the People: Uncovering the Hidden History of Cooperation, Cooperative Movements, and Communalism in America*, 2nd ed. (Oakland, CA: PM, 2012); John Curl, *History of Work Cooperation in America: Cooperatives, Cooperative Movements, Collectivity and Communalism from Early America to the Present* (Berkeley: Homeward, 1980).

18. Curl, *For All the People*.

19. Curl, *For All the People*, 291–296.

20. Virginie Pérotin, "Worker Co-operatives: Good, Sustainable Jobs in the Community," in *The Oxford Handbook of Mutual, Co-operative, and Co-owned Business*, ed. Jonathan Michie, Joseph R. Blasi, and Carlo Borzaga (Oxford: Oxford University Press, 2017), 132.

21. "Our History," International Cooperative Alliance, accessed August 18, 2022, https:// www.ica.coop/en/cooperatives/history-cooperative-movement.

22. SolidarityNYC, *Growing a Resilient City: Collaboration in New York City's Solidarity Economy*, http://solidaritynyc.org/wp-content/uploads/2013/02/Growing-A-Resilient-City -SolidarityNYC-Report.pdf; Michael Johnson, "A Night of Solidarity and Resilience in NYC," *Grassroots Economic Organizing*, March 8, 2013, https://geo.coop/story/night-solidarity -and-resilience-new-york-city.

23. Francisco Javier Forcadell, "Democracy, Cooperation and Business Success: The Case of Mondragón Corporación Cooperativa," *Journal of Business Ethics* 56, no. 3 (2005): 256.

24. Xabier Barandiaran and Javier Lezaun, "The Mondragón Experience," in *The Oxford Handbook of Mutual, Co-operative, and Co-owned Business*, ed. Jonathan Michie, Joseph R. Blasi, and Carlo Borzaga (Oxford: Oxford University Press, 2017), 280–282; Sharryn Kasmir, *The Myth of Mondragón: Cooperatives, Politics, and Working-Class Life in a Basque Town* (Albany: State University of New York Press, 1996), 33.

25. Forcadell, "Democracy, Cooperation and Business Success," 255; Barandiaran and Lezaun, "The Mondragón Experience," 279. Note that, as a result of its globalization, Mondragón has now acquired more than a hundred subsidiary businesses and joint ventures that have not yet been cooperatized. See Sharryn Kasmir, "The Mondragón Cooperatives and Global Capitalism," *New Labor Forum* 25, no. 1 (2016): 55.

26. "Cooperative University," Mondragon Unibertsitatea, accessed August 18, 2022, https:// www.mondragon.edu/en/meet-mu/cooperative-university.

27. Barandiaran and Lezaun, "The Mondragón Experience," 279; see generally Mondragón Corporation, *Mondragón Annual Report, 2018*, https://www.mondragon-corporation.com /wp-content/themes/mondragon/docs/eng/annual-report-2018.pdf.

28. Barandiaran and Lezaun, "The Mondragón Experience," 290. It has its detractors and critics, including some scholars, such as Sharryn Kasmir and June Nash, who believe it is more myth than reality, and a dangerous myth at that, one that undermines labor organization and more radical politics. See generally Kasmir, *The Myth of Mondragón.* I discuss this critique and address it in chapter 5 (discussing the myth of capitalism and communism).

29. Spencer Thompson, "Towards a Social Theory of the Firm: Worker Cooperatives Reconsidered," *Journal of Co-Operative Organization and Management* 3, no. 1 (June 2015): 8.

30. Sara Horowitz, with Andy Kifer, *Mutualism: Building the Next Economy from the Ground Up* (New York: Random House, 2021), 43, 91. OSS Project, "About Us," https://outerseedshadow.org.

31. Akuno and Nangwaya, *Jackson Rising*, 15.

32. See W. E. B. Du Bois, "A Negro Nation Within the Nation," *Current History* 42, no. 3 (1935): 265–270; Kali Akuno, *The Jackson-Kush Plan: The Struggle for Black Self-Determination and Economic Democracy*, n.d., accessed August 18, 2022, https://mronline.org/wp-content/uploads/2020/07/Jackson-KushPlan.pdf.

33. Akuno and Nangwaya, *Jackson Rising*, 3.

34. Akuno and Nangwaya, *Jackson Rising*, 15–16.

35. Ethan Miller, "Review of *The Solidarity Economy Alternative: Emerging Theory and Practice,* ed. Vishwas Satgar," *Antipode: A Radical Journal of Geography* (2014), accessed August 18, 2022, https://radicalantipode.files.wordpress.com/2014/07/book-review_miller-on-satgar1.pdf, 1.

36. Miller, "Review of *The Solidarity Economy Alternative,*" 1.

37. Vishwas Satgar, ed., *The Solidarity Economy Alternative: Emerging Theory and Practice* (Durban, South Africa: University of KwaZulu-Natal Press, 2014); Vishwas Satgar, ed., *Co-operatives in South Africa: Advancing Solidarity Economy Pathways from Below* (Durban, South Africa: University of KwaZulu-Natal Press, 2019); see COPAC, "Who We Are," https://copac.org.za/about-us/.

38. See generally Satgar, ed., *Co-operatives in South Africa.*

39. Miller, "Review of *The Solidarity Economy Alternative,*" 2.

40. Big Door Brigade, "About Big Door Brigade," http://bigdoorbrigade.com/about/. ("As part of and inspired by that group, Dean Spade created this website to lift up the significance of mutual aid as a strategy for survival and mobilization, and he continues to maintain it." Dean Spade, "Welcome," http://www.deanspade.net/.)

41. Big Door Brigade, "What Is Mutual Aid?," http://bigdoorbrigade.com/what-is-mutual-aid/.

42. Nembhard, *Collective Courage,* 55.

43. Nembhard, *Collective Courage*; Jia Tolentino, "Can I Help You? The Meaning of Mutual Aid During a Pandemic," *New Yorker,* May 18, 2020, 26; Giovanni Penna, "Mutual Aid in the Central Mediterranean: The Responses of Search and Rescue NGOs to Italy's and the EU's Governance of the Border," COMPAS WP-21-154, September 2021, https://www.compas.ox.ac.uk/wp-content/uploads/WP-2021-154-Penna-Mutual-Aid-in-the-Central-Mediterranean.pdf.

44. Dean Spade, *Mutual Aid: Building Solidarity During This Crisis (and the Next)* (New York: Verso, 2020), 7.

45. Tolentino, "Can I Help You?," 26.

46. See generally Judith Butler, *Notes Toward a Performative Theory of Assembly* (Cambridge. MA: Harvard University Press, 2015); Bernard E. Harcourt, "Political Disobedience," *Critical Inquiry* 39 (Autumn 2012): 33–55.

47.   Lynn Pitman, "History of Cooperatives in the United States: An Overview," University of Wisconsin Center for Cooperatives, Madison, Wisconsin, revised December 2018, https://resources.uwcc.wisc.edu/History_of_Cooperatives.pdf, 2.

48.   The Philadelphia Contributionship, https://1752.com.

49.   National Association of Mutual Insurance Companies, "About Mutual Insurance," https://web.archive.org/web/20210124082153/https://www.namic.org/about/mutuals.

50.   Lars-Fredrik Andersson, "Review of *Mutual Insurance 1550–2015: From Guild Welfare and Friendly Societies to Contemporary Micro-Insurers* by Marco H. D. van Leeuwen," *Continuity and Change* 33, no. 3 (December 2018): 447–449.

51.   Andersson, "Review of *Mutual Insurance 1550–2015*," 448.

52.   Johnston Birchall, "The Performance of Member-Owned Businesses Since the Financial Crisis of 2008," in *The Oxford Handbook of Mutual, Co-operative, and Co-owned Business*, ed. Jonathan Michie, Joseph R. Blasi, and Carlo Borzaga (Oxford: Oxford University Press, 2017), 577.

53.   Birchall, "The Performance of Member-Owned Businesses Since the Financial Crisis of 2008," 577.

54.   National Association of Mutual Insurance Companies, "About Mutual Insurance."

55.   Barbara Bowers, "State Farm: Behind the Veil," *Best's Review*, July 2001.

56.   Funding Universe, "History of State Farm Mutual Automobile Insurance Company," http://www.fundinguniverse.com/company-histories/state-farm-mutual-automobile-insurance-company-history/.

57.   Funding Universe, "History of State Farm Mutual Automobile Insurance Company."

58.   Michael Tipsord, *2019 Annual Report to State Farm Mutual Policyholders* (Bloomington, IL: State Farm Mutual Automobile Insurance Company, 2020).

59.   Tipsord, *2019 Annual Report to State Farm Mutual Policyholders*.

60.   Bowers, "State Farm: Behind the Veil."

61.   Joe Cahill, "State Farm's Edge? It's Private," *Crain's Chicago Business*, April 21, 2012, https://www.chicagobusiness.com/article/20120421/ISSUE01/304219977/state-farm-s-edge-over-allstate-it-s-private.

62.   Bowers, "State Farm: Behind the Veil."

63.   Silvio Goglio and Panu Kalmi, "Credit Unions and Co-Operative Banks Across the World," in *The Oxford Handbook of Mutual, Co-operative, and Co-owned Business*, ed. Jonathan Michie, Joseph R. Blasi, and Carlo Borzaga (Oxford: Oxford University Press, 2017), 145.

64.   Birchall, "The Performance of Member-Owned Businesses Since the Financial Crisis of 2008," 571.

65.   Goglio and Kalmi, "Credit Unions and Co-Operative Banks Across the World," 146.

66.   Goglio and Kalmi, "Credit Unions and Co-Operative Banks Across the World," 147; see generally Holger Blisse and Detlev Hummel, "Raiffeisenbanks and Volksbanks for Europe: The Case for Co-operative Banking in Germany," in *The Oxford Handbook of Mutual, Co-operative, and Co-owned Business*, ed. Jonathan Michie, Joseph R. Blasi, and Carlo Borzaga (Oxford: Oxford University Press, 2017), 398–411.

67.   Birchall, "The Performance of Member-Owned Businesses Since the Financial Crisis of 2008," 573.

68.   Goglio and Kalmi, "Credit Unions and Co-Operative Banks Across the World," 148.

69. Johnston Birchall and Lou Hammond Ketilson, *Resilience of the Cooperative Business Model in Times of Crisis* (Geneva: International Labour Organization, Sustainable Enterprise Programme, 2009), 3.

70. Birchall and Ketilson, *Resilience of the Cooperative Business Model in Times of Crisis*, 3.

71. Crédit Agricole Group, "Crédit Agricole," https://www.credit-agricole.com/en/business-lines -and-brands/all-brands/credit-agricole.

72. Anca Voinea, "How Does Crédit Agricole Stay Local While Operating Multinationally?," *Co-Operative News* (blog), September 5, 2018, https://www.thenews.coop/131687/sector /banking-and-insurance/credit-agricole-stay-local-operating-multinationally/.

73. Crédit Agricole Group, "History of the Crédit Agricole Group," https://www.credit -agricole.com/en/group/the-history-of-credit-agricole.

74. Crédit Agricole, "Governance Roadshows," December 16, 2021, https://www.credit-agricole .com/pdfPreview/191347.

75. Voinea, "How Does Crédit Agricole Stay Local While Operating Multinationally?"

76. Voinea, "How Does Crédit Agricole Stay Local While Operating Multinationally?"

77. "Finance and Economics: Farmers Unite; French Banking," *Economist*, July 21, 2001.

78. Land O'Lakes, *2019 Land O'Lakes, Inc. Annual Report* (Issuu, February 2020), https://issuu .com/landolakesinc1/docs/2019_landolakes_annual_report/, 1, 3.

79. Michael A. Boland, Brendan Cooper, and James M. White, "Making Sustainability Tangi- ble: Land O'Lakes and the Dairy Supply Chain," *American Journal of Agricultural Economics* 98, no. 2 (March 2016): 648–657.

80. Land O'Lakes, "What We Do," https://www.landolakesinc.com/What-We-Do.

81. Boland, Cooper, and White, "Making Sustainability Tangible," 654.

82. Land O'Lakes, *2019 Land O'Lakes, Inc. Annual Report*, 4.

83. KPMG, *Recreational Equipment, Inc. (Consolidated Financial Statements)* (Recreational Equip- ment, Inc., December 28, 2019), https://www.rei.com/assets/about-rei/financial-information /rei-fy19-issued-financial-statements/live.pdf, 3.

84. REI Staff, "REI History: It Started with an Ice Axe," *REI Co-Op Journal* (blog), March 13, 2016, https://www.rei.com/blog/camp/rei-history-it-started-with-an-ice-axe.

85. REI Staff, "REI History."

86. Birchall, "The Performance of Member-Owned Businesses Since the Financial Crisis of 2008," 575.

87. Mara Leighton, "The Perks of REI's Lifetime Membership Far Outweigh Its One-Time $20 Cost," *Business Insider*, March 23, 2019, https://www.businessinsider.com/rei-lifetime -membership-program-explainer-2017-3.

88. Recreational Equipment, Inc., *Recreational Equipment, Inc. Bylaws*, https://www.rei.com /assets/about-rei/governance/rei-bylaws/live.pdf, 5.

89. Leighton, "The Perks of REI's Lifetime Membership Far Outweigh Its One-Time $20 Cost."

90. Recreational Equipment, Inc., *Recreational Equipment, Inc. Bylaws*.

91. Leighton, "The Perks of REI's Lifetime Membership Far Outweigh Its One-Time $20 Cost."

92. Recreational Equipment Inc., "Working at REI," January 10, 2012, https://www.rei.com /newsroom/article/working-at-rei.

93. KPMG, *Recreational Equipment, Inc. (Consolidated Financial Statements)*, 9.

94.   Bourree Lam, "How REI's Co-Op Retail Model Helps Its Bottom Line," *Atlantic*, March 21, 2017, https://www.theatlantic.com/business/archive/2017/03/rei-jerry-stritzke-interview /520278/.

95.   *Capitalism: A Love Story*, directed by Michael Moore, Anne Moore, Rod Birleson, John Hardesty, and Jeff Gibbs (Montreal: Alliance Vivafilm, 2010), https://www.youtube.com /watch?v=LUpnFNUmfKw&has_verified=1.

96.   Michael Billeaux, Anne Reynolds, Trevor Young-Hyman, and Ayca Zayim, "Worker Cooperative Case Study: Isthmus Engineering & Manufacturing," Center for Cooperatives, University of Wisconsin–Madison, October 2011, https://www.ssc.wisc.edu/~wright/929 -utopias-2013/Real%20Utopia%20Readings/Billeaux%20et%20al%20Ishmus%20Engineering %20case%20study.pdf, 4.

97.   Billeaux et al., "Worker Cooperative Case Study," 4.

98.   IEM had annual revenues of $15 million as of 2009. See *Capitalism: A Love Story*.

99.   "Cooperatives in Wisconsin: The Power of Cooperative Action," University of Wisconsin–Madison, Center for Cooperatives, 2019, 5; Avery Edenfield, "Collective Management in a Cooperative: Problematizing Productivity and Power" (PhD diss., University of Wisconsin–Madison, 2016), 28.

100. Michael Billeaux et al., "Worker Cooperative Case Study," 5–6.

101. Michael Billeaux et al., "Worker Cooperative Case Study," 3.

102. Michael Billeaux et al., "Worker Cooperative Case Study," 6.

103. Michael Billeaux et al., "Worker Cooperative Case Study," 6.

104. Michael Billeaux et al., "Worker Cooperative Case Study," 8.

105. Michael Billeaux et al., "Worker Cooperative Case Study," 6.

106. Michael Billeaux et al., "Worker Cooperative Case Study," 15.

107. Michael Billeaux et al., "Worker Cooperative Case Study," 10.

108. Michael Billeaux et al., "Worker Cooperative Case Study," 16.

109. Michael Billeaux et al., "Worker Cooperative Case Study," 23.

110. Michael Billeaux et al., "Worker Cooperative Case Study," 22.

111. Michael Billeaux et al., "Worker Cooperative Case Study," 10.

112. Michael Billeaux et al., "Worker Cooperative Case Study," 12.

113. Michael Billeaux et al., "Worker Cooperative Case Study," 22.

114. Isthmus Engineering & Manufacturing," "Our Way of Saying Thanks to Healthcare Workers," accessed June 26, 2020, https://www.isthmuseng.com/news/our-way-of-saying-thanks-to -healthcare-workers/.

115. Janelle Orsi, William Lisa, and Sushil Jacob, *Legal Guide to Cooperative Conversations: A Business Owner's Legal Guide to Cooperative Conversion Including Conversion Models, Case Studies and Sample Documents* (Sustainable Economies Law Center, n.d.), 38; see also Ohio State University, "Business Structures 101," https://u.osu.edu/coopmastery/legal/alternative -business-structures/.

116. B Lab, "What's Behind the B?," https://usca.bcorporation.net/about-b-corps/.

117. "King Arthur Flour: Benefit Corporation Annual Report 2018," https://www.kingarthurbaking .com/sites/default/files/2019-06/2018-bcorp-report.pdf.

118. Middlebury Natural Foods Co-op, "Spotlight on King Arthur Flour," April 13, 2016, https:// middlebury.coop/2016/04/13/spotlight-king-arthur-flour/.

119. National Center for Employee Ownership (NCEO), "A Visual Guide to Employee Ownership," https://www.esopinfo.org/how-esops-work/. See generally Corey Rosen, "Statutory Employee Stock Ownership Plans in the USA," in *The Oxford Handbook of Mutual, Co-operative, and Co-owned Business*, ed. Jonathan Michie, Joseph R. Blasi, and Carlo Borzaga (Oxford: Oxford University Press, 2017), 412–425.

120. NCEO, "A Visual Guide to Employee Ownership."

121. Ben Wells, "Pros and Cons of Selling Your Business to Employees with an ESOP," Financially Simple, June 29, 2018, https://financiallysimple.com/should-you-sell-your-business-to-employees-pros-and-cons-of-esops/.

122. Claire Martin, "At King Arthur Flour, Savoring the Perks of Employee Ownership," *New York Times*, June 25, 2016, https://www.nytimes.com/2016/06/26/business/at-king-arthur-flour-savoring-the-perks-of-employee-ownership.html.

123. Martin, "At King Arthur Flour, Savoring the Perks of Employee Ownership."

124. Martin, "At King Arthur Flour, Savoring the Perks of Employee Ownership."

125. Note that not all ESOP companies really involve workers in decision making in a meaningful way, so only a limited set of ESOPs are included here. See John P. Bonin, Derek C. Jones, and Louis Putterman, "Theoretical and Empirical Studies of Producer Cooperatives: Will Ever the Twain Meet?," *Journal of Economic Literature* 31, no. 3 (1993): 1292.

126. Mark J. Kaswan, "US Worker Co-operatives," in *The Oxford Handbook of Mutual, Co-operative, and Co-owned Business*, ed. Jonathan Michie, Joseph R. Blasi, and Carlo Borzaga (Oxford: Oxford University Press, 2017), 531.

127. Ace Hardware Corporation, *2018 Annual Report*, 3–4.

128. Funding Universe, "History of Ace Hardware Corporation," http://www.fundinguniverse.com/company-histories/ace-hardware-corporation-history/.

129. Ace Hardware Corporation, *2018 Annual Report*, 1–5.

130. Ace Hardware Corporation, *2018 Annual Report*, 2.

131. Ace Hardware Corporation, *2018 Annual Report*, 3.

132. Joyce Mazero and Suzie Loonam, "Purchasing Cooperatives: Leveraging a Supply Chain for Competitive Advantage," *Franchise Law Journal* 29, no. 3 (2010): 149.

133. Clare O'Connor, "How Ace Hardware Turned Corner Stores Into a $4.7 Billion Co-Op," *Forbes*, March 2, 2015, https://www.forbes.com/sites/clareoconnor/2015/02/11/how-ace-hardware-turned-corner-stores-into-a-4-7-billion-co-op/.

134. "Ace Hardware Retailers Express Strong Satisfaction with Co-Op and Pride in the Ace Brand," Ace Hardware, accessed July 23, 2020, https://newsroom.acehardware.com/ace-hardware-retailers-express-strong-satisfaction-with-co-op-and-pride-in-the-ace-brand/.

135. Joseph R. Blasi, Richard B. Freeman, and Douglas L. Kruse, "Evidence: What the US Research Shows About Worker Ownership," in *The Oxford Handbook of Mutual, Co-operative, and Co-owned Business*, ed. Jonathan Michie, Joseph R. Blasi, and Carlo Borzaga (Oxford: Oxford University Press, 2017), 211–212.

136. Blasi, Freeman, and Kruse, "Evidence," 215–217.

137. See Bonin, Jones, and Putterman, "Theoretical and Empirical Studies of Producer Cooperatives"; Chris Doucouliagos, "Worker Participation and Productivity in Labor-Managed and Participatory Capitalist Firms: A Meta-Analysis," *Industrial and Labor Relations Review* 49, no. 1 (Oct. 1995): 58–77. Contrary to conventional belief, worker cooperatives

also may, as Spencer Thomson finds, "in fact have an advantage in implementing complex divisions of labor." Spencer Thompson, "Towards a Social Theory of the Firm: Worker Cooperatives Reconsidered," *Journal of Co-Operative Organization and Management* 3, no. 1 (June 2015): 10.

138. Thompson, "Towards a Social Theory of the Firm," 10.

139. See generally Richard C. Williams, *The Cooperative Movement: Globalization from Below* (London: Ashgate, 2007). Early findings consistent with this were reported in Bonin, Jones, and Putterman, "Theoretical and Empirical Studies of Producer Cooperatives," in 1993.

140. Birchall, "The Performance of Member-Owned Businesses Since the Financial Crisis of 2008," 574–575.

141. Birchall et al., *Resilience of the Cooperative Business Model in Times of Crisis*, 16–21.

142. Birchall, "The Performance of Member-Owned Businesses Since the Financial Crisis of 2008," 578.

143. Birchall, "The Performance of Member-Owned Businesses Since the Financial Crisis of 2008," 579.

144. Brian Van Slyke, "Pandemic Crash Shows Worker Co-Ops Are More Resilient Than Traditional Business," *Truthout*, May 8, 2020, https://truthout.org/articles/pandemic-crash -shows-worker-co-ops-are-more-resilient-than-traditional-business/.

145. See John Curl, *For All the People: Uncovering the Hidden History of Cooperation, Cooperative Movements, and Communalism in America*, 2nd ed. (Oakland, CA: PM, 2012), vi.

146. Bruno Roelants, Diana Dovgan, Hyungsik Eum, and Elisa Terrasi, *The Resilience of the Cooperative Model: How Worker Cooperatives, Social Cooperatives and Other Worker-Owned Enterprises Respond to the Crisis and Its Consequences* (CECOP, June 2012), 11.

147. Roelants et al., *The Resilience of the Cooperative Model*, 19.

148. Roelants et al., *The Resilience of the Cooperative Model*, 15.

149. Pérotin, "Worker Co-operatives: Good, Sustainable Jobs in the Community," 141.

150. Thomas Brzustowski and Francesco Caselli, "Economic Growth in a Cooperative Economy," *IDEAS Working Paper Series from RePEc*, 2021, https://www.proquest.com/working -papers/economic-growth-cooperative-economy/docview/2587466273/se-2, 5.

3. THE SIMPLICITY OF COOPERATION

1. Terry Mollner, "Mondragón: A Third Way," *Review of Social Economy* 42, no. 3 (1984): 261, https://doi.org/10.1080/00346768400000024.

2. Francisco Javier Forcadell, "Democracy, Cooperation and Business Success: The Case of Mondragón Corporación Cooperativa," *Journal of Business Ethics* 56, no. 3 (2005): 255.

3. Sharryn Kasmir, *The Myth of Mondragón: Cooperatives, Politics, and Working-Class Life in a Basque Town* (Albany: State University of New York Press, 1996), 34.

4. KPMG, "Recreational Equipment, Inc.: Consolidated Financial Statements, December 28, 2019 and December 29, 2018," https://www.rei.com/assets/about-rei/financial-information /rei-fy19-issued-financial-statements/live.pdf.

5. Kasmir, *The Myth of Mondragón*, 34.

6. Pierre Dardot and Christian Laval reject the bundle-of-rights approach that has been taken by American legal realists. They argue that the bundles approach is incoherent,

naïve, and elusive. The reason, they argue, is that there is a dominant hierarchy in which the right to the capital overshadows all the others. Pierre Dardot and Christian Laval, *Common: On Revolution in the Twenty-First Century*, trans. Matthew MacLellan (London: Bloomsbury, 2019), 326. Dardot and Laval argue that a use right is inadequate and toothless. They write, "according to our thesis—namely, *the establishment of rules of common use through the exercise of instituent praxis, and its extension into a form of instituent use that is based on the ongoing revision of these rules*—common use must be linked to co-decision concerning the rules, and the resulting co-obligation that flows from this process" (Dardot and Laval, *Common*, 326). I do not find this convincing and will need to address it at greater length later. It is worth noting here, though, that in political proposition five, Dardot and Laval write about economic associationism. They described the "social economy," which comes close to the idea of the cooperationist economy I am developing here.

7. Dardot and Laval, *Common*, 325.

8. See generally Wesley Hohfeld, *Fundamental Legal Conceptions as Applied in Judicial Reasoning*, ed. David Campbell and Philip Thomas (New York: Routledge, 2001).

9. International Cooperative Alliance (ICA), "Cooperative Identity, Values and Principles," https://www.ica.coop/en/whats-co-op/co-operative-identity-values-principles.

10. Albert O. Hirschman, *Exit, Voice, and Loyalty: Responses to Decline in Firms, Organizations, and States* (Cambridge, MA: Harvard University Press, 1970).

11. Rich Daly, "Small Investors Are Bigger Than You Think," *Forbes*, May 6, 2015, https://www.forbes.com/sites/richdaly/2015/05/06/small-investors-are-bigger-than-you-think/?sh=7535415f6308.

12. Cooperation Jackson, "Sustainable Communities Initiative," https://cooperationjackson.org/sustainable-communities-initiative.

13. Kasmir, *The Myth of Mondragón*, 34.

14. ICA, "Cooperative Identity, Values and Principles."

15. Virginie Pérotin, "Worker Co-operatives: Good, Sustainable Jobs in the Community," in *The Oxford Handbook of Mutual, Co-operative, and Co-owned Business*, ed. Jonathan Michie, Joseph R. Blasi, and Carlo Borzaga (Oxford: Oxford University Press, 2017), 132.

16. *Puget Sound Plywood, Inc. v. Commissioner of Internal Revenue*, 44 T.C. 305 (U.S.T.C., 1965).

17. *Puget Sound Plywood*, 309.

18. Daniel Tischer and John Hoffmire, "Moving Towards 100 Percent Employee Ownership Through ESOPs: Added Complexities in Add-on Transactions," in *The Oxford Handbook of Mutual, Co-operative, and Co-owned Business*, ed. Jonathan Michie, Joseph R. Blasi, and Carlo Borzaga (Oxford: Oxford University Press, 2017), 295.

19. Tischer and Hoffmire, "Moving Towards 100 percent Employee Ownership Through ESOPs," 295; Corey Rosen, "Statutory Employee Stock Ownership Plans in the USA," in *The Oxford Handbook of Mutual, Co-operative, and Co-owned Business*, ed. Jonathan Michie, Joseph R. Blasi, and Carlo Borzaga (Oxford: Oxford University Press, 2017), 417.

20. Kasmir, *The Myth of Mondragón*, 33.

21. Terry Mollner, "Mondragón: A Third Way," *Review of Social Economy* 42, no. 3 (1984): 261.

22. Bernie Sanders, *Guide to Political Revolution* (New York: Henry Holt, 2017), 60–61.

23. Erik Sherman, "How Many Workers Must Live in Poverty for McDonald's CEO to Make $21.8 Million?," *Forbes*, July 12, 2018, https://www.forbes.com/sites/eriksherman/2018/07

/12/how-many-workers-must-live-in-poverty-for-mcdonalds-ceo-to-make-21-8-million
/#a25a0b10926d.

24. Dardot and Laval, *Common*, 1.

25. Gustavo García López, "Saskia Sassen on Extractive Logics and Geographies of Expulsion," *Undisciplined Environments*, August 9, 2017, https://undisciplinedenvironments.org
/2017/08/09/saskia-sassen-on-extractive-logics-and-geographies-of-expulsion/.

26. See generally Alan Rappeport, Emily Flitter, and Kate Kelly, "The Carried Interest Loophole
Survives Another Political Battle," *New York Times*, August 5, 2022, https://www.nytimes
.com/2022/08/05/business/carried-interest-senate-bill.html.

27. See 26 U.S. Code § 1385(a)(1) (Amounts includible in patron's gross income); 26 U.S. Code
§ 61 (Gross income defined). There has also been a lot of litigation over whether cooperative member income is subject to self-employment tax, which is another potential
source of taxation. See generally "Subchapter T and How Money Flows Through a Cooperative," Co-opLaw.org, accessed August 18, 2022, https://www.co-oplaw.org/knowledge
-base/patronage/#Employment_and_self-employment_tax.

28. Katharina Pistor, *The Code of Capital* (Princeton, NJ: Princeton University Press, 2019), 3.

4. THE POLITICAL THEORY OF COÖPERISM

1. See, for example, Richard Sennett, *Together: The Rituals, Pleasures and Politics of Cooperation* (New Haven, CT: Yale University Press, 2013), tracing cooperation rituals back to
medieval times.

2. See, for example, Vera Zamagni, "A Worldwide Historical Perspective on Co-operatives
and Their Evolution," in *The Oxford Handbook of Mutual, Co-operative, and Co-owned Business*, ed. Jonathan Michie, Joseph R. Blasi, and Carlo Borzaga (Oxford: Oxford University
Press, 2017), 101–102.

3. Zamagni, "A Worldwide Historical Perspective on Co-operatives and their Evolution,"
102–104.

4. See, for example, Joseph R. Blasi and Douglas L. Kruse, "An American Historical Perspective on Employee Ownership," in *The Oxford Handbook of Mutual, Co-operative, and
Co-owned Business*, ed. Jonathan Michie, Joseph R. Blasi, and Carlo Borzaga (Oxford:
Oxford University Press, 2017), 114–116; Sennett, *Together* (discussing cooperation rituals
in communities of enslaved persons).

5. Lynn Pitman, "History of Cooperatives in the United States: An Overview," University of Wisconsin Center for Cooperatives, Madison, revised December 2018, https://
resources.uwcc.wisc.edu/History_of_Cooperatives.pdf, 1. Pitman offers the conventional
Western history of cooperatives in the following way:

Building on trade and social guild traditions, mutual aid and "friendly society" organizations sprang up to address the conditions of the times, and contributed to the
development of the cooperative business ideas. Robert Owen (1771–1858) and Charles
Fourier (1772–1837), searching for paths to a more harmonious, utopian society, articulated arguments that provided a broader rationale for cooperative organizations.

The more pragmatic William King (1786–1865) advocated the development of
consumer cooperatives to address working class issues. His self-published magazine,

"The Cooperator," provided information on cooperative practice as well as theory. King emphasized small cooperatives that could be started with capital supplied by members. He stressed the use of democratic principles of governance, and the education of the public about cooperatives.

The wave of consumer cooperatives that followed were part of a broader vision in which social needs could be met through cooperative action. The Rochdale Society of Equitable Pioneers, considered the prototype for the modern cooperative association, was organized in 1844.

6.   Pitman, "History of Cooperatives in the United States," 2.

7.   Sanjukta Paul at the University of Michigan is conducting research on the question of coordination rights under antitrust law, arguing that the legal framework should be more permissive with regard to certain cooperative arrangements. See her forthcoming book, *Solidarity in the Shadow of Antitrust: Labor and the Legal Idea of Competition* (Cambridge: Cambridge University Press, forthcoming 2023).

8.   Louis Blanc, *Organization of Work*, trans. Marie Paula Dickoré (Cincinnati: University of Cincinnati Press, 1911).

9.   Robert Owen, *A New View of Society: or, Essays on the Formation of the Human Character Preparatory to the Development of a Plan for Gradually Ameliorating the Condition of Mankind*, 3rd ed. (London: R. and A. Taylor, 1817); facsimile reproduction by the Free Press, Glencoe, Illinois, undated (a first essay was published in 1813, the full book was published with three additional essays revised in 1816-1817); Robert Owen, *Report: To the Committee of the Association for the Relief of the Manufacturing and Labouring Poor, Referred to the Committee of the House of Commons on the Poor Laws*, March 12, 1817, http://la.utexas.edu/users/hcleaver/368/368owenrptcom.html.

10.   Owen, *A New View of Society*, 129.

11.   Owen, *A New View of Society*, 33.

12.   Owen, *A New View of Society*, 42. Owen was paternalistic, as Peter Ranis notes in *Cooperatives Confront Capitalism: Challenging the Neoliberal Economy* (London: ZED, 2016), 8.

13.   Owen, *A New View of Society*, 71.

14.   Owen, *A New View of Society*, 123-124.

15.   Owen, *A New View of Society*, 73.

16.   Owen, *A New View of Society*, 74; see generally Gary Becker, *Human Capital: A Theoretical and Empirical Analysis, with Special Reference to Education*, 3rd ed. (Chicago: University of Chicago Press, 1993 [1975]).

17.   Owen, *A New View of Society*, 77.

18.   Karl Marx, "Critique of the Gotha Program," in *The Marx-Engels Reader*, 2nd ed., ed. Robert C. Tucker (New York: Norton, 1978), 536, https://www.marxists.org/archive/marx/works/1875/gotha/ch01.htm. For a more generous reading of Marx on cooperatives and an excellent review of the nineteenth-century proponents of worker cooperatives, see Ranis, *Cooperatives Confront Capitalism*, 2-13.

19.   Owen, *A New View of Society*, 65, 22, 129.

20.   Peter Kropotkin, preface to *The Conquest of Bread* (New York: Putnam, 1906); André Breton, *Ode à Charles Fourier* (Paris: Éditions de la Revue Fontaine, 1947); Roland Barthes, *Sade, Fourier, Loyola* (Paris: Éditions du Seuil, 1971); Herbert Marcuse, *Eros and Civilization:*

A Philosophical Inquiry Into Freud (Boston: Beacon, 1955); Hakim Bey, "The Lemonade Ocean and Modern Times" (Anarchist Library, 1991), http://theanarchistlibrary.org/library /hakim-bey-the-lemonade-ocean-modern-times.

21.   Charles Fourier, *The Theory of the Four Movements*, ed. Gareth Stedman Jones, trans. Ian Patterson (New York: Cambridge University Press, 1996 [1808]), 12.

22.   Fourier, *The Theory of the Four Movements*, 117.

23.   Pierre-Joseph Proudhon, *The System of Economic Contradictions, or the Philosophy of Poverty*, trans. Benjamin R. Tucker (Anarchist Library, 1847 [1946]), 254–255.

24.   Pierre-Joseph Proudhon, *What Is Property?*, ed. and trans. Donald R. Kelley and Bonnie G. Smith (Cambridge: Cambridge University Press, 1994), 205.

25.   Proudhon, *What Is Property?*, 14 (with quotation marks for emphasis in original); see also 215.

26.   Proudhon, *What Is Property?*, 36.

27.   Proudhon, *What Is Property?*, 215.

28.   Proudhon letter to Blanc, April 8, 1848, in *Property Is Theft! A Pierre-Joseph Proudhon Anthology*, ed. Iain McKay (Edinburgh: AK, 2011), 296; Proudhon letter response to Louis Blanc, December 28, 1849, in McKay, *Property Is Theft!*, 501.

29.   See Proudhon letter to Blanc on April 8, 1848, 501.

30.   Proudhon, letter of December 3, 1849, in McKay, *Property Is Theft!*, 479; see also Proudhon, Response to Louis Blanc, 28 December 1849, in McKay, *Property Is Theft!*, 501.

31.   Proudhon, *What Is Property?*, 195–197.

32.   See Proudhon letter to Marx dated May 17, 1846, in McKay, *Property Is Theft!*, 164.

33.   Proudhon, *What Is Property?*, 208. Proudhon writes of science, truth, laws, and order, concluding that the world is ordered, and therefore we do not need government or legislative power. Notice how close this is to François Quesnay and the Physiocrats, paradoxically. There is a similar reliance on natural order and scientific conceptions of human nature that leads to a displacement of the state. In his *System of Economic Contradictions*, Proudhon's argument is based on "the depths of our nature." McKay, *Property Is Theft!*, 171. It is indeed curious how such a similar faith in science and nature would lead Proudhon and Quesnay to such different politics.

34.   Proudhon letter to Marx dated May 17, 1846, in McKay, *Property Is Theft!*, 163.

35.   Pierre-Joseph Proudhon, entry of December 26, 1847, in private journal, in *Carnets de P. J. Proudhon*, vol. 2, trans. Mitchell Abidor (Paris: M. Rivière, 1960), 337: VI, 178, https:// www.marxists.org/reference/subject/economics/proudhon/1847/jews.htm.

36.   Proudhon, *Carnets de P. J. Proudhon*.

37.   Charles Gide, *Le Coopératisme: Conférences de propagande*, 5th ed. (Paris: Librairie du Recueil Sirey, 1929), 105–106.

38.   Adam Smith, *An Inquiry Into the Nature and Causes of the Wealth of Nations*, ed. Edwin Cannan (Chicago: University of Chicago Press, 1976); Adam Smith, *The Theory of Moral Sentiments* (New York: Penguin, 2010).

39.   For a useful discussion of the concept of "racial capitalism," with important references, see Olúfẹ́mi O. Táíwò and Liam Kofi Bright, "A Response to Michael Walzer," *Dissent*, August 7, 2020, https://www.dissentmagazine.org/online_articles/a-response-to-michael-walzer.

40.   W. E. B. Du Bois, "A Negro Nation Within the Nation," *Current History* 42, no. 3 (1935): 265.

41. Du Bois, "A Negro Nation Within the Nation," 265.

42. W. E. B. Du Bois, *Black Reconstruction, 1860–1880* (New York: Free Press, 1998), 362– 366.

43. Peter Kropotkin, *Mutual Aid: A Factor of Evolution* (New York: Dover, 2006).

44. Clarke A. Chambers, "The Cooperative League of the United States of America, 1916–1961: A Study of Social Theory and Social Action," *Agricultural History* 36, no. 2 (April 1962): 62.

45. Du Bois, "A Negro Nation Within the Nation"; the article was based on a speech Du Bois delivered on June 26, 1934, in New York City, at the time that he resigned from the NAACP. See W. E. B. De Bois, "A Negro Nation Within a Nation," BlackPast, March 13, 2012, https://www.blackpast.org/african-american-history/speeches-african-american-history/1934-w-e-b-du-bois-negro-nation-within-nation/.

46. Du Bois, "A Negro Nation Within the Nation," 269.

47. Du Bois, "A Negro Nation Within the Nation," 270.

48. Du Bois, "A Negro Nation Within the Nation," 265–270.

49. Du Bois, "A Negro Nation Within the Nation," 268.

50. Du Bois, "A Negro Nation Within the Nation," 269.

51. Du Bois, "A Negro Nation Within the Nation," 269.

52. Du Bois, "A Negro Nation Within the Nation," 270.

53. Du Bois, "A Negro Nation Within the Nation," 270.

54. Sennett, *Together*.

55. Kali Akuno and Ajamu Nangwaya, *Jackson Rising: The Struggle for Economic Democracy and Black Self-Determination in Jackson, Mississippi* (Wakefield, Quebec: Daraja, 2017), 37.

56. Cooperation Jackson, "Cooperation Jackson, Cooperation Vermont, the Marshfield Cooperative and PNLL," News and Media, February 17, 2022, https://cooperationjackson.org/blog/cooperationjackson-cooperationvermont-marshfieldcoop.

57. Ella Fassler, "Activists Are Sharing Land in Vermont with People Escaping Climate Disaster," *VICE Magazine*, June 29, 2021, https://www.vice.com/en/article/wx5zb9/activists-are-buying-land-in-vermont-to-help-people-escape-climate-disaster.

58. See Cooperation Humboldt, *Cooperation Humboldt: Building a Solidarity Economy on California's North Coast. Who We Are, What We Believe, and What We Do* (2020), https://cooperationhumboldt.com/wp-content/uploads/2020/09/CH-general-info-booklet-with-bleed-spreads.pdf.

59. Kropotkin, *Mutual Aid*.

60. Thomas Huxley, "The Struggle for Existence in Human Society," in *Collected Essays IX* (1888), https://mathcs.clarku.edu/huxley/CE9/Str.html.

61. Jia Tolentino, "Can I Help You? The Meaning of Mutual Aid During a Pandemic," *New Yorker*, May 18, 2020, 26.

62. Andrej Grubačić, "David Graeber Left Us a Parting Gift—His Thoughts on Kropotkin's *Mutual Aid*," *Truthout*, September 4, 2020, https://truthout.org/articles/david-graeber-left-us-a-parting-gift-his-thoughts-on-kropotkins-mutual-aid/.

63. David Graeber and Andrej Grubačić, "Introduction from the Forthcoming *Mutual Aid: An Illuminated Factor of Evolution* by David Graeber and Andrej Grubačić," in "David Graeber Left Us a Parting Gift—His Thoughts on Kropotkin's *Mutual Aid*," *Truthout*, September 4, 2020, https://truthout.org/articles/david-graeber-left-us-a-parting-gift-his-thoughts-on-kropotkins-mutual-aid/.

64. Graeber and Grubačić, "Introduction from the Forthcoming *Mutual Aid*."

65. Dean Spade, *Mutual Aid: Building Solidarity During This Crisis (and the Next)* (New York: Verso, 2020); Dean Spade, "Solidarity Not Charity: Mutual Aid for Mobilization and Survival," *Social Text 142* 38, no. 1 (March 2020): 131–151.

66. Simon Springer, *The Anarchist Roots of Geography: Toward Spatial Emancipation* (Minneapolis: University of Minnesota Press, 2016); Simon Springer, "Property Is the Mother of Famine: On Dispossession, Wages, and the Threat of Hunger," *Political Geography* 62 (2018): 201–203.

67. Larry Samuelson, "Game Theory in Economics and Beyond," *Journal of Economic Perspectives* 30, no. 4 (November 1, 2016): 116.

68. Alexander J. Stewart and Joshua B. Plotkin, "Collapse of Cooperation in Evolving Games," *Proceedings of the National Academy of Sciences* 111, no. 49 (December 9, 2014): 17558. In this paper, Stewart and Plotkin challenge the consensus by introducing the possibility of players changing the rewards they reap from cooperation over time.

69. See Samuelson, "Game Theory in Economics and Beyond," 116.

70. Samuelson, "Game Theory in Economics and Beyond," 115–116.

71. Samuelson, "Game Theory in Economics and Beyond," 122.

72. Samuelson, "Game Theory in Economics and Beyond," 122.

73. Eric Maskin, "How Can Cooperative Game Theory Be Made More Relevant to Economics? An Open Problem," in *Open Problems in Mathematics*, ed. John Forbes Nash, and Michael Th. Rassias (Cham, Switzerland: Springer International, 2016), 347, 348.

74. Maskin, "How Can Cooperative Game Theory Be Made More Relevant to Economics?," 347.

75. Samuelson, "Game Theory in Economics and Beyond," 123.

76. See, for example, Samuelson, "Game Theory in Economics and Beyond," 108.

77. Samuelson, "Game Theory in Economics and Beyond," 114; in a similar vein, the infrequency of worker cooperatives may be due to institutional bias toward capitalist firm formation. See Spencer Thompson, "Towards a Social Theory of the Firm: Worker Cooperatives Reconsidered," *Journal of Co-Operative Organization and Management* 3, no. 1 (June 2015): 10.

78. The difference is important, and there are key distinctions even if there is some "consilience between cooperative enterprises and cooperative solutions to game"; for instance, it is important to emphasize that cooperative enterprises value democratic participation, equality, and solidarity, but that none of those values is theorized into cooperative game theory. Roger A. McCain, "Cooperation and Effort, Reciprocity and Mutual Supervision in Worker Cooperatives," in *Advances in the Economic Analysis of Participatory and Labor-Managed Firms*, vol. 10, ed. Sonja Novkovic and Vania Sena (Bingley, UK: Emerald, 2007), 2.

79. Richard J. Sexton, "The Formation of Cooperatives: A Game-Theoretic Approach with Implications for Cooperative Finance, Decision Making, and Stability," *American Journal of Agricultural Economics* 68, no. 2 (May 1986): 214; Thomas Brzustowski and Francesco Caselli, "Economic Growth in a Cooperative Economy," *IDEAS Working Paper Series from RePEc*, 2021, https://www.proquest.com/working-papers/economic-growth-cooperative-economy/docview/2587466273/se-2, 3.

80. Sexton, "The Formation of Cooperatives," 224.

81. Samuelson, "Game Theory in Economics and Beyond," 124.

82. See Andrew Abbott, *Processual Sociology* (Chicago: University of Chicago Press, 2016). Abbott is not the only social theorist to place process at the heart of his sociology. Others who have emphasized this dynamic include the sociologists Norbert Elias and Pierre Bourdieu, whose work has also sometimes been labeled "processual."

83. Abbott, *Processual Sociology*, ix.

84. As Abbott writes, "individuals and social entities are not the elements of social life, but are patterns of regularities defined on lineages of successive events." Abbott, *Processual Sociology*, ix.

85. This reminds me of one of the labels on Dr. Bronner's soaps concerning "Dr. Gero Leson's Supply Chain ABCs": "Every stakeholder in your supply chain must make a decent living—be treated with respect! Don't create an island of happiness in a sea of misery!" See Kieran Dahl, "How a Decades-Old Hippie Soap Brand Became a Touchstone of Wellness Culture," *Vox*, May 8, 2019, https://www.vox.com/the-goods/2019/5/8/18535403/dr-bronners-soap -label-castile. The story behind Dr. Bronner's soaps is fascinating, and though they may not serve as a universal template, their politics, reflected in their political and charitable donations as well as in their famously wordy soap labels, exhibit a cooperationist ethic.

86. Johnston Birchall and Lou Hammond Ketilson, *Resilience of the Cooperative Business Model in Times of Crisis* (Geneva: International Labour Organization, Sustainable Enterprise Programme, 2009), 11.

87. Janelle Orsi, William Lisa, and Sushil Jacob, *Legal Guide to Cooperative Conversions: A Business Owner's Legal Guide to Cooperative Conversion Including Conversion Models, Case Studies and Sample Documents* (Sustainable Economies Law Center, n.d.), 3.

88. As the United States Court of Appeals for the Sixth Circuit made clear in *Simpson v. Ernst & Young*, in 1996, "if a worker cooperative chooses not to classify worker-owners as employees, it must give substantial management power to those worker-owners, and must adopt clear safeguards to prevent the devolution into a more hierarchical structure." Orsi, Lisa, and Jacob, *Legal Guide to Cooperative Conversions*, 45; see *Simpson v. Ernst & Young*, 100 F.3d 436 (6th Cir. 1996). On the role of the NLRB, see *NLRB v. North Arkansas Electric Cooperative, Inc.* 446 F.2d 602 (8th Cir, 1971); *NLRB v. Bell Aerospace Co.* 416 U.S. 267 (1974).

89. Thomas Piketty, *Capital and Ideology* (Cambridge, MA: Harvard University Press, 2020), 511.

90. RIPESS (Intercontinental Network for the Promotion of the Social Solidarity Economy; Réseau Intercontinental de Promotion de l'Économie Social Solidaire), "Charter of RIPESS," approved by the Board of Directors of RIPESS in Montevideo, Uruguay, October 20, 2008, http://www.ripess.org/wp-content/uploads/2017/08/RIPESS_charter_EN.pdf, 4.

91. REAS (Red de redes de economía alternativa y solidaria), "Carta de Principios de la Economía Solidaria," *Portal de Economía Solidaria*, May 2011, https://www.economiasolidaria.org/sites /default/files/pages_attachments/CARTA_ECONOMIA_SOLIDARIA_REAS.pdf.

92. REAS, "Carta de Principios de la Economía Solidaria," 8.

93. Richard D. Wolff, *Democracy at Work: A Cure for Capitalism* (Chicago: Haymarket, 2012); see also William Davies, "Corporate Governance Beyond Neoliberalism: Agency, Democracy, and Co-operation," in *The Oxford Handbook of Mutual, Co-operative, and Co-owned Business*, ed. Jonathan Michie, Joseph R. Blasi, and Carlo Borzaga (Oxford: Oxford University Press, 2017), 445-455; Raymond Williams, *The Long Revolution* (Peterborough, Ontario: Broadview, 2001).

94.   See generally Stephen A. Marglin and Juliet B. Schor, eds., *The Golden Age of Capitalism: Reinterpreting the Postwar Experience* (Oxford: Clarendon, 1992); Andrew Glyn, *Capitalism Unleashed: Finance, Globalization and Welfare* (New York: Oxford University Press, 2006).

95.   Thomas Piketty, *Capital in the Twenty-First Century* (Cambridge, MA: Harvard University Press, 2014); Piketty, *Capital and Ideology*; Lucas Chancel, Thomas Piketty, Emmanuel Saez, and Gabriel Zucman, *World Inequality Report 2022*, World Inequality Lab, https://wir2022.wid.world/www-site/uploads/2022/03/0098-21_WIL_RIM_RAPPORT_A4.pdf.

96.   Piketty, *Capital and Ideology*, 3.

97.   Karl Marx and Friedrich Engels, *The German Ideology, Including Theses on Feuerbach* (New York: Prometheus, 1998); see generally Emmet Kennedy, "'Ideology' from Destutt De Tracy to Marx," *Journal of the History of Ideas* 40, no. 3 (1979): 353–368; Guillaume Rouleau, "Le langage de l'idéologie. Sur l'idéologie dans *L'Idéologie allemande*" (mémoire, EHESS, August 25, 2022, on file with author). Guillaume Rouleau, a doctoral student at the EHESS, will be analyzing in more detail this genealogy of Piketty's (and others', such as Luc Boltanski's) use of the term *ideology*, so stay tuned for more.

98.   Georg Lukács, *History and Class Consciousness*, trans. Rodney Livingstone (Cambridge, MA: MIT Press, 1971); Antonio Gramsci, *Prison Notebooks*, vols. 1–3, ed. Joseph A. Buttigieg, trans. Joseph A. Buttigieg and Antonio Callari (New York: Columbia University Press, 2011); Max Horkheimer, "Traditional and Critical Theory," in *Critical Theory: Selected Essays*, trans. Matthew J. O'Connell et al. (New York: Continuum, 1972); Louis Althusser, "Ideology and Ideological State Apparatuses (Notes Towards an Investigation)," in *Lenin and Philosophy and Other Essays*, trans. Ben Brewster (New York: Monthly Review, 1971); see generally Steven Lukes, "In Defense of 'False Consciousness,'" *University of Chicago Legal Forum* 2011, article 3 (2011): 19–28, https://chicagounbound.uchicago.edu/cgi/viewcontent.cgi?article=1473&context=uclf.

99.   Karl Mannheim, *Ideology and Utopia: An Introduction to the Sociology of Knowledge*, trans. Louis Wirth and Edward Shils (New York: Harcourt, 1936).

100.   Piketty, *Capital and Ideology*, 123.

101.   Piketty, *Capital and Ideology*, 1.

102.   Piketty, *Capital and Ideology*, 113.

103.   Piketty, *Capital and Ideology*, 972.

104.   See, for example, Piketty, *Capital and Ideology*, 969, 1031.

105.   Piketty, *Capital and Ideology*, 7.

106.   Bernard E. Harcourt, *Critique and Praxis* (New York: Columbia University Press, 2020), 203–209.

107.   See Piketty, *Capital and Ideology*, 969.

108.   Katharina Pistor, *The Code of Capital* (Princeton, NJ: Princeton University Press, 2019).

109.   Piketty, *Capital and Ideology*, 7.

110.   Pistor, *The Code of Capital*, 4.

111.   Pistor, *The Code of Capital*, 205. One of the most important recent historical developments is that states have begun to recognize foreign laws of capital coding and, as a result, are increasingly willing to enforce legal protections established in other jurisdictions. This has been very powerful for coding capital because it has allowed lawyers to apply the most beneficial laws—the English common law and the laws of the state of New York—to

all states. Katharina Pistor refers to this as the "empire of law," suggesting the imperial dimension of English and New York law over other states. This allows capital holders to extend the advantages of capital beyond the local context. It allows states to "use their coercive powers to enforce" capital, and it "allow(s) domestic parties to opt into foreign law without losing the protections of local courts." Pistor, *The Code of Capital*, 7.

112. Pistor, *The Code of Capital*, x, 3.
113. Pistor, *The Code of Capital*, 183.
114. Pistor, *The Code of Capital*, x.
115. Michel Foucault, *The Birth of Biopolitics: Lectures at the Collège de France, 1978–1979*, ed. Michel Senellart, trans. Graham Burchell (New York: Picador, 2008), 161.
116. Hagen Henrÿ, "Co-operative Principles and Co-operative Law Across the Globe," in *The Oxford Handbook of Mutual, Co-operative, and Co-owned Business*, ed. Jonathan Michie, Joseph R. Blasi, and Carlo Borzaga (Oxford: Oxford University Press, 2017), 39.
117. Henry Hansmann, *The Ownership of Enterprise* (Cambridge, MA: Harvard University Press, 1996); Henry Hansmann and Reinier Kraakman, "The End of History for Corporate Law," *Georgetown Law Journal* 89, no. 2 (January 2001): 439–468; Henrÿ, "Co-operative Principles and Co-operative Law Across the Globe," 43; Antonio Fici, "The Essential Role of Co-operative Law and Some Related Issues," in *The Oxford Handbook of Mutual, Co-operative, and Co-owned Business*, ed. Jonathan Michie, Joseph R. Blasi, and Carlo Borzaga (Oxford: Oxford University Press, 2017), 539–549.
118. See Henrÿ, "Co-operative Principles and Co-operative Law Across the Globe," 40, 41 n.5; see generally Dante Cracogna, Antonio Fici, and Hagen Henrÿ, eds., *The International Handbook of Cooperative Law* (Heidelberg: Springer, 2013).
119. See, for example, Camille Kerr, "Choosing a Business Entity: A Guide for Worker Cooperatives," Democracy at Work Institute, U.S. Federation of Worker Cooperatives, 2014, https://institute.coop/resources/choosing-business-entity-guide-worker-cooperatives.

5. THE ECONOMIC THEORY OF COÖPERISM

1. John Stuart Mill, *Principles of Political Economy with Some of Their Applications to Social Philosophy*, Fifth London Edition, vol. 2 (New York: Appleton, 1920), bk. 4, chap. 7, § 6, 357–378.
2. Mill, *Principles of Political Economy*, 357–359.
3. Clarke A. Chambers, "The Cooperative League of the United States of America, 1916–1961: A Study of Social Theory and Social Action," *Agricultural History* 36, no. 2 (April 1962): 62.
4. Francis Fukuyama, "The End of History?" *National Interest*, no. 16 (Summer 1989): 4.
5. See generally Bernard E. Harcourt, *The Illusion of Free Markets: Punishment and the Myth of Natural Order* (Cambridge, MA: Harvard University Press, 2011).
6. See Harcourt, *The Illusion of Free Markets*; Fred L. Block, *Capitalism: The Future of an Illusion* (Berkeley: University of California Press, 2018).
7. *Oxford English Dictionary*, www.oed.com/view/Entry/27454.
8. *Oxford English Dictionary*, www.oed.com/view/Entry/27455.
9. Steven Levitt and Sudhir Alladi Venkatesh, "An Economic Analysis of a Drug-Selling Gang's Finances," *Quarterly Journal of Economics* 115, no. 3 (2000): 755–789; Edward Lazear

and Sherwin Rosen, "Rank Order Tournaments as Optimum Labor Contracts," *Journal of Political Economy* 89, no. 5 (October 1981): 841–864.

10.   Gustavo García López, "Saskia Sassen on Extractive Logics and Geographies of Expulsion," *Undisciplined Environments*, August 9, 2017, https://undisciplinedenvironments.org/2017/08/09/saskia-sassen-on-extractive-logics-and-geographies-of-expulsion/.

11.   Michel Foucault, *The Birth of Biopolitics: Lectures at the Collège de France, 1978–1979*, ed. Michel Senellart, trans. Graham Burchell (New York: Picador, 2008), 91.

12.   See generally Axel Honneth, *The Idea of Socialism*, trans. Joseph Ganahl (Malden, MA: Polity Press, 2017).

13.   See U.S. Department of the Treasury Bureau of Fiscal Service, *Public Debt Reports* (Washington, D.C., 2020), *TreasuryDirect*.gov, accessed April 11, 2020, https://www.treasurydirect.gov/govt/reports/pd/pd.htm.

14.   U.S. Government Accountability Office (GAO), *An Annual Report to Congress*, GAO-20-403SP (Washington, D.C., 2020), accessed April 11, 2020, https://www.gao.gov/assets/710/705327.pdf, 3.

15.   U.S. Congress, House, Coronavirus Aid, Relief, and Economic Security Act, H.R. 748, 116th Cong. (2020), § 4003. Coronavirus Aid, Relief, and Economic Security Act (CARES Act), Pub. L. No. 116-136, 134 Stat. 281 (2020).

16.   H.R. 748, § 1103(b)(1).

17.   H.R. 748, § 1106. Coronavirus Aid, Relief, and Economic Security Act (CARES Act), Pub. L. No. 116-136, 134 Stat. 297 (2020), §1106.

18.   H.R. 748, § 1107(a)(1). Coronavirus Aid, Relief, and Economic Security Act (CARES Act), Pub. L. No. 116-136, 134 Stat. 301 (2020), §1107(a)(1).

19.   H.R. 748, § 1107(a)(6) and (7).

20.   H.R. 748, § 5001. Coronavirus Aid, Relief, and Economic Security Act (CARES Act), Pub. L. No. 116-136, 134 Stat. 501 (2020), §5001.

21.   H.R. 748, p. 263.

22.   H.R. 748, p. 316.

23.   Emily Cochrane and Nicholas Fandos, "Senate Approves a $2 Trillion Virus Response," *New York Times*, March 26, 2020, https://www.nytimes.com/2020/03/25/us/politics/coronavirus-senate-deal.html.

24.   H.R. 748, § 4003 (b)(1) and (2). Coronavirus Aid, Relief, and Economic Security Act (CARES Act), Pub. L. No. 116-136, 134 Stat. 470 (2020), §4003 (b)(1).

25.   H.R. 748, § 4003 (c)(2)(E), (F), and (G). Coronavirus Aid, Relief, and Economic Security Act (CARES Act), Pub. L. No. 116-136, 134 Stat. 471 (2020), §4003 (c)(2)(E), (F), and (G).

26.   H.R. 748, § 4003 (d)(1). Coronavirus Aid, Relief, and Economic Security Act (CARES Act), Pub. L. No. 116-136, 134 Stat. 474 (2020), §4003(d)(1).

27.   H.R. 748, § 4112(a). Coronavirus Aid, Relief, and Economic Security Act (CARES Act), Pub. L. No. 116-136, 134 Stat. 498 (2020), §4112(a).

28.   H.R. 748, § 4117. Coronavirus Aid, Relief, and Economic Security Act (CARES Act), Pub. L. No. 116-136, 134 Stat. 500 (2020), §4117.

29.   "The Trump Administration and a Group of Major Airlines Agreed on a $25 Billion Bailout," in "Coronavirus Live Updates: Trump Halts U.S. Funding of World Health Organization," *New York Times*, April 14, 2020, https://www.nytimes.com/2020/04/14/us/coronavirus-updates.html?action=click&module=Spotlight&pgtype=Homepage#link-6a70d90d.

30. "The Trump Administration and a Group of Major Airlines Agreed on a $25 Billion Bailout."

31. Chris Isidore, "American Airlines Will Lay Off 19,000 Workers If It Doesn't Get Additional Federal Help," *CNN*, August 25, 2020, https://www.cnn.com/2020/08/25/business /american-airlines-job-cuts/index.html.

32. Tim Wu, "Don't Feel Sorry for the Airlines," *New York Times*, March 16, 2020, https://www .nytimes.com/2020/03/16/opinion/airlines-bailout.html.

33. Tim Wu and Yaryna Serkez, "These Companies Enriched Themselves: Now They're Getting a Bailout," *New York Times*, March 27, 2020, https://www.nytimes.com/interactive /2020/03/27/opinion/coronavirus-bailout.html.

34. H.R. 748, § 4003 (b)(4). Coronavirus Aid, Relief, and Economic Security Act (CARES Act), Pub. L. No. 116-136, 134 Stat. 470 (2020), §4003 (b)(4).

35. H.R. 748, § 2303, Coronavirus Aid, Relief, and Economic Security Act (CARES Act), Pub. L. No. 116-136, 134 Stat. 352 (2020), §2303, "Modifications for Net Operating Losses," 72 et seq.; see especially subsection (a) "Temporary Repeal of Taxable Income Limitation."

36. See *Net Operating Loss Deduction*, 26 U.S. Code § 172 (2020), accessed April 15, 2020, https://www.law.cornell.edu/uscode/text/26/172.

37. H.R. 748, § 2303(a)(1). Coronavirus Aid, Relief, and Economic Security Act (CARES Act), Pub. L. No. 116-136, 134 Stat. 353 (2020), §2303 (a)(1).

38. The Joint Committee on Taxation (JCT), *Estimated Revenue Effects of the Revenue Provisions Contained in an Amendment in the Nature of a Substitute to H.R. 748, the 'Coronavirus Aid, Relief, And Economic Security ('CARES') Act,' As Passed by the Senate on March 25, 2020, and Scheduled for Consideration by the House of Representatives on March 27, 2020*, JCX-11-20, March 26, 2020, https://www.jct.gov/publications.html?func=startdown&id=5252.

39. JCT, *Estimated Revenue Effects*, page 2, line C.5; page 1, line C.3. The *Washington Post* describes the tax change as follows: "Under the 2017 legislation, owners of businesses formed as "pass-through" entities and partnerships could deduct a maximum of $250,000 (or $500,000 in the case of couples) in losses from their 'nonbusiness' income. That change came with other measures aimed at lowering the tax obligations for these firms, including new deductions from their federal tax obligations. . . . Under the coronavirus relief legislation, the limit was suspended, enabling wealthy investors to use millions in losses to reduce their tax burdens. The policy also applies retroactively so losses in 2018 and 2019 can be 'carried back' against the past five years." Jeff Stein, "Tax Change in Coronavirus Package Overwhelmingly Benefits Millionaires, Congressional Body Finds," *Washington Post*, April 14, 2020, https://www.washingtonpost.com/business/2020/04/14 /coronavirus-law-congress-tax-change/.

40. Thomas A. Barthold, Joint Committee on Taxation to Honorable Sheldon Whitehouse and Honorable Lloyd Doggett, letter, April 9, 2020, https://www.whitehouse.senate.gov /imo/media/doc/116-0849.pdf; see Senator Sheldon Whitehouse, "Whitehouse, Doggett Release New Analysis Showing GOP Tax Provisions in CARES Act Overwhelmingly Benefit Million-Dollar-Plus Earners," press release, April 14, 2020, https://www.whitehouse .senate.gov/news/release/whitehouse-doggett-release-new-analysis-showing-gop-tax -provisions-in-cares-act-overwhelmingly-benefit-million-dollar-plus-earners.

41. Joint Committee on Taxation to Honorable Sheldon Whitehouse and Honorable Lloyd Doggett, April 9, 2020 (estimating the average benefit at $1.6 million). *Forbes* magazine estimates the tax change is likely to net about $1.7 million each for those approximately

43,000 taxpayers with annual earnings over \$1 million. *Forbes* calculated this by taking 82 percent of the tax revenue loss estimated for the tax change in the first JTC report (\$90 billion) and dividing that by the number of returns in that category (43,000). Shahar Ziv, "How Some Rich Americans Are Getting Stimulus 'Checks' Averaging \$1.7 Million," *Forbes*, April 14, 2020, https://www.forbes.com/sites/shaharziv/2020/04/14/why-are-rich -americans-getting-17-million-stimulus-checks/#1c29916a665b. As *Forbes* emphasizes, the \$1.7 million windfall is an average, with some individuals likely to get more and others less.

42.   Senator Sheldon Whitehouse, "Whitehouse, Doggett Release New Analysis Showing GOP Tax Provisions in CARES Act Overwhelmingly Benefit Million-Dollar-Plus Earn-ers," press release.

43.   Whitehouse, "Whitehouse, Doggett Release New Analysis."

44.   "U.S. Stocks Have Their Best Month Since 1987," *New York Times*, April 30, 2020, https:// www.nytimes.com/2020/04/30/business/stock-market-today-coronavirus.html#link-23f83d60.

45.   Andrew Van Dam, "Did a Third of the Economy Really Vanish in Just Three Months?," *Washington Post*, July 30, 2020, https://www.washingtonpost.com/business/2020/07/30/did -third-economy-really-vanish-just-three-months/.

46.   Barbara Kollmeyer, "An 'Extreme' August on the Stock Market Might Be Telling Us Something About the November Election," *Marketwatch*, September 1, 2020, https://www .marketwatch.com/story/an-extreme-august-on-the-stock-market-might-be-telling-us -something-about-the-november-election-2020-08-31.

47.   Claire Hansen, "Dow Rises Above 29000 for the First Time Since February," September 2, 2020, https://www.usnews.com/news/national-news/articles/2020-09-02/dow-rises-above -29000-for-the-first-time-since-february.

48.   Neil Irwin, "Everything Is Awful: So Why Is the Stock Market Booming?," *New York Times*, April 10, 2020, https://www.nytimes.com/2020/04/10/upshot/virus-stock-market -booming.html.

49.   Paul Krugman, "Crashing Market, Rising Stocks: What's Going On?," *New York Times*, April 30, 2020, https://www.nytimes.com/2020/04/30/opinion/economy-stock-market -coronavirus.html.

50.   Philip Mirowski, *Never Let a Serious Crisis Go to Waste* (New York: Verso, 2013).

51.   Matt Phillips, "The Bad News Won't Stop, but the Markets Keep Rising," *New York Times*, April 29, 2020, https://www.nytimes.com/2020/04/29/business/stock-markets.html.

52.   Wu, "Don't Feel Sorry for the Airlines."

53.   Eyal Press, "A Preventable Cancer Is on the Rise in Alabama," *New Yorker*, April 6, 2020, newyorker.com/magazine/2020/04/06/a-preventable-cancer-is-on-the-rise-in-alabama.

54.   Ronald J. Daniels and Marc H. Morial, "The Covid-19 Racial Disparities Could Be Even Worse Than We Think," *Washington Post*, April 23, 2020, https://www.washingtonpost .com/opinions/2020/04/23/covid-19-racial-disparities-could-be-even-worse-than-we -think/; APM Research Lab Staff, "The Color of Coronavirus: Covid-19 Deaths by Race and Ethnicity in the US," *APM Research Lab*, August 18, 2020, https://www.apmresearchlab .org/covid/deaths-by-race. The disparities have remained overall. See Latoya Hill and Samantha Artiga, "COVID-19 Cases and Deaths by Race/Ethnicity: Current Data and Changes Over Time," *KFF*, August 22, 2022, https://www.kff.org/coronavirus-covid-19 /issue-brief/covid-19-cases-and-deaths-by-race-ethnicity-current-data-and-changes -over-time/.

55. Columbia Center for Contemporary Critical Thought, "Covid-19 Response Projects," Columbia Law School, https://cccct.law.columbia.edu/content/covid-19-response-projects.

56. Bay City News Service, ""Controversial Post Leads to Calls for Antioch Commissioner's Removal,"*Napa Valley Register*, June 5, 2020, https://napavalleyregister.com/news/state-and -regional/controversial-post-leads-to-calls-for-antioch-commissioners-removal/article _926f1e0f-3762-5e42-a992-4e85cf206eed.html.

57. Whitehouse, "Whitehouse, Doggett Release New Analysis."

58. Bernard E. Harcourt, "Introducing the Birth of Biopolitics," *Foucault 13/13* (blog), Columbia Center for Contemporary Critical Thought, January 23, 2016, http://blogs.law.columbia .edu/foucault1313/2016/01/23/introducing-the-birth-of-biopolitics/.

59. Mirowski, *Never Let a Serious Crisis Go to Waste*, 89.

60. Mirowski, *Never Let a Serious Crisis Go to Waste*, 358.

61. *Oxford English Dictionary*, www.oed.com/view/Entry/37325.

62. *Oxford English Dictionary*, www.oed.com/view/Entry/37325.

63. *Oxford English Dictionary*, www.oed.com/view/Entry/37326.

64. I will set aside the term *socialism* for now. As Étienne Balibar shows, there are two violently opposed tendencies within the project of socialism: a statist tendency and one he calls, using the French term, *autogestionnaire*. The latter, he concedes, is a minor current; most thinkers for and against socialism essentially identify it with the statist version. See Étienne Balibar, "Régulations, insurrections, utopies: pour un 'socialisme' du XXIe siècle," in *Histoire interminable: D'un siècle l'autre: Écrits I* (Paris: La Découverte, 2020), 268. However, Balibar does trace those other genealogies of socialism as *autogestion* that have far more in common with cooperation, so I don't want to set aside the *autogestionnaire* variant and paint with too broad a brush.

65. Michael Hardt and Antonio Negri, *Commonwealth* (Cambridge, MA: Belknap, 2009); Michael Hardt and Antonio Negri, *Assembly* (New York: Oxford University Press, 2017); Pierre Dardot and Christian Laval, *Common: On Revolution in the Twenty-First Century*, trans. Matthew MacLellan (London: Bloomsbury, 2019).

66. Dardot and Laval, *Common*, 5.

67. Dardot and Laval, *Common*, 85.

68. Dardot and Laval, *Common*, 399–403.

69. Dardot and Laval, *Common*, 2; emphasis in original. See also 5.

70. Dardot and Laval, *Common*, 125.

71. Dardot and Laval, *Common*, 5.

72. Dardot and Laval, *Common*, 116–123.

73. Eben Moglen, "Anarchism Triumphant: Free Software and the Death of Copyright," *First Monday*, 2 August 1999, http://firstmonday.org/ojs/index.php/fm/article/view/684/594; Josh Lerner and Jean Tirole, "Some Simple Economics of Open Source," *Journal of Industrial Economics* 50, no. 2 (June 2002): 197–234; Yochai Benkler, "Peer Production, the Commons, and the Future of the Firm," *Strategic Organization* 15, no. 2 (2017): 264–274.

74. Richard Sennett, *Together: The Rituals, Pleasures and Politics of Cooperation* (New Haven, CT: Yale University Press, 2013).

75. Chambers, "The Cooperative League of the United States of America," 64–65 (quoting James Peter Warbasse, *The Destiny of the Co-operative Movement*, n.d., CLUSA files, Early Pamphlets, 1916–1919, Folder I).

76.   James Peter Warbasse, *Co-operative Democracy* (New York: MacMillan, 1923), 367, 373.

77.   Chambers, "The Cooperative League of the United States of America," 66.

78.   Chambers retraces the variegated ideological history of the Cooperative League in the following terms:

> The Cooperative League grew out of Jewish democratic socialism and fraternalism and out of Finnish radicalism. Under Warbasse's leadership the League's official theory was close to a benevolent form of anarchism that predicted the withering away of the state as the cooperative commonwealth was gradually established. With Bowen the great agricultural purchasing associations were brought into the League, which they soon dominated. With this development, during the terrible crisis of the depression decade, the League moved gently away from rigid neutralism toward social reform through political action, and tempered its earlier utopianism by more practical programs. With Lincoln and Voorhis, the League fully accepted the sector ideal of the Swedish cooperative movement without for a moment surrendering its reform urge. The League can be found today campaigning for every good cause of political and social liberalism. (Chambers, "The Cooperative League of the United States of America," 80–81)

79.   Chambers, "The Cooperative League of the United States of America," 65. Chambers cites Warbasse, *Co-operative Democracy*, 78.

80.   Chambers, "The Cooperative League of the United States of America," 77. Earlier, Warbasse had been in conflict with communist members, resulting in the factional separation of a whole core of communist members in 1930. See Chambers, "The Cooperative League of the United States of America," 67.

81.   See National Cooperative Business Association, https://ncbaclusa.coop.

82.   Martha Beatrice Webb, *The Cooperative Movement in Great Britain* (London: Swann Sonnenschein, 1891), 75–76 n.1.

83.   Webb, *The Cooperative Movement in Great Britain*, 67.

84.   Webb, *The Cooperative Movement in Great Britain*, 85.

85.   Paul Lambert, *La Doctrine coopérative*, 3rd ed. (Paris, 1963).

86.   G. D. H. Cole, *Socialist Thought: The Forerunners, 1789–1850* (London: MacMillan, 1953), https://files.libcom.org/files/A%20History%20of%20Socialist%20Thought%20Volume%201.pdf, 177; Mary Mellor, Janet Hannah, and John Stirling, *Worker Cooperatives in Theory and Practice* (Philadelphia: Open University Press, 1988), http://students.aiu.edu/submissions/profiles/resources/onlineBook/f2S3n5_Worker%20cooperatives%20in%20theory%20and%20practice%20(1988).pdf, 12–13.

87.   Mellor, Hannah, and Stirling, *Worker Cooperatives in Theory and Practice*, 12–13.

88.   Mellor, Hannah, and Stirling, *Worker Cooperatives in Theory and Practice*, 13.

89.   Paul Lambert, *Studies in the Social Philosophy of Co-operation*, trans. Joseph Létargez and D. Flanagan (Chicago: Cooperative League of the U.S.A., 1963), 165.

90.   Robert Sommer, Deborah Schlanger, Robert Hackman, and Steven Smith, "Consumer Cooperatives and Worker Collectives: A Comparison," *Sociological Perspectives* 27, no. 2 (1984): 144–146.

91.   For a debate between antigrowth and green growth, see, for example, Baptiste Mylondo and Xaiver Timbeau, "Is Green Growth an Illusion: For/Against—Baptiste Mylondo vs. Xavier Timbeau," *Philonomist*, December 12, 2018, updated March 4, 2022, https://www .philonomist.com/en/interview/green-growth-illusion.

92.   See, for example, Herman E. Daly and Joshua Farley, *Ecological Economics: Principles and Applications*, 2nd ed. (Washington, DC: Island, 2011); Tim Jackson, *Prosperity Without Growth: Economics for a Finite Planet* (London: Earthscan, 2009); Inge Røpke, "The Early History of Modern Ecological Economics," *Ecological Economics* 50 (2004): 293–314.

93.   Nicholas Georgescu-Roegen, *The Entropy Law and the Economic Process* (Cambridge, MA: Harvard University Press, 1971); Baptiste Mylondo, *Des caddies et des hommes: La consommation citoyenne contre la société de consommation* (La Dispute, 2005); Serge Latouche, *Petit traité de la décroissance sereine* (Paris: Fayard/Mille et Une Nuits, 2007); translated into English as Serge Latouche, *Farewell to Growth*, trans. David Macey (Cambridge, UK: Polity, 2010); Giorgos Kallis, *Degrowth* (New York: Columbia University Press, 2018); Giorgos Kallis, Christian Kerschner, and Joan Martinez-Alier, "The Economics of Degrowth," *Ecological Economics* 84 (2012): 172–180; Filka Sekulova, Giorgos Kallis, Beatriz Rodríguez-Labajos, and Francois Schneider, "Degrowth: From Theory to Practice," *Journal of Cleaner Production* 38 (2013):1–6; Christian Kerschner, "Economic De-growth vs. Steady-State Economy," *Journal of Cleaner Production* 18, no. 6 (2010): 544–551. For an overview and history of the degrowth movement, see generally Iris Borowy and Matthias Schmelzer, eds., *History of the Future of Economic Growth: Historical Roots of Current Debates on Sustainable Degrowth* (New York: Routledge, 2017); Diana Stuart, Ryan Gunderson, and Brian Petersen, *The Degrowth Alternative: A Path to Address Our Environmental Crisis?* (New York: Routledge, 2020).

94.   Kallis, *Degrowth*, 12.

95.   See generally "What Is Degrowth?," https://degrowth.info/en/degrowth; Giacomo D'Alisa, Federico Demaria, and Giorgio Kallis, eds., *Degrowth: A Vocabulary for a New Era* (New York: Routledge, 2015). There are interesting connections between degrowth and abolitionism, which I take up in the next chapter. See Erica Jung, "Rethinking Our Relationship to Land: Degrowth, Abolition, and the United States," September 28, 2020, https://www.degrowth.info/en/2020/09/rethinking-our-relationship-to-land-degrowth -abolition-and-the-united-states/#more-488463; Anastasia C. Wilson, "The Economics of Abolition," June 4, 2020, https://anastasiacwilson.com/2020/06/04/the-economics-of -abolition/; Jackie Wang, Anastasia Wilson, Alyxandria Goodwin, and Jasson Perez, "Abolitionist Economics: Moving Beyond Carceral Capitalism" (video), The New School for Social Research, March 24, 2021, https://www.youtube.com/watch?v=d4dpvLHyMg4.

96.   Matthias Schmelzer, Aaron Vansintjan, and Andrea Vetter, *The Future Is Degrowth: A Guide to a World Beyond Capitalism* (New York: Verso, 2022). See also Timothée Duverger, *La décroissance, une idée pour demain* (Paris: Sang de la Terre, 2011); Timothée Duverger, *Utopies locales. Les solutions écologiques et solidaires de demain* (Paris: Les Petits Matins, 2021). For information about the ecological cooperatives project of Longo Maï, see Pro Longo Maï (website), https://www.prolongomaif.ch; regarding TERA, see TERA (website), https://www.tera.coop.

6. THE SOCIAL THEORY OF COÖPERISM

1. PEW Center on the States, *One in 100: Behind Bars in America 2008*, https://www.pewtrusts.org/en/research-and-analysis/reports/2008/02/28/one-in-100-behind-bars-in-america-2008, 3; see generally Bernard E. Harcourt, *The Illusion of Free Markets* (Cambridge, MA: Harvard University Press, 2011), 196–202.

2. Right before the exponential explosion in incarceration, in 1973, Alfred Blumstein and Jacqueline Cohen hypothesized that there was a natural law of the stability of punishment, based on the fact that prison populations had remained so stable despite wildly fluctuation crime statistics. Alfred Blumstein and Jacqueline Cohen, "A Theory of the Stability of Punishment," *Journal of Criminal Law and Criminology* 64 (1973): 198–207. Tragically, their hypothesis was short-lived.

3. Matt Ford, "America's Largest Mental Hospital Is a Jail," *Atlantic*, June 8, 2015, https://www.theatlantic.com/politics/archive/2015/06/americas-largest-mental-hospital-is-a-jail/395012/.

4. That's the price we New Yorkers were paying in 2021 per person per year at Rikers Island, according to NYC Comptroller Scott Stringer. See "Comptroller Stringer: Cost of Incarceration per Person in New York City Skyrockets to All-Time High," New York City Comptroller, December 6, 2021, https://comptroller.nyc.gov/newsroom/comptroller-stringer-cost-of-incarceration-per-person-in-new-york-city-skyrockets-to-all-time-high-2/.

5. Mariame Kaba, *We Do This 'Til We Free Us* (Chicago: Haymarket, 2021); Mariame Kaba and Andrea J. Ritchie, *No More Police: A Case for Abolition* (New York: New Press, 2022); Dorothy E. Roberts, "Foreword: Abolition Constitutionalism," *Harvard Law Review* 133, no. 1 (2019): 1–122, https://harvardlawreview.org/wp-content/uploads/2019/11/1-122_Online.pdf; Rachel Kushner, "Is Prison Necessary? Ruth Wilson Gilmore Might Change Your Mind," *New York Times Magazine*, April 17, 2019, https://www.nytimes.com/2019/04/17/magazine/prison-abolition-ruth-wilson-gilmore.html; Derecka Purnell, *Becoming Abolitionists* (New York: Astra House, 2021); Derecka Purnell, "How I Became a Police Abolitionist," *Atlantic*, July 6, 2020, https://www.theatlantic.com/ideas/archive/2020/07/how-i-became-police-abolitionist/613540/; Derecka Purnell, "What Does Police Abolition Mean?," *Boston Review*, August 23, 2017; Amna Akbar, "Toward a Radical Imagination of Law," *New York University Law Review* 93, no. 3 (2018): 405–479; Amna Akbar, "Demands for a Democratic Political Economy," *Harvard Law Review Forum* 145, no. 1 (2020): 90–118; Patrisse Cullors, "Abolition and Reparations: Histories of Resistance, Transformative Justice, and Accountability," *Harvard Law Review* 132, no, 6 (2019):1684–1694; Che Gossett, *Abolitionist Entanglement: Ending the Grammars of Capture* (PhD diss., Rutgers University, 2021); Alexis Hoag, "Valuing Black Lives," *Columbia Human Rights Law Review* 51, no. 3 (2020): 983–1007; Allegra M. McLeod, "Prison Abolition and Grounded Justice," *UCLA Law Review* 62, no. 5 (2015): 1156–1239; Barbara Ransby, "The White Left Needs to Embrace Black Leadership," *Nation*, July 2, 2020, https://www.thenation.com/article/activism/black-lives-white-left/; Mariame Kaba and Andrea Ritchie, "We Want More Justice for Breonna Taylor Than the System That Killed Her Can Deliver," *Essence*, July 16, 2020, https://www.essence.com/feature/breonna-taylor-justice-abolition/; Dylan Rodriguez, "Abolition as Praxis of Human Being: A Foreword," *Harvard Law Review* 132, no. 6 (2019): 1575–1612; Keeanga-Yamahtta Taylor, "We Should Still Defund the Police," *New Yorker*, August 14, 2020, https://www.newyorker.com/news/our-columnists/defund-the-police; Harsha Walia, *Border and*

Rule: Global Migration, Capitalism, and the Rise of Racist Nationalism (Chicago: Haymarket, 2021). See also Dan Berger, Mariame Kaba, and David Stein, "What Abolitionists Do," *Jacobin*, August 24, 2017, https://perma.cc/K959-9FF5; Paul Butler, *Chokehold: Policing Black Men* (New York: New Press, 2018); Garrett Felber, "The Struggle to Defund the Police Is Not New," *Boston Review*, June 9, 2020, http://bostonreview.net/race/garrett-felber-struggle-abolish-police-not-new; Nicole Smith Futrell, "The Practice and Pedagogy of Carceral Abolition in a Criminal Defense Clinic, *NYU Review of Law and Social Change* 45 (2021): 159–196; Brandon Hasbrouck, "Abolishing Racist Policing with the Thirteenth Amendment," *UCLA Law Review* 67, no. 5 (2020): 1108–1129, https://www.uclalawreview.org/abolishing-racist-policing-with-the-thirteenth-amendment/; Angel E. Sanchez, "In Spite of Prison," *Harvard Law Review* 132, no. 6 (2019): 1650–1683; Ruth Wilson Gilmore and James Kilgore, "The Case for Abolition," *Marshall Project*, June 9, 2019, https://www.themarshallproject.org/2019/06/19/the-case-for-abolition; #8ToAbolition, https://www.8toabolition.com/; Naomi Murakawa, "Police Reform Works—for the Police," *Level*, October 21, 2020, https://level.medium.com/why-police-reform-is-actually-a-bailout-for-cops-ecf2dd7b8833; Dean Spade, "Solidarity Not Charity," *Social Text* 142 38, no. 1 (March 2020): 131–151; Dorothy Roberts, "Abolishing Policing Also Means Abolishing Family Regulation," *Imprint*, June 16, 2020, https://imprintnews.org/child-welfare-2/abolishing-policing-also-means-abolishing-family-regulation/44480; Harsha Walia, *Border and Rule* (Chicago: Haymarket, 2021); Monica Bell, "Black Security and the Conundrum of Policing," *Just Security*, July 15, 2020, https://www.justsecurity.org/71418/black-security-and-the-conundrum-of-policing/.

6.   Amna Akbar, "An Abolitionist Horizon for Police (Reform)," *California Law Review* 108, no. 6 (August 10, 2020): 103.

7.   Brendan O'Connor, "How to Build a Global Abolition Movement," *Vice*, December 7, 2020, https://www.vice.com/en/article/qjpjv7/how-to-build-a-global-movement-to-abolish-prison-police-v27n4; Amy Hall, "Beyond Punishment," *New Internationalist*, April 6, 2022, https://newint.org/features/2022/02/07/big-story-abolition-beyond-punishment; Myriam François, "Adama Traore: How George Floyd's Death Energized French Protests," *BBC*, May 19, 2021, https://www.bbc.com/news/world-us-canada-57176500.

8.   See Steve Crabtree, "Most Americans Say Policing Needs 'Major Changes,'" *Gallup News*, July 22, 2020, https://news.gallup.com/poll/315962/americans-say-policing-needs-major-changes.aspx; see also Berger, Kaba, and Stein, "What Abolitionists Do" (documenting the impact of abolitionist organizing).

9.   See Sara Fischer, "Obama: Broad Slogans Like 'Defund the Police' Lose People," *Axios*, December 1, 2020, https://www.axios.com/obama-slogan-defund-police-snapchat-interview-b8cddece-d76b-4243-948f-5dfccb2a3ec1.html. For an analysis of who agreed and disagreed with President Obama, see Rachel Ramirez, "Obama Said 'Defund the Police' Is a Bad Slogan: This Shouldn't Come as a Surprise," *Vox*, December 3, 2020, https://www.vox.com/2020/12/3/22150452/obama-defund-the-police-snappy-slogan.

10.   See Cheyanne M. Daniels, "GOP Lawmakers Adopt 'Defund' Rallying Cry for FBI, Not Police," *The Hill*, August 13, 2022, https://thehill.com/homenews/house/3599029-gop-lawmakers-adopt-defund-rallying-cry-for-fbi-not-police/.

11.   Slavoj Žižek, "Class Struggle Against Classism," *Philosophical Salon*, May 10, 2021, https://thephilosophicalsalon.com/class-struggle-against-classism/.

12.   Žižek writes: "In the case of antagonisms in relations between sexes and sexual identities, the struggle for emancipation does not aim at annihilating some of the identities but at creating the conditions for their non-antagonistic co-existence, and the same goes for tensions between ethnic, cultural or religious identities. The goal is to bring about their peaceful co-existence, their mutual respect and recognition. Class struggle does not function like that; it aims at mutual recognition and respect of classes only in its Fascist or corporatist versions. Class struggle is a "pure" antagonism: the goal of the oppressed and exploited is to abolish classes as such, not to enact their reconciliation." Žižek, "Class Struggle Against Classism."

13.   See Elizabeth Hinton, *America on Fire: The Untold History of Police Violence and Black Rebellion Since the 1960s* (New York: Liveright, 2021), 288: "Between fifteen and twenty-six million people participated in [the 2020] summer's nationwide demonstrations for racial justice, the largest social movement in American history. . . . Protests demanding justice . . . peaked in the first week of June, and eighty-seven hundred demonstrations across seventy-four countries around the world marched in solidarity."

14.   See Bernard E. Harcourt, *Critique and Praxis* (New York: Columbia University Press, 2020), 246. I am qualifying the concept of political liberalism (see John Rawls, *Political Liberalism* [New York: Columbia University Press, 1993]) with the term *legal* in order to emphasize the distinctly Western contemporary variant of political liberalism that emphasizes legal rights and the rule of law. Henceforth I will refer to this legal form of political liberalism, prevalent in the United States, simply as "contemporary liberalism." See Harcourt, *Critique and Praxis*, 244–255.

15.   In using the terms *race*, *class*, and *caste* in a more unified way, I would like to acknowledge and pay tribute to the internal contestation within race studies, and to draw productively from the different aspects of the concepts of race, class, and caste (and apartheid and "the new Jim Crow") while placing race at the forefront. See generally Oliver Cromwell Cox, *Caste, Class, and Race: A Study in Social Dynamics* (New York: Monthly Review, 1948); Gunnar Myrdal, *An American Dilemma: The Negro Problem and Modern Democracy*, vol. 1 (New York: Harper & Row, 1944); Isabel Wilkerson, *Caste: The Origins of Our Discontents* (New York: Random House, 2020); Charisse Burden-Stelly, "Caste Does Not Explain Race," *Boston Review*, December 15, 2020, http://bostonreview.net/race/charisse -burden-stelly-caste-does-not-explain-race.

16.   Akbar, "An Abolitionist Horizon for (Police) Reform," 102, 135–137; Hasbrouck, "Abolishing Racist Policing with the Thirteenth Amendment"; Kaba, *We Do This 'Til We Free Us*, 14–17; Purnell, *Becoming Abolitionists*, 5–6; Alex Vitale, *The End of Policing* (New York: Verso, 2017), 45–48.

17.   Dennis Childs, *Slaves of the State: Black Incarceration from the Chain Gang to the Penitentiary* (Minneapolis: University of Minnesota Press, 2018); Dorothy E. Roberts, "Constructing a Criminal Justice System Free of Racial Bias," *Columbia Human Rights Law Review* vol. 39, no. 1 (2008): 273; Bryan Stevenson, "A Presumption of Guilt," in *Policing the Black Man*, ed. Angela J. Davis (New York: Penguin Random House, 2017), 3–30.

18.   Angela Y. Davis, *Abolition Democracy: Beyond Empire, Prisons, and Torture* (New York: Seven Stories, 2005); Angela Y. Davis, *Are Prisons Obsolete?* (New York: Seven Stories, 2011); Ruth Wilson Gilmore, *Golden Gulag: Prisons, Surplus, Crisis, and Opposition in Globalizing*

California (Berkeley: University of California Press, 2007); Paul Butler, *Chokehold: Polic-ing Black Men* (New York: New Press, 2018); Allegra McLeod, "Prison Abolition and Grounded Justice," *UCLA Law Review* 62 (2015): 1156–1239; Rachel Kushner, "Is Prison Necessary? Ruth Wilson Gilmore Might Change Your Mind," *New York Times Magazine*, April 17, 2019. See also Michelle Alexander, *The New Jim Crow: Mass Incarceration in the Age of Colorblindness* (New York: New Press, 2010); Roberts, "Foreword: Abolition Con-stitutionalism," 29, 68–70; Stevenson, "A Presumption of Guilt"; Khalil Gibran Muham-mad, *The Condemnation of Blackness: Race, Crime, and the Making of Modern Urban American* (Cambridge, MA: Harvard University Press, 2010); Wilkerson, *Caste*; Loïc Wacquant, "Deadly Symbiosis: Rethinking Race and Imprisonment in Twenty-First-Century Amer-ica," *Boston Review*, April/May 2002, https://bostonreview.net/archives/BR27.2/wacquant .html#4. See generally Columbia Center for Contemporary Critical Thought, *Abolition Democracy 13/13* (blog), January 21, 2021, http://blogs.law.columbia.edu/abolition1313/.

19. As Aldon Morris has demonstrated, Du Bois's theoretical contributions at the time were deliberately marginalized. See Aldon D. Morris, *The Scholar Denied: W. E. B. Du Bois and the Birth of Modern Sociology* (Oakland: University of California Press, 2015). Thomas Wheat-land shows well how the members of the Frankfurt School had to dissimulate their ideas in order to get accepted and integrated in the American academy when they went into exile from Nazi Germany. See Thomas Wheatland, "The Frankfurt School's Invitation from Columbia University: How the Horkheimer Circle Settled on Morningside Heights," *Ger-man Politics and Society* 22, no. 3 (72) (Fall 2004): 1–32; Thomas Wheatland, "Critical Theory on Morningside Heights: From Frankfurt Mandarins to Columbia Sociologists," *German Politics and Society* 22, no. 4 (73) (Winter 2004): 57–87; Thomas Wheatland, *The Frankfurt School in Exile* (Minneapolis: University of Minnesota Press, 2009).

20. W. E. B. Du Bois, *Black Reconstruction in America, 1860–1880* (New York: Free Press, 1998 [1935]), 506.

21. Du Bois, *Black Reconstruction*, 698.

22. See generally *Hunter v. Underwood*, 471 U.S. 222 (1985), at 233 (reviewing the history of Article VIII, § 182, of the Alabama Constitution of 1901 on felon disenfranchisement, holding it unconstitutional, and stating that "we simply observe that its original enact-ment was motivated by a desire to discriminate against blacks on account of race, and the section continues to this day to have that effect"); Jeff Manza and Christopher Uggen, *Locked Out: Felon Disenfranchisement and American Democracy* (New York: Oxford University Press, 2006); Roberts, "Constructing a Criminal Justice System Free of Racial Bias," 279–280.

23. Du Bois, *Black Reconstruction*, 506.

24. Cedric Robinson, *Black Marxism: The Making of the Black Radical Tradition* (Chapel Hill: Uni-versity of North Carolina Press, 2000), 196. Amy Allen discusses this in her essay "Slavery, Work, and Property: Du Bois's Black Marxism," where she draws out other productive ele-ments and possible interpretations from the engagement with Marx, describing "the argu-mentative backbone of DuBois's text whereby the slave becomes the black worker, the slave rebellion a general strike, the Reconstruction Era the dictatorship of the proletariat in the states of the former Confederacy, and the subsequent dismantling of Reconstruction as a counterrevolution of property." Amy Allen, "Slavery, Work, and Property: Du Bois's Black

Marxism," *Abolition Democracy 13/13* (blog), November 29, 2020, http://blogs.law.columbia.edu/abolition1313/amy-allen-slavery-work-and-property-duboiss-black-marxism/.

25. Georg Rusche and Otto Kirchheimer, *Punishment and Social Structure* (New York: Columbia University Press, 1939), 55.

26. Rusche and Kirchheimer, *Punishment and Social Structure*, 102, 122–123.

27. Thorsten Sellin, foreword to *Punishment and Social Structure* by Georg Rusche and Otto Kirchheimer (New York: Columbia University Press, 1939), vi.

28. Rusche and Kirchheimer, *Punishment and Social Structure*, 5.

29. See, for example, Theodore G. Chiricos and Miriam A. Delone, "Labor Surplus and Punishment: A Review and Assessment of Theory and Evidence," *Social Problems* 39, no. 4 (1992): 431 (finding an "empirically plausible" relationship of labor surplus to punishment); Raymond J. Michalowski and Susan M. Carlson, "Unemployment, Imprisonment, and Social Structures of Accumulation: Historical Contingency in the Rusche-Kirchheimer Hypothesis," *Criminology* 37, no. 2 (1999): 237–238 (finding a weak but statistically significant effect of unemployment on prison admissions during the period 1933-1947 and a strong effect of unemployment on prison admissions during the period 1980-1992).

30. Davis, *Are Prisons Obsolete?*, 112.

31. Angela Y. Davis, "Political Prisoners, Prisons, and Black Liberation," in *If They Come in the Morning . . . Voices of Resistance*, ed. Angela Y. Davis (New York: Verso, 2016), 34.

32. Davis, "Political Prisoners, Prisons, and Black Liberation," 37.

33. George Jackson, "Towards the United Front," in *If They Come in the Morning . . . Voices of Resistance*, ed. Angela Y. Davis (New York: Verso, 2016), 157. See also George L. Jackson, *Blood in My Eye* (New York: Random House, 1972).

34. Jackson, *Blood in My Eye*, 99. The assassination of the Chicago Black Panther leader Fred Hampton under the guise of criminal law enforcement has recently gotten attention because of the film *Judas and the Black Messiah* (2021). But it was well understood at the time that his assassination at the hands of the Chicago Police Department, as well as his earlier arrest and incarceration for stealing $71 worth of ice cream, had little to do with the criminal law but were all about political struggle. His life and death illustrated Davis's argument. Leaders such as President Richard Nixon and FBI director J. Edgar Hoover perceived Fred Hampton as a political threat to the racial order in this country. For that reason, he was summarily executed by Chicago police officers, who used the enforcement of criminal law as pretext and cover. He was executed in part because Hoover and other political leaders realized that his imprisonment would likely render him even more politically powerful.

35. Samuel Kalman, "Policing the French Empire: Colonial Law Enforcement and the Search for Racial-Territorial Hegemony," *Historical Reflections/Réflexions Historiques* 46, no. 2 (2020): 2.

36. Davis, "Political Prisoners, Prisons, and Black Liberation," 39. Fanon also developed the notion that criminality is produced by colonization, that crime is the product of social ordering: "The Algerian's criminality, his impulsivity, and the violence of his murders are therefore not the consequence of the organization of his nervous system or of characterial originality, but the direct product of the colonial situation."

37. James Baldwin, "An Open Letter to My Sister, Angela Y. Davis," in *If They Come in the Morning . . . Voices of Resistance*, ed. Angela Y. Davis (New York: Verso, 2016), 19.

38. Baldwin, "An Open Letter to My Sister, Angela Y. Davis," 22.

39. Michel Foucault, Catharine von Bülow, and Daniel Defert, preface to "The Assassination of George Jackson" (Intolérable 3: Assassinat de George Jackson), in *Warfare in the American Homeland: Policing and Prison in a Penal Democracy*, ed. Joy James (Durham, NC: Duke University Press, 2007), 138. (The original French edition was published November 10, 1971.)

40. Michel Foucault, Catharine von Bülow, and Daniel Defert, "The Masked Assassination," in *Warfare in the American Homeland: Policing and Prison in a Penal Democracy*, ed. Joy James (Durham, NC: Duke University Press, 2007), 140.

41. Foucault, von Bülow, and Defert, "The Masked Assassination," 156.

42. Michel Foucault, *Penal Theories and Institutions: Lectures at the Collège de France, 1971–1972*, ed. Bernard E. Harcourt, trans. Graham Burchell (New York: Palgrave Macmillan, 2019).

43. Foucault, *Penal Theories and Institutions*, 190.

44. Foucault, *Penal Theories and Institutions*, 102. "The penal system–delinquency couple is an effect of the repressive system–seditious couple. An effect in the sense that it is a product, a condition of maintenance, a displacement, and an occultation of it." Foucault, *Penal Theories and Institutions*, 102–103.

45. Foucault, *Penal Theories and Institutions*, 190. See generally, Delio Vásquez, "Illegalist Foucault, Criminal Foucault," *Theory and Event* 23, no. 4 (October 2020): 935–972.

46. Foucault argued in a debate February 5, 1972: "Penal law was not created by the common people, nor by the peasantry, nor by the proletariat, but entirely by the bourgeoisie as an important tactical weapon in this system of divisions which they wished to introduce." Michel Foucault, "Sur la justice populaire," in *Dits et Écrits (1970–1075)*, vol. 2, ed. Daniel Defert, François Ewald, and Jacques Lagrange (Paris: Gallimard, 1994), 352; *Dits et Écrits (1954–1975)*, vol. 1, ed. Daniel Defert, François Ewald, and Jacques Lagrange (Paris: Quarto, 2001), 1220; Michel Foucault, "On Popular Justice," in *Power/Knowledge: Selected Interviews and Other Writings, 1972–1977*, ed. Colin Gordon, trans. Colin Gordon, Leo Marshall, John Mepham, and Kate Soper (New York: Pantheon, 1980), 22.

47. Michel Foucault, *La Société punitive: Cours au Collège de France (1972–1973)*, ed. Bernard E. Harcourt (Paris: Gallimard/Seuil, 2013); *The Punitive Society*, ed. Bernard E. Harcourt, trans. Graham Burchell (New York: Picador, 2015).

48. Michel Foucault, *Surveiller et Punir: Naissance de la prison*, ed. Bernard E. Harcourt, in *Michel Foucault: Oeuvres*, vol. 2, ed. Frédéric Gros (Paris: Gallimard/La Pléiade, 2015).

49. Foucault, *Surveiller et Punir*, 285 (my translation, drawing and correcting in part Michel Foucault, *Discipline and Punish: The Birth of the Prison*, trans. Alan Sheridan (New York: Vintage Books, 1975), 240).

50. Foucault, *Surveiller et Punir*, 285.

51. See Thomas Mathiesen, *The Politics of Abolition Revisited* (New York: Routledge, 2015). See generally Máximo Langer, "Penal Abolitionism and Criminal Law Minimalism: Here and There, Now and Then," *Harvard Law Review Forum* 134 (2020): 42–77.

52. Many people today no longer refer to the "criminal justice system" but instead use the term *criminal legal system*, a recognition that the processes themselves are not just. See, for example, Vivian Nixon and Daryl V. Atkinson, introduction to *What We Know: Solutions from Our Experiences in the Justice System*, ed. Vivian Nixon and Daryl V. Atkinson (New York: New Press, 2020), ix: "the [criminal justice] system has historically demonstrated a

failure to achieve true justice. As such, the editors intentionally use 'criminal legal system' to refer to the current system." I would go further because the term *system* also causes many misunderstandings. See Bernard E. Harcourt, "The Systems Fallacy: A Genealogy and Critique of Public Policy and Cost-Benefit Analysis," *Journal of Legal Studies* 47, no. 2 (June 2018): 419–447. I will therefore use, going forward, "criminal legal ordeal" or "criminal legal process" to capture the harrowing nature of the process and to counter the systems fallacy.

53. Roberts, "Constructing a Criminal Justice System Free of Racial Bias," 262.

54. Roberts, "Constructing a Criminal Justice System Free of Racial Bias," 267.

55. Roberts, "Constructing a Criminal Justice System Free of Racial Bias," 272–273. See generally Stuart Banner, "Traces of Slavery: Race and the Death Penalty in Historical Perspective," in *From Lynch Mobs to the Killing State: Race and the Death Penalty in America*, ed. Charles J. Ogletree Jr. and Austin Sarat (New York: New York University Press, 2006), 96, 98–99.

56. Roberts, "Constructing a Criminal Justice System Free of Racial Bias," 276.

57. Roberts, "Constructing a Criminal Justice System Free of Racial Bias," 284.

58. Gilmore, *Golden Gulag*.

59. Michelle Alexander, *The New Jim Crow: Mass Incarceration in the Age of Colorblindness* (New York: New Press, 2010). For a critique, see James Forman Jr., "Racial Critiques of Mass Incarceration: Beyond the New Jim Crow," *New York University Law Review* 87, no. 1 (February 2012): 101–146, which argues that analogy to Jim Crow masks important contributing factors and diminishes understanding of the old Jim Crow.

60. Loïc Wacquant, "The New 'Peculiar Institution': On the Prison as Surrogate Ghetto," *Theoretical Criminology* 4, no. 3 (2000): 377–389. "The task of defining, confining, and controlling African Americans in the United States has been successively shouldered by four 'peculiar institutions': slavery, the Jim Crow system, the urban ghetto, and the organizational compound formed by the vestiges of the ghetto and the expanding carceral system." Loïc Wacquant, "Deadly Symbiosis: Rethinking Race and Imprisonment in Twenty-First-Century America," *Boston Review*, April/May 2002, https://bostonreview .net/articles/loic-wacquant-deadly-symbiosis/. Although Wacquant contested the framework of the prison-industrial complex, arguing that it was too conspiratorial, that critique does not undermine the continuity on this question of breaking the link between crime and punishment.

61. Wacquant, "Deadly Symbiosis."

62. Carol S. Steiker and Jordan M. Steiker, "Sober Second Thoughts: Reflections on Two Decades of Constitutional Regulation of Capital Punishment," *Harvard Law Review* 109, no. 2 (1995): 355–438. Many other works focus on the political dimensions of legal doctrinal transformations. See, for example, Paul Butler, "Racially Based Jury Nullification: Black Power in the Criminal Justice System," *Yale Law Journal* 105, no. 3 (1995): 680 (documenting the political dimension of the criminal law as "one particularly destructive instrument of white supremacy" and proposing the use of jury nullification in certain cases involving Black defendants; one of the rare law review articles that begins with an epigraph by Malcolm X); Sarah Seo, *Policing the Open Road: How Cars Transformed American Freedom* (Cambridge, MA: Harvard University Press, 2019) (tracing how the policing of the open roads and legal regulation of automobiles contributed to the systematic

racialized policing of minorities). Note that I am trying to distinguish a body of scholarship that focuses on the political dimension of penal enforcement from the more classical legal or sociolegal scholarship that documents how politics influences the criminal law, such as William J. Stuntz's book, *The Collapse of American Criminal Justice* (Cambridge, MA: Harvard University Press, 2011) and his articles, such as "The Political Constitution of Criminal Justice," *Harvard Law Review* 119, no. 3 (2006): 780–851 and "The Pathological Politics of Criminal Law," *Michigan Law Review* 100, no. 3 (2001): 505–600.

63.   Keeanga-Yamahtta Taylor, *From #BlackLivesMatter to Black Liberation* (Chicago: Haymarket, 2016); Movement for Black Lives, *A Vision for Black Lives: Policy Demands for Black Power, Freedom, and Justice* (August 2016), https://m4bl.org/policy-platforms/; The Red Nation, *A Red Deal: Indigenous Action to Save Our Earth* (2020) ("We draw from Black abolitionist traditions to call for divestment away from the criminalizing, caging, and harming of human beings").

64.   Kaba, *We Do This 'Til We Free Us*, 3.

65.   Purnell, *Becoming Abolitionists*, 5; see also Purnell, *Becoming Abolitionists*, 62–63.

66.   See, for example, Kaba, *We Do This 'Til We Free Us*, 14: "Policing in the South emerged from the slave patrols in the 1700 and 1800s that caught and returned runaway slaves. In the North, the first municipal police departments in the mid-1800s helped quash labor strikes and riots against the rich. Everywhere, they have suppressed marginalized populations to protect the status quo." See also P. L. Reichl, "Southern Slave Patrols as a Transitional Police Type," *American Journal of Police* 7, no. 2 (1988): 51–77; Ailsa Chang and Chenjerai Kumanyika, "The History of Police in Creating Social Order in the U.S.," *NPR*, June 5, 2020, https://www.npr.org/2020/06/05/871083599/the-history-of-police-in-creating-social-order-in-the-u-s; Akbar, "An Abolitionist Horizon for (Police) Reform," 102, 135–137; Alex Vitale, *End of Policing* (New York: Verso, 2017), 45–48; "Abolition of Policing Workshop," *Critical Resistance*, https://criticalresistance.org/resources/abolish-policing-workshop/.

67.   Brandon Hasbrouck, "Abolishing Racist Policing with the Thirteenth Amendment," *UCLA Law Review* 67, no. 5 (July 2020): 1108–1129, https://www.uclalawreview.org/abolishing-racist-policing-with-the-thirteenth-amendment/. Other scholars, such as Monica Bell, emphasize the history of racial strife in policing to reveal the estrangement, detachment, and alienation from law enforcement felt by some communities of color. See Monica C. Bell, "Police Reform and the Dismantling of Legal Estrangement," *Yale Law Journal* 126 (2017): 2126–2148, where she argues that police reform efforts incorrectly diagnose procedural justice as a potential solution to friction between criminal justice and communities of color, suggesting instead that legal estrangement, the theory of detachment and alienation from law enforcement, forms a better foundation from which to launch reform efforts, and proposes a number of reforms to addresses feelings of estrangement, including better pay, reorganization, and shrinking police forces. Jeff Fagan and Dan Richman also focus on the withdrawal and alienation of affected communities. See Jeffrey Fagan and Daniel C. Richman, "Understanding Recent Spikes and Longer Trends in American Murders," *Columbia Law Review* 117, no. 5 (2017): 1235–1296, arguing that "harsh police tactics, social isolation and disadvantage, and unsolved murders contribute to the withdrawal of citizens and police from the co-production of security."

68.   Chang and Kumanyika, "The History of Police in Creating Social Order in the U.S."

69.   Roberts, "Foreword: Abolition Constitutionalism," 8.

70.   Bryan Stevenson, "A Presumption of Guilt," in *Policing the Black Man*, ed. Angela J. Davis (New York: Penguin Random House, 2017), 3–30; EJI Legacy Museum and Peace and Justice Memorial, Montgomery, AL, https://museumandmemorial.eji.org/.

71.   Childs, *Slaves of the State*, 62–63.

72.   Sarah Haley, *No Mercy Here: Gender, Punishment, and the Making of Jim Crow Modernity* (Chapel Hill: University of North Carolina Press, 2016).

73.   Haley, *No Mercy Here*, 7.

74.   Du Bois, *Black Reconstruction in America*, 136, quoting Carl Schurz, *Report on the Condition of the South* (1865); also quoted in Childs, *Slaves of the State*, 64.

75.   Muhammad, *The Condemnation of Blackness*; Butler, "Constructing the Thug," *Chokehold*, 17–46.

76.   The same can be said regarding racial segregation and policing. There is a directionality, feedback, etc., but the main problem to address is racial segregation, in a similar way. See Monica Bell, "Anti-Segregation Policing," *New York University Law Review* 95, no. 3 (June 2020): 650–765.

77.   See Alexis Hoag, "Valuing Black Lives: A Case for Ending the Death Penalty," *Columbia Human Rights Law Review* 51, no. 3 (2020): 985–1007.

78.   Bernard E. Harcourt, "Collapse of the Harm Principle," *Journal of Criminal Law and Criminology* 90, no. 1 (1999): 109–194; Harcourt, *Critique and Praxis*.

79.   See, for example, David Sklansky, *A Pattern of Violence: How the Law Classifies Crimes and What It Means for Justice* (Cambridge, MA: Harvard University Press, 2021).

80.   Instances of crime, as currently defined, can also be interpreted as forms of social ordering, along lines of race, gender, class, etc. In this sense, even a lot of what we call serious violent crime today can be understood as the product of a perceived need to enforce moral and political values: domestic violence, even homicides related to domestic violence, the drug trade, etc., can be understood as furthering gender- or race-inflected values. See Donald Black, "Crime as Social Control," *American Sociological Review* 48, no. 1 (1983): 34–45.

81.   One of the classic ways we try to bracket the political is to pretend that there is such a thing as the "criminal justice system," a system separate from these other social orderings. But that is simpleminded modeling that has no basis in reality and merely points us in the wrong direction. There is no criminal justice system that is severable from the social and racial order. See Harcourt, "The Systems Fallacy."

82.   Máximo Langer, for instance, argues for penal minimalism rather than abolitionism, but his argument follows a different order of questioning. I suggest we turn first to the question of what a cooperative world would look like and then ask what place there is for the criminal law. Langer goes to the second question first, taking present notions of harm as given, which leads him to penal minimalism. Despite these differences, I agree with Langer that "penal abolitionists, critical criminologists, and criminal law minimalists [should see] themselves as simpatico with each other, rather than as ideological or political opponents." Langer, "Penal Abolitionism and Criminal Law Minimalism," 56.

83.   Laura Kurgan, *Million Dollar Blocks*, Columbia Center for Spatial Research, https://c4sr.columbia.edu/projects/million-dollar-blocks.

84.   For this reason, I remain skeptical of the possibility of asking the question "What are the police for?" without first asking what society would look like with cooperation. But

see Tracey Meares and Tom Tyler, "The First Step Is Figuring Out What Police Are For," *Atlantic*, June 8, 2020, https://www.theatlantic.com/ideas/archive/2020/06/first-step-figuring-out-what-police-are/612793/.

85. Kaba, *We Do This 'Til We Free Us*, 3.

86. Obamacare, in contrast to a single-payer universal health-care system, is a private-market program that is unaffordable to many people and riddled with free-market abuses. To be sure, it is better than nothing and worth all the fight against Trump and the New Right, but it is hardly a viable solution for a just society.

87. Barbara Ransby, "The Class Politics of Black Lives Matter," *Dissent Magazine* (Fall 2015), https://www.dissentmagazine.org/article/class-politics-black-lives-matter.

88. Harsha Walia, *Border and Rule: Global Migration, Capitalism, and the Rise of Racist Nationalism* (Chicago: Haymarket, 2021), 215. As Seyla Benhabib reminds me, the term *worldmaking* comes from Hannah Arendt, *The Human Condition*, which elaborates on the notions of the "loss of world" and "loss of earth." The term has been used in philosophical discourse, especially by Nelson Goodman, in *Of Mind and Other Matters* (Cambridge, MA: Harvard University Press, 1984). See generally Adom Getachew, *Worldmaking After Empire: The Rise and Fall of Self-Determination* (Princeton, NJ: Princeton University Press, 2019).

89. Walia, *Border and Rule*, 215–216, quoting Toni Morrison, "Home," in *The House That Race Built: Original Essays by Toni Morrison, Angela Y. Davis, Cornel West, and Others on Black Americans and Politics in America Today*, ed. Wahneema Lubiano (New York: Vintage, 1998), 12.

90. Michel Foucault, "Alternatives to the Prison: Dissemination or Decline of Social Control?," *Theory, Culture and Society* 26, no. 6 (1976): 24. Special thanks to Daniele Lorenzini for this reference.

91. In more formal terms, restorative justice involves "a process whereby all the parties with a stake in a particular offence come together to resolve collectively how to deal with the aftermath of the offence and its implications for the future." T. F. Marshall, *Restorative Justice: An Overview* (London: Home Office Research Development and Statistics, 1999), 5. See generally Heather Strang and John Braithwaite, eds., *Restorative Justice and Civil Society* (Cambridge: Cambridge University Press, 2001); Theo Gavrielides, ed., *Routledge International Handbook of Restorative Justice* (New York: Routledge, 2019). For a wide-ranging and generous discussion and description of restorative justice, see Adriaan Lanni, "Taking Restorative Justice Seriously," *Buffalo Law Review* 69, no. 3 (2021): 635–681.

92. David B. Wexler, *Therapeutic Jurisprudence: The Law as a Therapeutic Agent* (Durham, NC: Carolina Academic Press, 1990); David B. Wexler and Bruce Winick, *Law in a Therapeutic Key: Developments in Therapeutic Jurisprudence* (Durham, NC: Carolina Academic Press, 1996); David B. Wexler, "The Development of Therapeutic Jurisprudence: From Theory to Practice," *Revista Jurídica Universidad de Puerto Rico* 68 (1999): 691–705; Natti Ronel and Ety Elisha, "A Different Perspective: Introducing Positive Criminology," *International Journal of Offender Therapy and Comparative Criminology* 55, no. 2 (2010): 305–325.

93. This may be, as Kaba suggests, because restorative justice "in some ways has been co-opted by the system." Kaba, *We Do This 'Til We Free Us*, 148.

94. John Braithwaite, "A Future Where Punishment Is Marginalized: Realistic or Utopian?," *UCLA Law Review* 46, no. 6 (1999): 1742.

95. In this, I think Foucault was entirely right. In his 1973 lectures on *The Punitive Society*, Foucault proposed a classification of punitive societies: societies that exclude and exile,

those that impose a sign on the body, those that imprison, and those that organize a redemption or seek compensation. Foucault, *The Punitive Society*, 248–249. Restorative justice, I believe, falls under the fourth model, societies that draw in the person who offends and impose obligations on them in the form of compensation and redemption.

96. Kaba, *We Do This 'Til We Free Us*, 104–118; Allegra McLeod, "Law, Critique, and the Under-commons," in *A Time for Critique*, ed. Didier Fassin and Bernard E. Harcourt (New York: Columbia University Press, 2019), 263–264; Allegra McLeod, "Envisioning Abolition Democracy," *Harvard Law Review* 132, no. 6 (2019): 1631–1632.

97. Kaba, *We Do This 'Til We Free Us*, 149.

98. McLeod, "Law, Critique, and the Undercommons," 268n34, 263.

99. McLeod, "Envisioning Abolition Democracy," 1632.

100. McLeod, "Law, Critique, and the Undercommons," 263.

101. McLeod, "Envisioning Abolition Democracy," 1632. For a critical discussion of these and other alternatives discussed below, see Langer, "Penal Abolitionism and Criminal Law Minimalism," 68–70.

102. McLeod, "Envisioning Abolition Democracy," 1623–1624.

103. Kaba, *We Do This 'Til We Free Us*, 107–109; McLeod, "Envisioning Abolition Democracy," 1624–1625, 1627.

104. McLeod, "Envisioning Abolition Democracy," 1614–1615.

105. On violence interrupters, see Purnell, *Becoming Abolitionists*, 144.

106. Alisa Bierria, Hyejin Shim, Mariame Kaba, and Stacy Suh, eds., *Survived and Punished: Survivor Defense as Abolitionist Praxis*, 2017, https://survivedandpunished.org/wp-content/uploads/2018/06/survivedandpunished_toolkitbw.pdf; Kaba, *We Do This 'Til We Free Us*, 116–117.

107. See generally Women of Color Against Violence eds., *Color of Violence: The INCITE! Anthology* (INCITE!, 2016).

108. Violence Intervention Program NYC (website), https://www.vipmujeres.org; Connect NYC (website), https://www.connectnyc.org.

109. Sherrilyn A. Ifill, "Reconciliation in the Twenty-First Century," in *On the Courthouse Lawn: Confronting the Legacy of Lynching in the Twenty-First Century* (Boston: Beacon Press, 2018), 173–176; Tammy Krause, "Reaching Out to the Other Side: Defense-Based Victim Outreach in Capital Cases," in *Wounds That Do Not Bind: Victim Based Perspectives on the Death Penalty*, ed. James Acker and David Karp (Durham, NC: Carolina Academic Press, 2006).

110. Sklansky, *A Pattern of Violence*.

111. Seyla Benhabib, "Democracy, Science and the State: Reflections on the Disaster(s) of Our Times," paper prepared for RESET Dialogues, May 2–7, 2020, Venice, Italy.

7. A DEFENSE OF COÖPERISM

1. Siblis Research, "Total Market Value of U.S. Stock Market," Siblis Research, https://siblisresearch.com/data/us-stock-market-value/.

2. U.S. Debt Clock.org, https://www.usdebtclock.org/.

3. Jesse Pound, "Global stock markets gained $17 trillion in value in 2019," *CNBC*, December 26, 2019, https://www.cnbc.com/2019/12/24/global-stock-markets-gained-17-trillion-in-value-in-2019.html.

4. Wolf Richter, "Stock-Market Margin Debt, After Plunging in Q4, Has Not Bounced Back Despite S&P 500 Historic Surge," *Wolf Street*, April 23, 2019, https://wolfstreet .com/2019/04/23/stock-market-margin-debt-after-plunging-in-q4-has-not-bounced-back -despite-sp-500-historic-surge/.

5. "U.S. and World Population Clock," United States Census Bureau, https://www.census .gov/popclock/.

6. U.S. Debt Clock.org, https://www.usdebtclock.org/world-debt-clock.html.

7. Jim Tankersley, "Federal Borrowing Amid Pandemic Puts U.S. Debt on Path to Exceed World War II," *New York Times*, September 2, 2020, https://www.nytimes.com/2020/09/02 /business/us-federal-debt.htm

8. See generally Thomas Piketty, *Capital in the Twenty-First Century* (Cambridge, MA: Harvard University Press, 2014).

9. Answath Damodaran, "Historical Returns on Stocks, Bonds and Bills—United States," Damodaran Online, http://pages.stern.nyu.edu/~adamodar/New_Home_Page/datafile /histretSP.html.

10. AEIdeas, "Chart of the Day: Historical Returns on Stocks, T-bills & T-bonds, 1928–2018: The Case for Privatizing Social Security?," American Enterprise Institute (blog), June 24, 2019, https://www.aei.org/carpe-diem/animated-chart-of-the-day-historical-returns-on -stocks-t-bill-and-t-bonds-1928-to-2018/. Based on data from "Historical Returns on Stocks" by Answath Damodaran.

11. U.S. Securities and Exchange Commission, "Compound Interest Calculator," https:// www.investor.gov/financial-tools-calculators/calculators/compound-interest-calculator.

12. One need only compare the GDP growth rates for the United States to the growth of the S&P 500 (including dividends) to see wealth extraction made possible by our tax and corporate laws. Compare GDP growth-rate data from the World Bank (see Macrotrends, "U.S. GDP Growth Rate 1961–2020," https://www.macrotrends.net/countries/USA/united-states /gdp-growth-rate) with S&P 500 data (Damodaran, "Historical Returns on Stocks").

13. Bernie Sanders, *Guide to Political Revolution* (New York: Henry Holt, 2017), 38–39.

14. See Sanders, *Guide to Political Revolution*, 8–9.

15. Pierre-Joseph Proudhon, *The System of Economic Contradictions, or the Philosophy of Poverty*, trans. Benjamin R. Tucker (Anarchist Library, 1847); Karl Marx, *The Poverty of Philosophy*, *with an introduction by Frederick Engels*, trans. H. Quelch (New York: Prometheus, 1995). On Marx's critique of utopian thinkers, see generally Roger Paden, "Marx's Critique of the Utopian Socialists," *Utopian Studies* 13, no. 2 (2002): 67–91.

16. Marx, foreword to *The Poverty of Philosophy*.

17. Karl Marx, *Capital*, vol. 3, trans. David Fernbach (New York: Penguin, 1981), 571–572.

18. Karl Marx, *Critique of the Gotha Program*, in *The Marx-Engels Reader*, 2nd ed., ed. Robert C. Tucker (New York: Norton, 1978), 536.

19. Karl Marx and Frederick Engels, *Manifesto of the Communist Party*, ed. Frederick Engels (New York: International, 1948), 30.

20. Sharryn Kasmir, *The Myth of Mondragón: Cooperatives, Politics, and Working-Class Life in a Basque Town* (Albany: State University of New York Press, 1996).

21. Kasmir, *The Myth of Mondragón*, 200.

22. June C. Nash, foreword to *The Myth of Mondragón: Cooperatives, Politics, and Working-Class Life in a Basque Town* (Albany: State University of New York Press, 1996), ix.

23.   Marx and Engels, *Manifesto of the Communist Party*, 44, 25.

24.   Bureau of Labor Statistics, January 20, 2022, https://www.bls.gov/news.release/pdf/union2 .pdf.

25.   See generally Piketty, *Capital and Ideology*, 788–799.

26.   Barbara Ransby, "The Class Politics of Black Lives Matter," *Dissent Magazine*, Fall 2015.

27.   In this sense, Lenin's writings at the end of his life offer better guidance, as do the economic writings and initiatives of Julius Nyerere. See Vladimir Lenin, "On Cooperation," *Pravda*, no. 115–116, May 26–27, 1923 (written January 4–6, 1923), reproduced in Vladimir Lenin, *Collected Works*, vol. 33, 2nd English ed. (Moscow: Progress, 1965), 467–475, https:// www.marxists.org/archive/lenin/works/1923/jan/06.htm); Julius Nyerere, "The Arusha Declaration" (written for the Tanganyika African National Union), February 5, 1967, https://www.marxists.org/subject/africa/nyerere/1967/arusha-declaration.htm.

28.   See, for instance, Proudhon to Marx, May 17, 1846, in *Property Is Theft! A Pierre-Joseph Proudhon Anthology*, ed. Iain McKay (Edinburgh: AK, 2011), 164; Proudhon to Blanc, April 8, 1848, in McKay, *Property Is Theft!*, 296; Proudhon letter response to Louis Blanc, December 28, 1849, in McKay, *Property Is Theft!*, 501. Dardot and Laval discuss at length the debate between Marx and Proudhon; see Dardot and Laval, *Common*, 79 et seq. Of course, the notion of the common was important to Marx from his early essay on the theft of wood (see my discussion of this in the course context of Michel Foucault's *The Punitive Society: Lectures at the Collège de France 1972–1972*, ed. Bernard E. Harcourt, trans Graham Burchell [New York: Picador, 2015], 265–300). Dardot and Laval discuss the theft of wood essay for a whole chapter, chapter 8 on "The 'Customary Law of Poverty.'" They also critique Hardt and Negri for returning to Proudhon. They argue that Hardt and Negri "make theft a central mode of accumulation that is independent of capital itself (as did Proudhon)." Dardot and Laval, *Common*, 126. To be sure, these are fascinating debates, but not necessary to a contemporary theory of cooperation in our interdependent world.

29.   Lenin, "On Cooperation."

30.   Lenin, "On Cooperation."

31.   Lenin, "On Cooperation." Ho Chi Minh similarly emphasized sequencing in his actions and writings. For Ho Chi Minh, as for Lenin, strategic alliances become the central issue. See generally Ho Chi Minh, *Down with Colonialism!*, ed. Walden Bello (New York: Verso, 2007).

32.   C. L. R. James, *Nkrumah and the Ghana Revolution* (Westport, CT: Lawrence Hill, 1977), 202.

33.   James, *Nkrumah and the Ghana Revolution*, 24.

34.   "Most cases of sexual abuse, for instance, go unreported, as do many cases of rape of adults; similarly, people in positions of power who engage in deceptive economic transactions and even many who physically harm others routinely evade any adverse consequences." Allegra McLeod, "Prison Abolition and Grounded Justice," *UCLA Law Review* 62 (2015): 1203, https://www.uclalawreview.org/wp-content/uploads/2019/09/McLeod _6.2015.pdf.

35.   Approximately 32.5 percent of property crimes and 40.9 percent of violent crimes were reported to the police in 2019. See Rachel E. Morgan and Jennifer L. Truman, "Criminal Victimization, 2019," U.S. Department of Justice, Office of Justice Programs, Bureau of Justice Statistics, September 2020, https://www.bjs.gov/content/pub/pdf/cv19.pdf.

36. Federal Bureau of Investigation, "Crime in the United States 2019: Clearances," https://ucr.fbi.gov/crime-in-the-u.s/2019/crime-in-the-u.s.-2019/topic-pages/clearances, table 25.

37. In the federal system in 2016, 67.7 percent of violent offense suspects were prosecuted in federal district court or disposed of by magistrates; 32.3 percent were not prosecuted. See Mark Motivans, "Federal Justice Statistics, 2016—Statistical Tables," U.S. Department of Justice, Office of Justice Programs, Bureau of Justice Statistics, September 2020, https://www.bjs.gov/content/pub/pdf/fjs16st.pdf, table 2.2. For property offenses, the rate was lower: 58.1 percent were prosecuted or disposed of and 41.9 percent were not.

38. I am thinking here of Ian Manuel, who was sentenced to life imprisonment without parole in Florida at the age of thirteen and served twenty-six years in prison, twenty of them in solitary confinement. See Bryan Stevenson, *Just Mercy: A Story of Justice and Redemption* (New York: Spiegel and Grau, 2015), chap. 8.

39. Sharon Dolovich, "Cruelty, Prison Conditions, and the Eighth Amendment," *New York University Law Review* 84, no. 4 (October 2009): 881–979; Sharon Dolovich, "Mass Incarceration, Meet COVID-19," *University of Chicago Law Review Online* 4 (November 2020).

40. The Sentencing Project, *Report of the Sentencing Project to the United Nations Special Rapporteur on Contemporary Forms of Racism, Racial Discrimination, Xenophobia, and Related Intolerance Regarding Racial Disparities in the United States Criminal Justice System*, April 19, 2018, https://www.sentencingproject.org/publications/un-report-on-racial-disparities/; Bruce Western, *Punishment and Inequality in America* (New York: Russell Sage Foundation, 2006); David Cole, *No Equal Justice: Race and Class in the American Criminal Justice System* (New York: New Press, 1999), 8–9. Regarding the role that race plays at nearly every step of the process in New York, from arrest to detention to bail to sentencing, see Besiki Luka Kutateladze, *Prosecution and Racial Justice in New York County* (Vera Institute for Justice, 2014), https://www.ojp.gov/pdffiles1/nij/grants/247227.pdf. Race also pervades the organization and provision of indigent defense. See Shaun Ossei-Owusu, "The Sixth Amendment Façade: The Racial Evolution of the Right to Counsel," *University of Pennsylvania Law Review* 167, no. 5 (April 2019): 1161–1239; Alexis Hoag-Fordjour, "White Is Right: The Racial Construction of Effective Assistance of Counsel," *NYU Law Review*, forthcoming, abstract at SSRN, https://papers.ssrn.com/sol3/papers.cfm?abstract_id=4179940. Race affects the predictive algorithms. See Sandra Mayson, "Bias In, Bias Out," *Yale Law Journal* 128, no. 8: (2018) 2218–2300. Even DNA databases are skewed: whites make up 62 percent of the U.S. population but only 49 percent of the disclosed DNA database; African Americans make up 13 percent of the population and 34 percent of the disclosed DNA database. See Erin Murphy, "The Racial Composition of Forensic DNA Databases," *California Law Review* 108, no. 6 (2020): 1847–1911. The evidence is truly overwhelming. For an article compiling the wealth of criminal justice–related articles establishing racial discrimination, see Radley Balko, "There's Overwhelming Evidence That the Criminal Justice System Is Racist. Here's the Proof," *Washington Post*, updated June 10, 2020, https://www.washingtonpost.com/graphics/2020/opinions/systemic-racism-police-evidence-criminal-justice-system/; and Radley Balko, "Twenty-One More Studies Showing Racial Disparities in the Criminal Justice System," *Washington Post*, April 9, 2019, https://www.washingtonpost.com/opinions/2019/04/09/more-studies-showing-racial-disparities-criminal-justice-system/.

41.   U.S. General Accounting Office (GAO), "Death Penalty Sentencing: Research Indicates Pattern of Racial Disparities," February1990, https://www.gao.gov/assets/220/212180.pdf; David Baldus and George Woodworth, "Race Discrimination and the Legitimacy of Capital Punishment," *DePaul Law Review* 53, no. 4 (2004): 1411–1495; see generally Alexis Hoag, "Valuing Black Lives: A Case for Ending the Death Penalty," *Columbia Human Rights Law Review* 51, no. 3 (2020): 992–996; Carol S. Steiker and Jordan M. Steiker, *Courting Death: The Supreme Court and Capital Punishment* (Cambridge, MA: Belknap, 2016), 110.

42.   Jennifer Eberhardt et al., "Looking Deathworthy: Perceived Stereotypicality of Black Defendants Predicts Capital-Sentencing Outcomes," *Psychological Science* 17, no. 5 (2006): 383–386.

43.   Even after controlling for locational variation and racial variation in crime participation, persons of African and Hispanic descent are stopped more frequently than whites. Andrew Gelman, Jeffrey Fagan, and Alex Kiss, "An Analysis of the New York City Police Department's 'Stop-and-Frisk' Policy in the Context of Claims of Racial Bias," *Journal of the American Statistical Association* 102, no. 479 (2007): 813–823.

44.   Alfred Blumstein, Jacqueline Cohen, and Daniel Nagin, "Report of the Panel on Research on Deterrent and Incapacitative Effects," in *Deterrence and Incapacitation: Estimating the Effects of Criminal Sanctions on Crime Rates*, ed. Alfred Blumstein et al. (Washington, DC: National Academy of Sciences, 1978), 42; Daniel Nagin, "General Deterrence: A Review of the Empirical Evidence," in *Deterrence and Incapacitation*, 95, 135; Steven Levitt, "Juvenile Crime and Punishment," *Journal of Political Economy* 106, no. 6 (December 1998): 1158n2 ("few of the empirical studies [regarding deterrence of adults] have any power to distinguish deterrence from incapacitation and therefore provide only an indirect test of the economic model of crime").

45.   Jeremy Bentham, *An Introduction to the Principles of Morals and Legislation*, 1781 ed., http://www.utilitarianism.com/jeremy-bentham/index.html.

46.   There are other problems as well. For instance, the rise of administrative law and its touchstones, reasoned decision making and judicial review, are not conducive to mercy and clemency, making it difficult to remedy some of the excesses of punishment. See Rachel Barkow, "The Ascent of the Administrative State and the Demise of Mercy," *Harvard Law Review* 121, no. 5 (March 2008): 1332–1365.

47.   Ruth Wilson Gilmore, *Golden Gulag: Prisons, Surplus, Crisis, and Opposition in Globalizing California* (Berkeley: University of California Press, 2007), 242. On "non-reformist reforms," see Ruth Wilson Gilmore and Craig Gilmore, "Restating the Obvious," in *Indefensible Space: The Architecture of the National Insecurity State*, ed. Michael Sorkin (New York: Routledge, 2007), 141; Amna Akbar, "Demands for a Democratic Political Economy," *Harvard Law Review Forum* 134, no. 1 (2020): 90–118; Jocelyn Simonson, "Police Reform Through a Power Lens," *Yale Law Journal* 130, no. 4 (2021): 778–1049.

48.   Dan Berger, Mariame Kaba, and David Stein, "What Abolitionists Do," *Jacobin*, August 24, 2017, https://perma.cc/K959-9FF5.

49.   Amna Akbar, "An Abolitionist Horizon for (Police) Reform," *California Law Review* 108, no. 6 (2020): 106.

50.   Jocelyn Simonson, "Police Reform Through a Power Lens," *Yale Law Journal* 130, no. 4 (2021): 778–1049.

51. Simonson, "Police Reform Through a Power Lens," draft version, on file with author.

52. Mariame Kaba, "Yes, We Mean Literally Abolish the Police," *New York Times*, June 12, 2020, https://www.nytimes.com/2020/06/12/opinion/sunday/floyd-abolish-defund-police.html.

53. Dorothy Roberts, "Foreword: Abolition Constitutionalism," *Harvard Law Review* 133, no. 1 (2019): 43, 114–115.

54. "Mathiesen explains that this distinction was introduced by André Gorz to analyze workers' strategies. [Mathiesen] finds it 'theoretically interesting' but argues that non-reformist reforms—such as reforms to give workers the power to decide their working conditions—are also not 'guaranteed against being absorbed by and consolidating the main system.'" Máximo Langer, "Penal Abolitionism and Criminal Law Minimalism: Here and There, Now and Then," *Harvard Law Review Forum* 134 (2020): 52–53. The Gorz text Mathiesen cites is André Gorz, *Stratégie ouvrière et néo-capitalisme* (Paris: Éditions du Seuil, 1964).

55. Angela Y. Davis, *Are Prisons Obsolete?* (New York: Seven Stories, 2003), 40. The Foucault quote is from Michel Foucault, *Discipline and Punish: The Birth of the Prison*, trans. Alan Sheridan (New York: Vintage, 1975), 234.

56. Foucault, *Discipline and Punish*, 234–235.

57. Mariame Kaba, *We Do This 'Til We Free Us* (Chicago: Haymarket, 2021), 15; Akbar, "An Abolitionist Horizon for (Police) Reform," 103.

58. Kaba, *We Do This 'Til We Free Us*, 15–16.

8. COOPERATION DEMOCRACY

1. Vanessa A. Boese, Nazifa Alizada, Martin Lundstedt, Kelly Morrison, Natalia Natsika, Yuko Sato, Hugo Tai, and Staffan I. Lindberg, *Democracy Report 2022: Autocratization Changing Nature?* (Gothenburg, Sweden: Varieties of Democracy Institute, 2022), https://v-dem.net/media/publications/dr_2022.pdf.

2. Ezekiel Kweku, "The Storming of the Capitol, One Year On," *New York Times*, January 6, 2022, https://www.nytimes.com/2022/01/06/opinion/jan-6-anniversary-package.html; Jimmy Carter, "Jimmy Carter: I Fear for Our Democracy," January 5, 2022, https://www.nytimes.com/2022/01/05/opinion/jan-6-jimmy-carter.html; Jedediah Britton-Purdy, "The Republican Party Is Succeeding Because We Are Not a True Democracy," *New York Times*, January 3, 2022, https://www.nytimes.com/2022/01/03/opinion/us-democracy-constitution.html; Rebecca Solnit, "Why Republicans Keep Falling for Trump's Lies," *New York Times*, January 5, 2022, https://www.nytimes.com/2022/01/05/opinion/republicans-trump-lies.html; Francis Fukuyama, "One Single Day. That's All It Took for the World to Look Away from Us," *New York Times*, January 5, 2022, https://www.nytimes.com/2022/01/05/opinion/jan-6-global-democracy.html.

3. Editorial Board, "Every Day Is Jan. 6 Now," *New York Times*, January 1, 2022, https://www.nytimes.com/2022/01/01/opinion/january-6-attack-committee.html.

4. Editorial Board, "Every Day Is Jan. 6 Now."

5. See, for example, Boese et al., *Democracy Report 2022*, 14.

6. PEW Center on the States, *One in 100: Behind Bars in America 2008*, https://www.pewtrusts.org/en/research-and-analysis/reports/2008/02/28/one-in-100-behind-bars-in-america-2008, 3;

see generally Bernard E. Harcourt, *The Illusion of Free Markets* (Cambridge, MA: Harvard University Press, 2011), 196–202.

7. My colleague and friend Jedediah Britton-Purdy argues for more expansive, robust, and participatory democracy throughout political life as a way to remedy the increasing polarization and breakdown of trust in society. See Jedediah Purdy, *Two Cheers for Politics: Why Democracy Is Flawed, Frightening—and Our Best Hope* (New York: Basic Books, 2022). In my view, however, his vision remains too tied to the procedural, to the mechanism of majority vote, as if participatory democracy will necessarily result in favorable outcomes. So long as a theory of participatory democracy does not infuse every aspect of our lives—including work, consumption, production, mutualism, etc.—and so long as the core values and principles of cooperation are not used to measure outcomes, simple majority vote even with robust participation will not be enough to save democratic practice.

8. Clarke A. Chambers, "The Cooperative League of the United States of America, 1916–1961: A Study of Social Theory and Social Action," *Agricultural History* 36, no. 2 (April 1962): 62.

9. James Peter Warbasse, *Co-operative Democracy* (New York: MacMillan, 1923), 367, 373.

10. Robin D. G. Kelley, preface to *Black and White: Land, Labor, and Politics in the South* by T. Thomas Fortune (New York: Atria Paperback, 2022), vii; Seth Moglen, introduction to *Black and White: Land, Labor, and Politics in the South* by T. Thomas Fortune (New York: Atria Paperback, 2022), xxiii–xxiv.

11. W. E. B. Du Bois, *Black Reconstruction in America, 1860–1880* (New York: Free Press, [1935] 1998), 179, 173, 131.

12. Du Bois, *Black Reconstruction in America*, 177.

13. Du Bois, *Black Reconstruction in America*, 670–672.

14. Du Bois, *Black Reconstruction in America*, 325.

15. Du Bois, *Black Reconstruction in America*, 182.

16. Du Bois, *Black Reconstruction in America*, 184.

17. See Derecka Purnell, *Becoming Abolitionists* (New York: Astra House, 2021), 117–119, distinguishing between the alliance of "liberal small-capitalist abolitionists," on the one hand, and the "Northern industrialist capitalists," on the other.

18. Du Bois, *Black Reconstruction in America*, 325.

19. "Translated from judicial activity in racial cases both before and after *Brown*, this principle of 'interest convergence' provides: The interest of blacks in achieving racial equality will be accommodated only when it converges with the interests of whites. However, the fourteenth amendment, standing alone, will not authorize a judicial remedy providing effective racial equality for blacks where the remedy sought threatens the superior societal status of middle and upper class whites." Derrick A. Bell Jr., "*Brown v. Board of Education* and the Interest-Convergence Dilemma," *Harvard Law Review* 93, no. 3 (1980): 523.

20. In the ensuing secondary literature on abolition democracy, few have disarticulated these different strands, with the notable exceptions of Robert Gooding-Williams and Derecka Purnell. I discuss Gooding-Williams shortly. By contrast to Purnell, I would suggest that the two historical conceptions also differ from a more ideal vision of abolition democracy that Du Bois maintained and that Angela Davis developed in her work. The larger distinction, I would argue, is between an ideal and the historical uses. Along those lines, the ideal, for Du Bois, was tied to a radical reenvisioning of political economy

along the lines of cooperation, as reflected in his essay from the same year titled "A Negro Nation Within the Nation," *Current History* 42, no. 3 (1935): 265-270. It is this ideal vision that has had the greatest influence, I believe, on abolitionism today.

21. Du Bois, *Black Reconstruction in America*, 182.

22. Du Bois, *Black Reconstruction in America*, 193.

23. Du Bois, *Black Reconstruction in America*, 190, 185, 186.

24. Du Bois, *Black Reconstruction in America*, 184, 185.

25. Robert Gooding-Williams, "Abolition Democracy 2/13," *Abolition Democracy 13/13* (blog), October 15, 2020, http://blogs.law.columbia.edu/abolition1313/2-13-abolition-democracy/. Alternatively, as Gooding-Williams discusses there, the uses of the term *abolition democracy* can be disambiguated by distinguishing between the ideal of abolition democracy and what might be called "compensated democracy." The first is more akin to the ideal of universal democracy. It involves the extension of the right to rule to all people. It is reflected in the expression "the rule of men" that Du Bois developed in *Darkwater*. W. E. B. Du Bois, *Darkwater: Voices from Within the Veil* (New York: Dover, 1999). The second, compensated democracy, focuses instead on people having a voice in the selection of government officials. It is more of a libertarian ideal and reflects a compromise with the people to make possible capitalist profit.

26. Robert Gooding-Williams, "Democratic Despotism and the New Imperialism," *Abolition Democracy 13/13* (blog), October 12, 2020, http://blogs.law.columbia.edu/abolition1313/robert-gooding-williams-democratic-despotism-and-the-new-imperialism/.

27. See especially Du Bois, *Black Reconstruction in America*, 634.

28. Du Bois, *Black Reconstruction in America*, 187.

29. Angela Y. Davis, *Abolition Democracy: Beyond Empire, Prisons, and Torture* (New York: Seven Stories, 2005), 92.

30. Angela Y. Davis, *Are Prisons Obsolete?* (New York: Seven Stories, 2011), 107.

31. Davis, *Are Prisons Obsolete?*, 111.

32. Dorothy Roberts, "Constructing a Criminal Justice System Free of Racial Bias: An Abolitionist Framework," *Columbia Human Rights Law Review* 39, no. 1 (2008): 285.

33. "Racism is integrally linked to capitalism," Davis states in June 2020. "And I think it's a mistake to assume that we can combat racism by leaving capitalism in place. As Cedric Robinson pointed out in his book *Black Marxism*, capitalism is racial capitalism. And of course, to just say for a moment, that Marx pointed out that what he called primitive accumulation—capital doesn't just appear from nowhere—the original capital was provided by the labor of slaves." See "Angela Davis: We can't eradicate racism without eradicating racial capitalism," *Democracy Now!*, June 14, 2020, https://youtu.be/qhh3CMkngkY.

34. Ruth Wilson Gilmore, *Golden Gulag: Prisons, Surplus, Crisis, and Opposition in Globalizing California* (Berkeley: University of California Press, 2007), 241.

35. Purnell, *Becoming Abolitionists*, 121.

36. See Purnell, *Becoming Abolitionists*, 185-191, 214-217; Liat Ben-Moshe, *Decarcerating Disability: Deinstitutionalization and Prison Abolition* (Minneapolis: University of Minnesota Press, 2020); Che Gossett, Nick Mitchell, Eric A. Stanley, and Liat Ben-Moshe, "Critical Theory, Queer Resistance, and the Ends of Capture," in *Death and Other Penalties: Philosophy in a Time of Mass Incarceration*, ed. Geoffrey Adelsberg, Lisa Guenther, and Scott Zeman (New York: Fordham University Press, 2015), 266-297.

37. Purnell, *Becoming Abolitionists*, 271.

38. Angela Davis, "We Can't Eradicate Racism Without Eradicating Racial Capitalism," *Democracy Now!*, June 14, 2020, https://www.facebook.com/watch/?v=256023612510210; see also Purnell, *Becoming Abolitionists*, 273–274.

39. See, for example, Mariame Kaba, *We Do This 'Til We Free Us* (Chicago: Haymarket, 2021); Dorothy E. Roberts, "Foreword: Abolition Constitutionalism," *Harvard Law Review* 133, no. 1 (2019): 1–122; Rachel Kushner, "Is Prison Necessary? Ruth Wilson Gilmore Might Change Your Mind," *New York Times Magazine*, April 17, 2019, https://www.nytimes.com /2019/04/17/magazine/prison-abolition-ruth-wilson-gilmore.html; Purnell, *Becoming Abolitionists*; Amna Akbar, "Toward a Radical Imagination of Law," *New York University Law Review* 93, no. 3 (2018): 405–479; Che Gossett, *Abolitionist Entanglement: Ending the Grammars of Capture* (PhD diss., Rutgers University, 2021); Alexis Hoag, "Valuing Black Lives," *Columbia Human Rights Law Review* 51, no. 3 (2020): 983–1007; Keeanga-Yamahtta Taylor, "We Should Still Defund the Police," *New Yorker*, August 14, 2020, https://www.newyorker .com/news/our-columnists/defund-the-police; Harsha Walia, *Border and Rule: Global Migration, Capitalism, and the Rise of Racist Nationalism* (Chicago: Haymarket, 2021); Brandon Hasbrouck, "Abolishing Racist Policing with the Thirteenth Amendment," *UCLA Law Review* 67, no. 5 (2020): 1108–1129, https://www.uclalawreview.org/abolishing-racist -policing-with-the-thirteenth-amendment/; Ruth Wilson Gilmore and James Kilgore, "The Case for Abolition," *Marshall Project*, June 9, 2019, https://www.themarshallproject .org/2019/06/19/the-case-for-abolition; Mariame Kaba and Andrea Ritchie, *No More Police: A Case for Abolition* (New York: New Press, 2022).

40. See Rose Braz, Bo Brown, Craig Gilmore, Ruthie Gilmore, Donna Hunter, Christian Parenti, Dylan Rodriguez, Cassandra Shaylor, Nancy Stoller, and Julia Sudbury, "The History of Critical Resistance," *Social Justice* 27, no. 3 (2000): 6–10; Joy James, ed., *The New Abolitionists: (Neo)Slave Narratives and Contemporary Prison Writings* (Albany: State University of New York Press, 2005); and notes *supra* and *infra*. By "the new abolitionism," I am referring to this wave of scholarship, organizing, and activism that, since the midtwentieth century, argues for the abolition of police, prisons, family regulation, the death penalty, and other manifestations of the punitive society. It had antecedents earlier in the United States and globally. See Garrett Felber, "The Struggle to Defund the Police Is Not New," *Boston Review*, June 9, 2020, http://bostonreview.net/race/garrett -felber-struggle-abolish-police-not-new (discussing the debate sparked by Bayard Rustin and George Houser at the inaugural Conference on Prison Problems in 1945 and the Quaker Fay Honey Knopp's 1976 *Instead of Prisons: A Handbook for Prison Abolitionists*, Prison Research Education Action Project, 1976); Máximo Langer, "Penal Abolitionism and Criminal Law Minimalism: Here and There, Now and Then," *Harvard Law Review Forum* 134 (2020): 47–57 (discussing the global and international movements for penal abolition beginning in the 1960s). I do not mean to elide those historical and global antecedents but rather to map a second movement of abolitionism and possibly of "abolition democracy."

41. See, for example, Davis, "We Can't Eradicate Racism Without Eradicating Racial Capitalism."

42. Stefano Harney and Fred Moten, *The Undercommons: Fugitive Planning and Black Study* (Wivenhoe, UK: Minor Compositions, 2013), 42.

43. Angela Y. Davis, Gina Dent, Erica R Meiners, and Beth E. Richie, *Abolition. Feminism. Now.* (Chicago: Haymarket, 2022); Alisa Bierria, Jakeya Caruthers, and Brooke Lober, eds., *Abolition Feminisms*, 2 vols. (Chicago: Haymarket, 2022). On the Combahee River Collective, see Keeanga-Yamahtta Taylor, *How We Get Free: Black Feminism and the Combahee River Collective* (Chicago: Haymarket, 2017); Keeanga-Yamahtta Taylor, "Until Black Women Are Free, None of Us Will Be Free," *New Yorker*, July 20, 2020, https://www.newyorker.com/news/our-columnists/until-black-women-are-free-none-of-us-will-be-free.

44. Davis, Dent, Meiners, and Richie, *Abolition. Feminism. Now.*, 61.

45. See Carol Gilligan, *In a Different Voice* (Cambridge, MA: Harvard University Press, 1982); Nel Noddings, *Caring: A Feminine Approach to Ethics and Moral Education* (Berkeley: University of California Press, 1982); Joan C. Tronto, *Caring Democracy: Markets, Equality, and Justice* (New York: New York University Press, 2013); Care Collective, *The Care Manifesto* (New York: Verso, 2020); Fabienne Brugère, *Care Ethics: The Introduction of Care as a Political Category*, trans. Armelle Chrétien, Olivia Cooper-Hadjian, and Brian Heffernan (Leuven, Belgium: Peeters, 2019); Miriam Ticktin, *Casualties of Care: Immigration and the Politics of Humanitarianism in France*, (Berkeley: University of California Press, 2011). For a recent treatment tracing the links to Hannah Arendt's notion of *amor mundi*, see Lucien Ferguson, "From Love to Care: Arendt's *Amor Mundi* in the Ethical Turn," *Political Theory*, July 2022, doi:10.1177/00905917221097426.

46. Derecka Purnell has a moving discussion of this in *Becoming Abolitionists* when she recounts reading and learning about Robin D. G. Kelley's ideas while she was organizing as a student at Harvard Law School. See Purnell, *Becoming Abolitionists*, 105–111.

47. Dean Spade, *Mutual Aid: Building Solidarity During This Crisis (and the Next)* (New York: Penguin, 2020), 40.

48. Bryan Stevenson, speaking on the *Ezra Klein Show*, "Bryan Stevenson on How America Can Heal," July 20, 2020, https://www.vox.com/21327742/bryan-stevenson-the-ezra-klein-show-america-slavery-healing-racism-george-floyd-protests (discussion of care and health at the 65:55 mark). Joe Margulies expresses something similar in his essay "Who Deserves to Be Forgiven?": "To approach each person in a spirit of forgiveness rather than condemnation, to treat them as a member of society rather than an outcast, will slowly unwind the punitive turn of the past fifty years." Joseph Margulies, "Who Deserves to Be Forgiven?," *Boston Review*, February 23, 2021, http://bostonreview.net/law-justice/joseph-margulies-who-deserves-be-forgiven.

49. Patrisse Cullors, "Abolition and Reparations: Histories of Resistance, Transformative Justice, and Accountability," *Harvard Law Review* 132, no. 6 (2019): 1694.

50. Kaba, *We Do This 'Til We Free Us*, 17.

51. Purnell, *Becoming Abolitionists*, 273, 274. Purnell quotes the mission statement of the Dream Defenders, which she helped found.

52. See "Why the World Should Take Note of the Swiss Apprenticeship Model," *Swissinfo.ch*, https://www.swissinfo.ch/eng/why-the-world-should-take-note-of-the-swiss-apprenticeship-model/45810312; Diana Elliott and Batia Katz, "Three Lessons from the Swiss Apprenticeship Model to Inform Our Post-COVID-19 Recovery," *Urban Institute*, July 20, 2020, https://www.urban.org/urban-wire/three-lessons-swiss-apprenticeship-model-inform-our-post-covid-19-recovery.

ACKNOWLEDGMENTS

1. Biodun Jeyifo, "An 'Illuminati' and Its Acolytes: Critical Theory in the Text and in the World," *British Journal of Sociology* 72, no. 3 (June 2021): 870.

2. Gayatri Chakravorty Spivak, "Can the Subaltern Speak?," in *Can the Subaltern Speak? Reflections on the History of an Idea*, ed. Rosalind C. Morris (New York: Columbia University Press, 2010), 27.

3. Jeyifo, "An 'Illuminati' and Its Acolytes," 869.

Bibliography

Abbott, Andrew. *Processual Sociology*. Chicago: University of Chicago Press, 2016.

Adams, Herbert B., ed. *History of Coöperation in the United States*. Baltimore: Johns Hopkins University, 1888.

Akbar, Amna. "An Abolitionist Horizon for Police (Reform)." *California Law Review* 108, no. 6 (2020): 1781–1846.

——. "Demands for a Democratic Political Economy." *Harvard Law Review Forum* 145, no. 1 (2020): 90–118.

——. "Toward a Radical Imagination of Law." *New York University Law Review* 93, no. 3 (2018): 405–479.

Akuno, Kali. *The Jackson-Kush Plan: The Struggle for Black Self-Determination and Economic Democracy.* n.d. https://mronline.org/wp-content/uploads/2020/07/Jackson-KushPlan.pdf.

Akuno, Kali, and Matt Meyer. *Jackson Rising Redux: Lessons on Building the Future in the Present.* Oakland, CA: PM, forthcoming.

Akuno, Kali, and Ajamu Nangwaya. *Jackson Rising: The Struggle for Economic Democracy and Black Self-Determination in Jackson, Mississippi.* Wakefield, Quebec: Daraja, 2017.

Alexander, Michelle. *The New Jim Crow: Mass Incarceration in the Age of Colorblindness*. New York: New Press, 2010.

Althusser, Louis. "Ideology and Ideological State Apparatuses (Notes Towards an Investigation)." In *Lenin and Philosophy and Other Essays*, trans. Ben Brewster, 85–126. New York: Monthly Review, 1971.

Andersson, Lars-Fredrik. "Review of *Mutual Insurance 1550–2015: From Guild Welfare and Friendly Societies to Contemporary Micro-Insurers*, by Marco H. D. van Leeuwen." *Continuity and Change* 33, no. 3 (December 2018): 447–449.

Aronoff, Kate, Alyssa Battistoni, Daniel Aldana Cohen, and Thea Riofrancos. *A Planet to Win: Why We Need a Green New Deal*. New York: Verso, 2019.

Baldus, David, and George Woodworth. "Race Discrimination and the Legitimacy of Capital Punishment." *DePaul Law Review* 53, no. 4 (2004): 1411–1495.

Baldwin, James. "An Open Letter to My Sister, Angela Y. Davis." In *If They Come in the Morning . . . Voices of Resistance*, ed. Angela Y. Davis, 19–23. New York: Verso, 2016.

Balibar, Etienne. *Histoire interminable. D'un siècle l'autre. Écrits I.* Paris: La Découverte, 2020.

Banner, Stuart. "Traces of Slavery: Race and the Death Penalty in Historical Perspective." In *From Lynch Mobs to the Killing State: Race and the Death Penalty in America*, ed. Charles J. Ogletree Jr. and Austin Sarat. New York: NYU Press, 2006.

Barandiaran, Xabier, and Javier Lezaun. "The Mondragón Experience." In *The Oxford Handbook of Mutual, Co-operative, and Co-owned Business*, ed. Jonathan Michie, Joseph R. Blasi, and Carlo Borzaga, 279–294. Oxford: Oxford University Press, 2017.

Bardet, Fabrice. *La Contre-révolution comptable: Ces chiffres qui (nous) gouvernent.* Paris: Les Belles Lettres, 2014.

Barkow, Rachel. "The Ascent of the Administrative State and the Demise of Mercy." *Harvard Law Review* 121, no. 5 (March 2008): 1332–1365.

Barthes, Roland. *Sade, Fourier, Loyola.* Paris: Éditions du Seuil, 1971.

Battistoni, Alyssa. "Living, Not Just Surviving." *Jacobin*, August 15, 2015. https://jacobinmag.com /2017/08/living-not-just-surviving/.

Becker, Gary. *Human Capital: A Theoretical and Empirical Analysis, with Special Reference to Education*, 3rd ed. Chicago: University of Chicago Press, 1993 [1975].

Beecher, Jonathan. *Charles Fourier: The Visionary and His World.* Berkeley: University of California Press, 1986.

Bell, Derrick A., Jr. "*Brown v. Board of Education* and the Interest-Convergence Dilemma." *Harvard Law Review* 93, no. 3 (1980): 518–533.

Bell, Monica. "Anti-Segregation Policing." *New York University Law Review* 95, no. 3 (June 2020): 650–765.

—. "Black Security and the Conundrum of Policing." *Just Security*, July 15, 2020. https://www .justsecurity.org/71418/black-security-and-the-conundrum-of-policing/.

—. "Police Reform and the Dismantling of Legal Estrangement." *Yale Law Journal* 126 (2017): 2054–2150.

Ben-Moshe, Liat. *Decarcerating Disability: Deinstitutionalization and Prison Abolition.* Minneapolis: University of Minnesota Press, 2020.

Benefit Corporation (B Lab). *What Is a Benefit Corporation?* 2020. https://benefitcorp.net/what-is -a-benefit-corporation.

Benkler, Yochai. "Peer Production, the Commons, and the Future of the Firm." *Strategic Organization* 15, no. 2 (2017): 264–274.

Bentham, Jeremy. *An Introduction to the Principles of Morals and Legislation.* http://www.utilitarianism .com/jeremy-bentham/index.html.

Berger, Dan, Mariame Kaba, and David Stein. "What Abolitionists Do." *Jacobin*, August 24, 2017. https://perma.cc/K959-9FF5.

Berry, Daphne. "The Worker Co-operative Form in the Home Care Industry in the USA." In *The Oxford Handbook of Mutual, Co-operative, and Co-owned Business*, ed. Jonathan Michie, Joseph R. Blasi, and Carlo Borzaga, 386–397. Oxford: Oxford University Press, 2017.

Bey, Hakim. "The Lemonade Ocean and Modern Times." Anarchist Library, 1991. http:// theanarchistlibrary.org/library/hakim-bey-the-lemonade-ocean-and-modern-times.

Bierria, Alisa, Jakeya Caruthers, and Brooke Lober, eds. *Abolition Feminisms.* 2 vols. Chicago: Haymarket, 2022.

Bierria, Alisa, Hyejin Shim, Mariame Kaba, and Stacy Suh, eds. *Survived and Punished: Survivor Defense as Abolitionist Praxis* (2017). https://survivedandpunished.org/wp-content/uploads/2018/06 /survived-and-punished-toolkit.pdf.

Big Door Brigade. "What Is Mutual Aid?" https://bigdoorbrigade.com/what-is-mutual-aid/.

Billeaux, Michael, Anne Reynolds, Trevor Young-Hyman, and Ayca Zayim. "Worker Cooperative Case Study: Isthmus Engineering & Manufacturing." Staff Paper, Center for Cooperatives,

University of Wisconsin–Madison, October 2011. https://www.ssc.wisc.edu/~wright/929 -utopias-2013/Real%20Utopia%20Readings/Billeaux%20et%20al%20Ishmus%20Engineering%20 case%20study.pdf.

Birchall, Johnston. "The Performance of Member-Owned Businesses Since the Financial Crisis of 2008." In *The Oxford Handbook of Mutual, Co-operative, and Co-owned Business*, ed. Jonathan Michie, Joseph R. Blasi, and Carlo Borzaga, 570–584. Oxford: Oxford University Press, 2017.

Birchall, Johnston, and Lou Hammond Ketilson. *Resilience of the Cooperative Business Model in Times of Crisis*. Geneva: International Labour Organization, Sustainable Enterprise Programme, 2009.

Black, Donald. "Crime as Social Control." *American Sociological Review* 48, no. 1 (1983): 34–45.

Blanc, Louis. *Histoire de la Révolution Française*. 2 vols. Cambridge: Cambridge University Press, 2011.

—. *L'Organisation du travail*. Scotts Valley, CA: CreateSpace Independent Publishing Platform, 2015. ISBN 978-1511511667.

—. *Organization of Work*. Trans. Marie Paula Dickoré. Cincinnati: University of Cincinnati Press, 1911.

Blasi, Joseph R., Richard B. Freeman, and Douglas L. Kruse. "Evidence: What the US Research Shows About Worker Ownership." In *The Oxford Handbook of Mutual, Co-operative, and Co-owned Business*, ed. Jonathan Michie, Joseph R. Blasi, and Carlo Borzaga, 211–226. Oxford: Oxford University Press, 2017.

Blisse, Holger, and Detlev Hummel. "Raiffeisenbanks and Volksbanks for Europe: The Case for Co-operative Banking in Germany." In *The Oxford Handbook of Mutual, Co-operative, and Co-owned Business*, ed. Jonathan Michie, Joseph R. Blasi, and Carlo Borzaga, 398–411. Oxford: Oxford University Press, 2017.

Block, Fred. *Capitalism: The Future of an Illusion*. Oakland: University of California Press, 2018.

—. *The Power of Market Fundamentalism: Karl Polanyi's Critique*. Cambridge, MA: Harvard University Press, 2016.

Blumstein, Alfred, and Jacqueline Cohen. "A Theory of the Stability of Punishment." *Journal of Criminal Law & Criminology* 64 (1973): 198–207.

Blumstein, Alfred, Jacqueline Cohen, and Daniel Nagin. "Report of the Panel on Research on Deterrent and Incapacitative Effects." In *Deterrence and Incapacitation: Estimating the Effects of Criminal Sanctions on Crime Rates*, ed. Alfred Blumstein et al. Washington, DC: National Academy of Sciences, 1978.

Boese, Vanessa A., Nazifa Alizada, Martin Lundstedt, Kelly Morrison, Natalia Natsika, Yuko Sato, Hugo Tai, and Staffan I. Lindberg. *Democracy Report 2022: Autocratization Changing Nature?* Gothenburg, Sweden: Varieties of Democracy Institute, 2022. https://v-dem.net /media/publications/dr_2022.pdf.

Boland, Michael A., Brendan Cooper, and James M. White. "Making Sustainability Tangible: Land O'Lakes and the Dairy Supply Chain." *American Journal of Agricultural Economics* 98, no. 2 (March 2016): 648–657. http://dx.doi.org/10.1093/ajae/aav062.

Bonin, John P., Derek C. Jones, and Louis Putterman. "Theoretical and Empirical Studies of Producer Cooperatives: Will Ever the Twain Meet?" *Journal of Economic Literature* 31, no. 3 (1993): 1290–1320.

Bonin, John P., and Louis Putterman. *Economics of Cooperation and the Labour-Managed Economy*. New York: Routledge, 2013.

Borowy, Iris, and Matthias Schmelzer, eds. *History of the Future of Economic Growth: Historical Roots of Current Debates on Sustainable Degrowth*. New York: Routledge, 2017.

Braithwaite, John. "A Future Where Punishment Is Marginalized: Realistic or Utopian?" *UCLA Law Review* 46, no. 6 (1999): 1727-1750.

Braudel, Fernand. *Civilisation matérielle, économie et capitalisme, XVe–XVIIIe siècle*. Vol. 2. Paris: Armand Colin, 2022.

—. *Civilization and Capitalism, 15th–18th Century*. Vol. 2, *The Wheels of Commerce*. New York: Harper and Row, 1982.

—. *Les jeux de l'échange*. Paris: Armand Colin, 1979.

Braz, Rose, Bo Brown, Craig Gilmore, Ruthie Gilmore, Donna Hunter, Christian Parenti, Dylan Rodriguez, Cassandra Shaylor, Nancy Stoller, and Julia Sudbury. "The History of Critical Resistance." *Social Justice* 27, no. 3 (2000): 6-10.

Breton, André. *Ode à Charles Fourier*. Paris: Éditions de la Revue Fontaine, 1947.

Brugère, Fabienne. *Care Ethics: The Introduction of Care as a Political Category*. Trans. Armelle Chrétien, Olivia Cooper-Hadjian, and Brian Heffernan. Leuven, Belgium: Peeters, 2019.

Brzustowski, Thomas, and Francesco Caselli. "Economic Growth in a Cooperative Economy." *IDEAS Working Paper Series from RePEc*. 2021. https://www.proquest.com/working-papers /economic-growth-cooperative-economy/docview/2587466273/se-2.

Burden-Stelly, Charisse. "Caste Does Not Explain Race." *Boston Review*, December 15, 2020. http:// bostonreview.net/race/charisse-burden-stelly-caste-does-not-explain-race.

Butler, Judith. *Notes Toward a Performative Theory of Assembly*. Cambridge, MA: Harvard University Press, 2015.

Butler, Paul. *Chokehold: Policing Black Men*. New York: New Press, 2018.

—. "Racially Based Jury Nullification: Black Power in the Criminal Justice System." *Yale Law Journal* 105, no. 3 (1995): 677-725.

Callon, Michel. *L'emprise des marchés. Comprendre leur fonctionnement pour pouvoir les changer*. Paris: Éditions La Découverte, 2017.

Care Collective. *The Care Manifesto*. New York: Verso, 2020.

Case, John, and Rosemary C. R. Taylor, eds. *Co-ops, Communes and Collectives: Experiments in Social Change in the 1960s and 1970s*. New York: Pantheon, 1979.

Chambers, Clarke A. "The Cooperative League of the United States of America, 1916-1961: A Study of Social Theory and Social Action." *Agricultural History* 36, no. 2 (April 1962): 59-81.

Chancel, Lucas, Thomas Piketty, Emmanuel Saez, and Gabriel Zucman. *World Inequality Report 2022*. World Inequality Lab. https://wir2022.wid.world/www-site/uploads/2022/03/0098-21 _WIL_RIM_RAPPORT_A4.pdf.

Chiapello, Eve. "Accounting and the Birth of the Idea of Capitalism." *Critical Perspectives on Accounting* 18, no. 3 (March 2007): 263-296.

Childs, Dennis. *Slaves of the State: Black Incarceration from the Chain Gang to the Penitentiary*. Minneapolis: University of Minnesota Press, 2018.

Chiricos, Theodore G., and Miriam A. Delone. "Labor Surplus and Punishment: A Review and Assessment of Theory and Evidence." *Social Problems* 39, no. 4 (1992): 421-446.

Clover, Joshua. "The Rise and Fall of Biopolitics: A Response to Bruno Latour." *Critical Inquiry* (blog), March 29, 2020. https://critinq.wordpress.com/2020/03/29/the-rise-and-fall-of-biopolitics -a-response-to-bruno-latour/.

Cole, David. *No Equal Justice: Race and Class in the American Criminal Justice System*. New York: New Press, 1999.

Cole, G. D. H. *Socialist Thought: The Forerunners, 1789–1850*. London: MacMillan, 1953.

Columbia Center for Contemporary Critical Thought. "Covid-19 Response Projects." Columbia Law School. https://cccct.law.columbia.edu/content/covid-19-response-projects.

Cooperation Humboldt. *Cooperation Humboldt: Building a Solidarity Economy on California's North Coast: Who We Are, What We Believe, and What We Do*. 2020. https://cooperationhumboldt.com /wp-content/uploads/2020/09/CH-general-info-booklet-with-bleed-spreads.pdf.

Cooperation Jackson. "Cooperation Jackson, Cooperation Vermont, the Marshfield Cooperative and PNLL." February 17, 2022. https://cooperationjackson.org/blog/cooperationjackson -cooperationvermont-marshfieldcoop.

Cox, Oliver Cromwell. *Caste, Class, and Race: A Study in Social Dynamics*. New York: Monthly Review, 1948.

Cracogna, Dante, Antonio Fici, and Hagen Henrÿ, eds. *The International Handbook of Cooperative Law*. Heidelberg, Germany: Springer, 2013.

Cullors, Patrisse. "Abolition and Reparations: Histories of Resistance, Transformative Justice, and Accountability." *Harvard Law Review* 132, no. 6 (2019): 1684–1694.

Curl, John. *For All the People: Uncovering the Hidden History of Cooperation, Cooperative Movements, and Communalism in America*. 2nd ed. Oakland, CA: PM, 2012.

——. *History of Work Cooperation in America: Cooperatives, Cooperative Movements, Collectivity and Communalism from Early America to the Present*. Berkeley, CA: Homeward, 1980.

D'Alisa, Giacomo, Federico Demaria, and Giorgio Kallis, eds. *Degrowth: A Vocabulary for a New Era*. New York: Routledge, 2015.

Daly, Herman E., and Joshua Farley. *Ecological Economics: Principles and Applications*. 2nd ed. Washington, DC: Island, 2011.

Damodaran, Answath. "Historical Returns on Stocks, Bonds and Bills—United States." Damodaran Online. http://pages.stern.nyu.edu/~adamodar/New_Home_Page/datafile/histretSP.html.

Daniels, Ronald J., and Marc H. Morial. "The COVID-19 Racial Disparities Could Be Even Worse Than We Think." *Washington Post*, April 23, 2020. https://www.washingtonpost.com/opinions /2020/04/23/covid-19-racial-disparities-could-be-even-worse-than-we-think/.

Dardot, Pierre, and Christian Laval. *Common: On Revolution in the Twenty-First Century*. Trans. Matthew MacLellan. London: Bloomsbury, 2019.

——. *Commun: Essai sur la révolution au XXIe siècle*. Paris: Éditions La Découverte, 2014.

Davies, William. "Corporate Governance Beyond Neoliberalism: Agency, Democracy, and Co-operation." In *The Oxford Handbook of Mutual, Co-operative, and Co-owned Business*, ed. Jonathan Michie, Joseph R. Blasi, and Carlo Borzaga, 445–455. Oxford: Oxford University Press, 2017.

Davis, Angela Y. *Abolition Democracy: Beyond Empire, Prisons, and Torture*. New York: Seven Stories, 2005.

——. *Are Prisons Obsolete?* New York: Seven Stories, 2011.

——. "Political Prisoners, Prisons, and Black Liberation." In *If They Come in the Morning . . . Voices of Resistance*, ed. Angela Y. Davis, 21–38. New York: Verso, 2016.

Davis, Angela Y., Gina Dent, Erica R. Meiners, and Beth E. Richie. *Abolition. Feminism. Now.* Chicago: Haymarket, 2022.

Debord, Guy. *Society of the Spectacle*. Trans. Ken Knabb. London: Rebel, 2002.

Dewey, John. *Lectures in China, 1919–1920.* Honolulu: University of Hawai'i Press, 1973.

Dolovich, Sharon. "Cruelty, Prison Conditions, and the Eighth Amendment." *New York University Law Review* 84, no. 4 (October 2009): 881–979.

Dolovich, Sharon. "Mass Incarceration, Meet COVID-19." *University of Chicago Law Review Online* 4 (November 2020).

Doucouliagos, Chris. "Worker Participation and Productivity in Labor-Managed and Participatory Capitalist Firms: A Meta-Analysis." *Industrial and Labor Relations Review* 49, no. 1 (October 1995): 58–77.

Droz, Jacques, ed. *Histoire générale de socialisme.* 4 vols. Paris: Presses Universitaires de France, 1997.

Du Bois, W. E. B. *Black Reconstruction in America, 1860–1880.* New York: Free Press, 1998.

——. *Darkwater: Voices from Within the Veil.* New York: Dover, 1999.

——. *Economic Co-operation Among Negro Americans: Report of a Social Study Made by Atlanta University, Under the Patronage of the Carnegie Institution of Washington, D.C., Together with the Proceedings of the Twelfth Conference for the Study of the Negro Problems, Held at Atlanta University, on Tuesday, May the 28th, 1907.* Atlanta: Atlanta University Press, 1907.

——. "A Negro Nation Within the Nation." *Current History* 42, no. 3 (1935): 265–270.

Durkheim, Emile. *Socialism and Saint Simon.* London: Routledge, 1959.

Duverger, Timothée. *La décroissance, une idée pour demain.* Paris: Sang de la Terre. 2011.

——. *Utopies locales. Les solutions écologiques et solidaires de demain.* Paris: Les Petits Matins, 2021.

Eberhardt, Jennifer, et. al. "Looking Deathworthy: Perceived Stereotypicality of Black Defendants Predicts Capital-Sentencing Outcomes." *Psychological Science* 17, no. 5 (2006): 383–386.

Edenfield, Avery. "Collective Management in a Cooperative: Problematizing Productivity and Power." PhD diss., University of Wisconsin-Madison, 2016.

Fagan, Jeffrey, and Daniel C. Richman. "Understanding Recent Spikes and Longer Trends in American Murders." *Columbia Law Review* 117, no. 5 (2017): 1235–1296.

Felber, Garrett. "The Struggle to Defund the Police Is Not New." *Boston Review,* June 9, 2020. http://bostonreview.net/race/garrett-felber-struggle-abolish-police-not-new.

Ferguson, Lucien. "From Love to Care: Arendt's *Amor Mundi* in the Ethical Turn." *Political Theory,* July 2022. doi:10.1177/00905917221097426.

Fici, Antonio. "The Essential Role of Co-operative Law and Some Related Issues." In *The Oxford Handbook of Mutual, Co-operative, and Co-owned Business,* ed. Jonathan Michie, Joseph R. Blasi, and Carlo Borzaga, 539–549. Oxford: Oxford University Press, 2017.

Foner, Eric. *Reconstruction: America's Unfinished Revolution, 1863–1877.* New York: Harper & Row, 1988.

——. *Second Founding: How the Civil War and Reconstruction Remade the Constitution.* New York: Norton, 2019.

Forcadell, Francisco Javier. "Democracy, Cooperation and Business Success: The Case of Mondragón Corporación Cooperativa." *Journal of Business Ethics* 56, no. 3 (2005): 255–274.

Fortune, T. Thomas. *Black and White: Land, Labor, and Politics in the South.* New York: Atria Paperback, 2022.

Forman, James, Jr. "Racial Critiques of Mass Incarceration: Beyond the New Jim Crow." *New York University Law Review* 87, no. 1 (February 2021): 101–146.

Foucault, Michel. "Alternatives to the Prison: Dissemination or Decline of Social Control?" *Theory, Culture & Society* 26, no. 6 (1976): 12–24.

—. *The Birth of Biopolitics: Lectures at the Collège de France, 1978–1979*. Ed. Michel Senellart. Trans. Graham Burchell. New York: Picador, 2008.

—. *Discipline and Punish: The Birth of the Prison*. Trans. Alan Sheridan. New York: Vintage, 1975.

—. *Naissance de la Biopolitique: Cours au Collège de France, 1978–1979*. Paris: EHESS/Gallimard/Seuil, 2004.

—. "On Popular Justice." In *Power/Knowledge: Selected Interviews and Other Writings, 1972–1977*, ed. Colin Gordon, trans. Colin Gordon, Leo Marshall, John Mepham, and Kate Soper. New York: Pantheon, 1980.

—. "Part 5: Right of Death and Power Over Life." In *The History of Sexuality*, Vol. 1, *An Introduction*, trans. Robert Hurley, 133–159. New York: Pantheon, 1978.

—. *Penal Theories and Institutions: Lectures at the Collège de France, 1971–1972*. Ed. Bernard E. Harcourt. Trans. Graham Burchell. New York: Palgrave Macmillan, 2019.

—. *The Punitive Society*. Ed. Bernard E. Harcourt. Trans. Graham Burchell. New York: Picador, 2015.

—. *Security, Territory, Population: Lectures at the Collège de France, 1977–1978*. Ed. Michel Senellart. Trans. Graham Burchell. Basingstoke, UK: Palgrave Macmillan, 2009.

—. *La Société punitive: Cours au Collège de France (1972–1973)*. Ed. Bernard E. Harcourt. Paris: Gallimard/Seuil, 2013.

—. "Sur la justice populaire." In *Dits et Écrits (1970–1075)*, Vol. 2, ed. Daniel Defert, François Ewald, and Jacques Lagrange. Paris: Gallimard, 1994.

—. *Surveiller et punir: Naissance de la prison*. Ed. Bernard E. Harcourt. In *Michel Foucault: Oeuvres*, Vol. 2, ed. Frédéric Gros. Paris: Gallimard/La Pléiade, 2015.

Foucault, Michel, Catharine von Bülow, and Daniel Defert. Preface to *The Assassination of George Jackson (Intolérable 3: Assassinat de George Jackson)*. In *Warfare in the American Homeland: Policing and Prison in a Penal Democracy*, ed. Joy James. Durham, NC: Duke University Press, 2007.

—. "The Masked Assassination." In *Warfare in the American Homeland*, ed. Joy James. Durham, NC: Duke University Press, 2007.

Fourier, Charles. *The Theory of the Four Movements*. Ed. Gareth Stedman Jones. Trans. Ian Patterson. New York: Cambridge University Press, 1996 [1808].

Franke, Katherine. *Repair: Redeeming the Promise of Abolition*. Chicago: Haymarket, 2019.

Frenkel, Sheera, et al. "U.S. Stocks Have Their Best Month Since 1987." *New York Times*, April 30, 2020. https://www.nytimes.com/2020/04/30/business/stock-market-today-coronavirus.html#link-23f83d60.

Fukuyama, Francis. "The End of History?" *National Interest*, no. 16 (Summer 1989).

Funding Universe. "History of Ace Hardware Corporation." http://www.fundinguniverse.com/company-histories/ace-hardware-corporation-history/.

—. "History of State Farm Mutual Automobile Insurance Company." http://www.fundinguniverse.com/company-histories/state-farm-mutual-automobile-insurance-company-history/.

Futrell, Nicole Smith. "The Practice and Pedagogy of Carceral Abolition in a Criminal Defense Clinic." *N.Y.U. Review of Law & Social Change* 45 (2021): 159–196.

García López, Gustavo. "Saskia Sassen on Extractive Logics and Geographies of Expulsion." *Undisciplined Environments*, August 9, 2017. https://undisciplinedenvironments.org/2017/08/09/saskia-sassen-on-extractive-logics-and-geographies-of-expulsion/.

Gavrielides, Theo, ed. *Routledge International Handbook of Restorative Justice*. New York: Routledge, 2019.

Gelman, Andrew, Jeffrey Fagan, and Alex Kiss. "An Analysis of the New York City Police Department's 'Stop-and-Frisk' Policy in the Context of Claims of Racial Bias." *Journal of the American Statistical Association* 102, no. 479 (2007): 813–823.

Georgescu-Roegen, Nicholas. *The Entropy Law and the Economic Process.* Cambridge, MA: Harvard University Press, 1971.

Getachew, Adom. *Worldmaking After Empire: The Rise and Fall of Self-Determination.* Princeton, NJ: Princeton University Press, 2019.

Gide, Charles. *Le Coopératisme: Conférences de propagande.* 5th ed. Paris: Librairie du Recueil Sirey, 1929.

Gillies, Benjamin. "Worker Cooperatives: A Bipartisan Solution to America's Growing Income Inequality." *Kennedy School Review* (blog), June 15, 2016. https://ksr.hkspublications.org/2016/06/15/worker-cooperatives-a-bipartisan-solution-to-americas-growing-income-inequality/.

Gilligan, Carol. *In a Different Voice.* Cambridge, MA: Harvard University Press, 1982.

Gilmore, Ruth Wilson. *Golden Gulag: Prisons, Surplus, Crisis, and Opposition in Globalizing California.* Berkeley: University of California Press, 2007.

Gilmore, Ruth Wilson, and Craig Gilmore. "Restating the Obvious." In *Indefensible Space: The Architecture of the National Insecurity State*, ed. Michael Sorkin. New York: Routledge, 2007.

Gilmore, Ruth Wilson, and James Kilgore. "The Case for Abolition." *Marshall Project*, June 9, 2019. https://www.themarshallproject.org/2019/06/19/the-case-for-abolition.

Glyn, Andrew. *Capitalism Unleashed: Finance, Globalization and Welfare.* New York: Oxford University Press, 2006.

Goglio, Silvio, and Panu Kalmi. "Credit Unions and Co-operative Banks Across the World." In *The Oxford Handbook of Mutual, Co-operative, and Co-owned Business*, ed. Jonathan Michie, Joseph R. Blasi, and Carlo Borzaga, 145–156. Oxford: Oxford University Press, 2017.

Goodman, Nelson. *Of Mind and Other Matters.* Cambridge, MA: Harvard University Press, 1984.

Gorz, André. *Stratégie ouvrière et néo-capitalisme.* Paris: Éditions du Seuil, 1964.

Gossett, Che. *Abolitionist Entanglement: Ending the Grammars of Capture.* PhD diss., Rutgers University, 2021.

Gossett, Che, Nick Mitchell, Eric A. Stanley, and Liat Ben-Moshe. "Critical Theory, Queer Resistance, and the Ends of Capture." In *Death and Other Penalties: Philosophy in a Time of Mass Incarceration*, ed. Geoffrey Adelsberg, Lisa Guenther, and Scott Zeman, 266–297. New York: Fordham University Press, 2015.

Gourevitch, Alex. *From Slavery to the Cooperative Commonwealth: Labor and Republican Liberty in the Nineteenth Century.* New York: Cambridge University Press, 2014.

Gramsci, Antonio. *Prison Notebooks.* Vols. 1–3. Ed. Joseph A. Buttigieg. Trans. Joseph A. Buttigieg and Antonio Callari. New York: Columbia University Press, 2011.

Grubačić, Andrej. "David Graeber Left Us a Parting Gift—His Thoughts on Kropotkin's *Mutual Aid*." *Truthout*, September 4, 2020. https://truthout.org/articles/david-graeber-left-us-a-parting-gift-his-thoughts-on-kropotkins-mutual-aid/.

Haley, Sarah. *No Mercy Here: Gender, Punishment, and the Making of Jim Crow Modernity.* Chapel Hill: University of North Carolina Press, 2016.

Hamburger, Philip. *The Administrative Threat.* New York: Encounter, 2017.

——. *Is Administrative Law Unlawful?* Chicago: University of Chicago Press, 2014.

Hansmann, Henry. *The Ownership of Enterprise.* Cambridge, MA: Harvard University Press, 1996.

Hansmann, Henry, and Reinier Kraakman. "The End of History for Corporate Law." *Georgetown Law Journal* 89, no. 2 (January 2001): 439–468.

Harcourt, Bernard E. "Collapse of the Harm Principle." *Journal of Criminal Law and Criminology* 90, no. 1 (1999): 109–194.

—. *Critique and Praxis*. New York: Columbia University Press, 2020.

—. *Exposed: Desire and Disobedience in the Digital Age*. Cambridge, MA: Harvard University Press, 2015.

—. *The Illusion of Free Markets: Punishment and the Myth of Natural Order*. Cambridge, MA: Harvard University Press, 2011.

—. "Radical Thought from Marx, Nietzsche, and Freud, Through Foucault, to the Present: Comments on Steven Lukes's *In Defense of 'False Consciousness.'*" *Chicago Unbound* (2011): 29–51.

—. "The Systems Fallacy: A Genealogy and Critique of Public Policy and Cost-Benefit Analysis." *Journal of Legal Studies* 47, no. 2 (June 2018): 419–447.

Hardt, Michael, and Antonio Negri. *Assembly*. New York: Oxford University Press, 2017.

—. *Commonwealth*. Cambridge, MA: Belknap, 2009.

Harney, Stefano, and Fred Moten. *The Undercommons: Fugitive Planning and Black Study*. Wivenhoe, UK: Minor Compositions, 2013.

Harvey, David. *The Enigma of Capital and the Crises of Capitalism*. New York: Oxford University Press, 2010.

Hasbrouck, Brandon. "Abolishing Racist Policing with the Thirteenth Amendment." *UCLA Law Review* 67, no. 5 (2020): 1108–1129.

Haskel, Jonathan, and Stian Westlake. *Capitalism Without Capital: The Rise of the Intangible Economy*. Princeton, NJ: Princeton University Press, 2018.

Henrÿ, Hagen. "Co-operative Principles and Co-operative Law Across the Globe." In *The Oxford Handbook of Mutual, Co-operative, and Co-owned Business*, ed. Jonathan Michie, Joseph R. Blasi, and Carlo Borzaga, 39–52. Oxford: Oxford University Press, 2017.

Hinton, Elizabeth. *America on Fire: The Untold History of Police Violence and Black Rebellion Since the 1960s*. New York: Liveright, 2021.

Hirschman, Albert O. *Exit, Voice, and Loyalty: Responses to Decline in Firms, Organizations, and States*. Cambridge, MA: Harvard University Press, 1970.

Ho Chi Minh. *Down with Colonialism!* Ed. Walden Bello. New York: Verso, 2007.

Hoag, Alexis. "Valuing Black Lives: A Case for Ending the Death Penalty." *Columbia Human Rights Law Review* 51, no. 3 (2020): 985–1007. http://hrlr.law.columbia.edu/hrlr/valuing-black-lives-a-case-for-ending-the-death-penalty/.

Hoag-Fordjour, Alexis. "White Is Right: The Racial Construction of Effective Assistance of Counsel." *New York University Law Review* 98 (forthcoming). Abstract at https://papers.ssrn.com/sol3/papers.cfm?abstract_id=4179940.

Hobsbawm, Eric. *The Age of Capital: 1848–1875*. New York: Vintage, 1996.

Hodgson, Geoffrey M. *Conceptualizing Capitalism: Institutions, Evolution, Future*. Chicago: University of Chicago Press, 2015.

Hogeland, Julie A. "The Economic Culture of U.S. Agricultural Cooperatives." *Culture & Agriculture* 28, no. 2 (December 2006): 67–79. https://doi.org/10.1525/cag.2006.28.2.67.

Hohfeld, Wesley. *Fundamental Legal Conceptions as Applied in Judicial Reasoning*. Ed. David Campbell and Philip Thomas. New York: Routledge, 2001.

Honneth, Axel. *Idea of Socialism*. Trans. Joseph Ganahl. Malden, MA: Polity, 2017.

Hoover, Melissa, and Hilary Abell. *The Cooperative Growth Ecosystem: Inclusive Economic Development in Action.* Democracy at Work Institute and Project Equity, n.d. https://institute.coop/sites/default/files/resources/Ecosystem%20Report.pdf.

Horkheimer, Max. "Traditional and Critical Theory." In *Critical Theory: Selected Essays*, trans. Matthew J. O'Connell et al. New York: Continuum, 1972.

Horowitz, Sara. *Mutualism: Building the Next Economy from the Ground Up.* New York: Random House, 2021.

Hoskins, DeAnna. "A New North Star." In *What We Know: Solutions from Our Experiences in the Justice System*, ed. Vivian Nixon and Daryl V. Atkinson, 239–244. New York: New Press, 2020.

Hughes, T., and E. V. Neales, eds. *A Manual for Co-operators.* Manchester, UK: Central Co-operative Board, 1881.

Huxley, Thomas. "The Struggle for Existence in Human Society." In *Collected Essays IX.* 1888. https://mathcs.clarku.edu/huxley/CE9/Str.html.

Ifill, Sherrilyn A. "Reconciliation in the Twenty-First Century." In *On the Courthouse Lawn: Confronting the Legacy of Lynching in the Twenty-First Century.* Boston: Beacon, 2018.

Irwin, Neil. "Everything Is Awful. So Why Is the Stock Market Booming?" *New York Times*, April 10, 2020. https://www.nytimes.com/2020/04/10/upshot/virus-stock-market-booming.html.

Jackall, Robert, and Henry M. Levin. *Worker Cooperatives in America.* Berkeley: University of California Press, 1984.

Jackson, George L. *Blood in My Eye.* New York: Random House, 1972.

—. "Towards the United Front." In *If They Come in the Morning . . . Voices of Resistance*, ed. Angela Y. Davis, 156–162. New York: Verso, 2016.

Jackson, Tim. *Prosperity Without Growth: Economics for a Finite Planet.* London: Earthscan, 2009.

James, C. L. R. *Nkrumah and the Ghana Revolution.* Westport, CT: Lawrence Hill, 1977.

James, Joy, ed. *The New Abolitionists: (Neo)Slave Narratives and Contemporary Prison Writings.* Albany: State University of New York Press, 2005.

Jeyifo, Biodun. "An 'Illuminati' and Its Acolytes: Critical Theory in the Text and in the World." *British Journal of Sociology* 72, no. 3 (June 2021): 869–870.

Kaba, Mariame. "Yes, We Mean Literally Abolish the Police. Because Reform Won't Happen," *New York Times*, June 12, 2020. https://www.nytimes.com/2020/06/12/opinion/sunday/floyd-abolish-defund-police.html.

—. *We Do This 'Til We Free Us.* Chicago: Haymarket, 2021.

Kaba, Mariame, and Andrea Ritchie. "We Want More Justice for Breonna Taylor Than the System That Killed Her Can Deliver." *Essence*, July 16, 2020. https://www.essence.com/feature/breonna-taylor-justice-abolition/.

Kallis, Giorgos. *Degrowth.* New York: Columbia University Press, 2018.

Kallis, Giorgos, Christian Kerschner, and Joan Martinez-Alier. "The Economics of Degrowth." *Ecological Economics* 84 (2012): 172–180.

Kalman, Samuel. "Policing the French Empire: Colonial Law Enforcement and the Search for Racial-Territorial Hegemony." *Historical Reflections/Réflexions Historiques* 46, no. 2 (2020): 1–8.

Kasmir, Sharryn. "The Mondragón Cooperatives and Global Capitalism." *New Labor Forum* 25, no. 1 (2016): 52–59.

—. *The Myth of Mondragón: Cooperatives, Politics, and Working-Class Life in a Basque Town.* Albany: State University of New York Press, 1996.

Kaswan, Mark J. "US Worker Co-operatives." In *The Oxford Handbook of Mutual, Co-operative, and Co-owned Business*, ed. Jonathan Michie, Joseph R. Blasi, and Carlo Borzaga, 527–538. Oxford: Oxford University Press, 2017.

Katznelson, Ira. *Fear Itself: The New Deal and the Origins of Our Time*. New York: Norton, 2013.

Kelley, Robin D. G. Preface to *Black and White: Land, Labor, and Politics in the South*, by T. Thomas Fortune, vii–xvi. New York: Atria Paperback, 2022.

Kennedy, Emmet. "'Ideology' from Destutt De Tracy to Marx." *Journal of the History of Ideas* 40, no. 3 (1979): 353–368.

Kerr, Camille. "Choosing a Business Entity: A Guise for Worker Cooperatives." Democracy at Work Institute, U.S. Federation of Worker Cooperatives. 2014. https://institute.coop/resources/choosing-business-entity-guide-worker-cooperatives.

Kerschner, Christian. "Economic De-growth vs. Steady-State Economy." *Journal of Cleaner Production* 18, no. 6 (2010): 544–551.

Knapp, Joseph G. *The Advance of American Cooperative Enterprise 1920–1945*. Danville, IL: Interstate, 1973.

—. *The Rise of American Cooperative Enterprise 1620–1920*. Danville, IL: Interstate, 1969.

Knopp, Fay Honey. *Instead of Prisons: A Handbook for Prison Abolitionists*. Prison Research Education Action Project. 1976.

Koopman, Colin. *How We Became Our Data*. Chicago: University of Chicago Press, 2019.

Krause, Tammy. "Reaching Out to the Other Side: Defense-Based Victim Outreach in Capital Cases." In *Wounds That Do Not Bind: Victim Based Perspectives on the Death Penalty*, ed. James Acker and David Karp. Durham, NC: Carolina Academic Press, 2006.

Kropotkin, Peter. *Mutual Aid: A Factor of Evolution*. New York: Dover, 2006 [1902].

—. Preface to *The Conquest of Bread*. New York: Putnam, 1906.

Krugman, Paul. "Crashing Market, Rising Stocks: What's Going On?" *New York Times*, April 30, 2020. https://www.nytimes.com/2020/04/30/opinion/economy-stock-market-coronavirus.html.

Kushner, Rachel. "Is Prison Necessary? Ruth Wilson Gilmore Might Change Your Mind." *New York Times Magazine*, April 17, 2019. https://www.nytimes.com/2019/04/17/magazine/prison-abolition-ruth-wilson-gilmore.html.

Lam, Bourree. "How REI's Co-Op Retail Model Helps Its Bottom Line." *Atlantic*, March 21, 2017. https://www.theatlantic.com/business/archive/2017/03/rei-jerry-stritzke-interview/520278/.

Lambert, Paul. *La Doctrine coopérative*. Brussels: Société Générale Coopérative, 1959.

—. *Studies in the Social Philosophy of Co-operation*. Trans. Joseph Létargez and D. Flanagan. Chicago: Cooperative League of the U.S.A., 1963.

Langer, Máximo. "Penal Abolitionism and Criminal Law Minimalism: Here and There, Now and Then." *Harvard Law Review Forum* 134 (2020): 42–77.

Lanni, Adriaan. "Taking Restorative Justice Seriously." *Buffalo Law Review* 69, no. 3 (2021): 635–681.

Latouche, Serge. *Farewell to Growth*. Trans. David Macey. Cambridge: Polity, 2010.

—. *Petit traité de la décroissance sereine*. Paris: Fayard/Mille et Une Nuits, 2007.

Lazear, Edward, and Sherwin Rosen. "Rank Order Tournaments as Optimum Labor Contracts." *Journal of Political Economy* 89, no. 5 (October 1981): 841–864.

Leighton, Mara. "The Perks of REI's Lifetime Membership Far Outweigh Its One-Time $20 Cost." *Business Insider*, March 23, 2019. https://www.businessinsider.com/rei-lifetime-membership-program-explainer-2017-3.

Leikin, Steven Bernard. *The Practical Utopians: American Workers and the Cooperative Movement in the Gilded Age*. Detroit, MI: Wayne State University Press, 2005.

Lenin, Vladimir. "On Cooperation." *Pravda* (No. 115–116), May 26–27, 1923 (written January 4–6, 1923). In *Collected Works*, by Vladimir Lenin, 2nd English ed., 33:467–475. Moscow: Progress, 1965. https://www.marxists.org/archive/lenin/works/1923/jan/06.htm.

Lerner, Josh, and Jean Tirole. "Some Simple Economics of Open Source." *Journal of Industrial Economics* 50, no. 2 (June 2002): 197–234.

Levitt, Steven. "Juvenile Crime and Punishment." *Journal of Political Economy* 106, no. 6 (December 1998): 1156–1185.

Levitt, Steven, and Sudhir Alladi Venkatesh. "An Economic Analysis of a Drug-Selling Gang's Finances." *Quarterly Journal of Economics* 115, no. 3 (2000), 755–789.

Lotringer, Sylvère, and Christian Marazzi, eds. *Autonomia: Post-Political Politics*. New York: Semiotext(e), 2007.

Lubiano, Wahneema, ed. *The House That Race Built: Original Essays by Toni Morrison, Angela Y. Davis, Cornel West, and Others on Black Americans and Politics in America Today*. New York: Vintage, 1998.

Lukács, Georg. *History and Class Consciousness*. Trans. Rodney Livingstone. Cambridge, MA: MIT Press, 1971.

Lukes, Steven. "In Defense of 'False Consciousness.'" *University of Chicago Legal Forum* 2011, article 3 (2011): 19–28. https://chicagounbound.uchicago.edu/cgi/viewcontent.cgi?article=1473&context=uclf.

Malthus, Thomas. *Essay on the Principle of Population*. Ed. Joyce E. Chaplin. New York: Norton, 2017.

Mannheim, Karl. *Ideology and Utopia: An Introduction to the Sociology of Knowledge*. Trans. Louis Wirth and Edward Shils. New York: Harcourt, 1936.

Manza, Jeff, and Christopher Uggen. *Locked Out: Felon Disenfranchisement and American Democracy*. New York: Oxford University Press, 2006.

Marcuse, Herbert. *Eros and Civilization: A Philosophical Inquiry Into Freud*. Boston: Beacon, 1955.

Marglin, Stephen A., and Juliet B. Schor, eds. *The Golden Age of Capitalism: Reinterpreting the Postwar Experience*. Oxford: Clarendon, 1992.

Margulies, Joseph. "Who Deserves to Be Forgiven?" *Boston Review*, February 23, 2021. http://bostonreview.net/law-justice/joseph-margulies-who-deserves-be-forgiven.

Marshall, T. F. *Restorative Justice: An Overview*. London: Home Office Research Development and Statistics, 1999.

Martin, Claire. "At King Arthur Flour, Savoring the Perks of Employee Ownership." *New York Times*, June 25, 2016. https://www.nytimes.com/2016/06/26/business/at-king-arthur-flour-savoring-the-perks-of-employee-ownership.html.

Martin, Reinhold. "Abolish Oil." *Places Journal*, June 2020. https://placesjournal.org/article/abolish-oil/.

Marx, Karl. *Capital*, Vol. 1. Trans. Ben Fowkes. New York: Vintage, 1976.

——. *Capital*, Vol. 3. Trans. David Fernbach. New York: Penguin, 1981.

——. "Critique of the Gotha Program." In *The Marx-Engels Reader*, 2nd ed., ed. Robert C. Tucker, 525–541. New York: Norton, 1978.

——. *Misère de la philosophie: Réponse à la philosophie de la misère de M. Proudhon*. Paris: A. Frank, 1847.

——. *The Poverty of Philosophy, with an introduction by Frederick Engels*. Trans. H. Quelch. New York: Prometheus, 1995.

Marx, Karl, and Friedrich Engels. *The German Ideology, Including Theses on Feuerbach*. New York: Prometheus, 1998.

——. *Manifesto of the Communist Party.* Ed. Frederick Engels. New York: International, 1948.

Maskin, Eric. "How Can Cooperative Game Theory Be Made More Relevant to Economics? An Open Problem." In *Open Problems in Mathematics*, ed. John Forbes Nash and Michael Th. Rassias. Cham, Switzerland: Springer International, 2016.

Mathiesen, Thomas. *The Politics of Abolition Revisited.* New York: Routledge, 2015.

Mayson, Sandra. "Bias In, Bias Out." *Yale Law Journal* 128, no. 8 (2018): 2218–2300.

Mazero, Joyce, and Suzie Loonam. "Purchasing Cooperatives: Leveraging a Supply Chain for Competitive Advantage." *Franchise Law Journal* 29, no. 3 (2010): 148–163.

McCain, Roger A. "Cooperation and Effort, Reciprocity and Mutual Supervision in Worker Cooperatives." In *Advances in the Economic Analysis of Participatory and Labor-Managed Firms*, Vol. 10, ed. Sonja Novkovic and Vania Sena, 185–203. Bingley, UK: Emerald, 2007. https://doi.org/10.1016/S0885-3339(06)10007-1.

McLeod, Allegra. "Envisioning Abolition Democracy." *Harvard Law Review* 132, no. 6 (2019): 1613–1649.

——. "Law, Critique, and the Undercommons." In *A Time for Critique*, ed. Didier Fassin and Bernard E. Harcourt, 252–270. New York: Columbia University Press, 2019.

——. "Prison Abolition and Grounded Justice." *UCLA Law Review* 62 (2015): 1156–1239. https://www.uclalawreview.org/wp-content/uploads/2019/09/McLeod_6.2015.pdf.

Meares, Tracey, and Tom Tyler. "The First Step Is Figuring Out What Police Are For." *Atlantic*, June 8, 2020. https://www.theatlantic.com/ideas/archive/2020/06/first-step-figuring-out-what-police-are/612793/.

Meiksins Wood, Ellen. *Origin of Capitalism.* New York: Verso, 2017.

Mellor, Mary, Janet Hannah, and John Stirling. *Worker Cooperatives in Theory and Practice.* Philadelphia: Open University Press, 1988.

Merrill, Thomas W. *The Chevron Doctrine: Its Rise and Fall, and the Future of the Administrative State.* Cambridge, MA: Harvard University Press, 2022.

Metzl, Jonathan M. *Dying of Whiteness: How the Politics of Racial Resentment Is Killing America's Heartland.* New York: Basic Books, 2019.

Michalowski, Raymond J., and Susan M. Carlson. "Unemployment, Imprisonment, and Social Structures of Accumulation: Historical Contingency in the Rusche–Kirchheimer Hypothesis." *Criminology* 37, no. 2 (1999): 217–250.

Michie, Jonathan, Joseph R. Blasi, and Carlo Borzaga, eds. *The Oxford Handbook of Mutual, Cooperative, and Co-owned Business.* Oxford: Oxford University Press, 2017.

Mill, John Stuart. "Chapters on Socialism." In *Principles of Political Economy.* Oxford: Oxford Paperbacks, 1998.

Miller, Ethan. *Reimagining Livelihoods: Life Beyond Economy, Society, and Environment.* Minneapolis: University of Minnesota Press, 2019.

——. "Review of *The Solidarity Economy Alternative: Emerging Theory and Practice*, edited by Vishwas Satgar." *Antipode: A Radical Journal of Geography* (2014): 1–7. https://radicalantipode.files.wordpress.com/2014/07/book-review_miller-on-satgar1.pdf.

Mirowski, Philip. *Never Let a Serious Crisis Go to Waste.* New York: Verso, 2013.

Moglen, Eben. "Anarchism Triumphant: Free Software and the Death of Copyright." *First Monday*, August 2, 1999. http://firstmonday.org/ojs/index.php/fm/article/view/684/594.

Moglen, Seth. Introduction to *Black and White: Land, Labor, and Politics in the South*, by T. Thomas Fortune. New York: Atria Paperback, 2022.

Mollner, Terry. "Mondragón: A Third Way." *Review of Social Economy* 42, no. 3 (1984): 260–271.

Moore, Michael, Anne Moore, Rod Birleson, John Hardesty, and Jeff Gibbs, dir. *Capitalism: A Love Story*. Documentary. Montreal: Alliance Vivafilm, 2010. https://www.youtube.com /watch?v=LUpnFNUmfKw&has_verified=1.

Morris, Aldon D. *The Scholar Denied: W. E. B. Du Bois and the Birth of Modern Sociology*. Oakland: University of California Press, 2015.

Morrison, Toni. "Home." In *The House That Race Built: Original Essays by Toni Morrison, Angela Y. Davis, Cornel West, and Others on Black Americans and Politics in America Today*, ed. Wahneema Lubiano. New York: Vintage, 1998.

Movement for Black Lives. *A Vision for Black Lives: Policy Demands for Black Power, Freedom, and Justice*. August 2016. https://policy.m4bl.org.

Muhammad, Khalil Gibran. *The Condemnation of Blackness: Race, Crime, and the Making of Modern Urban American*. Cambridge, MA: Harvard University Press, 2010.

Mulder, Catherine P. *Transcending Capitalism Through Cooperative Practice*. London: Palgrave Macmillan, 2015.

Murakawa, Naomi. "Police Reform Works—for the Police." *Level*, October 21, 2020. https://level .medium.com/why-police-reform-is-actually-a-bailout-for-cops-ecf2dd7b8833.

Murphy, Erin. "The Racial Composition of Forensic DNA Databases." *California Law Review* 108, no. 6 (2020): 1847–1911.

Mylondo, Baptiste. *Des caddies et des hommes: La consommation citoyenne contre la société de consommation*. La Dispute, 2005.

Mylondo, Baptiste, and Xaiver Timbeau. "Is Green Growth an Illusion? For/Against—Baptiste Mylondo vs. Xavier Timbeau." *Philonomist*, December 12, 2018. Updated March 4, 2022. https:// www.philonomist.com/en/interview/green-growth-illusion.

Myrdal, Gunnar. *An American Dilemma: The Negro Problem and Modern Democracy*. Vol. 1. New York: Harper & Row, 1944.

Nadeau, E. G. *The Cooperative Solution: How the United States Can Tame Recessions, Reduce Inequality, and Protect the Environment*. CreateSpace Independent Publishing Platform, 2012.

——. *Strengthening the Cooperative Community*. Madison, WI: Emile G. Nadeau, 2021.

Nadeau, E. G., and Luc Nadeau. *The Cooperative Society: The Next Stage of Human History*. Madison, WI: Emile G. Nadeau, 2016.

Nadeau, E. G., and David J. Thompson. *Cooperation Works!* Rochester, MN: Lone Oak, 1996.

Nagin, Daniel. "General Deterrence: A Review of the Empirical Evidence." In *Deterrence and Incapacitation: Estimating the Effects of Criminal Sanctions on Crime Rates*, ed. Alfred Blumstein et al. Washington, DC: National Academy of Sciences, 1978.

Negri, Antonio. *From the Factory to the Metropolis*. Trans. Ed Emery. Cambridge: Polity, 2018.

Nembhard, Jessica Gordon. *Collective Courage: A History of African American Cooperative Economic Thought and Practice*. University Park: Pennsylvania State University Press, 2014.

——. "A Long and Strong History with Southern Roots." In *Jackson Rising: The Struggle for Economic Democracy and Black Self-Determination in Jackson, Mississippi*, by Kali Akuno and Ajamu Nangwaya, 171–181. Wakefield, Quebec: Daraja, 2017.

Nixon, Vivian, and Daryl V. Atkinson. Introduction to *What We Know: Solutions from Our Experiences in the Justice System*, eds. Vivian Nixon and Daryl V. Atkinson, ix–xiv. New York: New Press, 2020.

NLRB v. North Arkansas Electric Cooperative, Inc. 446 F.2d 602 (8th Cir, 1971).

NLRB v. Bell Aerospace Co. 416 U.S. 267 (1974).

Noddings, Nel. *Caring: A Feminine Approach to Ethics and Moral Education.* Berkeley: University of California Press, 1982.

Nyerere, Julius. "The Arusha Declaration." Written for the Tanganyika African National Union. February 5, 1967. https://www.marxists.org/subject/africa/nyerere/1967/arusha-declaration .htm.

Ossei-Owusu, Shaun. "The Sixth Amendment Façade: The Racial Evolution of the Right to Counsel." *University of Pennsylvania Law Review* 167, no. 5 (April 2019): 1161–1239.

Orsi, Janelle, William Lisa, and Sushil Jacob. *Legal Guide to Cooperative Conversations: A Business Owner's Legal Guide to Cooperative Conversion Including Conversion Models, Case Studies and Sample Documents.* Sustainable Economies Law Center, n.d.

Owen, Robert. *A New Vision of Society: or, Essays on the Formation of the Human Character. Preparatory to the Development of a Plan for Gradually Ameliorating the Condition of Mankind,* 3rd ed. London: R. and A. Taylor, 1817.

——. *Report: To the Committee of the Association for the Relief of the Manufacturing and Labouring Poor, Referred to the Committee of the House of Commons on the Poor Laws.* March 12, 1817. http:// la.utexas.edu/users/hcleaver/368/3680wenrptcom.html.

Paden, Roger. "Marx's Critique of the Utopian Socialists." *Utopian Studies* 13, no. 2 (2002): 67–91.

Parker, Florence E. *The First 125 Years: A History of Distributive and Service Cooperation in the United States, 1829–1954.* Superior, WI: Cooperative League, 1956.

Pareto, Vilfredo. *Les Systèmes Socialistes: Cours professé à l'Université de Lausanne.* 2 vols. Paris: Giard et Brière, 1902.

Pencavel, John H., ed. *The Economics of Worker Cooperatives.* Cheltenham, UK: Edward Elgar, 2013.

Pérotin, Virginie. "Worker Co-operatives: Good, Sustainable Jobs in the Community." In *The Oxford Handbook of Mutual, Co-operative, and Co-owned Business,* ed. Jonathan Michie, Joseph R. Blasi, and Carlo Borzaga, 131–144. Oxford: Oxford University Press, 2017.

PEW Center on the States. *One in 100: Behind Bars in America 2008.* February 28, 2008. https:// www.pewtrusts.org/en/research-and-analysis/reports/2008/02/28/one-in-100-behind-bars -in-america-2008.

Phillips, Matt. "The Bad News Won't Stop, But the Markets Keep Rising." *New York Times,* April 29, 2020. https://www.nytimes.com/2020/04/29/business/stock-markets.html.

Piketty, Thomas. *Capital and Ideology.* Cambridge, MA: Harvard University Press, 2020.

——. *Le Capital au XXIème siècle.* Paris: Éditions du Seuil, 2013.

——. *Capital in the Twenty-First Century.* Cambridge, MA: Harvard University Press, 2014.

——. "Economist Thomas Piketty: Coronavirus Pandemic Has Exposed the 'Violence of Social Inequality.'" Interview by Amy Goodman and Nermeen Shaikj. *Democracy Now!* April 30, 2020. https://www.democracynow.org/2020/4/30/thomas_piketty.

Pistor, Katharina. *The Code of Capital.* Princeton, NJ: Princeton University Press, 2019.

Pitman, Lynn. "History of Cooperatives in the United States: An Overview." University of Wisconsin Center for Cooperatives, Madison, Wisconsin. Revised December 2018. https:// resources.uwcc.wisc.edu/History_of_Cooperatives.pdf.

Polanyi, Karl. *The Great Transformation.* Boston: Beacon, 1944.

Pound, Jesse. "Global Stock Markets Gained $17 Trillion in Value in 2019." *CNBC,* December 26, 2019. https://www.cnbc.com/2019/12/24/global-stock-markets-gained-17-trillion-in-value-in-2019.html.

Press, Eyal. "A Preventable Cancer Is on the Rise in Alabama." *New Yorker*, April 6, 2020. newyorker
.com/magazine/2020/04/06/a-preventable-cancer-is-on-the-rise-in-alabama.

Prichard, Alex. *Justice, Order and Anarchy: The International Political Theory of Pierre-Joseph Proudhon*.
New York: Routledge, 2013.

Proudhon, Pierre Joseph. "General Idea of Revolution." In *Property Is Theft! A Pierre-Joseph Proudhon Anthology*, ed. Iain McKay. Edinburgh: AK, 2011.

——. "On the Jews." In *Carnets de P. J. Proudhon*. Vol. 2. Paris: M. Rivière, 1960. https://www.marxists
.org/reference/subject/economics/proudhon/1847/jews.htm.

——. *Qu'est-ce que la propriété?* (1840). Paris: Livres de Poche, 2009.

——. *Système des contradictions économiques, ou Philosophie de la misère* (1846). Paris: Garnier Frères,
1850.

——. *The System of Economic Contradictions, or the Philosophy of Poverty* (1846). Trans. Benjamin R.
Tucker. Anarchist Library, 1847.

——. *What Is Property?* Ed. and trans. Donald R. Kelley and Bonnie G. Smith. Cambridge: Cambridge
University Press, 1994.

Purnell, Derecka. *Becoming Abolitionists*. New York: Astra House, 2021.

——. "How I Became a Police Abolitionist." *Atlantic*, July 6, 2020. https://www.theatlantic.com
/ideas/archive/2020/07/how-i-became-police-abolitionist/613540/.

——. "What Does Police Abolition Mean?" *Boston Review*, August 23, 2017.

Quesnay, François. *Oeuvres économiques complètes et autres textes*. Ed. Christine Théré, Loïc Charles,
and Jean-Claude Perrot. 2 vols. Paris: Institut National d'Études Galilées, 2005.

——. *Oeuvres économiques et philosophiques*. Ed. Auguste Oncken. Darmstadt, Germany: Scientia
Verlag Aalen, 1965.

Ranis, Peter. *Cooperatives Confront Capitalism: Challenging the Neoliberal Economy*. London: ZED, 2016.

Ransby, Barbara. "The Class Politics of Black Lives Matter." *Dissent Magazine*, Fall 2015. https://
www.dissentmagazine.org/article/class-politics-black-lives-matter.

——. "The White Left Needs to Embrace Black Leadership." *Nation*, July 2, 2020. https://www
.thenation.com/article/activism/black-lives-white-left/.

Rawls, John. *Political Liberalism*. New York: Columbia University Press, 1993.

Red Nation. *A Red Deal: Indigenous Action to Save Our Earth*. 2020. https://therednation.org
/about-maisha/.

Reichl, P. L. "Southern Slave Patrols as a Transitional Police Type." *American Journal of Police* 7,
no. 2 (1988): 51–77.

Resnick, Stephen, and Richard Wolff. *Knowledge and Class*. Chicago: University of Chicago Press,
1987.

Ricardo, David. *The Works and Correspondence of David Ricardo: On the Principles of Political Economy and Taxation*. Ed. Piero Sraffa. Indianapolis, IN: Liberty Fund, 2004.

Roberts, Dorothy. "Abolishing Policing Also Means Abolishing Family Regulation." *Imprint*, June 16,
2020. https://imprintnews.org/child-welfare-2/abolishing-policing-also-means-abolishing-family
-regulation/44480.

——. "Constructing a Criminal Justice System Free of Racial Bias." *Columbia Human Rights Law
Review* 39, no. 1 (2008): 261–285.

——. "Foreword: Abolition Constitutionalism." *Harvard Law Review* 133, no. 1 (2019): 1–122. https://
harvardlawreview.org/wp-content/uploads/2019/11/1-122_Online.pdf.

Robinson, Cedric. *Black Marxism: The Making of the Black Radical Tradition*. Chapel Hill: University of North Carolina Press, 2000.

Rodriguez, Dylan. "Abolition as Praxis of Human Being: A Foreword." *Harvard Law Review* 132, no. 6 (2019): 1575–1612.

——. *Forced Passages: Imprisoned Racial Intellectuals and the U.S. Prison System*. Minneapolis: University of Minnesota Press, 2006.

Roelants, Bruno, Diana Dovgan, Hyungsik Eum, and Elisa Terrasi. *The Resilience of the Cooperative Model: How Worker Cooperatives, Social Cooperatives and Other Worker-Owned Enterprises Respond to the Crisis and Its Consequences*. CECOP, June 2012.

Ronel, Natti, and Ety Elisha. "A Different Perspective: Introducing Positive Criminology." *International Journal of Offender Therapy and Comparative Criminology* 55, no. 2 (2010): 305–325.

Rosen, Corey. "Statutory Employee Stock Ownership Plans in the USA." In *The Oxford Handbook of Mutual, Co-operative, and Co-owned Business*, ed. Jonathan Michie, Joseph R. Blasi, and Carlo Borzaga, 412–425. Oxford: Oxford University Press, 2017.

Rouleau, Guillaume. "Le langage de l'idéologie. Sur l'idéologie dans *L'Idéologie allemande*." Mémoire, EHESS, August 25, 2022. On file with author.

Røpke, Inge. "The Early History of Modern Ecological Economics." *Ecological Economics* 50 (2004): 293–314.

Rusche, Georg, and Otto Kirchheimer. *Punishment and Social Structure*. New York: Columbia University Press, 1939.

Sabel, Charles Frederick, and William H. Simon. "Democratic Experimentalism." In *Searching for Contemporary Legal Thought*, ed. Justin Desautels-Stein and Christopher Tomlins. New York: Cambridge University Press, 2017.

Samuelson, Larry. "Game Theory in Economics and Beyond." *Journal of Economic Perspectives* 30, no. 4 (Fall 2016): 107–130. https://doi.org/10.1257/jep.30.4.107.

Sanchez, Angel E. "In Spite of Prison." *Harvard Law Review* 132, no. 6 (2019): 1650–1683.

Sanders, Bernie. *Guide to Political Revolution*. New York: Henry Holt, 2017.

Satgar, Vishwas, ed. *Co-operatives in South Africa: Advancing Solidarity Economy Pathways from Below*. Durban, South Africa: University of KwaZulu-Natal Press, 2019.

——, ed. *The Solidarity Economy Alternative: Emerging Theory and Practice*. Durban, South Africa: University of KwaZulu-Natal Press, 2014.

Seo, Sarah. *Policing the Open Road: How Cars Transformed American Freedom*. Cambridge, MA: Harvard University Press, 2019.

Sexton, Richard J. "The Formation of Cooperatives: A Game-Theoretic Approach with Implications for Cooperative Finance, Decision Making, and Stability." *American Journal of Agricultural Economics* 68, no. 2 (May 1986): 214–225. https://doi.org/10.2307/1241423.

Sherman, Erik. "How Many Workers Must Live in Poverty for McDonald's CEO to Make $21.8 Million?" *Forbes*, July 12, 2018. https://www.forbes.com/sites/eriksherman/2018/07/12/how-many-workers-must-live-in-poverty-for-mcdonalds-ceo-to-make-21-8-million/#a25a0b10926d.

Shukur, Omavi. "The Criminalization of Black Resistance to Capture and Policing." Columbia Law School, New York, August 2022. Article on file with author.

Siblis Research. "Total Market Value of U.S. Stock Market." Siblis Research. https://siblisresearch.com/data/us-stock-market-value/.

Simpson v. Ernst & Young, 100 F.3d 436 (6th Cir. 1996).

Simonson, Jocelyn. "Police Reform Through a Power Lens." *Yale Law Journal* 130, no. 4 (2021): 778–1049.

Sklansky, David. *A Pattern of Violence: How the Law Classifies Crimes and What It Means for Justice.* Cambridge, MA: Harvard University Press, 2021.

Smith, Adam. *An Inquiry Into the Nature and Causes of the Wealth of Nations.* Ed. Edwin Cannan. Chicago: University of Chicago Press, 1976.

—. *The Theory of Moral Sentiments.* New York: Penguin, 2010.

Sommer, Robert, Deborah Schlanger, Robert Hackman, and Steven Smith. "Consumer Cooperatives and Worker Collectives: A Comparison." *Sociological Perspectives* 27, no. 2 (1984): 139–157. https://doi.org/10.2307/1389015.

Sonnichsen, Albert. *Consumers' Coöperation.* New York: Macmillan, 1919.

Spade, Dean. *Mutual Aid: Building Solidarity During This Crisis (and the Next).* New York: Verso, 2020.

—. "Solidarity Not Charity: Mutual Aid for Mobilization and Survival." *Social Text* 142 38, no. 1 (March 2020): 131–151.

Spivak, Gayatri Chakravorty. "Can the Subaltern Speak?" In *Can the Subaltern Speak? Reflections on the History of an Idea,* ed. Rosalind C. Morris, 21–78. New York: Columbia University Press, 2010.

Springer, Simon. *The Anarchist Roots of Geography: Toward Spatial Emancipation.* Minneapolis: University of Minnesota Press, 2016.

—. "Property Is the Mother of Famine: On Dispossession, Wages, and the Threat of Hunger." *Political Geography* 62 (2018): 201–203.

Steiker, Carol S., and Jordan M. Steiker. *Courting Death: The Supreme Court and Capital Punishment.* Cambridge, MA: Belknap, 2016.

—. "Sober Second Thoughts: Reflections on Two Decades of Constitutional Regulation of Capital Punishment." *Harvard Law Review* 109, no. 2 (1995): 355–438.

Stein, Jeff. "Tax Change in Coronavirus Package Overwhelmingly Benefits Millionaires, Congressional Body Finds." *Washington Post,* April 14, 2020. https://www.washingtonpost.com/business/2020/04/14/coronavirus-law-congress-tax-change/.

Steinbaum, Marshall. "Why Are Economists Giving Piketty the Cold Shoulder?" *Boston Review,* May 12, 2017. https://bostonreview.net/articles/marshall-steinbaum-beyond-piketty/.

Schmelzer, Matthias, Aaron Vansintjan, and Andrea Vetter. *The Future Is Degrowth: A Guide to a World Beyond Capitalism.* New York: Verso, 2022.

Sekulova, Filka, Giorgos Kallis, Beatriz Rodríguez-Labajos, and Francois Schneider. "Degrowth: From Theory to Practice." *Journal of Cleaner Production* 38 (2013): 1–6.

Sellin, Thorsten. Foreword to *Punishment and Social Structure,* by Georg Rusche and Otto Kirchheimer. New York: Columbia University Press, 1939.

Sennett, Richard. *Together: The Rituals, Pleasures and Politics of Cooperation.* New Haven, CT: Yale University Press, 2013.

Stewart, Alexander J., and Joshua B. Plotkin. "Collapse of Cooperation in Evolving Games." *Proceedings of the National Academy of Sciences* 111, no. 49 (December 9, 2014): 17558–17563.

Stevenson, Bryan. *Just Mercy: A Story of Justice and Redemption.* New York: Spiegel and Grau, 2015.

—. "A Presumption of Guilt." In *Policing the Black Man,* ed. Angela J. Davis, 3–30. New York: Penguin Random House, 2017.

Strang, Heather, and John Braithwaite, eds. *Restorative Justice and Civil Society.* Cambridge: Cambridge University Press, 2001.

Stuart, Diana, Ryan Gunderson, and Brian Petersen. *The Degrowth Alternative: A Path to Address Our Environmental Crisis?* New York: Routledge, 2020.

Stuntz, William J. *The Collapse of American Criminal Justice.* Cambridge, MA: Harvard University Press, 2011.

——. "The Pathological Politics of Criminal Law." *Michigan Law Review* 100, no. 3 (2001): 505–600.

——. "The Political Constitution of Criminal Justice." *Harvard Law Review* 119, no. 3 (2006): 780–851.

Táíwò, Olúfẹ́mi O., and Liam Kofi Bright. "A Response to Michael Walzer." *Dissent*, August 7, 2020. https://www.dissentmagazine.org/online_articles/a-response-to-michael-walzer.

Taylor, Keeanga-Yamahtta. *From #BlackLivesMatter to Black Liberation.* Chicago: Haymarket, 2016.

——. *How We Get Free: Black Feminism and the Combahee River Collective.* Chicago: Haymarket, 2017.

——. "Until Black Women Are Free, None of Us Will Be Free." *New Yorker*, July 20, 2020. https://www.newyorker.com/news/our-columnists/until-black-women-are-free-none-of-us-will-be-free.

——. "We Should Still Defund the Police." *New Yorker*, August 14, 2020. https://www.newyorker.com/news/our-columnists/defund-the-police.

Thomas, Frank. "The Emergence of Multi-Stakeholder Co-operatives in the Movement of Farm Machinery Co-operatives (CUMAs) in France." In *The Oxford Handbook of Mutual, Co-operative, and Co-owned Business*, ed. Jonathan Michie, Joseph R. Blasi, and Carlo Borzaga, 499–511. Oxford: Oxford University Press, 2017.

Thomas, Kendall. "Envisioning Abolition: Sex, Citizenship, and the Racial Imaginary of the Killing State." In *Sensible Politics: The Visual Culture of Nongovernmental Activism*, ed. Meg McLagan and Yates McKee, 257–275. New York: Zone, 2012.

Thompson, Spencer. "Towards a Social Theory of the Firm: Worker Cooperatives Reconsidered." *Journal of Co-Operative Organization and Management* 3, no. 1 (June 2015): 3–13. https://doi.org/10.1016/j.jcom.2015.02.002.

Ticktin, Miriam. *Casualties of Care: Immigration and the Politics of Humanitarianism in France.* Berkeley: University of California Press, 2011.

Tischer, Daniel, and John Hoffmire. "Moving Towards 100 percent Employee Ownership Through ESOPs: Added Complexities in Add-on Transactions." In *The Oxford Handbook of Mutual, Co-operative, and Co-owned Business*, ed. Jonathan Michie, Joseph R. Blasi, and Carlo Borzaga, 295–307. Oxford: Oxford University Press, 2017.

Tolentino, Jia. "Can I Help You? The Meaning of Mutual Aid During a Pandemic." *New Yorker*, May 18, 2020. https://www.newyorker.com/magazine/2020/05/18/what-mutual-aid-can-do-during-a-pandemic.

Tronto, Joan C. *Caring Democracy: Markets, Equality, and Justice.* New York: New York University Press, 2013.

University of Wisconsin–Madison, Center for Cooperatives. "Cooperatives in Wisconsin: The Power of Cooperative Action." 2019. https://resources.uwcc.wisc.edu/About%20Co-ops/Cooperatives_in_Wisconsin_FINAL_small.pdf.

Van Slyke, Brian. "Pandemic Crash Shows Worker Co-Ops Are More Resilient Than Traditional Business." *Truthout*, May 8, 2020. https://truthout.org/articles/pandemic-crash-shows-worker-co-ops-are-more-resilient-than-traditional-business/.

Vásquez, Delio. "Illegalist Foucault, Criminal Foucault." *Theory and Event* 23, no. 4 (October 2020): 935–972.

Vitale, Alex S. *The End of Policing.* New York: Verso, 2017.

Vogel, Steve. *Freer Markets, More Rules.* Ithaca, NY: Cornell University Press, 1996.

—. *Marketcraft: How Governments Make Markets Work.* New York: Oxford University Press, 2018.

Voinea, Anca. "How Does Crédit Agricole Stay Local While Operating Multinationally?" *Coop News,* September 5, 2018. https://www.thenews.coop/131687/sector/banking-and-insurance /credit-agricole-stay-local-operating-multinationally/.

Wacquant, Loïc. "Deadly Symbiosis: Rethinking Race and Imprisonment in Twenty-First -Century America." *Boston Review,* April/May 2002. https://bostonreview.net/archives/BR27.2 /wacquant.html#4.

—. "The New 'Peculiar Institution': On the Prison as Surrogate Ghetto." *Theoretical Criminology* 4, no. 3 (2000): 377–389.

Wadsworth, James J. "Cooperative Unification: Highlights from 1989 to Early 1999." United States Department of Agriculture. September 1999. https://www.rd.usda.gov/sites/default /files/rr174.pdf.

Walia, Harsha. *Border and Rule: Global Migration, Capitalism, and the Rise of Racist Nationalism.* Chicago: Haymarket, 2021.

Warbasse, James Peter. *Co-operative Democracy.* New York: MacMillan, 1923.

—. *The Destiny of the Co-operative Movement.* n.d. CLUSA files, Early Pamphlets, 1916–1919, Folder I.

Ward, Benjamin. "The Firm in Illyria: Market Syndicalism." *American Economic Review* 48, no. 4 (September 1958): 566–589.

Ward, Colin. *Anarchism: A Very Short Introduction.* New York: Oxford University Press, 2004.

Webb, Martha Beatrice. *The Cooperative Movement in Great Britain.* London: Swann Sonnenschein, 1891.

Weitzman, Martin L. *The Share Economy.* Cambridge, MA: Harvard University Press, 1986.

Wells, Ben. "Pros and Cons of Selling Your Business to Employees with an ESOP." Financially Simple, June 29, 2018. https://financiallysimple.com/should-you-sell-your-business-to-employees -pros-and-cons-of-esops/.

West Virginia v. EPA, 597 U.S. __ (2022).

Western, Bruce. *Punishment and Inequality in America.* New York: Russell Sage Foundation, 2006.

Wexler, David B. "The Development of Therapeutic Jurisprudence: From Theory to Practice." *Revista Jurídica Universidad de Puerto Rico* 68 (1999): 691–705.

—. *Therapeutic Jurisprudence: The Law as a Therapeutic Agent.* Durham, NC: Carolina Academic Press, 1990.

Wexler, David B., and Bruce Winick, *Law in a Therapeutic Key: Developments in Therapeutic Jurisprudence.* Durham, NC: Carolina Academic Press, 1996.

Wheatland, Thomas. "Critical Theory on Morningside Heights: From Frankfurt Mandarins to Columbia Sociologists." *German Politics & Society* 22, no. 4 (73) (Winter 2004): 57–87.

—. *The Frankfurt School in Exile.* Minneapolis: University of Minnesota Press, 2009.

—. "The Frankfurt School's Invitation from Columbia University: How the Horkheimer Circle Settled on Morningside Heights." *German Politics & Society* 22, no. 3 (72) (Fall 2004): 1–32.

Whitehouse, Sheldon. "Whitehouse, Doggett Release New Analysis Showing GOP Tax Provisions in CARES Act Overwhelmingly Benefit Million-Dollar-Plus Earners." Press Release, April 14, 2020. https://www.whitehouse.senate.gov/news/release/whitehouse-doggett-release -new-analysis-showing-gop-tax-provisions-in-cares-act-overwhelmingly-benefit-million-dollar -plus-earners.

Wilkerson, Isabel. *Caste: The Origins of Our Discontents*. New York: Random House, 2020.

Williams, Richard C. *The Cooperative Movement: Globalization from Below*. London: Ashgate, 2007.

Wolff, Richard D. *Democracy at Work: A Cure for Capitalism*. Chicago: Haymarket, 2012.

Wolin, Sheldon. *Politics and Vision: Continuity and Innovation in Western Political Thought*. Princeton, NJ: Princeton University Press, 2004.

Women of Color Against Violence, eds. *Color of Violence: The INCITE! Anthology*. INCITE!, 2016.

World Bank. "U.S. GDP Growth Rate 1961–2020." *Macrotrends*. https://www.macrotrends.net /countries/USA/united-states/gdp-growth-rate.

Wright, Erik Olin. *Envisioning Real Utopias*. London: Verso, 2010.

Wu, Tim. "Don't Feel Sorry for the Airlines." *New York Times*, March 16, 2020. https://www .nytimes.com/2020/03/16/opinion/airlines-bailout.html.

Wu, Tim, and Yaryna Serkyz. "These Companies Enriched Themselves. Now They're Getting a Bailout." *New York Times*, March 27, 2020. https://www.nytimes.com/interactive/2020/03/27 /opinion/coronavirus-bailout.html.

Xifaras, Mikhaïl. "The Role of Law in Critical Theory." *Praxis 13/13* (blog), December 2, 2018. https://blogs.law.columbia.edu/praxis1313/mikhail-xifaras-the-role-of-the-law-in-critical -theory-the-role-of-property-in-the-commons/.

Zamagni, Vera. "A Worldwide Historical Perspective on Co-operatives and Their Evolution." In *The Oxford Handbook of Mutual, Co-operative, and Co-owned Business*, ed. Jonathan Michie, Joseph R. Blasi, and Carlo Borzaga, 97–113. Oxford: Oxford University Press, 2017.

Ziv, Shahar. "How Some Rich Americans Are Getting Stimulus 'Checks' Averaging $1.7 Million." *Forbes*, April 14, 2020. https://www.forbes.com/sites/shaharziv/2020/04/14/why-are-rich -americans-getting-17-million-stimulus-checks/#2c6dacc3665b.

Name Index

Subject Index

Page locators in *italics* refer to figures and tables